Entrepreneurship

Entrepreneurship

**Price Institute for
Entrepreneurial Studies**

Edited by
Joshua Ronen

LexingtonBooks
D.C. Heath and Company
Lexington, Massachusetts
Toronto

Library of Congress Cataloging in Publication Data
Main entry under title:

Entrepreneurship.

Includes index.
1. Entrepreneur—Addresses, essays, lectures. I. Ronen, Joshua.
HB615.E62   1982   338'.04   82–47950
ISBN 0–669–05715–0

Copyright © 1983 by D.C. Heath and Company

Published simultaneously in Canada

Printed in the United States of America

International Standard Book Number: 0–669–05715–0

Library of Congress Catalog Card Number: 82–47950

Contents

Foreword   *Harold Price*   vii

Preface   *William J. Baumol*   ix

Chapter 1   **Introduction**   *Joshua Ronen*   1

Part I   *Theoretical Analysis of Entrepreneurial Behavior*   13

Chapter 2   **Innovation in Large and Small Firms**
Kenneth J. Arrow   15

Chapter 3   **Toward Operational Models of Entrepreneurship**
William J. Baumol   29

Chapter 4   **The Effects of Financing Opportunities and Bankruptcy on Entrepreneurial Risk Bearing**
Jerry R. Green and *John B. Shoven*   49

Chapter 5   **Entrepreneurial Concepts, Definitions, and Model Formulations**   *Harold N. Shapiro*   75

Chapter 6   **Organizational Innovation: The Transaction-Cost Approach**   *Oliver E. Williamson*   101

Part II   *An Empirically Based Framework*   135

Chapter 7   **Some Insights into the Entrepreneurial Process**
Joshua Ronen   137

Part III   *Entrepreneurship in Yugoslavia and the Soviet Union*   175

Chapter 8   **Entrepreneurship under Labor Participation: The Yugoslav Case**   *Abram Bergson*   177

Chapter 9   **On the Nature and Location of Entrepreneurial Activity in Centrally Planned Economies: The Soviet Case**   *Herbert S. Levine*   235

Part IV   *Commentaries*   269

Chapter 10   **The Neglect of the Entrepreneur**
                 Harold Demsetz   271

Chapter 11   **Entrepreneurs and the Entrepreneurial Function:**
                 A Commentary   *Israel M. Kirzner*   281

Chapter 12   **Entrepreneurial Activity in a Complex Economy**
                 Mordecai Kurz   291

Chapter 13   **Economics and Entrepreneurs**
                 Sherwin Rosen   301

                 Index   311

                 About the Contributors   319

                 About the Editor   323

Foreword

The belief born with the Kenseyian revolution that economic bliss is just around the corner and that the only thing required is fine tuning, tax, and regulatory policy to make any economist's dream come true has now fallen into disrepute. The malaise lies to a large degree in the neglect of the entrepreneur. The goal was assumed to be given and clear, the means specified and unambiguous. In such a means-oriented world as we witness in the aftermath of World War II, the entrepreneur is an anachronism. The manager, the administrator, and the efficiency expert reign supreme.

By now we have come to realize that we cannot manufacture economic growth simply by managing business, by use of efficient bureaucratic rules. Innovation and creativity are needed to solve the problems of society. We face the sort of environment in which the entrepreneur can and should flourish and pave the ground for a new economic order. By discovering hitherto unidentified needs of society, by exploiting hitherto neglected resources, he leads himself and society to prosperity.

But where do we find and how do we channel entrepreneurial talent? Is it born? Can it be cultivated? Could those involved with it be taught to sharpen that gift, to make it work for them and their surroundings? Mindful of the power of government, it would seem at first glance that the tools available to it (tax incentives, reduced regulation, monetary policy, and so on) can be used to fuel entrepreneurial force. But does the mere existence of the favorable climate ensure entrepreneurial activity? Not any more than the existence of a basketball and court guarantees game and players. Too little is known now about entrepreneurs to conclude that they will necessarily take advantage of available opportunities.

Typically, the entrepreneur is seen as an individual who owns and operates a small business—a "momma and poppa" business. This view excludes (1) the person who does not own but just runs the business and (2) the executive who owns a large business. Thus a proper definition of the *entrepreneur* must be broad enough to include all entrepreneurs.

The individual who owns and operates a small business may or may not be an entrepreneur. For example, can the owner of a bus company under contract with New York City to transport school children be considered an entrepreneur? Scrutiny would reveal that engaging in scheduling, administration, and the like, he should be considered a manager: he does not seek and find new markets, create new products, and deal with risks.

There are some who suggest that entrepreneurship is like the caveat about pornography: "You know it when you see it." Others say entrepreneurship is similar to artistic creativity in that it defies formalization. Thus, a workable definition of the word *entrepreneurship* needs to be formulated. Ronen, in chapter 7, deals with the problem in an interesting way. The entrepreneur, he argues, is part of a process that starts with discovery or, if you will, creative inspiration, diffusion of the discovery, and ultimately conversion of the discovery into a reality. The last step in this process appears to be the logical basis for defining the entrepreneur: a person who identifies an opportunity and gives it an existence. With this definition in hand the question of whether entrepreneurship can be encouraged and/or taught can be answered in the affirmative. The issues that now require deeper understanding are: (1) where and how does one find new ideas; (2) how does one go about implementing a new idea? At the moment very little is known about these questions. Only after we have gained a better understanding of entrepreneurship as a whole can a rational policy at the national level be formulated.

The efforts of the Price Institute for Entrepreneurial Studies are directed toward addressing these important questions. The institute's work can be considered entrepreneurial in its own right. It addresses a discerned need in society, a vacuum in the market for ideas currently unfilled. This, in the opinion of the institute, is an opportunity, though not one that is motivated by the classic, self-interest argument. The institute is currently in the implementing phase of the entrepreneurial process as defined by Ronen. Success is the ultimate criterion by which entrepreneurial endeavor is judged. It is the institute's fervent hope that ultimately it will be judged to be an *entrepreneur*.

Harold Price
Chairman
Price Institute for
Entrepreneurial Studies

Preface

The great productivity crisis of the past fifteen years has brought with it renewed concern over entrepreneurship. The rate of productivity growth in the U.S. has fallen precipitately from its level in the first half of the 1960s and has remained about half that of the leading industrial countries of Western Europe, and a third that of Japan. A great deal of effort has been devoted to finding explanations for this fact, as a first step toward formulating an effective productivity policy. The shadow that hangs over all this is the fear that, for some reason, the American entrepreneurial spirit has gone into decline, and that the preeminence of the U.S economy is threatened by a newly emerging army of entrepreneurs marching forth from the societies of Japan, Taiwan, Hong Kong, South Korea, and Singapore.

One disturbing feature of this hypothesis is that no one has succeeded in devising a means of testing it. No variable represents the exercise of entrepreneurship in the econometric models designed to seek out the sources of the productivity slowdown. Nor does it often enter into the theorists' mathematical models, which, as they are hypothetical in character, should be capable of including any economic phenomenon their authors wish to embrace. The entrepreneur, in short, is an invisible man. His role is respected, his importance acknowledged, his significance for effective economic policy is stressed; yet, he eludes the grasp of the analyst.

Clearly, this is an unsatisfactory state of affairs.

It is not difficult to offer conjectures explaining the entrepreneur's general absence from standard economic analysis. My own hypothesis is that the primary cause is the necessarily ill-defined character of entrepreneurship itself. Entrepreneurship is the generic term we use to encompass the exercise of daring, imagination, vision—the abilities needed to seize opportunities overlooked by those whose thoughts run in conventional patterns. In short, *predictability* is almost the antonym of *entrepreneurship*. Because unpredictability is one of its essential features, entrepreneurship is inherently difficult to take into account in systematic analysis, which relies on stable patterns and repeated behavior in representing its actors.

If this view of the matter is valid, it helps account for the current place of entrepreneurship in formal economic analysis. However, this hardly makes the situation more comfortable, for this view of the matter also reinforces our intuitive judgment about the entrepreneur's importance. What would an economy be like with all boldness, imagination, and vision expunged from its workings? It would soon become flat, stale, and unprofitable, a place of stagnation.

It was the vision of Harold Price—himself an entrepreneur, not an economist—that put underway the attempts represented in this book to remedy the unsatisfactory status of entrepreneurship in economic analysis. In 1979, he founded the Price Institute for Entrepreneurial Studies as a vehicle for stimulating research into the subject. Moreover, not content just to found the organization, he immersed himself in its work, participating in its conferences and watching over its progress while not in any way interfering with the analytic integrity of its research activities. Operating under the valuable day-to-day guidance of Ed and Gloria Appel, the organization rapidly began to function effectively.

Academic leadership was put into the capable hands of Professor Joshua Ronen of New York University, who, in consultation with Harold Price, decided that they would do whatever was necessary to attract a set of first-rate scholars. The table of contents of this volume shows beyond any doubt how successful these efforts were.

To get significant research under way, it was decided to advance simultaneously on every front. Empirical work was undertaken with the aid of a rich body of historical data and contemporary interviews. Imaginative institutional analysis was provided by examining the forms of entrepreneurship that emerge outside the sphere of capitalist industrialized economies. Theoretical models were constructed that not only assign a place to the entrepreneur, but also seek to analyze how his behavior is influenced by other variables in the system and how his consequent behavior can, in turn, influence the workings of the system itself. In short, this was no modest effort—its ambition was to bring about a major breakthrough, a first step toward integrating the entrepreneur fully into operational and systematic economic analysis. In my judgment, they have succeeded admirably—though that must be left for the reader to judge.

The crucial question is, what will happen next? This is by no means a foregone conclusion. There have been moments before when entrepreneurship entered the forefront of economic thought, as when Schumpeter made his now-classic contribution on the subject. Yet no one found in that work the stimulus to follow through. It is as though Schumpeter had found a new vein of priceless ideas, but mined it thoroughly, leaving no scraps for extraction by others.

I believe this volume is very different. Every contribution is as much a program for future research as it is a report on a fully explored subject. It is an invitation to other scholars to plunge in and carry on in an arena of obvious importance in which fruitful directions are now more clearly indicated.

In all this, it seems clear that the Price Institute will continue both to be a focal point for such work and to provide the required stimulation. For that, and for the accomplishments it has already accumulated, our profession owes a heavy debt.

William J. Baumol
Princeton and New York Universities

1

Introduction

Joshua Ronen

This book offers the results of a concerted scholarly effort to reassess the role of a creative entrepreneurship vital to the needs of our time. A few introductory remarks may highlight for the reader some of the special perceptions of the individual contributors—not necessarily, however, in the order of the table of contents.

Entrepreneurship has long beguiled and tantalized economic theorists. Tackling the many-sidedness of the entrepreneurial way, the scholars here present a fascinating medley of speculations. Does a unified theme emerge? We believe so. While preserving a much-desired diversity of perspective, the authors' suggestive insights spell out a plausible view of the determinants of entrepreneurial force. My own contribution, I trust, will seem consistent, stemming as it does from actual interviews with a group of businessmen.

Those interviewed were selected for leadership qualities that seemed recognizably entrepreneurial. Thus, the entrepreneur is seen as the explorer of novel ventures. Mindful of uncertain consequences, he limits downside risk by seeking out projects with a calculated maximum of loss, such as will not, finally, threaten survival, while holding promise of large returns. To reduce uncertainty he will engage in market testing and in research and development.

But having refused the temptation of the more secure low-risk return, the adventuresome entrepreneur must bear in mind the threat of bankruptcy. To minimize this threat, he innovatively devises whatever financing arrangements will lure capital. Rarely does this individual reside in the large, bureaucratic organization.

Risk of Bankruptcy

This finding—that fear of bankruptcy prompts financial innovation—should be considered in conjunction with the analysis by Jerry Green and John Shoven. It is they who show how institutional rules governing bankruptcy might well deter risky investment. Their chapter views the underlying mechanism that generates inducements for the entrepreneur to create new financing instruments, to exploit regulatory loopholes, and to spread risk, perhaps in some ingeniously new direction. When there is bankruptcy risk, the structure of the financial contract is shaped by the way in which uncertainties unfold. The successful entrepreneur will know how to tailor the financing arrangements to the pattern in which uncertainty is resolved.

Thus, my chapter and that of Green and Shoven together build a scenario in which is synthesized the Knightian and Schumpeterian constructions. A specific application of the Schumpeterian entrepreneurial function is seen in the businessman's implementing of flexible strategies to accommodate needs of equity and of debt owners. At the same time, the entrepreneur must be conscious of the potential risk—the Knightian perspective.

Locus of Control

Also evident in my series of interviews is the importance of the entrepreneur's perception of his special talents as a decisive influence on events. Typically, entrepreneurs believe outcomes are contingent on their own actions. If one has a sharp alertness to opportunity, will he not believe himself master of his own fate? And if such alertness (attention, cognitive readiness, perceptual sensitivity, sagacity) is viewed as a scarce resource, then its supply must be responsive to perceived rewards. But those non-entrepreneurs characterized as "external" on the basis of their locus of control (attributing outcomes more to chance than to their own skill and action) will find little incentive to allocate their supply of alertness to activities whose effects they see as determined not by their conscious effort, but by the arbitrary will of others or the vagaries of fate. The perceived locus of control is in turn closely related to the strong urge—expressed by the interviewees—for that financial independence that releases one from the control of others. Being "internal" implies belief that one's own skill might well guarantee freedom to *choose* one's goals and to be responsible for success or failure. How such perception of control can be endogenously induced (and with it the supply of entrepreneurial talent or spirit), whether through socialization, parentally encouraged independence, evolution of cultural and religious beliefs, removal of any conditioning effect of constraint in one's choice of ends or in the means to accomplish those ends—this is a matter for social psychologists to grapple with.

Organizational Entrepreneurship

Whatever the genesis, perceived control, alertness, a sense of independence, and above all a passion for novelty together with the acceptance of risk are the traits not only of Green and Shoven's venturesome entrepreneur (seeking ways to avoid bankruptcy) but of Oliver Williamson's organizational innovator as well. Alertness to paths for profit can produce entrepreneurial manifestations in a number of areas, notably organizational structure. Williamson's chapter examines various hypotheses regarding the antecedents of organizational change and settles on transaction-cost savings as responsible for the incentives to shift from one governance structure to another. Entrepreneurs alert to the implications of new forms of mediating exchanges for profit have been responsible, according to Williamson, for major changes in the interfaces among markets (forward, backward, lateral integration) that not only advantaged the innovator but produced social benefits as well. Eli Whitney, Cyrus McCormick, Andrew Carnegie, Henry Ford, and others are viewed by Williamson as giant organizational entrepreneurs.

Skillfully, Williamson scans business history to document how growth of organizations was predicated upon balance among: (1) cost of adapting interfaces to changing circumstances; (2) degree to which economies of scale are exhausted by self-requirements; (3) degree to which economies of scope are sacrificed by undertaking one's own production; and (4) incentive dysfunctions and other dysfunctions of internal organization. The notion that organizational entrepreneurs resourcefully alter governance structures leads Williamson to suggest that a more permissive public policy and attitude, —that is, a reduced regulatory environment—would foster both organizational and technological innovation. The regulatory bodies should exhibit not hostility, but positive encouragement of change to promote efficiency. Again we see how the supply of entrepreneurial talent—this time implementing new organizational forms—is endogenous to the economic system and can be stimulated by a climate that will ensure the entrepreneur's freedom to innovate, to choose his means, and most importantly, to reap his due rewards.

Of striking interest in Williamson's chapter is the notion that uncertainty, the frequency of transactions, and the degree to which idiosyncratic investments (both physical and human) are made jointly determine whether a unified governance structure, the firm, emerges, and what size it is. Thus a firm would grow and integrate activities and transactions if such are of a recurring nature and idiosyncratic (in the sense that the specific identities of the parties to the exchange affect costs). Internal organization is then changed to allow adaptation to unfolding events. Economies of communication and of trust are attempted by the development of specialized language and signals.

Curiously, herein lies one of the problems of large organizations. Asset specificity favors the production within the firm of services and products whose qualities are considered important and not easily checkable by an autonomous purchaser. However, information would then have to be duplicated and control systems installed to compensate for incomplete awareness by one member of activities and objectives of others in the same organization. Because the nature and degree of knowledge differs across individuals, the cost of generating, transmitting, and assimilating information is high. Moral hazard and the possibility of guile complicates the attainment of coordination and trust. Design of incentive contracts to distribute risk optimally and minimize shirking becomes difficult. A threat to entrepreneurial activity thus inheres in jointness in production, in the sense that actions of many individuals within the organization are interdependently required to supply a good or service within a setting in which no one is wholly informed about the actions, objectives, and degree of honesty of others. No individual member can have, or perceive being able to have, control over all actions necessary to produce a desired consequence; nor would any one member be certain of reward, since no reliable measure of individual contribution can be produced. The joint work of many produces the good or service. In such an environment, what is there to lure the entrepreneurially inclined to be alert to innovative opportunities?

Locus of Entrepreneurial Research and Development

It is in this context that Kenneth Arrow addresses the very interesting question of the locus of research innovation. In my own interviews, it seemed evident that bolder entrepreneurs found the large organization stifling, the need to justify plans and investments inhibiting. This pointed to the strong possibility that mutual self-selection links the novelty-seeking, independent-minded entrepreneur with the small firm, the managerial type with the larger organization.

Is there promise of further refinement? Are there fields of specialization within the entrepreneurial investment in innovation? And is the locus of these entrepreneurial specializations systematically associated with size and complexity of organization? Arrow's fascinating chapter suggests that investments in innovation can be fruitfully decomposed into two specializations. The less costly and more original (novel) innovations are initiated by small firms, those involving greater development costs, but of a less radical kind, by the larger firms. This very specialization creates opportunities for trade in firms—takeovers, mergers.

The hypotheses behind these interesting observations are: (1) Large firms can avail themselves of larger and more stable capital supply, from both internal and external sources, than small firms; this is made possible because of activity diversification and economies of scale in attention-directing and information-gathering by outside suppliers of funds. (2) When responsibility for decisions on necessary research and development is shared, from need to seek approval for capital expenditure, the information provided as the basis for the approval becomes degraded as it passes through the communications channels. The more lengthy the chain of communication within the firm, the more extensive the degradation, becoming even more severe when such information must cross the firm's boundary. Inevitably, information degradation in large organizations is greater than in small, and is most severe when financing is sought from external capital sources. Moreover, degradation may result from the communication channels as such, with their limited capacity; and from incentive effects that reduce the reliability of transmission. In the latter case, entrepreneurs cherishing novel concepts may be tempted for personal gain to present information misleadingly, especially since the consequences of research and development become visible only after great lapse of time; even then (and even with the initiator still around), it would be hard, within the uncertain setting of such research and development, to pinpoint responsibility either for failure, or for success.

These hardly disputable premises lead Arrow to his conclusion: on average one would expect firms to specialize so as to correlate optimal development scales of projects with firm size and complexity. Once a market for research outcomes is introduced, Arrow further speculates, smaller firms will tend to specialize more in research and in more modest development processes, while larger firms will specialize in the larger developments, with a lesser proportion of their budget going into the research phase. Indeed they will tend to buy from smaller firms a considerable fraction of their research basis for subsequent development of innovations.

Which firms, then, will stay small and which will grow? Are there characteristics that identify each set? Mordecai Kurz—who, together with Harold Demsetz, Israel Kirzner, and Sherwin Rosen, provides a commentary in this book—suggests that Arrow's conclusions and mine would seem complementary: we perceive small firms as led by entrepreneurs, large ones by industrial managers. I would even venture the possibility that the bureaucratic internal capital-allocation mechanism within the large firm, together with its degrading of information, is itself endogenously induced by the mutual self-selection I have already discussed. The entrepreneur and the small firm seek each other out. The managerial-type individuals, preferring the executive suites of large organizations, hardly encourage alert entrepreneurs to cast permanent anchor anywhere near them.

This reinforces Arrow's supplementary hypothesis that a larger firm will find it harder to allocate capital to very novel ventures since prior information of the internal capital-allocation mechanism may not equip it to evaluate novelties very well. In fact, it could be contended that, because of mutual self-selection, internal capital allocators tend to be less entrepreneurial, exhibiting very little passion for novelty. By spinning off innovation-research activity into small units partially controlled by the organization and immunized from the internal capital-allocation mechanism, the large organization can gain first access to research outcomes while avoiding some of the information degradation otherwise encountered.

The Averaging of Risk and Novelty-Seeking

Why would the large organization exhibit a complex internal capital-allocation mechanism that discourages investment in novel research concepts? Could not decision-making power in such large organizations, with ownership typically diffused and requiring a high degree of monitoring (where incentive problems inhere in the agency relation), be shared by a larger group of individuals than in proprietorships or small organizations, thus effecting checks and balances on management actions? In such an environment, that salient entrepreneurial quest for novelty that might indeed characterize a given decision maker within the organization would likely be blunted by the shared decision making, attenuated by the lesser passion for novelty of decision makers not so entrepreneurially inclined. Only some sort of average degree of novelty seeking is allowed to come into play. Interest (and funds) are diverted away from the more innovative and uncertain projects.

Contrast this with the small business, where decision making is the sole domain of the individual entrepreneur. His actions, unencumbered by need to seek consent or approval, can give full expression to his eagerness to commit resources to innovative research and to his willingness to assume the attendant risks. Clearly, the entrepreneurial investment would here loom larger.

In the large organization, risk-sharing spells a lesser risk for each. The single entrepreneur can more easily act on his own greater willingness to take the risk involved: he has no highly risk-averse partners to veto a go-ahead. Thus, in the large organization only the "lowest common" willingness to take risk figures in the decision to invest. Offsetting this, however, is the greater ability of the large organization to garner resources.

Within the large private-sector organization of the Western business world, some sharing of risk, profit, and decision-making is typical. We encounter a more extreme form of such sharing in the East European country of Yugoslavia. Abram Bergson's comprehensive and illuminating chapter focuses on risk taking, particularly in the form of innovations, under the prevailing labor participatory system of Yugoslavia, referring more especially to the period prior to the 1974–1976 reforms.

In the Yugoslav socialistic enterprise workers share profits with management, though rewards to all are differentiated in accordance with labor quality. All are residual claimants and risk bearers. There are indications that the enterprise aims more or less (as Western theory assumes) to maximize the net income of each worker; but in the socialistic environment this is subject to constraints on staff curtailment. Such workers might be expected to be less affluent than the owners of private enterprise in a capitalistic society, and so more likely to exhibit risk aversion. Coupled with relative inability to diversify job investments, this implies risk avoidance and therefore a lesser tendency to invest in innovative projects than evidenced by owners in private Western business.

The Yugoslav enterprise appears to be a limiting case. The large organization of our own free-enterprise society does have some risk sharing and some participatory decision making. Thus, we see a continuum from our single entrepreneur on the one extreme (exhibiting a marked tendency for investment in innovation) to the Yugoslav enterprise, with its extensive profit and risk sharing, at the other. Somewhere in the middle is the large Western enterprise which together with a degree of risk avoidance offers a moderate willingness to invest internal resources in development of relatively safe innovations.

Bergson concludes, in fact, that if the Yugoslav self-managed firm is in practice *more* entrepreneurial than might have been anticipated, it probably is less so than the typical private enterprise of the Western world.

The Ultimate Bureaucracy

The information degradation hypothesized by Arrow to exist in large organizations, together with the relatively high risk aversion manifest in group decision making both in the large organization of the West and in Yugoslav enterprise, reaches a maximum in the Soviet enterprise. This is ably documented in Herbert Levine's chapter. Here the interface between the potentially entrepreneurial individual and the large or small organization—an interface projected as critical throughout my own interviews, skillfully analyzed by Arrow, and placed in the context of the Yugoslav environment by Bergson—is now carried by Levine one logical step further to the Soviet state bureaucracy.

Levine tells us about information degradation and its costs when approval is sought for research ideas: not only how long such ideas "stand in line," but also how layers and levels of communication and approval distort objectives and misdirect attention. Hierarchical referral, bureaucratic relay, and the vast difference in technical knowledge between performers and high ministerial authorities impede communication and degrade the information flow from innovator to grantor of approval. In the large Western enterprise, it is in the interest of the internal capital allocators and external capital-market investors to specialize in evaluating technical research concepts in various fields. For the numerous layers of administrators in the Soviet bureaucracy, such specialization is neither rewarding nor feasible—other functions demand time.

Risk aversion among decision makers certainly exacts a toll on entrepreneurial innovation in the large Western organization and in the Yugoslav enterprise. In the totalitarian-state bureaucracy, the prevention of "innovation by invasion," documented by Levine as a manifestation of risk aversion, may in fact also indicate realistic risk assessment: an innovation turned sour can spell disaster for an entrenched force.

Entrepreneurship in the Soviet Union is plagued by more than information degradation and risk aversion. Decision-making autonomy—a sine qua non in the quest for novelty—is curtailed to a much greater degree than in Western enterprise. Without freedom, the entrepreneurial individual could hardly attribute results to his own talents—any link has been severed, exploration is not seen to be rewarded. The American businessman's confidence in the success of the novel venture, so strongly emphasized in my interviews, will not likely be found in a centralized economy.

Levine points to still another factor in the Soviet economy: application by the central planning authority of extreme pressure, which filters down to managers required to fulfill—and over-fulfill—performance targets, especially in production. In addition to curtailed autonomy, the enterprise directors and managers below them will have little or no time for alertness to novel opportunity. Alertness, even among the most entrepreneurial, must be a function of time not devoted to the routine.

This constant state of excess aggregate demand in the Soviet economy gives rise to rigid incentive schemes narrowly based on deviations from performance targets. This year's good performance becomes next year's target. Rewards from any innovation are thus diminished; the implementation of the new may interrupt current schedules, nibble away at possible bonuses from production above target. More importantly, if the innovation should fail to produce, the manager runs considerable risk (possibly more than the Yugoslav counterpart) of losing managerial status, together with such perquisites as the privileged vacation, and the like.

In this environment, the very large enterprise under surveillance of state and party bureaucracy dominates; mutual self-selection between the individual and the organization cannot come into play. But where is there the small enterprise for the entrepreneur? Will he then become a member of the "second economy?"

If, as the picture Levine has drawn shows, Soviet enterprise managers have little incentive to experiment with the new, they might slacken the implementing of any innovations pressed upon them by governmental or party bodies. The new entrepreneurial firms responsible for diffusing scientific ideas into the production process, removed from the operating conditions, will likely be of only little avail.

The Tyranny of the Runner-Up

It becomes clear that in the Soviet economy the enterprise manager is subjected to considerable risk; not so the enterprise, or the ministry. There is no
threat of bankruptcy. The bureaucracy's power to avert invasion from competitive innovation prevents the kind of creative destruction that Levine
believes to be the major manifestation of entrepreneurial activities in the
West. But how will that large organization in the West protect itself from
innovative invasion? It may collaborate with whatever kind of bureaucracy
there is and invite regulatory protection in return for exchange in the political market. This, in Baumol's imaginative chapter, was the theme for the
modeling of entrepreneurial growth and demise.

Baumol sees regulations and administrative barriers as impeding the
activities of the entrepreneur, deterring innovation, and protecting what
exists from competition. All are seen as endogenously created at the urging
of runners-up threatened by the pressure of competition. Unlike the Soviet
state's curb on entrepreneurial innovation (designed to protect the bureaucracies), the Western economy's regulatory constraint is viewed as a policy
variable whose systematic manipulation becomes worthy of inquiry. Autonomy provides the entrepreneur of the West with the *ability* to act on his urge
to innovate; perceived net rewards offer *incentives* to do so. Thus, regulatory constraint and taxes (determining net rewards) become the variables of
interest in Baumol's dynamic model of entrepreneurship.

The model yields a prognosis of recurring fluctuation in economic rate
of growth from acceleration to deceleration to stagnation. But while an
increase in the tax burden slows the rate of growth of entrepreneurship (and
with it rate of growth of national income), it does not affect the amplitude
of fluctuations. On the other hand, tightening regulatory constraints lowers
the ceiling that determines the high point of fluctuations. For Baumol, constraints spell the more serious threat.

At the core of the analysis lies a difficult problem noted by Baumol: the
dimensions of interest, namely, entrepreneurial activity and consequently
financial return, remain operationally undefined. Hence comes the necessity to introduce assumptions regarding the relation between entrepreneurship and economic growth and financial returns. Two such important
assumptions are: (1) Productive entrepreneurship (contributing primarily to
overall growth with everyone benefiting from the resulting prosperity)
yields diminishing returns. Ultimately, this gives rise to competitive entrepreneurship (nibbling away at the share of others to increase one's own
share of activity), at which time runners-up invite regulatory protection. (2)
The supply of *autonomous* entrepreneurship stimulated by the success of
other entrepreneurs is such that inducement is less than one for one. As first
approximations, both assumptions are clearly plausible. But we must con-

sider, eventually, the type of explosive entrepreneurial innovation that yields increasing returns in rate of economic growth as well as in autonomously induced future entrepreneurial action. These possibilities are consistent with the random outburst of entrepreneurial talent said by Baumol to drive the economy out from a point of stagnant equilibrium, parallel to the random proliferation of research concepts held by Arrow to be possibly a function of previous innovations and also to the complex and largely random process of initiation or invention described in my own chapter.

Common to all these angles of vision on the entrepreneurial process is the phenomenon of change. The entrepreneur has thus far emerged as surveying simultaneously the environment and his organization in search of advantageous opportunities, recognizing that he can benefit from alteration in the existing economic arrangements, that is, from change. Hence, the reality of change in the prevailing system must be considered in the modeling of the entrepreneur and of his influence on the economic structure. Such modeling, it would appear, requires that the flows between entrepreneur and environment be explicitly admitted. It is Harold Shapiro's chapter that formalizes this notion of change and provides us with a method for modeling flows within the economic system. Shapiro's approach imbues the model of innovative change with a sense of the entrepreneur's connectedness with his environment.

Regulations and the Public Interest

Noteworthy too is Kurz's observation that a large subset of public regulations is not of the kind instigated by the runner-up business firm. Any such regulations are designed, rather, to protect the public interest and induce the production of public goods, and by correction of informational defects to facilitate the conduct of financial markets and implement rules for the disclosure of products or information. Kurz argues that this large set of regulations not specifically addressed by Baumol need not put a limit on incentives or entrepreneurial activity, but may in fact bring about an increase in such, even in tandem with enhancement of social welfare. (Examples Kurz cites include innovative engine design by the Japanese to conform to U.S. clean-air regulation.)

Kurz's insight is rich in implications. It could well be thought, for example, that some regulation might be necessary to build public confidence in financial markets by requiring disclosure about the conduct of firms; such public confidence would furnish a better environment for entrepreneurial action. Contrariwise, some regulations designed to further social welfare might induce entrepreneurial activities that do not merit encouragement—for example, those involving legal or accounting skills meant to avoid levies of any kind. Future research should attempt a finer discrimination between regulations that discourage and those that encourage. As Kurz argues, the view held by some supply-side supporters that *all* regulations serve no public need and result only in restrictions on entrepreneurial incentive may indeed be over-simplified.

Reflections on Team Entrepreneurship

Perhaps Baumol's most interesting suggestions draw upon the experience both of the Israeli kibbutz and the Japanese firm. Consider again that the quest for novelty and (in the initial stages) the willingness to bear risk were held necessary conditions for entrepreneurial action among the business leaders I interviewed. Baumol points out that grave risks to workers attend the success of labor-saving innovations. Why not then offer to these workers the job security guaranteed in the Israeli kibbutz or the Japanese firm, thus promoting innovation while at the same time eliminating protection of inept runners-up by subjecting them to competitive invasion and giving full play to creative destruction. Curiously, this discriminatory allocation of risk (much to be borne by the enterprise, little by the worker) reverses the pattern of immunity-responsibility prevalent in the Soviet economy, where enterprises are immune to the threat of bankruptcy, while the enterprising managers are subject to grave consequences.

But how about the risk attending the *failure* of non-labor-saving innovations? Surely, many of the innovations in the kibbutz and the Japanese firm are of this kind! Here, the relatively low willingness to bear risk (possibly characteristic of a group's average risk tendencies) may be well accommodated by the low risk borne by any one individual—low by dint of the risk-sharing that prevails. But distribution of risks requires in most cases the building of reserves in good times to compensate for rough times; this would tend to blunt the large rewards otherwise flowing to innovation.

Are we witnessing here the kind of substitutability between quest for novelty and financial reward I implied might exist among my interviewees? Do nonfinancial rewards loom large in the Japanese firm and the Israeli kibbutz? But why did Bergson not discover similar bursts of innovation in the Yugoslav *poduzeće?* Are there organizational characteristics nourishing the quest for novelty in the Japanese firm and in the Israeli kibbutz that are not to be found in the Yugoslav enterprise? Exciting lines of inquiry are suggested here.

Task interdependencies and specialization require teams. Teamwork is also made necessary by the collectivity of skill and motivation going into production; by the difficulty (or high cost) of observing effort and skill in individual team members; and, especially in the case of innovative tasks, by the need for *diversity* of knowledge and skill to enhance creativity. Indeed, these factors may supplement and reinforce those that Williamson argues replace market transactions by organizations (asset idiosyncrasy, transaction frequency, uncertainty). But teamwork requires information transmission and coordination, both costly. Increasing returns geared to scale of networks for information transmission and coordination may well explain the increased size, over time, of organizations, as Arrow has suggested. But are there implications of accentuated need for such coordination in team entrepreneurship?

To speculate: within teams, the pursuit of self-interest—pillar of traditional doctrine—by any member of the team is blocked by relative ignorance as to motives of other members and by ignorance of possible actions on which depend the outcome of the teamwork (and, thus, the ultimate rewards to any given member). The greater such ignorance or uncertainty regarding others' actions, the greater the degree of mutual distrust and alienation likely to be exhibited among members. (Could the open workroom of the Japanese plant be intended to reduce distrust?)

An individual's incentive to innovate within a team is thus impeded because: (1) he does not necessarily reap benefits, and (2) he has lesser (actual and perceived) control over the means to make innovation successful. With others' actions and goodwill necessary, uncertainty deters entrepreneurial acts.

In this setting, knowledge of each other, a mutual trust and intimacy, can become important stimulants to team entrepreneurship. The two characteristics are much cited as typifying the Israeli kibbutz. The larger the size of teams, the greater their multiplicity, the more need for coordination of every kind. If a newly acquired mutual perception reveals the identity of any members who are untrustworthy, these can be weeded out; the individual member, with deeper understanding, could more correctly specify what actions satisfy his own self-interest. The investment required for this particular kind of knowledge acquisition in the smaller organization is apt to be less: teams are smaller, pursuit of self-interest and reaping of rewards more certain. Here may be a lesson for the large organization from the Japanese and Israeli experience: stimulate mutual knowledge and greater familiarity; also, perhaps, accord freedom to teams to implement different modes of organizing work and schemes of profit and risk sharing, and so bring to bear whatever organizational and financial innovativeness are latent in the most entrepreneurial of the team. The rugged-individualism brand of entrepreneurship of the past may well have to be balanced by attention to the larger organism, the team, in recognition of increasingly complex business realities.

Part I
Theoretical Analysis of Entrepreneurial Behavior

2 Innovation in Large and Small Firms

Kenneth J. Arrow

Introduction

This essay is intended to begin the elaboration of a theme: the interaction between the observed sizes of firms and their internal decisionmaking procedures. This theme is a major one in the symphony of enterpreneurial activity. The entrepreneur, as the maker and changer of economic and productive life, is usually envisaged as an individual. In the neoclassical tradition, he (or, rarely, she) is the lightning calculator, the individual who rapidly scans the field of alternative productive processes and chooses the optimum at any given set of prices. In the Austrian tradition, most notably in the work of Schumpeter,[1] he is endowed with a special psychology that makes him all the more an individual in the strict sense of the word—he cannot be replaced by a machine or by a multiplicity of individuals, who would inevitably slow him down. "He travels fastest who travels alone," says an ancient proverb.

However, the individual entrepreneur-proprietor does not loom nearly as large today as suggested by these accounts. The large—even giant—firm is a massive presence on the economic landscape. These large firms not only predominate in the static allocation of resources, but are the sources of much of the world's change. They share fully with others as the sources and users of innovations.

This is not to deny the continued importance of the relatively small firm and the individual inventor. Indeed, the coexistence of large and small firms is itself an interesting intellectual question. If, in fact, large firms do have advantages over smaller ones, why are small firms not eliminated in the competitive struggle? More generally, if there are differential advantages to one size or another of firm, why do firms not converge to the optimal size?

The presence of large firms creates logical difficulties for the concept of property and for the reward structure of the individual, as Berle and Means[2] pointed out almost fifty years ago. The sharp calculating eye of the neoclassical entrepreneur was for his own profits, and even those who gave a more psychological interpretation to entrepreneurial motives could hardly deny that revenue was essential among them. But an employee, however entrepreneurial in spirit, does not have property rights and cannot claim profits,

15

the residual revenues after contractual claims. Much ingenuity can go into alternative compensation schemes, but the maker of decisions about innovations can no longer be simply identified with the recipient of rewards (and taker of losses) from them.

Of equal, or even greater, significance is the diffuse control structure of the large firm. Essentially, no one can make decisions without limits even within the framework of feasibility. Even a chief executive officer is restricted, partly because of the need to adhere to well-defined operating procedures, and partly because limits on span of control prevent him from making more than a limited range of decisions with limited information. In large firms, entrepreneurship has sociological as well as psychological and economic dimensions.

The remarks thus far show that entrepreneurial activity, however defined, operates in different ways in large firms than in small ones. I will concentrate here on entrepreneurship as Schumpeter conceived it—the process of innovation. The basic decisions are the recognition of promising ideas and the financing of their development. We want to discuss how these decisions operate in firms of varying sizes.

An economist would not, of course, discuss any issues of decision making by firms without taking account of market relations. Since the development of innovations is an investment, the most relevant market is the capital market. However, innovations are, by their nature, rather odd commodities from a neoclassical viewpoint. They tend to be indivisible. Their development is attended by uncertainty—if everything about an innovation were known, it would not be an innovation. What is still more, the properties and economic potential of an innovation are by its nature likely to be better known to the innovator than to a prospective source of financing.

In short, the supply of capital for innovation is not modeled well by conventional competitive market theory. Indeed, most of the analysis in this chapter will center about the methods of financing innovation and their implications.

The chapter is organized as follows: In the next section, I review in the sketchiest way the idea that large firms are really significant in the economy and constitute a phenomenon about which we cannot be indifferent. I then describe an idealized model of the process of innovation (oversimplified of course) designed to serve as a basis for subsequent discussion. The heart of the paper follows, an attempt to understand the factors in the decision to innovate and (what is essentially equivalent) the financing of the innovative activity. In particular, I stress the systematic variation of these decisions with firm size and complexity. It is concluded that there is likely to be a tendency toward specialization—less costly and more original innovations will come from small firms, and those involving higher development costs but less radical departures in principle will come from larger firms. This specialization creates opportunities for trade, as all specialization does; in this case, the trade will frequently be in firms as such—that is, takeovers and mergers.

The Significance of Large Firms

From the popular viewpoint, the concentration of economic power is one of the most obvious aspects of the economic world. In mainstream neoclassical economics, it hardly appears—especially in more abstract versions of the neoclassical system (for instance, Arrow and Hahn).[3] Of course, the presence of natural monopoly is recognized, and this is the basis for the doctrine of price regulation. Even here, many economists consider that there is sufficient competition from substitute products to make natural monopoly an unimportant concept.

The trouble is that the analytic tools of neoclassical economics are not well adapted to departures from perfect competition. There are two pillars to the edifice: the optimizing behavior of the firm and household, and the equilibrating forces of the markets that link them. Optimizing behavior can indeed be discussed under conditions of market power; the theory of monopoly is rich in implications. But the concept of imperfectly competitive markets is very hard to define. Various ad hoc constructions, such as Chamberlin's notion of monopolistic competition,[4] have appeared, but they suffer from inconsistencies. Game theory has supplied a formal framework that, in principle, replaces markets by more general forms of interactions, but it has not yet succeeded in producing a *general* theory comparable in power to the theory of general competitive equilibrium.

Hence, there is a bias toward analyzing the competitive case. As we know, this analysis requires, if taken literally, that the production possibility sets be convex. In particular, it requires constant or diminishing returns to scale. The latter case suggests a bias toward small firms—under free entry, the smaller the better. Constant returns, on the other hand, is neutral toward the size of firms. If two firms merge, the owners will (under perfect competition) be neither better off nor worse off than they were before. Under perfect markets, including perfect capital markets, the profits of two different activities will simply be additive.

A good deal of the empirical literature on firm sizes has been devoted to arguing that the competitive model is adequate in practice—that is, there are not many markets dominated by one or two firms. This may well be true; it follows that the static efficiency characteristics of competitive equilibrium can be postulated to hold in the real world. This is very far from denying the existence of very large firms or from explaining this phenomenon.

For it is certainly a fact. Depending on what measures you use, 500 firms constitute half or more of the nonagricultural economy.[5] It is frequently argued that the indices of concentration have not shown much secular rise, at least not for 75 years or so. However, this misses the point. The economy has grown enormously in this period. If it were merely a question of replication—that is, if the economy were expanding homogeneously—we would expect the number of firms to increase in the same proportion. Since firms differ in size, for whatever reason, we would expect the *proportion* of firms of a given size to be constant, while the total number increases.

To be sure, the expansion of the economy has not been merely a replication. The fact that per capita income is rising—and, more strongly, that factor productivity (output per unit input) is or was rising—implies a change in the proportions of the economy. But one component of growth in the market remains sheer size—population or total factor supply (capital and labor). One might expect, then, that the number of firms would be proportional to the extensive growth of the economy (its size in population or inputs), while the size of each firm might be expected to grow with the intensive growth (for example, output per capita or per unit factor supply). This is what has happened (roughly) to the distribution of individual income. It can be expressed as the constancy of the Lorenz curve—that is, the proportion of total income received by a given proportion of the population arrayed by income level (for example, the upper tenth of income recipients) is a constant.

But this is not what has happened with the distribution of firm sizes. The proportion of total sales or income received by a fixed *number* of firms has more or less remained constant.[6] Therefore, the proportion of income received by a fixed proportion of firms starting from the top (say, an upper decile again) has increased.

In short, we find that the size of each firm has increased more than proportionally to intensive growth. If intensive growth is identified with productivity (either of labor or of total inputs), it follows that not only the outputs but also the inputs of the average firm have risen. This implies that the forces determining the sizes of firms (in particular the economies of scale and the size of the market) have so shifted as to make larger firms more advantageous.

The increasing costs of innovation are a possible candidate, and the later analysis in this chapter implicitly makes the case for this proposition. At this point, however, I only with to establish that there has been a significant shift to larger sizes of firms and that this shift has systematic economic consequences and causes.

One obvious feature of larger firms (as contrasted with smaller contemporary firms or even with the same firms when they were smaller) is that they are more complex. They are not simply scale expansions of smaller firms, any more than the economy as a whole is a scale expansion of its earlier historical self. Even if the added activities are similar in nature to the original ones, random fluctuations would make coordinating activities profitable. More broadly, growth usually involves disaggregation of activities and differentiation of products and activities.[7] No doubt these tendencies can ultimately be explained in terms of indivisibilities and other causes of increasing returns to scale. The complexity requires additional control functions at the central level.[8]

Coordinating activities themselves are costly; not only do they directly involve the use of resources (managerial and supporting personnel, associated equipment, space, and communication channels), but they also impose costs upon decision making at lower levels by creating delays and requiring additional communication costs. They are undertaken because the costs of coordination are exceeded by the benefits.[9] As Coase has argued, these benefits are relevant only if they are not obtainable by coordinating separate activities in the marketplace, through prices.[10]

This point can be emphasized by considering the multidivisional firm and the role of transfer pricing. A large firm is organized into profit centers, each of which operates as virtually a separate firm. Transactions between them are market transactions, and payments between them are made at current market prices or (if no suitable market exists) at transfer prices mimicing market prices. Presumably the opportunities for direct (as op- posed to market oriented) coordination of activities have been exhausted within the profit centers. What distinguishes the large firm, however, from a collection of smaller firms is that many resource-allocation decisions are still made at a central level—particularly capital formation. A profit center is responsible for its own decisions on current flows, but in general it cannot make its own investment decisions, except possibly for very trivial ones. Indeed, it is surprising how often decisions on investment require the approval of the Board of Directors, while decisions of at least equal impor- tance relating to pricing and production are decentralized to much lower levels.

There is, in short, an internal centralized mechanism for allocating available investment funds to specific projects among the various profit centers. The internal capital-allocation mechanism is not, properly speak- ing, a market—that is, a profit center cannot borrow any amount at a fixed rate of interest. Rather, the project it proposes must be examined by the allocating authority for feasibility and profitability.

It would not be correct to contrast this allocation mechanism with an external capital market thought of as a true market in the textbook sense. Much, though not all, external financing is also project-specific and rationed. A bank does not lend by buying securities from anonymous sellers, but by lending to particular firms and individuals and often by looking at the particular project that the lender wishes to finance.

(We will not here study why capital allocation is so largely centralized, even in an otherwise decentralized firm. Part of the reason, certainly, must be the relatively slow feedback. The head of a profit center is not personally liable for the costs of bad investments. Considering job mobility, he may not be around to take any consequences when an investment is realized.)

It is important to distinguish the existence or absence of an internal capital allocation (in this sense) from the presence or absence of external financing. The supply of capital available for internal allocation can come either from retained profits in the various profit centers or from the outside. Large firms in general have an advantage in access to the outside capital market. One reason is the principle of insurance. Investing as they do in a variety of projects, their earnings are apt to be more stable and, therefore, the riskiness of their securities is reduced. Another reason is an economy of scale in attention and information-gathering from the viewpoint of the suppliers of funds. A large firm is a greater demander, and it therefore pays potential investors to concentrate their attention on that firm's activities rather than scattering it in one-shot transactions over many firms, for each of which there will be relatively little opportunity to use the information.

Diversification of activities also implies a more stable source of internal funds. Hence, in general, large firms will have a disproportionately larger and more stable internal capital supply than smaller firms will.

A Model of the Innovation Process

Innovations are infinitely variable; indeed, they include all alterations in knowledge of current production relations between inputs and outputs. Most are very small, but those are not the ones we are concerned with here. We wish to stress those large enough that deliberate decisions are needed to proceed along the path of innovation. An innovation may never be realized as a product; if it is so realized, it may not remain in production very long. The process of innovation is, virtually by definition, filled with uncertainty; it is a journey of exploration into a strange land.

We take as a primitive of the system a stream of *concepts*—ideas for innovation. These occur to individuals both within firms and elsewhere. A concept may or may not prove to be feasible. If it is feasible, it may or may not prove to be profitable. These determinations require investment, and it is these investment decisions that we are investigating.

For simplicity, we will distinguish two further stages after the concept, those of *research* and of *development*. Somewhat arbitrarily, we will think of research as determining the feasibility of the concept and development as determining its profitability.

In this model, the concepts are random events, not controllable and unaffected by policy. They will, of course, depend on many factors, but especially on the state of knowledge in the relevant specialty. This in turn, may be influenced by previous innovations in the same intellectual area.

Decisions are made at the next two stages. First, research is needed to determine if the concept can be translated into actuality. The research may be more or less costly to carry out. When it is completed, it yields information about the prospects for development in the following sense. At the start of the development process, there will be a relation between the profitability of the innovation when it is finally introduced (possibly zero or even negative) and the amount invested in development. This relation depends on the information gathered in the research phase—that is, the profitability of the innovation at any given level of development expenditure will vary with the information obtained from research. Further, the relation of profitability to development cost is uncertain even given the research outcome.

To put it in a slightly different language, the research outcome is purchased by the research expenditure. The profitability of innovation after development is a random variable with a probability distribution conditional on both the research outcome and the decision about development expenditure. Given this distribution, the firm has the problem of choosing the optimal development expenditure. The optimal level might be (and frequently is) zero; but if it is not zero, it is frequently a very large amount.

In this simple model, there are two points at which decisions are made: (1) to engage in research and (2) to determine the optimal level of development expenditure. In the first decision, the information potentially available to the decision makers consists of the concept and publicly available information. In the second, it consists of the concept and the research outcome together with publicly available information. Of course, this oversimplifies the process in many ways. The sharp distinction between research and development is overstated; furthermore, the development process itself is sequential. Instead of a single decision establishing development expenditures for an entire project, there are repeated reassessments based on information revealed by the development process itself. However, our simplification will be adequate for our purposes here.

What must be insisted upon is the privacy of the information and its relation to the locus of decision making. The two relevant pieces of information, to repeat, are the initial concept and the research outcome. They are received in the first instance by some particular individuals. If these individuals were the decision makers, there would be no difficulty in principle. The decisions made (to engage in research and to choose the optimal level of development expenditures) would be optimal given the information available.

But the individuals concerned are members of organizations, small or large. The decisions to be made involve the allocation of resources. Some of these decisions might be structurally delegated to them. However, as the amounts involved increase, there will be more and more need for approval at higher levels. The internal capital-allocation mechanism will become involved. The lower levels who have the relevant information cannot make the final decisions; their scope of authority is often restricted to making recommendations.

The important question then becomes, how is the information initially available communicated to the capital-allocation mechanisms? There are two classes of reasons why information cannot be conveyed without cost: (1) communication channels have limited capacity; and (2) there are incentive effects that reduce the reliability of information transmission.

1. The specialists who have the concepts and undertake the research have more knowledge of the context than others. An engineer has had training that may not be available to the generalist who allocates resources. Thus, any information conveyed will not be understood as well by the recipient as by the sender.

Second, the specialists have spent more time with the project than any reviewing agency with many other responsibilities could. The capacity to absorb information is always limited. Hence, again there is a degradation of information with transmission.

There may, to be sure, be situations in which the central mechanism has better information in some respects than the specialists. It might have better knowledge of other similar concepts and might well have better understanding of the commercial—as opposed to technical—possibilities. However, there will always be a degradation of the technical information, so that the probability distribution of outcomes of the development process (for given development costs) will on the average be wider.

2. Within a given firm it may be assumed, as a first approximation, that there is no distortion of the information; the specialist presents the information as well as he or she can. However, if information has to cross the boundaries of the firm (for instance, to attract capital from outside investors), the incentive increases to present information misleadingly. Negative aspects might be slurred over, probabilities of success exaggerated.

As a second approximation, there can be some distortion even within the firm. There is some incentive to increase the importance of one's work, to make it appear more valuable in potentiality and thereby earn material and nonmaterial rewards. As in any investment activity, the individual bears limited financial responsibility for failure. Furthermore, for research and development over extended periods of time, the feedback is so slow that the individual is not apt to be in the same position when the program shows results. Finally, the responsibility for success and failure in any position— but especially in one involving such uncertainties as those of research and development—is very hard to assess. That a project failed by no means proves that it should not have been undertaken.

From these considerations, the following implications may be drawn: (1) When responsibility for decisions on research and development is shared because of a need for approval of capital expenditures, the information used in making these decisions is apt to be degraded from its initial state. (2) The longer the chain of communication involved in the approval of projects, the more the information is apt to be degraded. (3) When the chain of communication crosses the boundary of the firm, the degradation of information is apt to be much more severe.[11]

The Decision to Innovate and Firm Size

We can now draw the threads of the analysis together. In particular, the different strategic responses of small firms and large firms to the emergence of research concepts will be analyzed. For simplicity, I speak as if there were just two discrete sizes of firm; of course, there is a continuum of firm sizes and a parallel continuum of innovation strategies.

Innovation has been described as a two-stage decision process. As usual, the appropriate analysis must proceed in reverse order of time. That is, we must first study the decision on development expenditure given the research concept and the research outcome, then analyze the decision to engage in research.

Suppose, then, that we compare a large and a small firm, both of which engaged in research starting from the same concept and observed the same research outcome. The small firm is well informed about the development possibility function—that is, the function relating expected profitability to a given level of development expenditures. It can therefore calculate an optimal level of development expenditures. However, if the amount is large enough, it will not be able to finance it from its own capital funds. It could seek capital from outside. Assume, however, that it has fully utilized whatever general borrowing power it has. Then it has to seek financing based on the project itself. However, for reasons adduced in the last section, the transmission of information across the boundary of the firm will be accompanied by considerable degradation. It follows that capital will be available from the outside only on unfavorable terms (if at all) so that the scale of development expenditures will be less than optimal. Indeed, if the amount of development funds required is very large, it will be essentially impossible to finance the project by borrowing.

A small firm can in many cases obtain outside financing by sale of equity. When the amounts involved are large relative to the initial size of the firm, the transaction amounts to selling the development prospects and is likely to be accompanied by a change in control. (I will take up the possibility of sale of research findings in the next section.)

A large firm facing the same research concept and research outcome will have much less severe restrictions on funding. However—as usual in economic affairs—there is no pure gain without offsets. The difficulties of communicating with an external capital market are replaced by those of communicating with the internal capital-allocation mechanism. As we have seen, the information loss in the large firm is greater than that in the small firm, but less than that involved in reaching the external market. Therefore, the larger firm will tend to invest suboptimally in development expenditures. However, it will do better than the small firm for large development expenditures that the large firm can finance but the small firm cannot; it will do less well on expenditures small enough that the small firm can also finance them.

As an additional hypothesis, it might be supposed that the information loss in the large firm is greater for proposals with greater novelty. The prior information of the internal capital-allocation mechanism may not equip it to evaluate novelties very well. The smaller firm, having less information loss, may be able to accept greater novelty more easily (provided it can finance the development process). Hence, there may be a bias against greater originality in large firms.

It may be objected that a large firm is not more capable of financing large expenditures than a small one. It has larger resources, but it also has larger demands of all kinds. Hence, it is no more capable of financing a given large expenditure for development than the small firm, as it has other large development expenditures competing for the scarce funds. This is an important point. But there are at least two reasons why we would expect the financing ability of large firms to grow more than proportionately to their size: (1) as we have already seen, large firms have disproportionate access to the external capital market without reference to specific projects. Hence, the pool of available capital is more than proportionately larger. Further (as also noted) the size of the financing available is likely to be statistically steadier, decreasing the probability that a demand for a large amount of development expenditures will coincide with a transient shortage of capital funds. (2) If there are a number of potential demands for development expenditures, the demand will also be statistically steadier. There is a high probability that an above-average demand for development expenditures in one area will be offset by a below-average demand in another. This potential offsetting is less available in small firms.

Basically, then, the superiority of large firms in financing rests on the operations of the insurance principle, though it is aided by economies of information to companies that supply capital to the large firms.

We have first analyzed in dynamic programming form the effects of firm size on the development decision, given the outcome of the research phase. From the above reasoning, for each research concept and each re-search outcome there is an expenditure on development and a probability distribution of profitabilities in production. These will be affected (as indicated) both by the development profitability function and by the availability of capital, which, in turn, is conditioned by the problems of information transmission. Hence, there will be a probability distribution of anticipated profitabilities taking account of both development expenditures and subsequent profitabilities in production. It has been argued that, on the average, small firms will be superior if the optimal development costs are low and large firms will be superior if costs are large.

Now consider the decision to engage in research. (Again, for the time being, ignore the possibility that the research outcome can be sold.) Before engaging in research, the development profitability function is itself unknown; nevertheless there will be expectations of it. In probability language, the development profitability function (itself a random variable expressing the distribution of profitability in production conditional on development expenditures) is taken as conditional on research outcome after that is known and as unconditional (more precisely, conditional on research concept but not on outcome) before research is undertaken.

Given the research concept, it may be expected (though without certainty) that subsequent development expenditures will be low if the project is at all feasible. In that case, it follows that small firms will be more likely to undertake the research than large firms. The opposite is the case if the unconditional distribution implies that development expenditures are likely to be high. Already at the point where the decisions to undertake research are made, there is differential selection among firms of differing sizes.

Thus, on the average one would expect firms to specialize in projects whose optimal development scales are correlated with the size of the firm. Projects anticipated to lead to large expenditures will on the whole be less than optimally funded, because large firms have higher transmission losses for information.

If the supplementary hypothesis advanced above is correct (that larger firms will find it harder to allocate capital to very novel ventures), then it is also true that very novel research concepts will be less likely to lead to research projects in large firms than in small.

Finally, it must be pointed out that the correlation in research undertaken between firm size and optimal level of development expenditures, though positive, will be far from perfect. The level of development expenditures, as repeatedly emphasized, will depend on the research outcome. Research, by its nature, is uncertain. It can easily happen that a research program is undertaken with a probability distribution of optimal development expenditures whose expectation is relatively small before the research outcome is observed. The distribution conditional on research outcome may be quite different, possibly with a large expectation. This is a far from rare event. Of course, the opposite can also occur; if the correct distributions are held, it must occur comparably frequently.

It can therefore happen that a small firm undertakes a line of research whose outcome would optimally involve a much larger development expenditure than it is prepared to undertake. It will either pursue the development on a much smaller scale than optimal, or it will discontinue it altogether if there are sufficient increasing returns to scale in the development process.

A Market for Research Outcomes

This concluding section seeks to remove one limitation of the preceding. The research outcome may itself be the object of a market transaction. Selling ideas is not entirely as simple as selling goods, but they are valuable to at least some potential buyers. Establishment and transfer of property rights can take several forms. The research outcome might be patentable, in which case the sale is straightforward. Alternatively, the buyer might value a whole constellation of working knowledge embodied in the firm. In that case, the sale of the research outcome could be equivalent to the sale of the whole firm.

From the discussion thus far, the natural sellers of research outcomes would be small firms that, after observing the outcome, determine that optimal expenditures on development exceed the financial capacity of the firm. In view of the uncertainty about development costs at the moment of the research concept, such situations can arise easily. The buyers might be individuals or groups of individuals in the external capital market who wish to secure their investment in such an uncertain situation by equity acquisition rather than bonds. More likely, however, it is the large firms in similar fields who constitute the natural demand side of the innovation market, whether research outcomes are sold in the form of patents or of whole firms.

The existence of markets for research outcomes alters the incentive structures for undertaking research within both large and small firms. For small firms, it lessens the inhibition on starting research for which large development expenditures are likely. If this came to pass, they do not find the research useless—they can sell the outcome to a large firm. One must still reckon with a loss of information as it passes across the boundaries between the large and small firms. Hence, the incentives for the research are less than they would be within the large firm. Since the large firm is well informed, it is also true that the loss of information is less than it would be between the small firm and the general external-capital market, so that the possibility of sale to large firms is not negligible, as we have assumed the external financing of expensive developments by small firms to be.

The existence of markets for research outcomes also alters the incentives for research within large firms—for the worse. For now the firm has an alternative supply of research outcomes on which to base its development of innovations. The constraints on its total development expenditures imply that anticipated availability of research outcomes on the market will reduce the incentive to use only internally generated research outcomes.

There are limits to relying on the market for research inputs into the development process. For example, internal research capability is complementary to externally purchased research outcomes. It is needed to evaluate them and to synthesize them with other research outcomes, whether internal or external. But clearly some substitution takes place.

If this analysis is meaningful, it suggests a division of labor according to firm size. Smaller firms will tend to specialize more in the research phase and in smaller development processes; larger firms will devote a much smaller proportion of their research and development budget to the research phase. They will specialize in the larger developments and will buy a considerable fraction of the research basis for their subsequent development of innovations.

While anecdotes are no substitute for good statistical analysis, a striking number of innovations have been produced by giant corporations on the basis of ideas (and perhaps some production) by small firms.

Notes

1. J.A. Schumpeter, *Business Cycles,* vol. I (New York and London: McGraw-Hill, 1939), pp. 94–109.

2. A.A. Berle, Jr., and G.C. Means, *The Modern Corporation and Private Property* (New York: Macmillan, 1932).

3. K.J. Arrow, and F.H. Hahn, *General Competitive Analysis* (San Francisco and Edinburgh: Holden-Day and Oliver & Boyd, 1971).

4. E.H. Chamberlin, *The Theory of Monopolistic Competition,* 6th ed. (Cambridge, Mass.: Harvard University Press, 1950).

5. See, for example, table 3.1, p. 40, in F.M. Scherer, *Industrial Market Structure and Economic Performance* (Chicago: Rand McNally, 1970).

6. For the period from 1899 to 1939, see G.W. Nutter, *The Extent of Enterprise Monopoly in the United States 1899-1939* (Chicago: University of Chicago Press, 1951). For more recent trends or lack thereof, see W.F. Mueller and L.G. Hamm, "Trends in Industrial Market Concentration 1947 to 1970." *Review of Economics and Statistics* 56 (1974):511–520.

7. G.J. Stigler, "The Division of Labor is Limited by the Extent of the Market," *Journal of Political Economy* 56 (1951):185–193.

8. A. Chandler, Jr., *The Visible Hand: The Managerial Revolution in American Business* (Cambridge, Mass.: Harvard University Press, 1977).

9. For more complete discussion, see K.J. Arrow, *The Limits of Organization* (New York: Norton, 1974): Ch. 2.

10. R.H. Coase, "The Theory of the Firm." *Economica N.S.* 4 (1937):368–405.

11. In order not to interrupt the main line of the argument, I have left rather vague the concept of the profitability of the innovation, which appears as an output of the development process. It is not necessary that the innovation give rise to market power—that is, that it be a commodity with some distinct differentiation from others and on which, therefore, a monopoly profit can be earned. (Of course, this possibility is not excluded either.) But even if the product, or a close substitute, is one already produced, an innovation may amount to a cost reduction. Hence, the firm will earn a rent on the superior productivity induced by the innovation. It must be recognized, however, that the knowledge embodied in an innovation cannot fully be made property. It is apt to be copied by others, and, as the knowledge spreads, the price of the product will decline. Hence, the anticipated profitability must take account of the declining rent from the innovation.

3 Toward Operational Models of Entrepreneurship

William J. Baumol

The subject of entrepreneurship looms as a continuing reproach to the theory of the firm and to the formal analysis of economic growth. In each of these areas, the entrepreneur is universally acknowledged to play a leading role; yet, he seems always to remain invisible in the models used to analyze them. It is not that analysts wish to ignore him; rather, it is he who always seems to elude them.

This chapter begins with an attempt to explain this phenomenon, then proceeds to consider what one can do about it. Finally, it offers a very preliminary theoretical model that tries to describe the influences that determine the supply of entrepreneurship and its influence on economic growth. The model is tractable analytically and promises that some more sophisticated variant will lend itself to a deeper analysis of policy in the future.

Specifically, it will be argued in this chapter that the main reason entrepreneurial activity has generally eluded economic analysis (as well as teaching in the business schools) is that, by its very nature, such activity cannot be standardized and, therefore, cannot be described in general terms. This means that attempts to offer a detailed and general characterization of such activity are virtually doomed to fail. But this problem does not preclude another useful avenue of investigation: a study of the influences that encourage or discourage the heterogeneous and undescribed set of activities that constitute entrepreneurship. While entrepreneurship itself cannot be standardized, influences such as tax policy can be and their effects therefore lend themselves to systematic analysis.

The model offered in this chapter is intended to permit such an analysis. It starts off from the premise that the supply of entrepreneurial talent is, from the viewpoint of economic theory, subject to a number of exogenous influences. For one thing, the supply of entrepreneurial talent itself is subject to stochastic influences, being in part the product of genetics. Second, entrepreneurial supply is obviously affected by cultural conditions, educational systems, attitudes toward economic success, degree of acceptance of something like a Protestant work ethic, and the like.

I am extremely grateful to the Price Institute for Entrepreneurial Studies, its director, Joshua Ronen, and its sponsor, Harold Price, whose interest in the subject stimulated the writing of this chapter. The foundation's support also greatly facilitated its completion.

There are also endogenous influences that are more interesting analytically. It is suggested, for instance, that the very success of entrepreneurship tends to create opposition to it and leads to attempts to subvert it. By their very nature, successful entrepreneurs leave runners-up in their wake and threaten their economic viability. The latter naturally seek to protect themselves by imposing constraints on the exercise of entrepreneurship, which initially inhibit it and can ultimately succeed in curbing it altogether. A society in which this occurs is threatened with stagnation, which itself discourages the exercise of entrepreneurship. When an economy falls into such a stagnant equilibrium, only fortuitous developments or deliberate policy measures can revive the process of growth and set the economy upon an upward path once more. This process may produce a set of long-term fluctuations (not really cycles) in which periods of growth and stagnation are interspersed. The model shows how impediments to entrepreneurship, such as taxes and various constraints imposed by runners-up, affect the intertemporal path of economic growth and the supply of entrepreneurs.

On the Analytic Intractability of Entrepreneurship

By its very nature, entrepreneurial activity is not routine. It involves exercise of imagination, departure from standard practice, acuteness of perception that permits the rapid recognition of new opportunities (as Israel Kirzner has emphasized), and the use of innovative means to take advantage of them.

Indeed, we can define entrepreneurial activities residually as those economic acts that are not subject to standardization and obey no systematic and persistent principles. This by itself should indicate why entrepreneurship has resisted formal analysis and teaching in the schools. One can, of course, discuss particular entrepreneurial acts *retrospectively*—but if history is not our main concern, how can one analyze or teach acts whose nature is not yet known and whose effectiveness relies to a considerable degree on the difficulty others have in foreseeing them?

Worse than that. Imagine that it becomes possible to analyze a particular entrepreneurial activity and to teach it to a generation of eager students. By this very process the activity becomes routine and managerial. That is, the very success of the analysis deprives the activity of its entrepreneurial character. If this is so, it literally becomes impossible to analyze entrepreneurial activity. It must forever elude us because the moment it is recognized and understood it is, by that act alone, transmuted into something else.[1] Here we have a sort of Heisenberg uncertainty principle that attains an ultimate extreme. To observe the subject is to make it disappear.

If this view of the matter is accepted, it becomes clear why the entreprenuer is absent from our formal economic models. More important, from our point of view, is the implication that he is very unlikely to achieve much greater visibility in firm-theoretic models in the future. Since we cannot hope to describe what he does, we cannot expect to produce a formal construct in which his influence on product design, marketing strategy, and the other ingredients of the firm's behavior enters the matter explicitly.

This is not meant to imply that theoretical investigation of entrepreneurship is pointless—on the contrary, this chapter is intended to suggest the reverse. Rather, the argument indicates that the theoretical analysis of entrepreneurship must be reoriented to avoid the obstacles we have been discussing. We might not be able to analyze the entrepreneur's choice of strategy, his goals and attitudes, or the determinants of his way of thinking. But I believe it possible to investigate what influences encourage or discourage his activity. If we can identify the actions that constituted entrepreneurial behavior in the past, we can hope to study empirically the variables that influence the supply of entrepreneurship. One can then construct theoretical models spelling out such relationships and hope to test and improve them with the aid of empirical evidence on past entrepreneurial behavior.

In such models, one can focus on variables whose magnitudes can readily be affected by public policy. One cannot reject the hypothesis that religious beliefs and cultural conditions make a substantial difference in the degree to which entrepreneurial activity is considered a desirable or undesirable way to spend one's time. But cultural conditions and religious attitudes are not quickly and easily modified by government act; indeed, most of us prefer it so. On the other hand, a plausible hypothesis is that the volume of entrepreneurial activity will be influenced by the nature and magnitude of taxes on business and individual incomes, by the character of regulatory restraints upon the behavior of firms, and by a variety of other variables whose magnitudes are either determined by government directly, or are easily influenced by it.

A useful analysis of entrepreneurship should devote the bulk of its attention to influences that can readily be affected by policy. This is appropriate even if it is admitted that in the last analysis intractable determinants such as cultural circumstances are far more potent in their effects than taxes or regulatory constraints. As I have suggested elsewhere ["Entrepreneurship in Economic Theory," *American Economic Review*, 58, 2 (May 1968), pp. 70–71] an analogy is illuminating here. To me, one of the prime elements of genius in the *General Theory* lies in Keynes' deliberate decision to emphasize an admittedly secondary influence upon the level of investment over one that he considers more powerful but that is clearly less amenable to control by public policy. Specifically, Keynes tells us that one of the prime determinants of the volume of investment is the state of business expectations, the degree of optimism that prevails in the business community. But the investment function in the Keynesian model makes no use of an expectations variable; instead, he assigns the starring role to the interest rate. Though many have since questioned the power of interest rates to change the level of investment, it is clear that Keynes's decision made it possible to use his model to derive the fiscal and monetary principles now referred to as Keynesian policy.

As I wrote in my earlier paper on entrepreneurship,

> . . . such a theoretical analysis [of the determinants of entrepreneurship that are amenable to influence by the public sector] can be of enormous significance for policy. . . . I remain convinced that encouragement of the entrepreneur is the key to the stimulation of growth. The view that this must await the slow and undependable process of change in social and psychological climate is a counsel of despair for which there is little justification. Such a conclusion is analogous to the view that all we can do to reduce spending in an inflationary world is to hope for a revival of the Protestant ethic and acceptance by the general public of the virtues of thrift . . . that is precisely why I [advocate] careful study of the rewards of entrepreneurship. Without awaiting a change in the entrepreneurial drive exhibited in our society, we can try to learn how one can stimulate the volume and intensity of entrepreneurial activity, thus making the most of what is permitted by current morés and attitudes. If the theory succeeds in no more than showing us something about how that can be done, it will have accomplished very much indeed." ["Entrepreneurship in Economic Theory," *American Economic Review,* 58, 2 (May 1968), p. 71.] Reprinted with permission.

Elements of the Model

Rewards to Entrepreneurship

Entrepreneurship is rewarded differently in different societies. Profits or other forms of earnings are not the only way entrepreneurial activities are recognized. In other cultures, it can be encouraged by the award of medals, special titles (for instance, the "Order of Lenin") or even titles of nobility. The rewards may even be intangible and unofficial, taking the form of peer approval (as presumably happens in a small integrated community that is also the productive unit—for instance, a kibbutz).

Even in a market economy, entrepreneurship can be pursued as part of a search for power or because of a love of accomplishment. But, obviously, money *is* a prime reward of entrepreneurial effort. We will therefore engage in what is, surely, a permissible oversimplification and treat the money earnings of the entrepreneur as the variable that his activities are designed to pursue. In selecting this as our focus we are, of course, following the precedent of standard economic analysis. But, in any event, the analysis can be adapted to substitute some alternative form of reward as the prime objective of the entrepreneur if the model is to be modified to make it applicable to some other sort of economic organization.

The earnings pertinent to our discussion are, presumably, earnings after taxes. It is this observation that permits us to assign a role to taxes that is amenable to analysis. We will simply write out explicitly the amount of tax deducted from gross earnings and then have that variable at our disposal for formal consideration.

A more difficult problem (and one that, it must be conceded, will not be dealt with here in a satisfactory manner) is the determination of gross entrepreneurial earnings. The reason for this stems from the inherent difficulty of describing the activities of the entrepreneur. Presumably, different entrepreneurial activities, even if completely successful, will bring in different rewards. Therefore, if we cannot characterize those activities, we cannot hope to provide a generic characterization of the financial return to entrepreneurship.

We must also characterize the effects upon nonentrepreneur businessmen of an expansion in entrepreneurial activity. While it is not necessary for our formal analysis, the following scenario may be suggestive: entrepreneurs have two avenues by which they can pursue increased earnings. Let us call them *productive* and *competitive* entrepreneurship. The first encompasses the introduction of new techniques, new products, ways to eliminate inefficiency, and so forth. In short they can engage in the sorts of innovation emphasized by Schumpeter and the elimination of the departures from equilibrium emphasized by Kirzner, all of which increase the real output of the industry, Y_t. This component of the entrepreneur's activities, the one that has been emphasized in the literature, increases dY_t/dt. If entrepreneurs receive their share, this becomes one of the components of their total earnings.

However, entrepreneurs can also benefit by increasing their *share* of the pie, and there is no reason to believe that they will be reluctant to do so. Battles over market share and other zero-sum conflicts are surely not outside the scope of entrepreneurial activities. To someone whose primary objective is the accumulation of wealth, it may for all practical purposes be irrelevant whether this is accomplished by means that, in effect, extract it from competitors or through activities that, incidentally, bring prosperity to others.[2]

As a first approximation, therefore, it may be assumed that the share of total output in an industry going to its entrepreneurs *as a class* will increase with the number of entrepreneurs. But the reward per entrepreneur need not behave in this way. The latter is affected by two offsetting influences. On the one hand, the growth-stimulating effects of entrepreneurship will encounter diminishing returns precisely analogous to those we attribute to other inputs. That is, other things being equal, the value of $(dY_t/dt)/E_t$ will be smaller the larger the value of E_t at any given moment. As the field of entrepreneurship grows more crowded, the unused opportunities that the individual entrepreneur perceives may become increasingly scarce or decreasingly valuable. Since his share of Y_t depends on his contribution to dY_t/dt, the decline in the latter as the number of entrepreneurs increases will tend to reduce his share of the former.

On the other hand, there is the possibility that as diminishing returns to productive entrepreneurship set in, more effort will be devoted to competitive entrepreneurship and that this will (at least to some extent) offset any tendency to a declining share of Y_t to each successful entrepreneur.

As a first approximation, then, we will assume that the gross financial return per entrepreneur is monotonically related to Y_t and that its after-tax counterpart, $(1 - T)Y_t$, is an appropriate indicator of his returns.

Institutionalized Constraints

There is a second major component of our story. High taxes are only one type of policy measure that discourages entrepreneurship. A second impediment to entrepreneurship is, at least potentially, far more significant to the vigor of our economic mechanism. This consists of a growing body of laws, regulations, and administrative actions that impose limits on the activities of the entrepreneur. Rules that restrict entry, delay innovations by subjecting them to bureaucratic preconditions, protect firms from the effects of competition, and in other ways circumscribe the entrepreneur can discourage his activity as much as increasingly onerous taxes.

In an analysis like ours, the extent of such restrictions is usually taken as a matter of historical accident—in short, as an exogenous factor. I believe this view is seriously misleading. I believe it is the very success of entrepreneurship that stimulates the imposition of such constraints, and that failure to take account of the connection leaves us more poorly prepared to deal with a major threat to our economy.

A glance at the emergence of constraints of the sort we are discussing will confirm that they are generally introduced at the urging of business firms and others threatened by the pressures of competition. In international trade, tariffs and quotas are instituted under pressure from industries that feel threatened by competition from importers—all too often because they are relatively inefficient and their productive techniques are obsolete. Internally, regulatory restrictions have also grown in response to the representations of those who are unable to prosper in an atmosphere of unrestricted competition. In this respect, it is noteworthy that a very high proportion of pricing issues brought before U.S. regulatory agencies in the postwar period involved, not efforts to force price reductions upon the regulated firms (as one might have expected), but on the contrary, attempts to require them to undertake price increases they did not want. This obviously, was not the work of consumer groups incensed at excessive prices made possible by market power. Rather, it was the work of disgruntled rivals seeking to impose rules of gentlemanly competition—which, in essence, means no competition of all. Thus, contrary to all common sense, regulators have found themselves pushed out of the role of defending the interests of consumers and into that of protecting firms unable to survive the heat of full competition. One such agency, in an outburst of candor, once described its role as that of a giant handicapper whose task was to prevent those in the best competitive position from damaging the market position of their rivals.

The antitrust program has, to some degree, undergone a similar evolution. From the point of view of general economic prosperity, the extraordinary success of a business firm is something very much to be desired and encouraged. It would seem, however, that to the antitrust authorities this is (at the very least) ground for suspicion, if not per se evidence of wrongdoing. Business enterprises that are runners-up in the competitive battle increasingly use the antitrust laws to bring their successful rivals to heel and, incidentally, to extract some compensation for their own ineptitude in the form of the triple damage payments required of a firm found guilty of excessive success in its competitive endeavors.

The point in all this is that constraints upon entrepreneurship are not a matter of happenstance. They result at least partly from the efforts of the runners-up. The more threatened the runners-up feel, the more strongly they can be expected to demand that something be done to protect them from the unfairness that is the source of their discomfort. Rallying their employees about them, they can be expected to request (and get) special laws, regulations, and acts of administrative intervention designed to protect their interests. The result can perhaps be referred to (paraphrasing Kahn) as the tyranny of the runners-up, which can be a very effective impediment to the growth of the economy.

So far, entrepreneurship has not been mentioned in this part of the story, but its relevance should be clear. To the extent that entrepreneurial success occurs at the expense of rivals, it stimulates precisely the kind of protection that has just been discussed. What is less clearcut is the sequence in which this process occurs. As a prototype, we can focus on the following scenario. If an economy finds itself with a scarcity of entrepreneurship, an increase in the supply of entrepreneurs will initially contribute primarily to overall growth, with enough total yield that virtually everyone benefits from the resulting prosperity. Such a Paretian improvement elicits little opposition and little or no demand for constraints upon entrepreneurial activity.

However, as the number of entrepreneurs grows, diminishing returns to productive entrepreneurship set in and the share of activity devoted to competitive entrepreneurship rises. Competition now begins to hurt, and the runners-up become vocal. The stage is then set for the workings of our dynamic model.

Toward a Dynamic Model of Entrepreneurship

We turn next to our formal model. First, we should emphasize once more that this model is no more than a crude prototype. It vastly oversimplifies a set of relationships that are far more complex and subtle. Yet, it is this oversimplification that permits us to derive concrete results, at least some of which suggest policy measures that may be able to stimulate entrepreneurship and economic growth.

Turning to specifics, our model is composed of three basic relationships. The first determines the severity of the constraint upon entrepreneurship; the second relates entrepreneurship to the rate of economic growth; and the third relates the supply of entrepreneurship to entrepreneurial income, taxes and the severity of regulatory constraint. We employ the following variables:

Y_t = the total income produced by the industry in period t.

E_t = the supply of entrepreneurial time in period t.

C_t = the constraint on entrepreneurship in t.

$$E_t < C_t \qquad (3.1)$$

This notation immediately gives rise to several difficulties, which I will note but make no attempt to overcome. First, there is no simple and obvious way to measure—or even observe—the magnitude of E_t, the volume of entrepreneurial activity. Since it certainly refers to an extremely heterogeneous set of actions, the use of a single symbol to represent it is already a serious distortion of the facts. However, if used retrospectively it does not necessarily run into the problem of indescribability. It is certainly possible, at least in principle, to describe what *used* to constitute entrepreneurship yesterday. It is just that we cannot determine what tomorrow's entrepreneur (or even today's) will be up to. That means that our strictures on this subject, even if valid, do not condemn to futility an attempt to measure the supply of entrepreneurship in the past.[3]

Besides this, the suggestion that there is a quantifiable ceiling, C_t, upon the number of hours of entrepreneurial activity at any time is an extremely

crude formalization of a set of complex and varied constraints that constitute no fixed limit, but rather make the increased exercise of entrepreneurship increasingly difficult. It does, however, give us a very rough way of
approaching the issue that, as we will see, is at least analytically tractable.

Our three relationships can now be described directly. Using a differ-
ence-equation approach with discrete time periods we have:

Supply of Entrepreneurship:

$$E_t = \begin{cases} \min\left[f((1-T)Y_t), C_t\right] & \text{for } E_t \geq E_{t-1} \\ R(E_{t-1}) & \text{for } E_t < E_{t-1} \end{cases} \qquad (3.2)$$

Output Growth Function:

$$Y_{t+1} - Y_t = g(E_t) \qquad (3.3)$$

The Ceiling of Entrepreneurial Activity:

$$C_{t+1} = C(E_t) \qquad (3.4)$$

where

$$f' > 0, \quad 0 \leq R' \leq 1, \quad g' > 0. \qquad (3.5)$$

Let us examine these in turn. Relationship (3.2) states that the supply of
entrepreneurship has an autonomous component, $R(F_t)$, and an induced
component, $f((1 - T)Y_t) - R(E_t)$, that depends on the economy's disposable personal income $(1 - T)Y_t$ (since entrepreneurial income is, presumably, a monotonically rising function of this magnitude). This supply is,
however, constrained by the ceiling, C_t, in accord with (3.1). Here R_t can be
described as autonomous innovative activity—entrepreneurship that arises,
as it were, spontaneously, out of exuberance and what D.C. McLelland
refers to as "the need for achievement." Like $f(\cdot)$, $R(\cdot)$ is stochastic—
influenced by cultural elements and other variables beyond the scope of our
model. $R(\cdot)$ need not be a constant. It may well, for example, be an increasing function of E_t if the increased number of successful entrepreneurs
lures more persons into following their example. This, and the plausible
premise that the marginal propensity to induce entrepreneurship is less than
unity, is what is implied by $0 \leq R' < 1$.

Relationship (3.3) has an obvious interpretation—it makes the *rate of
growth* of output an increasing function of the supply of entrepreneurship.
There is no point in repeating the arguments underlying this view of the

matter, which certainly go back to Schumpeter (and, arguably, to much earlier writers).

Finally, relationship (3.4), the ceiling on entrepreneurship, follows the behavior postulated in the preceding section. We assume that constraint (3.1) is not very restrictive when the magnitude of E_t is small, but that as E_t rises it becomes increasingly constraining, either absolutely or only relatively. That is, we may have

Case 1:

$$C_E = \frac{\partial C}{\partial E} < 0 \qquad (3.5a)$$

meaning that a rise in entrepreneurial activity (at least beyond some point) elicits so sharp a reaction that, in the future, even maintenance of the same quantity of entrepreneurial activity is effectively prevented. Alternatively, the erosion of the scope for entrepreneurship may be more moderate, yielding a relationship involving

Case 2:

$$0 < C_E < 1 \qquad (3.5b)$$

in which the constraints dampen the growth of entrepreneurial activity, but do not bring it directly to a halt.

In figure 3-1, C_1C_1 and C_2C_2 are possible constraint curves corresponding to the two cases. We now examine the implications for the time path of the supply of entrepreneurship.

The Time Path of E_t

Case 1: The Absolute-Constraint Case

Relationships (3.2) to (3.5), then, constitute our model. As is well known, such a difference equation model implicitly determines the behavior of its variables over time. That is, equations (3.2) to (3.5) permit us to determine how the supply of entrepreneurship and the growth of the economy's output will change with the passage of time, starting from any initial state of affairs. We will describe the time path of the variables E_t and Y_t with the aid of a phase diagram—a diagram showing the relation between E_{t+1} and E_t for any period—whose analysis is very similar to that of the cobweb diagram.

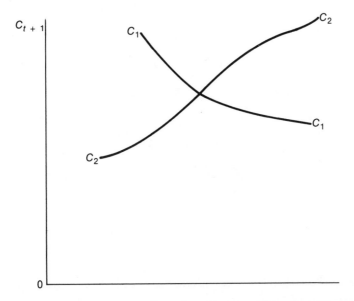

Figure 3-1. Constraint Curves for the Absolute Constraint Case (C_1C_1) and for the Relative-Growth Constraint Case (C_2C_2)

To derive expressions for the curves of the diagram, we must first eliminate Y_t from relationships (3.2) and (3.3) to express the workings of the system entirely in terms of the behavior of E_t. For this purpose, we begin by noting that by relationship (3.5), $E_t = f((1 - T)Y_t)$ is monotonically increasing in Y_t and so, if it is continuous, it has the unique inverse

$$Y_t = f^{-1}(E_t) \equiv F(E_t) \quad F' > 0. \tag{3.6}$$

Substituting this into (2-3), we obtain

$$F(E_{t+1}) = g(E_t) + F(E_t). \tag{3.7}$$

This gives us

$$F'dE_{t+1} = (g' + F')dE_t$$

that is,

$$\frac{dE_{t+1}}{dE_t} = \frac{g'(E_t) + F'(E_t)}{F'(E_{t+1})} > 1 \tag{3.8}$$

if F' is approximately constant.

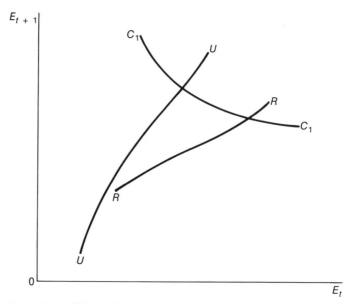

Figure 3-2. Phase Diagram for the Absolute Constraint Case

Equation (3.7) determines E_{t+1} as a function of E_t—the relationship we are seeking. In figure 3-2, our phase diagram, it is drawn in as the upper curve UU. In the same figure the curve $C_1 C_1$ [the case I constraint curve given by equation (3.4)] is reproduced from figure 3-1. Finally, RR in figure 3-2 represents $E_t = R(E_{t-1})$ in (3.2). As we will see next, these three curves correspond, respectively, to the upswing, peak, and downswing phases of what amounts to a set of long-term fluctuations (cycles) in the supply of entrepreneurship. Such cycles can be expected to characterize our case 1, where absolute limitations on the growth of entrepreneurship produce a CC curve with a negative slope.

To see how the time path of E_t is determined by these curves, we must insert a 45° line into our diagram (see figure 3-3). As usual, the 45° line permits us to transfer values from the vertical to the horizontal axis.

Suppose, now, that the supply of entrepreneurship has been rising, so that, in accord with (3.2), curve UU is the relevant relationship between E_t and E_{t+1}. Then, if at some initial date $t = 0$, that supply happens to be given by E_0, in the next period we will have a supply of entrepreneurship represented by E_1, as indicated by the height of point a.

Moving directly to the right of point a up to the 45° line (point b) we transfer E_1 to the horizontal axis (the point directly below b). Then, in the next period we obtain a value of E_2 given by the height of point c. Thus, the

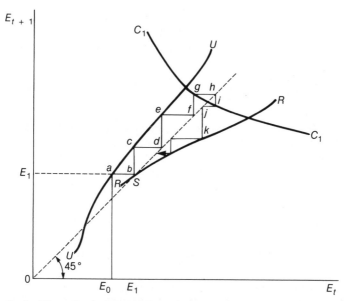

Figure 3-3. Time Path and Phase Diagram for the Absolute Constraint Case

time path of entrepreneurship continues upward in the same way, traversing points *a, b, c, d, e,* and *f,* in turn.

At point *g,* however, the upward rise of E_t runs into the constraint curve. There, because of the negative slope of C_1C_1, the path turns cyclical and experiences a downturn (*h, i*). Because E_t is decreasing, in accord with equation (3.2) the curve RR becomes the relevant relationship between E_t and E_{t+1}. The path of E_t consequently moves along *j, k, . . .* toward point *S,* where RR crosses the 45° line.

If, as drawn, RR has a nonnegative slope less than unity, *S* will be a point of stable equilibrium.[4] It is an equilibrium at which the supply of entrepreneurship is low and, by (3.3), the rate of growth of the economy's output is correspondingly small. It is, in short, a position of relative stagnation.

If this model were deterministic, the economy would remain in that position until some fortuitous event from outside the model were by happenstance to move the value of E_t back toward the circumstances under which curve UU once more determines behavior. But the model is *not* deterministic. E_t is in fact a random variable, and the values given by the time path in our diagram represent mean (expected) values for the pertinent distribution, or some other index of typical value. Thus one can anticipate that, over time, actual values of E_t will deviate from that corresponding to point S. Ultimately, at some unpredictable date, one can expect this random process to yield a fortuitous rise in E_t of significant magnitude, and this will restart the rising portion of the fluctuation process. Once more the economy will proceed upward along a path such as a, b, c, d, . . ., and the entire process will begin all over again.

Thus, in this world an economy is condemned to rough replications of its previous history, with time intervals of varying duration spent at equilibrium point S with its attendant stagnation. Moreover, since each upswing is likely to start off at an initial point, E_0, that differs from its predecessor, the subsequent cycle will normally not be a perfect replication of its predecessor. This becomes all the more likely in view of the probability that our three curves (most notably CC) can be expected to shift over time. As a result, this nonlinear dynamic model will produce an intertemporal behavior pattern characterized by irregular fluctuations rather than by the precise replication of upswings and downswings that constitute a sequence of cycles.

The two principal engines of the fluctuation process are, first, the (random) outbursts of entrepreneurial talent that ultimately (at some unpredictable date) drive the economy from a point of stagnant equilibrium, and, second, the ultimate growth in opposition by the runners-up and their success in imposing impediments to the supply and exercise of entrepreneurship.

By substituting our results for E_t into (3.3), we can also deduce the corresponding time path for national income, Y_t. Since, by (3.3), it is the *rate of growth* of Y_t (rather than its level) that varies monotonically with E_t we see that the fluctuations in E_t bring with them corresponding fluctuations in the rate of change in output. For example, the interval during which E_t follows UU is a period of rapid growth; that corresponding to RR is one involving a *deceleration* in the rate of growth, but not necessarily a decline in the economy's total output. Similarly, the period when the economy is at S is likely to be characterized by fairly steady but very slow growth, and in that respect can be considered stagnant only in a relative sense.

Case 2: The Relative-Growth Constraint

We can now deal rather quickly with our second case, that in which the ceiling on entrepreneurship slows down its growth rather than depressing it absolutely. Here, in accord with figure 3–1 and equation (3.5b), our phase diagram becomes that depicted in figure 3–4. Curve RR is included for completeness, but it is distinctly possible that it will no longer play any role in the history of our variables. Starting, as before, at some arbitrarily chosen

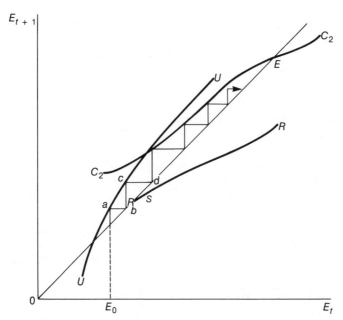

Figure 3–4. Time Path and Phase Diagram with a Relative-Growth
Constraint

initial value E_0, we see that E_t initially follows the explosive growth path, *a,
b, c, . . .,* found in case 1. Beyond *d,* however, the paths diverge qualita-
tively. Now, as it enters the region governed by *CC,* E_t continues to move
upward, but the expansion is damped and asymptotically approaches *E,* the
point of stable equilibrium. Point *E* can also be looked upon as a point of
relative stagnation if at the same time other industries (or other economies)
are in the phase governed by *UU.* Here the economy will remain indefinitely
unless either of two events occurs: (1) an exogenous event shifts *UU* out-
ward and, perhaps, changes its shape or (2) the random component of E_t
happens to produce a substantial decrease in the value of E_t. In the latter
case, *RR* now takes over and E_t will move steadily downward toward *S,* as
in case 1.

In comparing cases 1 and 2, several differences merit emphasis. The
first is obvious: case 1 produces long cycles of activity, whereas case 2 shows
a damped tendency toward stagnation. A second, more subtle difference is
found in the duration of the period during which *CC* governs the time path
of E_t. In case 1, *CC* serves only as a ceiling off which the time path bounces
and from which E_t promptly departs. In case 2, after a (possibly brief) initial period, *CC* effectively constrains the time path, in principle forever

after. Thus in case 1, regulation, antitrust, and other constraints upon entrepreneurial activity are ineffective at almost all times. This certainly seems implausible, and suggests that the case 1 model is, at least in this form, unacceptably oversimplified.[5]

Taxes versus Constraints as Influences on Entrepreneurship

Let us now see how our model can be used to study the effects of taxes and constraints, the two impediments to the supply of entrepreneurship that we have discussed. The following paragraphs concern themselves more with the method of analysis than with policy implications. They are intended primarily to show how other such influences can be dealt with in future work using more sophisticated models.

The representation of a tightening of constraints is obvious enough. It is shown by a lowering of the constraint curve (as from C_1C_1 to $C_1'C_1'$ in figure 3-5 or from C_2C_2 to $C_2'C_2'$ in figure 3-6. Of course, the shift need not be a parallel one.

On the other hand, a rise in tax rate seems likely to reduce the slope of UU, and presumably also its absolute level (the shift to $U'U'$ in figures 3-5 and 3-6). Intuitively, the reason is clear. Upon the imposition of a higher tax rate, a growth in entrepreneurship will (other things being equal) generate a smaller rise in *disposable* income than it would have otherwise. This, in turn, will decrease the induced rise in entrepreneurship, E_{t+1}.

Now the significance of the difference in the shift effects of a tax increase and of a tightening of constraints is that there is a corresponding difference in the qualitative characteristics of the time path of E_t. It is easy to verify that the shifting of UU that controls the expansion phase of our fluctuations slows the rate of growth of entrepreneurship. However, it does not affect the amplitude of the fluctuations—that is, the high-water mark of the economy's achievement remains unchanged, it only takes longer to get there.

On the other hand, tightening the constraints affects the time path of E_t more fundamentally. It actually lowers the ceiling that determines the high point of the fluctuations, and means the economy can never reach the level of prosperity it would otherwise have attained.

This, then, suggests that more onerous tax rates and severer constraints do both discourage entrepreneurship. However, their workings are quite different and, at least in this simple model, it is tempting to consider the constraints as the more serious threat. Whether one should be prepared to take such a conclusion very seriously must, of course, depend on what this model has omitted. But that is beyond the scope of this paper.

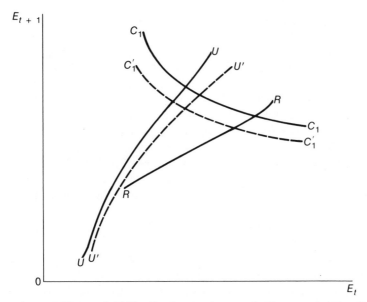

Figure 3–5. Effects of Shifts in Constraints and Changes in Tax Rate in the Absolute Constraint Case

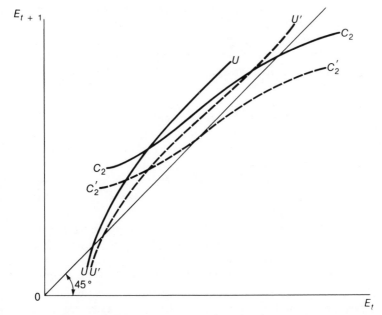

Figure 3–6. Effects of Shifts in Constraints and Changes in the Tax Rate in the Relative-Growth Constraint Case

Some Preliminary Ruminations on Policy Implications

Despite the reservations just expressed, speculations about the policy implications implicit in the model may, perhaps, be suggestive. The key problem identified by our discussion has its roots in competitive (as contrasted with productive) entrepreneurship. That is, its source is the fact that the economic growth it stimulates is not shared universally, and that entrepreneurs sometimes profit directly at the expense of their rivals.

To some extent this is inevitable and desirable. One of the great virtues of the free-market mechanism is its intolerance of inefficiency, particularly on the part of business firms—and inefficiency is relative. If the enterprise is highly innovative, cuts costs severely, and introduces product changes that attract customers away from their rivals, those rivals will be hurt unless they can quickly come up with equally desirable innovations of their own. Any attempt to amend the market mechanism in a way that protects laggards from the penalties of their incompetence is, in my view, likely to prove detrimental to the general welfare.

But runner-up business firms are not the only source of opposition to innovative activity. The Luddite inclinations of some labor organizations are very well publicized. Union opposition to labor-saving innovations is often considered a prime impediment to technological progress. It is, in fact, easy to sympathize with the reservations of workers who fear for their jobs and their living standards. In the end, even Ricardo was forced to concede that they had a valid point.

It is here that the experience of the Japanese and the kibbutz is most suggestive. In both there are arrangements that offer workers considerable assurance that they have little to fear from technical change. Job-security assurances do not have to be extracted by force after bitter quarrels—they are granted routinely and as a matter of course.

It may well be argued that such assurances are invitations to inefficiency and thus produce the same problems as protective measures for inefficient firms. But there are at least two basic differences. First, while humanitarian considerations can easily justify a program of protection and welfare for individual people, there is hardly any such justification for a program of welfare for indigent business enterprises.

The second difference is more to the point. Suppose we assume (though the evidence is far from conclusive) that job security does lead to laxness and reduced work effort on the part of labor—say, that it reduces output per labor-hour by an (improbable) 30 percent. But suppose it simultaneously hastens the introduction of new productive techniques sufficiently to increase rate of growth in productivity by, say, 2 percent per year. It is obvious that before long this second influence will overtake and ultimately swamp the former, adding substantially to the economy's output stream in the long run.

In contrast, protection accorded to the inefficient business firm has no such stimulating effect upon productivity. On the contrary, it dries up the very pressures for innovation to which we look for the stimulation of growth. If firms can survive and prosper without striving for improvement in techniques, then one can expect the rate of innovation to decline—precisely the thing we want to avoid.

This suggests that a program to promote economic growth should include at least one, if not both, of the following approaches. First, it may seek to emulate the example of Japanese industry and the kibbutz and try to expand the Paretian character of the growth process— that is, try to make the diffusion of its benefits greater, more obvious, and more certain.

Alternatively (or perhaps simultaneously) one can undertake a program of education intended to make clearer the heavy costs to everyone of the constraints upon entrepreneurship extracted from society by the runners-up. If the general public, legislators, and regulators can be led to recognize the heavy price we pay for them, then the supply of entrepreneurship can perhaps be freed from its impediments.

Notes

1. This is not meant to deny the value of an empirical study of entrepreneurial behavior. Enormous benefits can be yielded by its contribution to the understanding, teaching, and effectiveness of management activities, even if it tells us less than we would hope about future entrepreneurial behavior.

2. Indeed, to the extent that wealth is measured by comparison to the position of others, the person who pursues wealth will prefer means that increase his own absolute wealth at the expense of others.

3. There are, as a matter of fact, several promising studies on this subject currently underway. One is being carried out by Lance E. Davis of the California Institute of Technology, and another by Peter Bearse of the City University of New York.

4. As will be recalled, this means that the supply of *autonomous* entrepreneurship may be stimulated (and will certainly not be discouraged) by the example of successful entrepreneurs. In other words, one entrepreneur induces the birth of others, but the inducement ratio is less than one for one. Ten additional entrepreneurs, thus, stimulate the appearance of fewer than ten (autonomous) entrepreneurs. It is surely quite implausible that this premise, $0 \leq R < 1$, will not be satisfied.

Incidentally, it is to be noted that the smaller the slope of RR, the more rapid will be the decline of E_t in the pertinent phase of its history. In particular, in the limiting case where $R = 0$, E_t will fall directly to S once the downturn begins.

5. I am grateful to Mordecai Kurz for pointing out this curious feature of case 1 to me.

4

The Effects of Financing Opportunities and Bankruptcy on Entrepreneurial Risk Bearing

Jerry R. Green and
John B. Shoven

General Introduction

Initiating new ventures often requires outside financing. In this chapter, we discuss the form this financing can take. We show how the risk of bankruptcy shapes the financial contract, and how the contract can be used to regulate the subsequent choices of the entrepreneur.

Clearly, some entrepreneurial ideas have such a large profit potential that an informed financier can be attracted without difficulty. Other ideas are so poor that they cannot be financed even at the best of terms. We deal with the middle ground: projects whose profitability depends on the cost of capital.

To the extent that short-run policies such as tax rates, depreciation rules, and investment credits effect the net returns of the entrepreneur and the financier, they will have an impact upon the criteria for selecting projects. Perhaps a more important channel for stimulating entrepreneurship is by providing, in the longer run, a history of successful innovations. These can serve as a point of focus for individuals with entrepreneurial talent and encourage their efforts in that direction. In this way, the flow of potential projects can be increased.

In this chapter, the existence of the entrepreneurial ideas is taken as given. We might imagine that the prevailing business climate generates ideas of variable quality. An efficient economic system could select the socially valuable ones, finance them, and reject the others. In the real world, and in the simplified models of it we study here, this ideal is not achievable. A variety of market imperfections stands in the way. The interests of the entrepreneur and the financier are not coincident if the finance takes the

An earlier draft was presented at the Price Institute for Entrepreneurial Studies Conference, Toronto, Canada, September 22–24, 1980.

form of debt. If it is an equity interest, the incentives for managerial effort have been dulled by the presence of a silent partner. For these reasons, it is natural to expect that the system will err. Some projects will be financed when superior ones are rejected.

Some of the causes of project selection bias are natural byproducts of the financing process. Specifically, projects in small firms cannot offer a lender a risk-free return because of the size of the firm and the risks involved. Bankruptcy will loom as a possibility at the time the financing takes place. Moreover, bankruptcy entails real costs, that is, if it could be avoided, the real return to the project under those circumstances would be higher. The second key ingredient in our recipe is the simplicity of the financial contracts we allow, relative to the complexity of the relevant uncertainties. This is the primary cause of real bankruptcy possibilities. Conversely, potential bankruptcy costs are a primary determinant of the cost of finance.

The temporal resolution of uncertainties is as important as the size of the risk. The central issue is whether uncertainties are resolved before or after debt repayments are scheduled.

We show that the prospect of bankruptcy may make debt finance so expensive that it results in the premature termination of socially beneficial ventures. Moreover, such a situation cannot always be rescued by a friendly takeover.

The tendency for debt-financed ventures to overemphasize the upper tail of profit possibilities (as opposed to, say, expected returns), is well known. Although this is true when the venture is in place, the opposite bias exists when the finance still has to be attracted. Excessively safe ventures may be chosen by the entrepreneur because he can obtain financing for these on much better terms.

In most actual ventures, some discretionary choices are made after the finance has been arranged and the project actually initiated. We will assume that the entrepreneur retains control of the firm in these matters. Having locked-in his financial base, there may be a divergence between his interests and those of his creditors. Such problems can be perceived at the date the financing is arranged. We show that sometimes (but not always) the structure of the initial financing can be arranged so that the potential for conflicting interests is mitigated, or even avoided.

Our work is aimed at the interplay between the entrepreneur's decisions and the manner in which the venture is financed. The complexity of the situations we are attempting to describe requires that we take a highly stylized viewpoint. At this stage, we proceed through a set of examples designed to shed light on the timing of scheduled debt repayments, senior versus subordinated obligations, bankruptcies, takeovers, and the investment decision itself.

Description of Assumptions

It is easiest to begin by setting out some of the central assumptions. The detailed structure of our model is then described in the following sections.

The effects of uncertainty on the conduct of the new venture can be manifested in risk sharing and risk avoidance. We will concentrate entirely on the latter. Specifically, we will assume that all participants are risk neutral, thereby eliminating the issue of risk sharing. Furthermore, to simplify the examples, we assume a zero rate of real interest in discounting future cash flows.

Bankruptcy possibilities arise in our model because of the potential insolvency of the venture. Because bankruptcy entails a cost in real resources (for instance, lawyers' time in arranging a reorganization or receivership) there will be a collective benefit if this outcome can be avoided. We will see, however, that problems arise because of the limitations of financial instruments and the dynamics of decision making in the conduct of the new enterprise.

A principal assumption concerns the competitive structure of the model. Potential lenders are assumed to behave in a perfectly competitive fashion. One can imagine that the entrepreneur proposes a set of financing terms and that these are accepted whenever they offer the lenders, on average, their competitive return.

We further suppose that the entrepreneurs and financiers have the same information about the nature of the undertaking, the decisions that will be faced at later stages, the relevant risks, and the possible needs for further capitalization. If additional borrowing is undertaken, the claim of the new lenders on future cash flows is strictly junior to the commitments made to the initial financiers. Subject to this priority, however, additional financing is obtained on competitive terms, as was the initial financing.

Finally, we assume that the entrepreneur retains sole control of the venture once it has started. Any subsequent decisions, real or financial, will be made in his own best interest. Moreover, the other participants in the enterprise know, at the time their commitment is made, that its future conduct will be determined in this way.

Available Financial Instruments

In the world we have just described, there is a very simple optimal financing package: all capital is equity capital, sharing equally in all profits and losses. By avoiding any debt obligations, the potential for bankruptcy is eliminated. All owners will obviously agree on the decisions to be taken;

and, as risk sharing is irrelevant, full efficiency can be achieved. There are a variety of reasons why this does not happen in reality. First, the incentives for efficient management are blunted to the extent that the entrepreneur is not the only marginal beneficiary of improved performance. Institutional restrictions, risk averse behavior, and differential information (all assumed away in our model) are other possibilities. Substantial equity participation by outside investors is often observed, but as our focus will be on the conflicts between holders of different financial claims, the analysis will proceed by treating all outside finance as if it took the form of debt. The terms on which loans are made will be determined as part of the solution of the model.

The nature of the debt contract is central to all of our results. Therefore, it is worthwhile to pause and consider the modeling of these obligations in detail. We assume that promised repayments cannot be made dependent upon any events that befall in the project, or upon any future decisions to be taken by the entrepreneur. This entails two consequences. First, debt repayment cannot be tailored to match the available cash flow. If it is insufficient, either the deficit must be financed by further borrowing on competitive terms, or the debt is in default and bankruptcy is declared. Second, if the cash flow exceeds the amount required for debt service, no restriction on dividends can be imposed. In our simple examples, any such excess will be garnered by the entrepreneur. Because all parties have complete information at the outset, this will be foreseen, and it will be reflected in the equilibrium financial arrangements.

In reality, of course, both of these restrictive assumptions are often circumvented. Complex debt contracts can be written. Convertible debt, mortgage bonds, and other instruments have equity characteristics that help protect the lenders while avoiding the real costs of bankruptcy. Direct restrictive covenants are used to avoid some of these problems as well. These facts only demonstrate the severity of the issue. In some cases, these more complex debt instruments effectively act as equity by eliminating the possibility of bankruptcy and removing the conflicting interests that distort investment decisions. However, no contract except real equity participation can always be flexible enough to entirely avoid the problem. Therefore, our use of rather extreme assumptions should be viewed as a stylized way of studying the consequences of incompleteness in the financial contracting process, rather than as an attempt to depict actual financial arrangements.

Structure of the Model

With these preliminaries out of the way, we can now describe our model. The project is assumed to require $1 of additional debt capital that must be raised at the outset. Once initiated, the net cash flows before subtracting debt repayments are described by a tree structure as they evolve over time. For example,

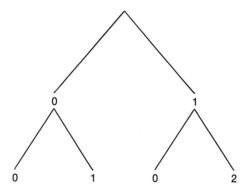

means that at the next date, a cash flow of either 0 or 1 will be realized, and at a subsequent date the possibilities are either 0 or 1, or 0 or 2. Unless otherwise specified, the probabilities of branches emanating from the same node of the tree will be assumed equal.

Some of our examples also involve decisions on the conduct of the project at subsequent dates. These form an important part of our analysis, and they will be indicated by the diamond symbol at the node where the decision is taken. For example,

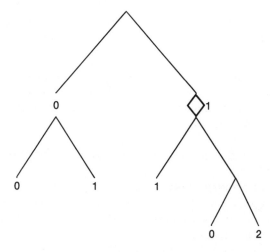

means that if a cash flow of 1 is realized at the first date, the entrepreneurs can choose between a sure cash flow of 1 and a risky prospect with the same mean.

Finally, some subsequent decisions might require new capital beyond the initial $1. If so, these will be indicated by the symbol "$(K = \ )$" next to the corresponding branch of the tree. For example,

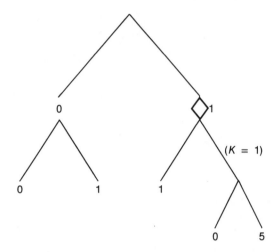

means that to choose the risk option requires an additional unit of capital, but the safe option can be pursued without further costs.

Equilibrium

Because the entire tree structure describing the prospects of the venture is common knowledge to lenders at the start, the future conduct of the entrepreneur is perfectly predictable. An equilibrium is a complete dynamic description of the financial arrangements and real decisions, and has the following two properties:

1. At any time, the entrepreneur will always behave in his own best interest. Furthermore, he has a rational perception of the consequences of any action he might take.
2. Lenders, knowing that this is true, use it to compute the anticipated return on their investments. It is this expectation that must meet the competitive standard.

This type of equilibrium is called perfect in the game-theoretic literature because it is internally consistent and the participants are completely rational.

Examples Using the Model

Example 1

We begin with the simplest example of financing when bankruptcy is possible.

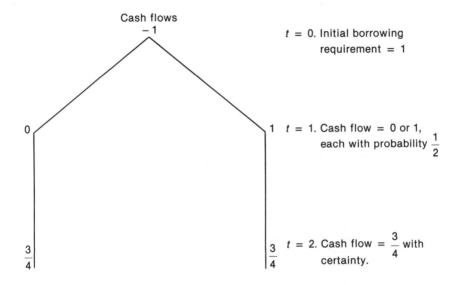

Cash flows

$t = 0.$ Initial borrowing
requirement $= 1$

$t = 1.$ Cash flow $= 0$ or 1,
each with probability $\frac{1}{2}$

$t = 2.$ Cash flow $= \frac{3}{4}$ with
certainty.

By assumption, the entrepreneur cannot finance the $1 initial cost with his own funds, and must seek external sources. Bonds are issued with required payments D_1 and D_2 in payment periods 1 and 2, respectively. The cash flow structure is as pictured. Our zero interest rate and risk neutrality assumptions imply that the project has a total economic value of 1 1/4 and a surplus of 1/4.

Our assumptions about the occurrence of bankruptcy and its associated real costs are as follows: If the contractual obligation to debt holders is positive at time 1, and if the worse event is realized, there will not be any cash to pay them. We assume that this state of affairs leads to a bankruptcy. The remaining cash flow prospect (which in this case is a sure 3/4 at date 2) is sold to another firm or individual, but at an unavoidable cost of C. Thus the debt holders can recover only $3/4 - C$.

One may ask why the debt holders should press for a forced sale of the firm, rather than letting the original entrepreneur continue operation, which will give them 3/4 with certainty. Rationality should lead them to this benign course of action. Forced bankruptcies, however, do exist in the world, and it is the real costs of bankruptcy that drive all the examples in this paper. Many bankruptcies are avoided (or at least postponed) because debt holders are lenient in pressing their claims, extend credit, or carry accounts receivable. This only attests to the magnitude of the real costs they are attempting to avoid. Nevertheless, we must assume that there is some divergence of interests between debt and equity, lest we implicitly convert the former into the latter and obviate the need for this entire analysis. The simplicity of these examples should not belie the difficulty of realizing such coordination in practice.

Suppose first that the entrepreneur tries to avoid a bankruptcy at time 1 by setting $D_1 = 0$. We assume that the equity holder (entrepreneur) cannot be contractually prevented from paying dividends in a period in which cash flows permit such after all current debt obligations have been paid. Thus, if the cash flow in period 1 turns out to be unity, and if D_1 has been set at zero, the equity holders will declare the \$1 as a dividend. The total return to the debtholders will be 3/4 (the certain return in period 2) but this is insufficient to compensate them for their initial outlay. The problem is that while $D_1 = 0$ is compatible with the avoidance of bankruptcy costs, it is not compatible with offering lenders competitive terms.

Because of the above arguments, D_1 must be positive in any equilibrium. This implies that bankruptcy will occur with probability 1/2. In the event that the cash flow of the company in period 1 is zero, the firm's value is just $3/4 - C$, since bankruptcy costs must be paid. All of this goes to the bondholders. To offer the lenders a competitive rate of return, the better branch must have an expected present value of $1\ 1/4 + C$. Debt repayments cannot be set at levels above the maximum cash flow (that is, $D_1 \leq 1, D_2 \leq 3/4$), so the condition for competitive lending terms is

$$\min(1, D_1) + \min(\frac{3}{4}, D_2) = 1\frac{1}{4} + C \qquad (4.1)$$

Possible solutions are shown in figure 4–1.

If C, the bankruptcy costs, is less than 1/2, any financial terms on segment $\overline{AB}$ are feasible. The project can be undertaken, and the residual value or profit to the entrepreneur is

$$\frac{1}{2}((1 - D_1) + (\frac{3}{4} - D_2)) = \frac{1}{4} - \frac{C}{2} \qquad (4.2)$$

An all-equity venture, on any financial structure that prevents the possibility of bankruptcy, will have a value of 1/4. However, as we have seen, if the project is financed with debt, it can only proceed if bancruptcy costs are less than 1/2. Furthermore, there is a 50 percent probability that the bankruptcy costs will be paid.

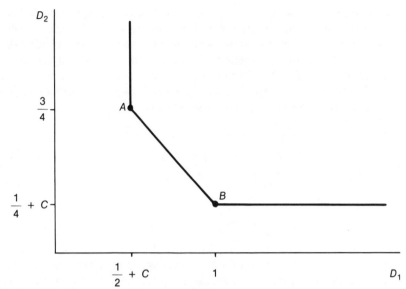

Figure 4–1. Required Promised Repayments to Finance Venture in
Example 1

Example 2

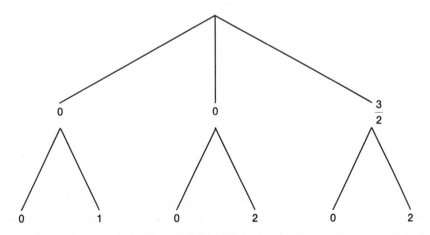

In the second example of our model, there are three possible outcomes
at $t = 1$, with all branches equally likely at each t. What this example

illustrates is that bankruptcy can spread or spill over from one branch to another because of the constraints on financial structure. To obtain a competitive return, debt holders must increase their terms to offset the bankruptcy that occurs in one branch. However, this increase in terms may doom other probability branches (that is, lead them to bankruptcy).

In this example, assume that only the left branch leads to bankruptcy. In that case, the debt must be structured so that

$$\frac{1}{3}(\frac{1}{2} - C) + \frac{2}{3}D_1 + \frac{1}{3}D_2 = 1$$

or

$$\frac{2}{3}D_1 + \frac{1}{3}D_2 = \frac{5}{6} + \frac{1}{3}C \tag{4.3}$$

Since $D_2 \le 2$, this requires $D_1 > 0$. Thus the firm is insolvent along the middle branch. Any attempt to save the project along the middle branch by refinancing with junior debt will fail. If such an attempt is to succeed,

$$\frac{1}{2}(2 - D_2) \ge D_1 \tag{4.4}$$

since the probability of the $2 payoff in period 2 is 1/2. Condition (4.3), in conjunction with $D_1 \le 3/2$, $D_2 \le 2$, requires that the debt terms be on the line segment $\overline{AB}$ in figure 4-2. Condition (4.4), however, requires that the terms be on or below $\overline{CD}$. Therefore, even though the middle branch has an expected present value of one, it will lead to bankruptcy.

Given that both the left and center branches involve default, the condition to offer debtholders a competitive return can be written as

$$\frac{1}{3}(\frac{1}{2} - C) + \frac{1}{3}(1 - C) + \frac{1}{3}D_1 + \frac{1}{6}D_2 = 1$$

$$D_1 \le \frac{3}{2}, \qquad D_2 \le 2 \tag{4.5}$$

This has feasible solutions along line segment $\overline{EF}$ in figure 4-3 as long as $C \le 1/2$. It should be noted that $\overline{EF}$ is strictly northeast of $\overline{AB}$ in figure 4-2. That is, the competitive lending terms have been increased to offset the now 2/3 chance of incurring bankruptcy costs.

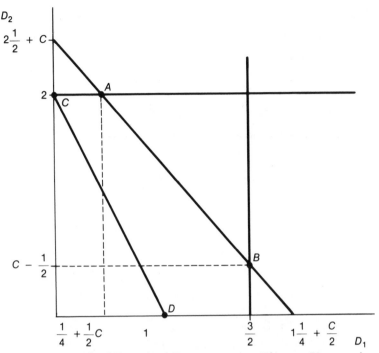

Figure 4-2. Required Promised Repayments to Finance Venture in
Example 2: Only Left Branch in Default

Example 3

It is often observed that bankruptcy provisions can bias equity holders
toward riskier prospects, since limited liability effectively insures them
against extremely low or negative cash-flow outcomes [see, for example,
Bulow and Shoven (1978)]. The extreme example of this occurs in a firm
with (temporarily) adequate cash flow, but a negative net worth. If the
equity holders are prohibited from paying dividends in such a situation,
their best alternative strategy is to invest in extremely risky projects, in the
hope of giving the firm some chance to survive.

While the above argument is relevant for an ongoing concern, the focus
in our model is rather on the financial arrangements of a new venture. We
show in this example how the incentives for risktaking can be reversed when
we look at the problem of *ex ante* financing. The choice among projects can
be influenced by the cost of capital. As lenders have complete information

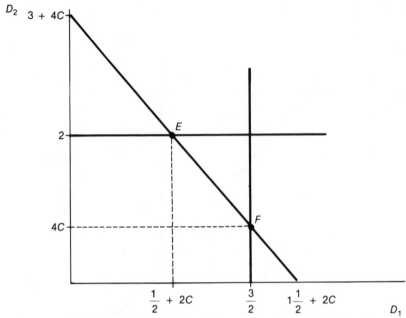

Figure 4–3. Required Promised Repayments to Finance Venture in
          Example 2: Left and Middle Branches in Default

about future prospects, they can offer better terms to entrepreneurs who
can demonstrate that their debt is less risky. In order to avoid bankruptcy
costs, the safer of two projects may be preferred, even if the expected present value of its cash flows (excluding bankruptcy costs) is somewhat less
than that of a risky project.

   We compare two projects with the same expected present value of cash
flow.

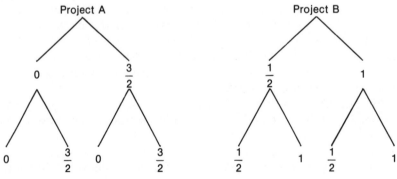

The competitive return constraint for the lender for project A is

$$D_1 + \frac{1}{2}D_2 = 1\frac{1}{4} + C$$

$$D_1 \le \frac{3}{2} \qquad D_2 \le \frac{3}{2} \qquad\qquad (4.6)$$

This can be financed as long as $C \le 1$ along the line segment $\overline{AB}$ in figure 4-4. The return to the equity is

$$\frac{1}{2}(\frac{3}{2} - D_1) + \frac{1}{4}(\frac{3}{2} - D_2) = \frac{1}{2}(1 - C) \qquad\qquad (4.7)$$

Project B, the safer project with the same expected present value, can be financed with debt by setting $D_1 = D_2 = 1/2$. There is no possibility of

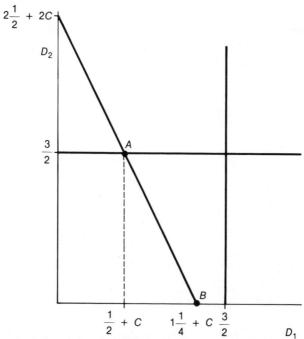

Figure 4-4. Required Promised Repayments to Finance Venture in Example 3

bankruptcy, and therefore, no premium need be included in the terms of the loan. The entrepreneur can realize a higher expected present value given by

$$\frac{1}{2}(\frac{1}{2}) + \frac{1}{2}(\frac{1}{2}) = \frac{1}{2} > \frac{1}{2}(1 - C) \qquad \text{for } C > 0 \qquad (4.8)$$

Therefore, project B will be preferred. The lesson is that bankruptcy costs impose a kind of nonconvexity in the evaluation of projects, favoring those whose cash flows do not threaten default.

Examples 4 and 5 should be viewed in parallel. They address the issue of whether the entrepreneur can effectively commit himself to the socially superior course of action through his prior financial arrangements, even though the actual decision will be taken at a later date when he retains control and when he might have the incentive to act against the bondholders' interests. This type of financial strategy is possible, as in example 4; but it is not always the case, as example 5 will demonstrate.

Example 4

Example 4 involves a choice at time $t = 1$ of a safe or a risky investment, as shown below. The entrepreneur can choose between a project that pays a certain \$1 and one with a 50–50 chance of 0 or 3/2.

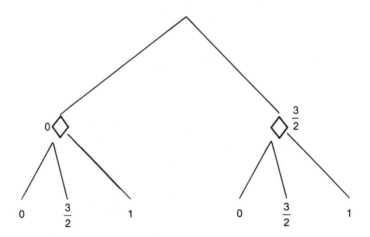

The safer project clearly has a higher expected present value. However, with the initial financing set at $t = 0$, the question we now ask is whether the entrepreneur will choose the safe or risky profit at $t = 1$. Can the entrepreneur, by suitably structuring the initial financing package, make it credible that *ex post* he will not opt for the risky (inferior) alternative despite its better upper tail?

Suppose the entrepreneur announces at time $t = 0$ that he will choose the risky investment at $t = 1$. The cash-flow pattern is thus identical to project A in example 3. If the worse event happens at $t = 1$, the firm will go bankrupt and its value will be $1 - C$, rather than $3/4 - C$. The possible financing is thus given by

$$\frac{1}{2}D_1 + \frac{1}{4}D_2 + \frac{1}{2}(1 - C) = 1$$

or

$$D_1 + \frac{1}{2}D_2 = 1 + C \qquad (4.9)$$

If we set D_1 to $3/2$, then $D_2 = 2C - 1$. The value to the entrepreneur is

$$\frac{1}{4}(\frac{3}{2} - 2C + 1) = \frac{1}{4}(\frac{5}{2} - 2C) = \frac{5}{8} - \frac{C}{2} \qquad (4.10)$$

If, after obtaining this financing, the entrepreneur considers switching to the safe choice, the value of his choices at the decision juncture are

$$\text{Risky: } \frac{1}{2}(\frac{3}{2} - D_2)$$

$$\text{Safe: } 1 - D_2 \qquad (4.11)$$

Therefore, he will have an incentive to contradict his promise of choosing the risky option if

$$1 - D_2 > \frac{3}{4} - \frac{D_2}{2}$$

or

$$D_2 < \frac{1}{2}$$

The lowest D_2 can be is $2C - 1$. Therefore, if $C \geq 3/4$, there will never be an incentive for switching, and we will have a perfect equilibrium in the sense that precommitments will be kept. If $C < 3/4$, the announced choice may not be followed, depending on whether $D_2 < 1/2$.

Now, let us examine the case where the entrepreneur commits himself in advance to the safe strategy along the right branch. In this case, the debt requires that

$$\frac{1}{2}(D_1 + D_2) + \frac{1}{2}(1 - C) = 1$$

or

$$D_1 + D_2 = 1 + C \qquad (4.12)$$

A natural question, of course, is why not set the financing at $D_1 = 0$ and $D_2 = 1$, thereby eliminating the risk of bankruptcy. This financing, however, is obviously not compatible with equilibrium. With this financial structure, it would be in the interest of the entrepreneur to choose the risky investment. Note that the entrepreneur's profit with a precommitment to the safe strategy is

$$\frac{1}{2}(\frac{5}{2} - D_1 - D_2) = \frac{1}{2}(\frac{3}{2} - C)$$

$$= \frac{3}{4} - \frac{C}{2} \qquad (4.13)$$

which dominates the $5/8 - C/2$ yielded by the precommitment to the risky move. The question we want to examine is whether the commitment can be made credible. At $t = 1$, the prospects are valued at

$$\text{Safe:} \quad 1 - D_2$$

$$\text{Risky:} \quad \frac{1}{2}(\frac{3}{2} - D_2) \qquad (4.14)$$

For small D_2, the safe strategy dominates, for larger D_2, the risky strategy gives the larger return. Since $D_1 \leq 3/2$, $D_2 \geq C - 1/2$. Safe is at least as good as risky as long as

$$1 - D_2 \geq \frac{1}{2}(\frac{3}{2} - D_2)$$

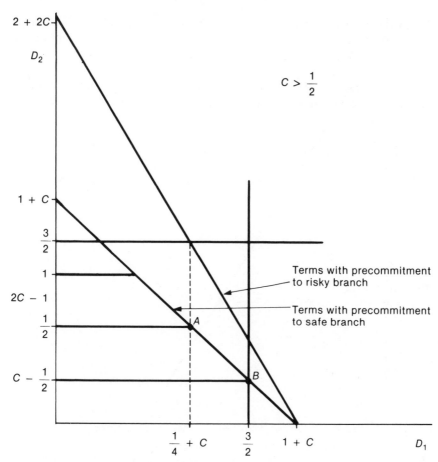

Figure 4–5. Two Self-Enforcing Promised-Repayment Plans to Finance Venture in Example 4

or

$$D_2 \le \frac{1}{2}$$

Collecting our results, we see that a credible precommitment to the safe investment can be made as long as $C - 1/2 \le D_2 \le 1/2$. Clearly C must be less than unity. The financial terms are illustrated in figure 4–5.

It shows that the financial terms are better for the entrepreneur if he can make the safe commitment. This can be done only along the segment

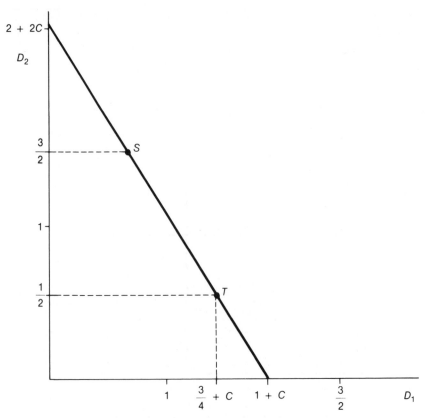

Figure 4–6. Equilibrium-Financing Plans Consistent with Safe
Precommitment in Venture in Example 4

$\overline{AB}$ if $C < 1$. Note that for small C, the risky precommitment is credible
only for some financial terms. This is because the entrepreneur's *ex post*
incentive is to choose safe if D_2 is less than $1/2$. The financial plans along
$\overline{ST}$ in figure 4–6 are equilibrium conditions, however.

Example 5

This example is very similar to the previous one. However, here the entrepreneur cannot make a believable precommitment to the socially optimal
choice. The only financing obtainable is that based on the assumption that
the risky option will be chosen at $t = 1$, even though it has a lower expected

return. The inflexibility of the debt contract (as we have modeled it) makes it impossible to avoid the *ex post* financing bias towards risk.

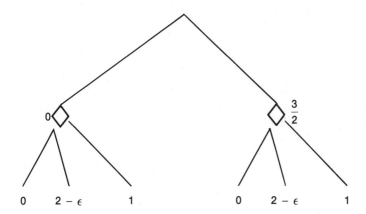

The e parameter is a small positive number present simply to demonstrate that the result mentioned above is possible even when the risky option is strictly inferior (as opposed to equal) in expected value. The debt conditions are

$$D_1 + \frac{1}{2}\min{(D_2, 2 - \epsilon)} = 1 + C \qquad (4.15)$$

if a risky precommitment has been made and

$$D_1 + \min{(D_2, 1)} = 1 + C \qquad (4.16)$$

if the safe precommitment had been made.

Assuming that the entrepreneur has made a precommitment to the risky strategy and obtains finance on that basis, the value of the firm is

$$\frac{1}{2}(\frac{3}{2} - D_1 + \frac{1}{2}(2 - \epsilon - D_2)) = \frac{3}{4} - \frac{\epsilon}{4} - \frac{C}{2} \qquad (4.17)$$

whereas the entrepreneur's position is worth

$$\frac{1}{2}(\frac{5}{2} - (D_1 + D_2)) = \frac{3}{4} - \frac{C}{2} \qquad (4.18)$$

if a safe precommitment can be credibly made. The safer strategy is more valuable to the entrepreneur and has a higher return; however, it cannot be sustained as an equilibrium.

Consider a safe precommitment. At the decision node, the choice facing the entrepreneur is

$$\text{Safe:} \quad 1 - D_2$$

$$\text{Risky:} \frac{1}{2}(2 - \epsilon - D_2) = 1 - \frac{D_2}{2} - \frac{\epsilon}{2} \qquad (4.19)$$

Risky will be chosen if

$$1 - \frac{D_2}{2} - \frac{\epsilon}{2} > 1 - D_2$$

or

$$D_2 > \epsilon$$

To make D_2 as small as possible with the safe precommitment, D_1 is set to 3/2 and D_2 to $C - 1/2$. However, if $C - 1/2 > \epsilon$, there is no way to make the safe precommitment valid, and the risky option must be chosen even though it is socially less valuable.

Example 6

One phenomenon of great practical importance in many new ventures is the possibility of a takeover by a large corporation. Reasons for takeovers are quite varied. We will consider only one in this example. The need for more capital to finance a good investment project can be better met by a large outside investor than by the original entrepreneur, who must issue additional risky debt.

As in the examples above, the point to be emphasized is that the foresight of all concerned will influence the initial financing and, hence, the subsequent behavior of the entrepreneur. Debt must be so contracted that the takeover will be beneficial both to the outside firm and to the entrepreneur. Only in this case can it be rationally predicted. The cash-flow structure is as follows:

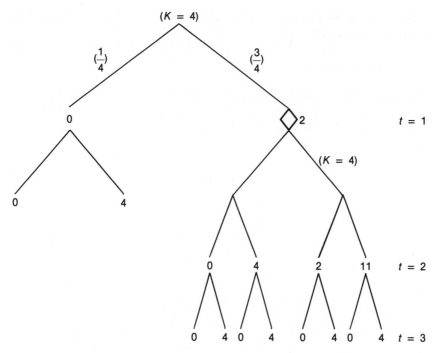

$C = 1$

To find the financing plan that gives the entrepreneur the highest expected profit, we must consider cases that depend on whether or not the original lenders perceive that a takeover will occur at $t = 1$. Within each case, we will compute the relevant values to the entrepreneur and the outside firm as they depend on the subsequent actions chosen.

1. No Takeover, Entrepreneur Declines New Project. Let us first assume that no takeover is perceived, and that the new investment will not be undertaken by the entrepreneur using a new debt issue. Lenders then perceive the expected value of the promised repayment sequence (D_1, D_2, D_3), with $D_1 \leq 2$, $D_2 \leq 4$, and $D_3 \leq 4$, to be

$$\frac{1}{4}(2 - C) + \frac{3}{4}D_1 + \frac{3}{8}(2 - C) + \frac{3}{8}D_2 + \frac{3}{16}D_3 \qquad (4.20)$$

For this to be feasible, its value must at least be 4, or

$$\frac{3}{4}D_1 + \frac{3}{8}D_2 + \frac{3}{16}D_3 = \frac{27}{8}$$

If the entrepreneur behaved as predicted and did not finance the additional investment, his initial expectation could be computed by taking $D_1 = 2$, $D_2 = 4$, $D_3 = 2$, which gives a value of 3/8. Other financing plans satisfying (4–20) would have the same value.

2. No Takeover, Entrepreneur Accepts Project. Will the failure to invest be verified? From the viewpoint of a new lender, the cash flow remaining in the new investment after D_2 and D_3 have been repaid will be

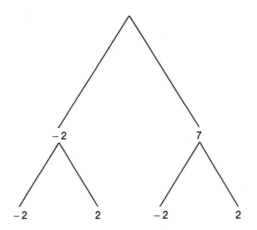

The left-hand branch yields nothing to new debt holders. The original lenders would insist on a bankruptcy to get back 3 out of the 4 they are owed. [They would receive the cash flow (2) and the net bankruptcy value of the remaining firm $(1/2 \cdot 4 - 1 = 1)$]. Note that bankruptcy could not be avoided by issuing debt at this point to cover the cash-flow deficit.

On the right-hand branch, the residual cash flow is worth 8 $(7 + 1/2 \cdot 2)$ to new lenders. Back at the decision point $(t = 1)$ their expectation is just 4; therefore, the financial package is just barely feasible.

Will the entrepreneur borrow on these terms and thereby invalidate the beliefs of lenders who financed the original investment? No. The new loan repayments would wipe out all of the profit, even in the most favorable of circumstances. Therefore, if investors believed that the entrepreneur will not finance his future investment, they would demand terms under which this belief could be verified *ex post.*

3. No Takeover Anticipated, Entrepreneur Seeks Takeover Offer at $t = 1$. Now we introduce the possibility that even though a takeover was not anticipated by lenders, *ex post* the entrepreneur seeks a takeover by a large firm at $t = 1$. In such a situation, the outstanding debt obligations must be honored. The parent firm cannot repurchase the debt at market values reflecting default risk and then proceed with the takeover, because the expectation of this will cause the market price to reflect the full default-free value. With the debt structure (2,4,2) shown above, the parent firm would have a gross expected return of $1/2(2) + 1/4(4) + 1/2(11) + 1/4(4) =$ 8 1/2. The debt obligations are worth 6 and the additional capital requirements are worth 4, making it impossible to compensate the entrepreneur at all. Therefore, a takeover is not financially possible with this debt structure.

4. Takeover Anticipated, Terms Defined by Opportunity Cost of the Entrepreneur. On the other hand, suppose that we assume that the original lenders believe from the beginning that there will be a takeover. Can this be verified *ex post?* The lender in this case thinks that in the worse event they will recover 1, because the firm will be worth 2 and the bankruptcy costs absorb 1 (by assumption) in this example. In the better event, the debt is made riskless because of the takeover. Therefore, the breakeven value for lenders is given by

$$\frac{1}{4} + \frac{3}{4}(D_1 + D_2 + D_3) = 4 \qquad (4.21)$$

Consider, for example, the solution $D_1 = 2$, $D_2 = 3$, $D_3 = 0$. Note that these terms are strictly better than those considered above, where a takeover was not feasible.

To see whether takeover will occur here, we have to find out the maximum value realizable by equity if (contrary to lenders beliefs) the entrepreneur does not submit to the takeover. This maximum must be computed for both the case in which the entrepreneur tries to undertake the additional investment and that in which he does not. First, assume that the entrepreneur chooses not to make the additional investment when it is possible. Their net prospects at $t = 1$ after debt repayments are,

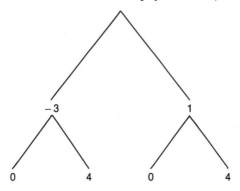

Clearly the left-hand branch results in bankruptcy, so we are left with an overall expected value of 3/2. If they do invest, they must raise 4 units of

capital to be repaid out of the net proceeds remaining after senior debt obligations are met:

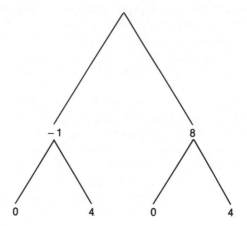

Let these junior obligations be denoted d_2, d_3. If there is to be no default on this junior debt, we must have $d_2 \leq 1$ on the left-hand branch. Were $d_2 >$ 1, the obligations would exceed the remaining expected value of the firm on the left-hand branch. However, $d_2 = 1$ implies that $d_3 \geq 6$ is required to satisfy the breakeven condition for junior lenders. This is clearly unfeasible, so junior debt must be risky if it is viable at all. Risky junior debt will get no payoff on the left-hand branch because the senior debt will force a bankruptcy that will leave zero value remaining. The breakeven condition for junior debt is, thus,

$$\frac{1}{2}d_2 + \frac{1}{4}d_3 = 4 \qquad (4.22)$$

Take, for example, $d_2 = 8$, $d_3 = 0$. Under this option, the value to equity is entirely due to the payoff of 4 they receive on the rightmost branch at $t = 3$. The value viewed from $t = 1$ is just 1, which compares unfavorably to the "don't invest" option of 3/2. To summarize, given that the debt is structured according to the belief that a takeover will occur, the best policy the entrepreneur can follow in resisting a takeover is not to make the new investment, yielding an expected value of 3/2 from the potential takeover point onward. The takeover firm must give him at least 3/2 if he will yield control.

5. Takeover Anticipated, Is It Profitable? Will there be a successful takeover? The debt is worth 3, the new investment is worth 4, and equity costs 3/2, which is its opportunity cost as computed in sub-section 4 above. Total outlay will be 8 1/2 (exactly equal to the gross value of the project) so the takeover is a borderline case.

It is easy to modify the example slightly to make takeover strictly superior. For example,

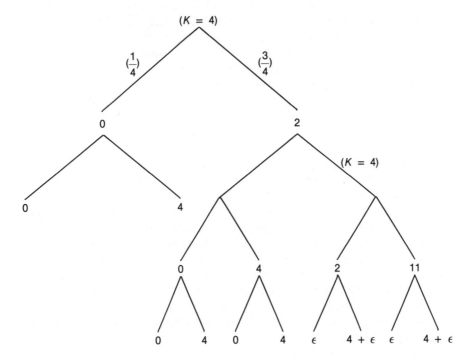

for $1/2 > \epsilon > 0$. It is still better (given no takeover) for the entrepreneur not to invest and get 3/2 than to undertake the investment and get $1 + \epsilon$. His reservation value is not increased at all; thus, the cost of the takeover is still the same. The value is, of course, higher, and so it is strictly preferred and can be confidently predicted by the initial lenders.

Conclusion

Through a series of highly stylized examples, we have illustrated that the interaction of the entrepreneur and his financiers can lead to socially inferior outcomes, even though both parties have complete information and identical attitudes toward risk. This result comes from the rigidity of the debt contract and the fact that once the initial financing is set, neither the entrepreneur nor the financier are interested in maximizing the total (social) return of the venture. Despite the fact that everyone rationally understands the incentives faced by the other participants, costly bankruptcies might occur and less than optimal investments might be undertaken.

Our framework of analysis has been kept extremely simple to highlight the results. In fact, however, we believe that the type of outcomes we have derived are even more likely in a more realistic environment. For example, taxes have not entered our examples; but these clearly affect bankruptcies and takeovers in a monumental manner. First, for a firm with its primary financing set, a tax system with symmetrical loss offsets the variance of net cash flows, lowering the value of the entrepreneur's position and encouraging bankruptcy. At the same time, as tax-loss carry-forwards are forfeited in bankruptcy, but assumed in a takeover within the same industry, the tax system favors takeovers relative to bankruptcies. Similarly, differential risk aversion and asymmetric information can add to the likelihood of nonoptimal outcomes.

We have not highlighted all of the results generated by models of the type presented. One that others have noted (White 1980) deals with the principle of investment diversification. Risk-averse investors place a premium on assets that have a negative covariance with the individual's existing portfolio. If one is risk neutral (as in this model) covariance is a matter of indifference. Here, however, once financing is set, the entrepreneur may strictly prefer additional investments that have a positive covariance with the cash flows of the existing firm. The reason is clear—namely, total variance increases the value of the claimant of the upper tail, that is to say the equity holders or the entrepreneur. As we saw in our examples 3 through 5, this result would likely be reversed if we considered the problem before the financing was fixed.

The class of problem examined here is very relevant for fledgling firms seeking either bank financing or venture capital. These enterprises almost always face a nonnegligible bankruptcy probability, and the idea of entrepreneurial talent is frequently embodied in one individual. The lenders may have information regarding the prospects of the firm, but must leave control in the hands of the entrepreneur. The question we have addressed is whether entrepreneurs and such informed, competitive lenders can cooperate in initiating and financing ventures in a socially efficient manner.

References

Bulow, J., and Shoven, J. "The Bankruptcy Decision." *Bell Journal of Economics,* 9, 2 (Autumn 1978):437–456.

White, M.J. "Public Policy Toward Bankruptcy: Me-First and Other Priority Rules." *Bell Journal of Economics,* 11, 2 (Autumn 1980): 550–564.

5 Entrepreneurial Concepts, Definitions, and Model Formulations

Harold N. Shapiro

Introduction

This chapter concerns a variety of ideas that relate to the formulation and possible understanding of problems concerning entrepreneurial activities. It is intended as a rough map of the terrain, with some indication of roads that might be traveled. There is much conjecturing as to what might be seen on such a journey, but this is not the report of an actual trip.

Though economic theory as a science, and its application as an art form, are much advanced (with reference to our current social complex), the very basic role of the entrepreneur, its definition, its measurement, and the determination of its influence and implications, has not received a deserving share of investigative effort. Certainly, it would be presumptuous to assume that the efforts represented by this modest book could fulfill this need. Rather, it is the hope of this and the other chapters to renew and sharpen the focus on those problem areas that relate to the entrepreneur and his activities.

Quite independently of any formal definitions, the entrepreneur functions and performs within, and is motivated by, the economic, social, political, and cultural frameworks in which the entrepreneurial activity is imbedded. In a sense, all of economic theory is an effort at uncovering and understanding the relevant economic framework. Moreover, psychology, sociology, government, and history all contribute to the determination of the rules under which the entrepreneur operates and of the forces that operate on him.

Viewed from this perspective, the avowed objective of studying entrepreneurism is much easier stated than achieved. Indeed, it appears to imply an almost prohibitive awareness and command of both the facets and dynamics of modern society. Prohibitive not only from the point of view of the intellectual capacity of the investigator, but also simply because much of the required factual information does not exist. How then does one cope with the difficulty of organizing the analysis of this complex situation in the face of such intellectual and informational handicaps. We begin our answer to this by setting as our goal the establishment of a general framework for model formulation and objective specification. Within this framework we could then seek a useful, idealized model of the entrepreneurial situation. The sense of *idealization* is that elements of structure and dynamics are singled out to serve as a framework for formulating and analyzing problems arising in the real world. This so-called model need not be "real" in any reasonable sense of the word. Rather, its *raison d'etre* rests heavily on the requirement that it be useful. Stated differently, the analysis of real-world problems, via this model leads to useful decisions and conclusions. Of course, the exact meaning of *useful* is quite variable, and it is meant to include both the affirmation of experimental decision making and the definition and assessment of new situations. In this regard, experience dictates that it is necessary to extract considerable information from reality on which to base the details of the model structure. One can dream of reality in an academic cloister, but it cannot be created there simply by making a model. Nor can such a model by itself justify any claim to the understanding of reality.

Since the notion of model plays a central role in most efforts to quantize a real-world situation, it is appropriate to pause and consider what meaning is conveyed here by this word. A model is a composite object, $\mathfrak{M}$, which in some sense is intended as a description of a situation $\mathcal{S}$. At least, purely linguistically, the intent is to say that "$\mathfrak{M}$ is a model of $\mathcal{S}$." And what is $\mathfrak{M}$? To begin with, it contains a list of specified *elements* which have been assigned specific designations, (that is, names or symbols). Such elements can have many different categories. A most useful type is that of an object X that has been carried over from $\mathcal{S}$ to the model. X may represent an actual object in $\mathcal{S}$ or some agglomeration of several elements of $\mathcal{S}$. For example, if the real situation $\mathcal{S}$ under consideration is a visit to the dentist, the model $\mathfrak{M}$ might include such objects as the dentist, the waiting room, the dentist chair, and, of course, the drill. As an agglomerated element of the model, one might include all of the office help under one idealized object: the nurse. Thus far these elements are physical in that they stem from real people or objects. A second important category includes elements that are conceptual in nature. For example, in our dental illustration above, our model $\mathfrak{M}$ might include "pain," "nature of the dental problem," and "competence of the dentist."

Concomitant with the delineation of the elements, various numerical quantities are introduced to specify some descriptive feature of one or more of the objects. For example, a code number to distinguish whether the dentist is right handed or left handed, a numerical measure of the sharpness of the drill, the position of the drill, a measure of pain level, and so on. Initially, the main distinction in the category of these quantities is that some are constant, whereas others may vary with time.

Thus we are led to the fact that for many models, time itself is an important quantity that must be present as an ingredient of the model.

With time and the other descriptive aspects of the model specified, we can now talk about a *state* of the system. By this we refer to the aggregate of the values of all these descriptive quantities at a fixed instant of time. In particular, the aggregate of values that correspond to that time at which the analysis of $\mathfrak{M}$ is initiated is called the *initial state*.

Finally, the model $\mathfrak{M}$ must contain some specification of the circumstances that induce changes in the state of the system and rules for calculating these changes. In doing this we are incorporating into $\mathfrak{M}$ some estimate of the *dynamics* of the system $\mathcal{S}$. For example, when the dentist starts to drill, the pain level may change, and some rule would be provided to calculate this change. It is important to note that, in general, the rules of dynamics may be of two kinds, usually referred to as *deterministic* and *stochastic*. A *deterministic law* is one that always responds to a given stimulus for change, in the presence of a given state, with exactly the same evolving changes of state. For example, in this category we have most of the elementary laws of physics. On the other hand, a *stochastic law* is one that allows for more than one possible outcome as a result of a given stimulus for change, in the presence of a given state, but that specifies the probabilities with which each of the possible evolutions may occur.

Thus far, the real situation $\mathcal{S}$ has been replaced by a model $\mathfrak{M}$ consisting of (1) objects, (2) descriptive state parameters, and (3) specification of dynamics. How does one proceed to use this to study $\mathfrak{M}$? For this one needs one more essential entity, an *objective!* By this one can mean a large variety of things, and for the moment we leave it vague. However, in addition to the selection of the objective, one has to specify some corresponding mode of measurement that we call the *objective function*. In some sense the objective function measures the extent to which the system "achieves the objective," as estimated via the model.

To remove a small amount of the vagueness concerning objectives, note first that there are many categories of objectives. However, from the broadest possible point of view these can be grouped to correspond to two general problem areas that we will refer to as *direct problems* and *inverse problems*. The direct problems are those in which the model parameters are set and one wishes to study the evolution of the system as a function of the initial state. In the inverse problems, one has some assessment (from reality) of both the initial state and the outcome and wishes to fit one or more of the model parameters so as to have the model account for the observed transition. In practice, then, ideally the utilization of a model is a combination of direct and inverse problems. First, one uses the available data concerning reality to estimate the model parameters. Then one uses these values to predict, or to assess, new or related situations.

Even with the specification of an objective, there remain many decisions concerning the utilization of the model. With respect to the actual implementation of the model, two distinct procedures are available: *simula-*

tion or *mathematical analysis.* The extent to which the latter is useful is dictated by how intrinsically mathematical and how simple is the model. In general, with the occurrence of any degree of complexity, weakness of intellect quickly forces one to simulative procedures. With this, one literally lives through or flows through the paths of the model from a prescribed initial state to the outputted state at some specified time or event. If the model is deterministic, a single such "run" yields the unique output that results from a given input. However, if the model is stochastic, a single run gives only a sample from a larger collection of possible outcomes. This is because of the fact that in traveling through the model, when a local stochastic component is reached, an outcome is chosen according to the specified probabilities. (A rare event may actually occur!) One must then reprocess the model (over and over again) with the same initial conditions, so as to obtain the relative frequencies of the possible outcomes. (Of course, the question of how many repetitions are required to establish this information is itself a critical and difficult one.) Once one is armed with this distribution of outcomes one can return to some mode of analysis that focuses on the relevant objective functions.

In this chapter we will attempt to formulate a general *abstract* model that is structured to accommodate a wide variety of entrepreneurial situations and objectives. Moreover, it is hoped that the model itself will enhance the very formulation of such problems. Further, it is hoped that the different views of what is an entrepreneur and how entrepreneurial activity is measured can coexist within the framework of a single model. Then, within this conception, these differences are essentially accounted for by a combination of

1. which portion of the model is in focus?
2. what is the objective?
3. how is the objective measured?
4. how can the utilization of the model be measured? Can it be risked? Is this a proper application?

Thus comes our thesis that the different concepts of entrepreneurism are not intrinsic to reality but stem from different views of reality and the different modes of analysis and assessment that correspond to these views.

We will attempt to give all of the above ideas some precision within the framework of the abstract model that will be presented. But, in any case, of what service can such a development be to the entrepreneur, whoever and whatever he may be? Here, the point of view is twofold. On one hand, from a local point of view, this type of analysis would be invaluable for evaluation and decision making. In this regard, our position is that the intangible aspect of the entrepreneur resides in how he estimates the parameters of reality. Once this is done, these may be processed optimally, by rational means, for the purpose of decision making. On the other hand, viewing things globally, one could use this type of analysis to study, understand, and construct the environment in which entrepreneurial activity flourishes.

Before proceeding with the above program, a warning is in order. We've already noted that the main measure of efficacy of such methods is whether or not they are useful. One must beware of attempting conclusions of causality (that is, of the form "phenomenon A *causes* phenomenon B"). Such assertions require complicated analysis and testing of precise dynamical laws, and they are rarely achieved in social or economic situations. Rather one attempts to establish the possible existence of some relationship between the quantities under consideration, a so-called correlation. Thus, for example, numerical data may show such a correlation between smoking and cancer of the prostate. However, a statement of causality would require that one hypothesize some physiological model of "how the smoke gets there." With these remarks we wish only to focus on the danger of confusing causality with correlation. For the pragmatic approach to economic systems, which we are proposing, correlation is quite adequate as a guide to decision making *as long as it works!*

Basic Concepts

The formulation of a general model of an economic or entrepreneurial flow system (EFS) requires the delineation of a multitude of concepts. In the following, we will set these down with some attempt at exaggerated generality, so as to cover a wide range of potential cases. In practice, the specialization of this to a relevant model will be much simplified.

To begin with, an EFS is an aggregation of objects consisting of

1. a finite collection of *nodes* $P_1, \ldots, P_n$
2. a finite collection of *directed graphs* $G_1, \ldots, G_m$, on the nodes $P_1, \ldots, P_n$.

Note that each of the graphs G_k consists of a collection of directed edges connecting various pairs of the nodes P_i. An instance of this may be noted as

$$P_i \xrightarrow{\hspace{1cm} x \hspace{1cm}} P_j$$

and indicates that in the subsystem delineated by G_k, there is a possible flow x from P_i to P_j. We might also have

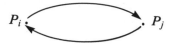

which indicates the existence of an additional flow from P_j back to P_i.

For example, if the nodes P_i correspond to a collection of relevant economic organizations (banks, factories, transportation, or idealizations thereof) G_1 might be the commodity graph, and G_2 the capital graph. Thus if F = a factory, B = a bank, and R = a retail outlet, a simplified system might show

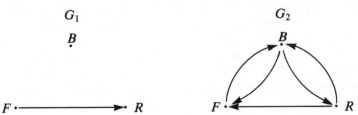

This asserts that in G_1 commodities flow from the factory F to the retail outlet R. Also, from G_2, both the factory and the store receive capital from the bank B and make payments to the bank. Here we note the flow of capital from R to F, representing the flow of payments for goods received. Using a solid line for G_1 and a broken line for G_2, the picture can be consolidated to

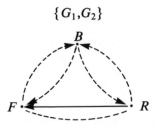

More complicated systems may be built up from simpler ones. In the above, adding a consumer group C, we have

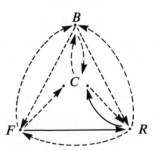

where there is a flow of funds to factory workers, some of which goes to the bank as deposits, and some for purchases at R. There is also a capital flow in the form of loans from the bank to C and a return flow of interest and repayment.

In the above type of modeling, a flow edge in a given graph may itself be an idealization of some composite. For example, the commodity flow from F to R may consist of a mix of many products, and the capital flow from B to R may consist of both loans and interest on deposits. If the practical situation requires the consideration of a more refined decomposition of a flow, this is easily achieved by using additional directed graphs.

Thus, in the system EFS(G_1, . . . ,G_m), the number m is a quick measure of the complexity or degree of flow detail in the model. We call m the degree of the system. In any event, causal disturbances are propagated from one graph to another via the nodes. Thus a degree 0 system is totally disconnected (that is, no flow at all) and a degree 1 system has only a single agglomerated flow.

In each graph G_k, any directed edge or *channel* that appears is presumed to have a name x with which is associated one or more numerical measurements. Thus, in the above example we might have:

x_{1FR} = the number of commodity units on order from F by R

x_{2FR} = the amount R owes F

x_{2FB} = the amount F owes B

x_{2RB} = the amount R owes B

x_{2BF} = the amount of unused credit F has at B

x_{2BR} = the amount of unused credit R has at B

and so forth. As implied in the above, the numerical description of the flow, in a given channel, might require a vector. For example, in the above, the G_1 channel from F to R might use a vector x_{1FR} whose components give the number of units on order of each type of commodity.

The specification of a set of values for all the flow parameters associated with all the channels of the graphs G_1, . . . , G_m, specifies all the *external* state parameters of the system (that is, external to the nodes). There still remains the requirement of establishing the *internal* state parameters. That is, roughly, those quantities that are necessary for processing what occurs "inside a node" in relating inflow to outflow. Furthermore, such internal parameters of different nodes may be linked even without the presence of a direct channel (from one to the other) in any of the graphs. For example, the shortage of a raw material can affect the supply of a component at a factory. A simple formal device enables us to treat internal parameters as a part of the external parameters and, at the same time, to handle interactions between them that can occur without the presence of channels. We introduce an additional (fictitious) node P_0, which we will call "the internal-state control node," and an additional graph G_0, in which

P_0 is connected in both directions to every other node with internal parameters.

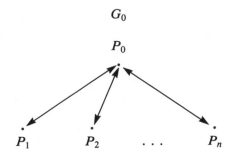

Then, to the channel from P_i to P_0 in G_0 we attach all the parameters y_{i00} required to describe the system operations that are internal to the node P_i. To the channel from P_0 to P_i we assign these same parameters, that is, formally $y_{0i0} = y_{i00}$. Thus, in particular, viewing P_0 as an ordinary node, any processing that is described there provides a link between the internal states of different nodes. (If no such links are required, an alternative procedure for handling internal parameters at P_i would be by adjoining a closed loop that starts and ends at P_i.)

Henceforth, we will assume that the system has the form described above. Then, a specification of all the external flow parameters associated with all channels of all graphs provides a deterministic description of the state of the system. In general, however, the state may be known only stochastically. Namely, we have only the current joint distribution function of the state parameters. This is a distribution function

$$F(x_{ijk}, i = 0, \ldots, n, \quad j = 0, \ldots, n, \quad i \neq j, \quad k = 0, \ldots, m)$$

over all the channel parameters, which gives the probabilities of their possible values via

$$Pr(x_{ijk} \leq \omega_{ijk}, i, j, k, i \neq j) = F(\omega_{ijk}, i, j, k, i \neq j).$$

This joint distribution function may "separate" into distribution functions of subsets of the x_{ijk} as a reflection of their statistical independence.

Thus, in general, the state of the system (which we denote by S) is described by the joint distribution function F. This state S may vary with time and is therefore written as $S = S(t)$. (Time may be either a discrete or continuous parameter.) Concomitantly the corresponding distribution function $F = F_t$ depends on t.

The flows of the various graphs G_k, $k = 1, \ldots, m$, interact at the nodes P_i, $i = 1, \ldots, n,$ and the description of this interaction, and how it affects the various flows, is the specification of the *dynamics* of the system. Roughly, focusing on a fixed P_{i*}, $i* > 0$, the x_{ji*k}, $j \neq 1*$, $j = 1, \ldots, n,$ $k = 1, \ldots, m,$ describe what is flowing into P_{i*}, and similarly the x_{i*jk} describe what is flowing out of P_{i*}. Also, x_{i00} gives the current internal state of each P_i. The local dynamics at P_{i*} is given by some laws (that is, rules or formulas):

$$x'_{i*\hat{j}\hat{k}} = \Phi_{i*\hat{j}\hat{k}}(x_{i*\hat{j}\hat{k}}, x_{ji*k}, x_{j00}) \qquad (5.1)$$

$$x'_{ji*\hat{k}} = \Psi_{ji*\hat{k}}(x_{i*jk}, x_{ji*k}, x_{j00}) \qquad (5.2)$$

for all $\hat{j} = 1, \ldots, n,$ $\hat{k} = 1, \ldots, m;$ as well as (5.1) for $\hat{j} = k = 0.$ If the state S of the system is described initially by a distribution function $F = F(x_{ijk})$, the transformation described above induces, in principle, a new joint distribution function $F' = F'(x'_{ijk})$ associated with the new state S'. As described above, the dynamical laws (5.1) and (5.2) are deterministic. These could also be stochastic in that changes of various kinds only occur with prescribed probabilities.

All of the above provides the description of a system with "decision-free dynamics." Once initialized at a given time t_0, that is, $S(t_0)$ given, the distribution of the state of the system $S(t)$ is completely determined for all times thereafter (that is, $t > t_0$). In order to attempt to further bridge the gap to reality we must include the possibility of introducing a change into the system. Here, *change* is meant to denote an alteration made at a given time $t*$, which injects some processing upon $S(t*)$ that is *external to the model,* thereby replacing it by a new system $S(t)$ with specified initial condition $S(t*)$. The key phrase in this definition of change is "exterior to the model." For example, a model might have an internal descriptive parameter x'_{i00} at a node P_{i*}, such that the model dynamics requires that if $x'_{i00} < C,$ (some constant), eliminate the node P_{i*}, (for example, the available funds of a firm become very negative and it goes out of existence). If this occurs and P_{i*} is eliminated, this "happening" is internal to the model and is not a change in the sense we have described. The constant $C,$ in the above, is part of the model, and if at some time $t*$ one arbitrarily changes its assigned value (leaving everything else the same) this *is* a change in the sense of the above.

Hence, in addition to the specification of the model $\mathfrak{M}$, we provide a collection of admissible changes to the system, which we denote by $\mathfrak{J}$, for *transformation.* If T is an element of $\mathfrak{J}$, it carries with it a description of some change of the system, and it is often referred to as a *transition operator.* In general such a transition operator involves some combination of the following:

1. nodes added to or deleted from the system
2. channels added to or deleted from the system
3. new categories of flows, that is, new graphs added
4. changes in the distribution function F_t
5. changes in fixed state parameters
6. changes in the dynamical laws.

In practice, one often starts with a given collection of possible external *decisions* $\mathfrak{D}$, which are available for imposition on the system. Then, to each such δ there corresponds a $T_\delta \in \mathfrak{I}$, which describes the changes that are induced by this decision.

The above description of an economic flow system with associated decisions and transition operators provides a general structure that can be used to format a wide variety of entrepreneurial problems. However, the analysis of such a system, from the point of view of decision making, depends on the choice of an *objective function*. That is, the *analyzer* or *decision maker* must specify his values or point of view. In classical terms there are such simple options as:

1. risk per unit cost
2. gain per unit cost
3. loss per unit cost

as well as many other more sophisticated measures. Here, it is important to note that "answers" also depend on the point of view. Who is a better entrepreneur, or what is a better entrepreneur, or what is a better entrepreneurial risk, or even what is an entrepreneur, is a function of point of view. Also, clearly, point of view may be a complicated mix of various primitive options, such as those given above. The decision maker can also utilize a "meta-view" in which the objective function partially values the system in terms of the evaluation sensitivity to a given spectrum of basic objective functions. (In simple terms, if the basic objective functions are too sensitive to inputs or yield differing decisions (under the same inputs), this reduces the utility of the system.)

Though we will not pursue the general question of objective functions, we will return to it from time to time in later sections.

Entrepreneurs, Entrepreneurism, and Entrepreneurial Activity

In the previous section we developed a framework within which one can define the essence of a wide range of interactive economic systems or components thereof. This provides a "world" in which we can attempt to identify, define, and measure such concepts as *entrepreneur* and *entrepreneurial activity*. Once again we note that since such definitions must depend subjectively on point of view and the part of the world under consideration, the presentation given here is basic and illustrative and is not intended as generic.

Given a system EFS(t) such as described in the previous section, what do we mean by an "entrepreneurial activity" relative to this system? We adopt the following:

> *Definition:* An *entrepreneurial activity* relative to a system $S(t)$ is any activity whose objective is to change the system.

The sense of the word *change* in this definition is as described in the previous section. It is also assumed that for any such changes under consideration, the corresponding transition operators have been well defined within the framework of the system.

For semantic completeness we add:

> *Definition:* An individual who initiates an entrepreneurial activity is an *entrepreneur*.

We see at the very outset that the assessment of how much of an entrepreneur an individual is depends on the assessment that is made of the magnitude of the entrepreneurial activity. This in turn will depend on the point of view that is manifested by the choice of objective functions (or manifests itself in that choice). In general terms, some of the elements that may be incorporated into the objective function are measures of:

1. magnitude of the attempted change
2. success of the attempt
3. cost of the attempt
4. risk of the attempt.

What the entrepreneur does is to introduce a strategy of change into the existant system, whose purpose might be one or more of the following:

1. increase the productivity of the system
2. decrease the cost of part of the system
3. produce accrual of personal wealth
4. produce an increase of social values.

How this is valued, and to what extent, is then a function of:

1.   who is doing the evaluation
2.   the objective of the evaluation (for example, investment, etc.)
3.   the nature of the induced entrepreneurial flow.

Initially, we can also perceive several possibly useful measures of the entrepreneurial activity:

(α) = the *percentage* of proposed change, with respect to some measure of the system

(β) = the *expected return* to the entrepreneur

(γ) = the *expected return* to others.

Pursuing (α) above, we note that whereas the entire system may be very large, the interest of the entrepreneur is usually centered on a smaller subsystem. Hence the percentage change in question must be related to this subsystem. However, even this is not a universal truth. Peception of entrepreneurial goals and their measurement will depend on the point of view, or focus, of the observer (or decision maker) or evaluator. (The evaluator may or may not be the entrepreneur.) For example, one might go to some Mediterranian island, inhabited by a grape-growing culture, and organize a wine industry based on this grape output. To the local populace and business community such an action would be deemed entrepreneurial, especially if new risk capital, equipment, organization, and employment are involved. However, to the worldwide wine industry this might well be deemed just a small promotional activity. From this we see that two factors play an interactive role in determining such judgments: (1) the actual magnitude of the economic change which occurs, and (2) the order of this change relative to the frame of reference of the evaluator of this activity.

At this point, we arrive at a clear need to specify a notion of *focus,* as a pre-input to a formal specification of any measure of entrepreneurial activity. In behalf of this, we tentatively propose:

Definition: Within the framework of a given EFS(t) a *focus* is a subset Σ of the nodes $P_1, \ldots, P_n$ and of the channels of all the graphs G_k, $k = 0, \ldots, m$. A *valuated-focus* is a focus Σ, together with a function $v(\sigma)$ defined over all nodes and channels, and such that $v(\sigma)$ vanishes for all $\sigma \notin \Sigma$. This function $v(\sigma)$ represents a set of numerical weights that measures the relative importance to the evaluator of the elements of the system.

In essence, *focus* corresponds to a subsystem of nodes and channels. This subsystem may not necessarily be "closed" in that some of the nodes of Σ can have flow lines entering or leaving that do not connect to other nodes of Σ. (Also, there may be channels that are devoid of nodes.) Such nodes will be called *boundary nodes* of the subsystem, and the related flows, *boundary flows*.

Having chosen a subsystem Σ as focus, it is in the context of Σ that the evaluator has decided to assess an entrepreneurial action in the original EFS. Two distinctly different possibilities can arise. First, and most natural, we can have the entrepreneurial change occur within Σ, that is, either internal to the nodes of Σ or relative to some of the nonboundary flows of Σ. The second possibility is that the entrepreneurial activity is outside Σ and relates to Σ only via boundary flows. In either case, the observer or evaluator who has specified the focus then attaches relative weights to the elements of Σ so as to define the function $v(\sigma)$. Once the evaluator has established this valuated focus he can proceed to incorporate the function $v(\sigma)$ into his objective functions, so as to properly reflect his point of view.

It is important to note that evaluations usually take place *outside* the EFS under consideration. In general, the evaluator is not an integral part of the model. However, the evaluator as an entrepreneur or coentrepreneurial activity can be integrated into the picture in terms of what we will call *meta-models*.

In any event, the problems connected with carrying out the above program, in actual cases, are many and difficult. However, most of these difficulties can probably be overcome. In the following (or in the future) we will ultimately descend from the very general and consider a variety of special entrepreneurial problems in illustrative settings. This in turn will serve to indicate how the method can be applied and to highlight the subsidiary questions that must be answered.

The Art Form of Model Making

Before leaving our general speculations concerning model formulation and application, the natural question arises as to how one goes about doing this. Though somewhere, ultimately, one must attempt it, it is not at all clear that this can be communicated (between mere mortals). In most areas, experience seems to show that the construction of appropriate and useful models is an art form practiced by only a limited number of talented individuals. However, a few qualitative principles can be delineated, and we propose to spend a few lines discussing one or two of these that apply especially to our setting and problems.

In our general description of an economic flow-system model, some distinction is made between internal and external state variables. The choice of emphasis and balance between these two types of entities relates to how detailed or how coarsely the various aspects of reality are to be treated. If one visualizes an ideal model, in which one attempts to treat reality with maximum detail, we have the problem of *complexification*. To make the model manageable one can visualize various kinds of simplification. First, a whole collection of nodes can be contracted into a single node. The various external variables involved are replaced by new idealized external and internal variables. The graphs of the model are modified to adapt to the new node structure, and corresponding new dynamics are specified. We refer to this process as *contraction* or *agglomeration*. For the opposite process whereby a node is "blown up" into a larger component, we will use our previous term, *complexification*.

An extreme case of agglomeration occurs when the entire model is reduced to a single node. In this case, there are no external variables, and the graphs of our system are all trivial, (just a single node with no edges). Consequently, all variables and dynamics are internal. An example of this is found in the model proposed by Baumol (ch. 3). There, the single node is the entire economic system, and the three internal descriptive variables are (at time t)

Y_t = a measure of economic activity

E_t = a measure of entrepreneurial activity in the system

C_t = an upper constraint on entrepreneurial activity.

The internal dynamics that specifies how these variables evolve with time, is given sequentially via the relations:

$$E_t = \begin{cases} \min (f(\alpha Y_t), C_t) & \text{if } Y_t \geq Y_{t-1} \\ E(E_{t-1}) & \text{if } Y_t < Y_{t-1} \end{cases} \tag{5.3}$$

$$Y_t = Y_{t-1} + g(E_{t-1}) \tag{5.4}$$

$$C_t = C(E_{t-1}). \tag{5.5}$$

The constant α, and the functions $f(\cdot)$, $E(\cdot)$, $g(\cdot)$, $C(\cdot)$, are parameters of the dynamics, and are not to be confused with internal variables. Initial values are given for E_0 and Y_0 and the above relations then determine the sequential evolution of the values of E_t and Y_t.

A second example of agglomeration is given by the model of Green and Shoven (ch. 4). There we have two nodes B and F, corresponding respectively to the business entity and the financial community. There is only one graph—flow of capital to and from each node.

B .   . F

The external variables include the flow of loans from F to B and the repayments from B to F. The internal variables involve the cash balance of B at each point in time. The corresponding internal dynamics is given in terms of a "tree" that specifies both the probability with which the cash position of B develops and the decisions available to the management of B. The external dynamics is that of an "equilibrium rule," in terms of which F attempts to establish a loan-repayment schedule that depends both on the cost of bankruptcy and on perfect information concerning the internal dynamics of B.

The above two models suggest the introduction of the quantity r = the *rank* of the model as given by the number of nodes. Thus the Baumol model is of rank $r = 1$, and the Green-Shoven model is of rank $r = 2$. For obvious reasons the complexity of the model tends to increase with r.

Concerning the Baumol Model

As noted in the above, the model of Baumol (ch. 3) describes the state of the economic system under consideration via the vector (E_t, Y_t, C_t), and specifies the dynamics by the relations (5.3), (5.4), (5.5). In Baumol's original presentation the constant $\alpha = 1 - T$ where T is a tax rate, but this interpretation is really inessential (at this level) since the constant α could be subsumed under the notation of the function f. More significant perhaps is the observation that C_t is really not an independent state variable because of the relation (C). Thus the vector (E_t, Y_t) describes the state of the system completely, and only (E_0, Y_0) need be specified initially.

As observed by Baumol, in the presence of either a steadily rising or steadily falling economy, the model really determines the functional form of E_t. Namely, assuming that f is monotone, the inverse function f^{-1} is defined; and we note that from (5.4) and (5.5), knowing the pair (E_{t-1}, Y_{t-1}) yields the values of Y_t and C_t. Then using the values of E_{t-1}, Y_{t-1}, C_t, in (5.3) we obtain E_t. Thus the pair (E_{t-1}, Y_{t-1}) yields the pair (E_t, Y_t). Taking $\alpha = 1$ (no loss of generality) and assuming f to be monotone increasing we see that in fact

$$E_t = C(E_{t-1})$$

if both

$$g(E_{t-1}) \geq 0, \text{ and } Y_{t-1} \geq g(E_{t-1}) + f^{-1}(C(E_{t-1})), \qquad (5.6)$$

$$E_t = f(Y_{t-1} + g(E_{t-1}))$$

if both

$$g(E_{t-1}) \geq 0, \text{ and } Y_{t-1} < g(E_{t-1}) + f^{-1}(C(E_{t-1})), \qquad (5.7)$$

$$E_t = E(E_{t-1})$$

if

$$g(E_{t-1}) < 0. \tag{5.8}$$

Thus we see that the state space is divided into regions in each of which the functional form of E_t, as a function of E_{t-1} and Y_{t-1}, is determined. Since these regions are determined completely by the pair (E_{t-1}, Y_{t-1}) it follows that (5.6), (5.7), (5.8) define a function $\varphi(u, v)$, of two variables, such that

$$E_t = \varphi(E_{t-1}, Y_{t-1}). \tag{5.9}$$

Clearly, (5.4) is explicitly of the form

$$Y_t = \Psi(E_{t-1}, Y_{t-1}), \tag{5.10}$$

where

$$\Psi(u, v) = v + g(u).$$

If, as we've seen, the input functions explicitly determine the qualitative rise and fall of the economy and entrepreneurism, what mystery is left for this model to reveal? The answer lies in the determination of which functional form applies as time evolves. More precisely, also, how this depends on the explicitly input functions f, C, E. For the case of the region described by (5.8) above, the condition on $g(E_{t-1})$ that defines this region is also a function of E_{t-1} alone. For the cases of (5.6) and (5.7) the region determination appears to depend on both E_{t-1}, and Y_{t-1}. Thus we see that as long as we stay in a single region we are simply calculating from inputs. The critical times are those when the state forces us to switch from one region to another. These are the shocks or discontinuities in the flow of the system. It is the determination and prediction of the pattern (if any) of these that is the only partially nontrivial aspect of the model. Note further that in the vicinity of such times, the analysis must be more combinatorial in nature. The tools of calculus (differentiation and so on) cannot be applied (as Baumol does).

One should never be carelessly supercilious in the consideration of even the simplest aspects of the simplest models. Even for a model of the Baumol form, the sequential evolution of the discontinuities described above can be difficult to analyze and determine (and surprising). To illustrate this, we consider a special numerical case of Baumol's model, as given by (5.3), (5.4), and (5.5), wherein the underying functions of the model are as follows:

$$f(v) = v, \quad C(u) = \frac{10}{u}, \quad g(w) = w - 5, \quad \alpha = \frac{1}{2}.$$

We define $E(x)$ to be any function such that for all real x,

$$1 \le E(x) \le 2. \tag{5.11}$$

Then the condition $E(x) \le C(x)$ is automatically satisfied.

The regions $R_i = R_i(t)$ corresponding to (5.6), (5.7) and (5.8), are given by

$$R_1(t): \left\{ E_{t-1} \ge 5, \ Y_{t-1} + E_{t-1} - 5 \ge \frac{20}{E_{t-1}} \right\}$$

$$R_2(t): \left\{ E_{t-1} \ge 5, \ Y_{t-1} + E_{t-1} - 5 < \frac{20}{E_{t-1}} \right\}$$

$$R_3(t): \left\{ E_{t-1} < 5 \right\}.$$

Presuming that it is satisfied initially, the requisite condition, $E_t \le C_t$, is satisfied for all t. In R_1 or R_2 we have $E_{t-1} \ge 5$, which implies

$$C_t = 10/E_{t-1} \le 2.$$

Hence $E_t \le C_t \le 2$, and we must move into $R_3(t+1)$. There, since $1 \le E(x) \le 2$, we remain. That is, the sequence is either $R_1 R_3^\infty$ or $R_2 R_3^\infty$ or R_3^∞, where $R_3^\infty = R_3 R_3 R_3. \ldots$

Summarizing the above, we see that apart from a possible finite initial segment, the region transitions must ultimately terminate with R_3^∞.

The above example is not meant as an effort to use the Baumol-type model to reveal anything about entrepreneurism. Rather, it serves as a small indication, a specimen, of the kind of extended analysis and experimentation that is needed in order to understand the structural gestalt of even the simplest of models. For even the simplest of interactive models can have hidden connectives that are implications of the structure. In the Baumol model the state variables E_t and Y_t are independent in general. As a consequence, in general, the recursions (5.9) and (5.10) would have to be unraveled all the way back to the initial states in order to relate E_t and Y_t or to give E_t as a function of E_{t-1} and the initial state. However, this is not a function in the proper sense since it also requires a variable with infinite domain, in order to specify the time t. On the other hand, it is not hard to show that the information obtained for the special example given above implies that these E_t can be given as a function of E_{t-1} and the initial data alone.

If models of this type are to be applied, one would have to understand exactly what produces this phenomenon. Though this precise effect will probably not occur very often it suggests the more general possibility that in these models the number of consecutive times that the model transitions are in the same region is bounded as a function of the initial data. (Conditions for theorems of this type are not hard to envisage.) These and other (as yet undiscovered) effects would have to be well in hand before one could even attempt model experiments relating to reality.

Though the above barely touches on the implications of the Baumol model itself, we move on next to briefly note some of its more global implications. It is in fact a suggestive illustration of a much larger class of models that we may view as corresponding to natural generalizations of the functional recursions (5.9) and (5.10). Namely, retaining the state description (E_t, Y_t) we can envisage these recursions as having the form

$$E_t = \Phi(E_{t-1}, E_{t-2}, \ldots, E_{t-e}; Y_{t-1}, \ldots, Y_{t-d}) \qquad (5.12)$$

$$Y_t = \Psi(E_{t-1}, \ldots, E_{t-b}; Y_{t-1}, \ldots, Y_{t-c}) \qquad (5.13)$$

where $b, c, d,$ and e are positive integers. They represent the "time-depth" into the past, on which the current values depend. From (5.9) and (5.10) we see that the original Baumol system has $b = c = d = e = 1$. The integer $a = \max(b, c, d, e)$ measures the deepest penetration into the immediate past required to describe the recursive determination of the current state. The original Baumol model is Markovian in that $a = 1$.

Thus we arrive at a view of a generalized Baumol model as a completely prescribed recursion. For any special realization of this, the area for analysis that remains is that of studying properties of the sequence E_t as a function of initial conditions.

Clearly, the number of models encompassed by relations of the type (5.12) and (5.13) is quite unlimited. We indulge in one more brief example, not so much for its intrinsic value but to illustrate the further point that the model relationships may arise as implicit rather than explicit. If one thinks of the entrepreneurial activity E_t as part of the overall economic activity Y_t, so that $E_t \leq Y_t$, we can view

$$\tilde{Y}_t = Y_t - E_t$$

as measuring the nonentrepreneurial component of the economic activity. Then, we may consider the model as having *two nodes,* the entrepreneurial and the nonentrepreneurial. One flow relation gives Y_t as a function of the immediate past via

$$\tilde{Y}_t = \tilde{\Phi}(E_{t-1}, \tilde{Y}_{t-1}). \qquad (5.14)$$

Similarly, we may have E_t as a function of Y_t and the immediate past, in the form

$$E_t = \tilde{\Psi}(\tilde{Y}_t, \tilde{Y}_{t-1}, E_{t-1}). \qquad (5.15)$$

Introducing (5.14) into (5.15) yields

$$E_t = \tilde{\Psi}(\tilde{\Phi}E_{t-1}, \tilde{Y}_{t-1}), E_{t-1}, \tilde{Y}_{t-1})$$

or

$$E_t = \hat{\Psi}(E_{t-1}, \tilde{Y}_{t-1}). \qquad (5.16)$$

These relations are, of course, quite explicit. However, a small change of viewpoint changes this completely. If the model is such that one desires to specify E_t as a function of Y_t and the immediate past, we have

$$E_t = \tilde{\Lambda}(E_{t-1}, Y_t, \tilde{Y}_{t-1}),$$

or retaining the Baumol relation (5.4)

$$E_t = \tilde{\Lambda}(E_{t-1}, E_t + \tilde{Y}_t, \tilde{Y}_{t-1}),$$

which is of the form

$$E_t = \Lambda(E_t, E_{t-1}, \tilde{Y}_{t-1}). \qquad (5.17)$$

This implicit relationship must then be solved for E_t.

The above evolution of the Baumol-type model remains completely deterministic. Baumol notes certain difficulties that this produces; in particular, that the model may permanently produce a decreasing economy. To offset this Baumol proposes that the model flow might be thought of as that of the mean of some distribution of states. Actually, this would not resolve the aforementioned difficulties. Rather, one must make the flow of possible states a stochastic phenomenon. (This, in fact, is the spirit of the Green-Shoven model, ch. 4). To illustrate, we might alter the Baumol model so that

$$E_t = \begin{cases} \min(f(\alpha Y_t), C_t) \text{ with probability } p \text{ if } Y_t \geq Y_{t-1} \\ E(E_{t-1}) \text{ with probability } q \text{ if } Y_t < Y_{t-1} \end{cases} \qquad (5.18)$$

where (5.4) and (5.5) are retained as before, and

$$p + q < 1. \qquad (5.19)$$

The remaining probability $r = 1 - p - q$ might be distributed among "irrational" increase or decrease in the amount of entrepreneurism. That is,

$$E_t = E_{t-1} + h, \tag{5.20}$$

where

$$h = \left\{ \begin{array}{l} c_1 \text{ with probability } r/2 \\ -c_2 \text{ with probability } r/2 \end{array} \right\} \tag{5.21}$$

$c_1 \geq 0, c_2 \geq 0$. In fact, more generally, one might prescribe a distribution function $F(h)$ on $(-\infty, \infty)$ such that $F(-\infty) = 0$, and $F(\infty) = r$, to describe the probability distribution of the values of h, (that is, the "distribution of irrationality" of the system's behavior).

Given an initial state (E_0, Y_0) the above model generates for each sequence time t a distribution function $G_t(w)$ that describes the probability distribution of the values of E_t (that is, $\Pr(E_t \leq w) = G_t(w)$). Of course, for the simple model given, $G_t(w)$ will turn out to be a step function with a finite number of jumps.

The above answers some of the difficulties of the original Baumol model, associated with stagnation of the system. Here it is clear that the probability is zero of being stuck *indefinitely* with such conditions as a steadily decreasing economy. Further, in such a framework one can easily formulate criteria for when the model parameters describe an optimistic environment for entrepreneurial activity, such as

$$\Pr(\varlimsup_{t \to \infty} E_t = \infty) = 1.$$

(In fact, it is fairly easy to see that this can be proved under various special assumptions.) Such an assertion would have the character of a Borel-Cantelli Lemma for this system. Similarly we could ask whether or not

$$\Pr(\varlimsup_{t \to \infty} Y_t = \infty) = 1.$$

Still more refined measures of the model could be formulated that would have the nature of a law of the iterated logarithm for the system. These would ask for the determination of those functions $\varphi(t)$ such that

$$\Pr(\varlimsup_{t \to \infty} E_t/\varphi(t) = \infty) = 1. \tag{5.22}$$

Since it is not a priori clear whether or not a zero-one law holds here, (5.22) might be replaced by

$$\Pr(\varlimsup_{t \to \infty} E_t/\varphi(t) = \infty) \geq \beta. \tag{5.23}$$

What Does One Do With A Model

The actions of the entrepreneur and those of the evaluator may take place using as a background the EFS model in which the parameters are known to all. In an actual "real" case, the basic questions under consideration may then be questions of *strategy*. To invest or not invest? If so, how much? Which of several alternatives is preferable, or what is the optimal mix of these alternatives? What is the optimal timing for the proposed actions? Such considerations, in a sense, "lie on top of" the underlying model. Thus, a formalization of these decision-theoretic questions requires a model-formulation all its own, which we refer to as the *meta-model*.

Less formally, the meta-model can be viewed as the plan of how one uses the model for evaluative purposes or as the design of experiment. This could be a combination of one or more procedures.

One such procedure is to use the underlying model as the basis of some game in which one player who is exterior to the model is the evaluator. A *move* for this first player might consist of one or more of the following:

1. A choice of values for certain model parameters.
2. Activation or deactivation of a component of the model.
3. A choice between two or more specified models (in a sense this includes 1 and 2).
4. A choice between two or more objective functions, or more specifically, a choice of parameters in a given objective function.

The second player is the economic-flow system itself, or rather its representation by the model. With its parameters fixed, the model provides an output vector that is input to the objective functions chosen by the first player. The output of these objective functions is a distribution function of the possible payoffs to the first player.

The above can be viewed either as a type of game in normal, rectangular form, or as one in extensive form. In the former case, each move, μ, of the first player produces a response from the model that is a specified probability distribution of outcomes, and this is converted to a probability distribution of payoffs, $P_\mu(w)$, corresponding to the outcome w. That is, the model is announcing the strategy it will use in response to the first player's move μ [this is the vector $P_\mu(w)$]. The first player then desires to determine some optimal strategy in the form of a probability distribution on his possible moves μ. This then calls for some specification, in the meta-model, of a *principle of optimality*. In this regard, there is a current fondness for equilibria criteria. Namely, a principle in which each player has a strategy that guarantees him a certain stable situation (profit or loss) regardless of what the other player (or players) does. This is, for example, the viewpoint of statistical decision theory, where the game is viewed as being between man (the statistician) and nature (the producer of data). This point of view is our legacy from Von Neumann and the theory of games. It is not as appropriate as some of its more slavish followers might like to think. (Perhaps some future academician writing about this period will title his work, "The Von Neumann Curse or Life on a Saddle Point.") In any event, such equilibria may fail to properly account for risk and the rewards that may result therefrom.

Viewed as a game in extensive form, moves in the meta-model on the part of the first player (the external evaluator) are made sequentially in response to the replies from the model (the second player). Here again some principle of optimality is required. Also, again, in this setting an equilibrium principle can arise in the form of a specification of some desirable class $\mathcal{R}$ of response configurations from the model, which the first player is trying to reach. Such a class (and the corresponding principle) might be *local* in nature in that the objective of the first player is simply to arrive at some response in $\mathcal{R}$ (from the second player). If cost factors are associated with the *time* it takes to reach $\mathcal{R}$, *where* you reach and *how long it takes* will be an integral part of the principle of evaluation. The utilization of $\mathcal{R}$, by the optimality principle, is *global* if the configurations of $\mathcal{R}$ are not specific model responses but patterns of such responses (for example, apparent stagnation, periodicity, or stability of any kind). Here the evaluation principle might include the cost of various types of errors that this utilization of the model might produce. Statistics itself is filled with examples of these ideas, and perhaps a most striking one is Wald's theory of the sequential-probability-ratio test and its optimality.

In contrast to principles of strategy that seek optimality objectives, the content of the evaluator's meta-model may be simply that of applying a prescribed procedure of assessment, which is not of a gaming nature. This might include

1. For some given initial conditions, calculating the distribution of model states at specified times,
2. Varying one or more model parameters so as to get some feeling for the sensitivity of output to the values of these parameters.
3. Varying model parameters so as to produce a given model output (for example, as with what investment and product volume is required to obtain a desired profit level).
4. Utilizing two or more models, corresponding to different entrepreneurial structurings, to see which yields a better output.

Here the model is used simply to represent the structure of reality and to process various sets of values of the input parameters. The assessment of the outputs may then range from the purely subjective to the use of esoteric objective functions. This less sophisticated approach to model utilization is also probably the most useful. For it is not likely that (in the near future) any bona fide method will be available for valid assessments of the parameters of reality (especially after they have been idealized for modeling purposes). The intuition of the entrepreneur or evaluator, based on possibly undefinable experience and instinct, will be the best source of such estimates. The model structure then serves him as a processor and provides a more precise view of the implications of his basic assessments.

From a pure theoretical and philosophical point of view there is no a priori reason for stopping evaluative efforts at the categorical level of the meta-model. One could formulate an indefinite hierarchy of meta-meta-models, and so on, in which one provides games over evaluative procedures (that is, games over games). Something in this spirit does occur in reality, as for example in the case of two competing entrepreneurs at the meta-model level, and an evaluator (possibly a bank or investment instrument) at the meta-meta-model level, which must compare them. Of course, it must remain as part of the art form of modeling as to whether all or part of a meta-model structure should be "projected down" and included in the model. In any event, the principle of model hierarchies should be handled with great care and used mainly in the presence of some raison d'etre that stems from reality. For indeed, there may be some kind of theorem, lurking in the background, which asserts that the farther away from the original model one gets, in such a hierarchy, the less sensitive is the overall evaluative procedure to the inputs.

Concluding Contemplations and Assorted Disclaimers

At this point, it would seem appropriate to look back on what has been presented here and review both its nature and its intent. Though in a formal sense this chapter is an essay, it is a totally subjective presentation of a point of view. Also, in anticipation of criticism and rejection, it is pedantic, repetitious, and almost argumentative. It is not, nor is it intended to be, a scholarly work. Rather, it was conceived as a collection of somewhat related thoughts, motivated by the contemplation of the task of initiating studies of entrepreneurial activities.

Since this objective has the character of breaking new ground, a proper beginning is to indulge in a free flow of imagination. A first thought was to set down some tentative, albeit primitive, language that might be useful for addressing the problem of formulating entrepreneurial models. The reason for desiring a special language for this purpose is to reduce the level of ambiguity inherent in our everyday real-world language. In this way, we could hope to strengthen implications concerning entrepreneurism that we attempt to realize via the use of language. The content of the second section constitutes a modest attempt to provide such a language, and this is followed in the next section by a conceptualizing and defining of explicit notions of entrepreneurial activity and entrepreneur.

All of this is presented in the spirit of personal introspection and trauma. Initially, the impression one has is of attempting an interaction between science and reality in which something is to be created out of nothing. More precisely, the confrontation with the prospect of engaging in an investigation of entrepreneurism is characterized by various questions:

1. Is this a bona fide field?
2. Can anything be done?
3. Can anything be achieved?
4. What does it mean to achieve something here?
5. How should one go about developing a relevant investigative route?
6. What directions should one take?
7. What are the *chances* for success?

Though the contemplations presented above really prove nothing (or at most little) they have produced some very definite subjective feelings. Foremost among these is that entrepreneurial activity *is* probably a bona fide and potentially productive area of investigation. There is certainly no difficulty in generating a large amount of investigative activity.

For this last conclusion we are really indebted to Baumol. Although his model is primitive, it is seminal! Although, in its present form it is not likely to shed much light on the subject, it does suggest whole lines of development that might conceivably be productive. The material in the fifth section has been presented to give some feeling for the feasibility of analyzing such models and extending their range.

With regard to the above, it appears that the important missing link is to reality. Though we can conceive of how to experiment with the structure of models, the question is still open as to what is the reality to be modeled. Thus, although we are not prepared to definitely answer any of the questions that have been raised, we can point to a suggested continuation of effort. Modeling investigations should be continued in conjunction with and motivated by a data-gathering effort.

In final conclusion, it should be noted (as is probably already quite evident) that this author is not an economist either by talent or training and is an entrepreneur only by fantasy. Thus all of the thoughts contained herein were stimulated by listening to the professional members of the group. A special debt is owed to J. Cherny and J. Ronen for many valuable discussions and idea swappings. Also, very special gratitude and thanks to our one real entrepreneur, Mr. Harold Price, who not only made this acitivity possible, but who personally instilled into it a high level of communicability and good fellowship.

6 Organizational Innovation: The Transaction-Cost Approach

Oliver E. Williamson

The possibility that organizational innovation is an economically important phenomenon is ignored or dismissed by most economists. At best, organizational innovation is no more than a poor second cousin to technological change. To be sure, many business historians hold the contrary view. A few microeconomists likewise maintain that the conventional theory of the firm, which has been sanitized of interesting organizational features, is not wholly adequate. But the overall view is as I have described.

This chapter has two purposes. I endorse the proposition that organizational change during the past 150 years has been substantial and economically significant, and I contend that efficiency has been the main force driving this change. Specifically, economizing on transaction costs is the key concept that has been hitherto neglected (or referred to only incidentally) in prior studies of organizational change. Once the transaction is made the basic unit of analysis, and attention is focused on the economic importance of devising efficient governance structures for mediating transactions, a wide array of organizational changes fall into place within a common economizing framework.

Some Background

Changing Organizational Forms

A comprehensive enumeration of the leading organizational innovations is beyond the scope of this paper. I am persuaded by Alfred Chandler, however, that the 1840s mark the beginning of a great wave of organizational change that has brought us the modern corporation. According to Stuart Bruchey, the fifteenth-century merchant of Venice would have understood the organizational structure and the methods of managing men, records, and investment used by Baltimore merchants in 1790 (Bruchey 1956, pp.

This chapter was prepared for presentation at the Conference on Entrepreneurship held in Toronto in September 1980 under the auspices of the Price Institute for Entrepreneurial Studies. It has since been revised with the benefit of comments from Alfred Chandler, Douglass North, Andrew Oswald, Richard Nelson, and Peter Temin.

370–371). These practices evidently remained quite serviceable until after the 1840s (Chandler 1977, p. 16).

To be sure, the early 1800s witnessed the transformation of the all-purpose merchant to one who specialized in a single line of goods (Porter and Livesay 1971, pp. 6–10). Factory organization, in the form of the integrated textile mill and the Springfield Armory, made their appearance during this same period. Until the 1840s, however, "the armories and textile mills remained the exception" (Chandler 1977, p. 75).

Significant organizational innovations that occurred after 1840 include: (1) the development of line and staff organizational techniques; (2) the development and refinement of cost accounting and capital accounting; (3) selective integration between manufacturing and earlier supply stages and (more interestingly) selective forward integration by manufacturers into distribution; (4) the moving assembly line and related flow-management techniques; (5) the development of the multidivisional structure to manage separable lines of business; and (6) the extension of the multidivisional structure to manage diversified (conglomerate) organization. Important innovations in mass retailing included the development of the department store, the mail-order house, the chain store, and the discount house. New forms of market mediation included the commodity dealer and the wholesale jobber. Arbitration, mediation, and franchise law were important legal developments. Entrepreneurial figures who contributed significantly to these and related organizational changes include Eli Whitney, Cyrus McCormick, J. Edgar Thomson, John Wanamaker, James Duke, Gustavus Swift, Andrew Carnegie, Theodore Vail, George Eastman, Henry Ford, Pierre du Pont, Alfred P. Sloan, and Royal Little.[1] Many other figures, large and small, also contributed to these evolutionary developments.

Perceived Importance

Neither these organizational changes nor organizational innovation in general has attracted the widespread interest of economists. To be sure, Joseph Schumpeter (1942) held otherwise: "The fundamental impulse that sets and keeps the capitalist engine in motion comes from the new consumers' goods, the new methods of production or transportation, the new markets, the new forms of industrial organization that capitalist enterprise creates" (p. 83). There are other exceptions. Kenneth Arrow (1971) observes that "Truly among man's innovations, the use of organization to accomplish his ends is among both his greatest and his earliest" (p. 224). Arthur Cole (1968) contends that "if changes in business procedures and practices were patentable, the contributions of business change to the economic growth of the nation would be as widely recognized as the influence of mechanical innovations or the inflow of capital from abroad'' (pp. 61–62). Chandler (1977) evidently agrees. In his judgment, ''far more economies result from the careful coordination of flow through the processes of production and distribution than from increasing the size of producing or distributing units in terms of capital facilities or number of workers'' (p. 490). However, aside from the Research Center in Entrepreneurial History at Harvard, which was established in 1948 and closed its doors a decade later, there has not been a concerted effort to work through and establish the importance of organizational innovation.

There are three main reasons for this. First, many organizational changes take the rather unexciting form of realigning the interfaces between successive stages of production and distribution. It is difficult to arrest the public imagination with such events. Contrast the public celebration in Menlo Park in 1879, when Edison's grounds and laboratory were bathed in light to announce the development of the electric light bulb, or the television coverage of the first manned space flights. Second, as Cole observed, organizational innovations are not patentable. I conjecture, however, that the most important reason for the neglect of organizational innovation is the third, that business history has not had ''the support of an established system of theory'' (Larson 1950, p. 135).

The lack of a theoretical framework to which Henrietta Larson referred in 1950 was also a concern of James Soltow in 1968. Although there have since been significant contributions to business history,[2] and economic historians have given renewed attention to the importance of institutional change,[3] only limited headway has been made in fashioning a framework within which to interpret organizational change. Accordingly, changes from one organizational structure to another are explained on the grounds that the earlier structure was inadequate.

A framework for studying organizational change is needed if the reasons for these purported inadequacies are to be unraveled. The argument advanced here is that transaction-cost savings are responsible for the economic gains realized by shifting from one governance structure to another; furthermore, that (at least for the extreme cases) the circumstances that will support such gains can be ascertained a priori. Examining the underlying dimensions of the transaction (or related set of transactions) in question is crucial to the assessment.

Although characterizing the firm as a production function is a convenient and useful abstraction,[4] such an approach suppresses much of the interesting action that accounts for the high-performance features of an enterprise economy. It facilitates marginal analysis within a narrow economizing framework at the expense of organizational and comparative institutional analysis. The peformance differences between capitalist and noncapitalist firms in developed economies, however, are less explained by technology than by differences in organization. This suggests a broader approach to the study of economics in which the firm is expressly treated as a governance structure.[5]

Transaction-Cost Economics

Transaction-cost economics relies on different behavioral assumptions and employs a more microanalytic level of analysis than does received microtheory. Both have ramifications for the study of organizational innovation.

Transaction Costs

At a very general level, transaction costs can be thought of as "costs of running the economic system" (Arrow 1969, p. 48). A *transaction* occurs, when a good or service is transferred across a technologically separable interface. One stage of processing or assembly activity terminates, and another begins. A well-working interface, like a well-working machine, is one where these transfers occur smoothly. In mechanical systems, we look for frictions: Do the gears mesh? Are the parts lubricated? Is there needless slippage or other loss of energy? The economic counterpart of friction is transaction cost: Do the parties to the exchange operate harmoniously, or are there frequent misunderstandings and conflicts that lead to delays, breakdowns, and other malfunctions? Transaction-cost analysis supplants the usual preoccupation with technology and steady-state production (or distribution) expenses, with an examination of the *comparative costs of planning, adapting, and monitoring task completion under alternative governance structures.*

The study of transaction-cost economizing is thus a comparative institutional undertaking in which the properties of alternative governance structures are assessed—where, by governance structure, I have reference to the institutional frameworks within which the integrity of transactions is decided. The object is to match governance structures to the attributes of transactions in a discriminating way. To do this, both microanalytic attention to differences among governance structures and microanalytic definition of transactions are needed.

Behavioral Assumptions

Although Adam Smith is widely held responsible for the fiction that individuals are self-interest seeking and high-powered optimizing agents, Smith in fact maintained a wider view of economic man (Coase 1976). His skepticism about the corporate form of organization reflects this (Smith 1922, bk. 5, ch. 1, pt. 3). As Melvin Copeland (1932) put it, Smith "recognized, in a general way at least, the limitations on the ability of a single human mind to comprehend the perplexing details and the interacting variables which constantly are influencing the welfare of a particular enterprise large in scale, non-routine in character. He realized the jeopardy resulting to investors' capital from ill-management" (p. 597). Expressed in terms of the behavioral assumptions employed here, Smith held that the large corporate form experienced inherent disabilities because of bounded rationality on the one hand and the hazards of opportunism on the other.

Bounded rationality is related to the familiar assumption of optimizing, but it expressly recognizes that intendedly rational human agents experience severe limits in formulating and solving complex problems (Simon 1957, p. 198). Accordingly, problems must not be permitted to outrun individual capacities—which explains Smith's preference for small enterprise. But there is another possibility, which Smith implicitly dismissed: new structures might conceivably be devised that permitted individual capacities to be aggregated to better advantage.

The assumption that human agents are given to opportunism is related to the more familiar assumption of self-interest seeking, but extends this to include self-interest seeking with guile. If agents were honest and candid, self-interest seeking would pose no contractual problems. Principals would simply extract promises from agents that they will behave in a stewardship fashion. This strategem will not work, however, if some agents are dishonest or, more generally, if they disguise preferences, distort data, obfuscate issues, and otherwise confuse transactions and it is very costly to distinguish opportunistic from nonopportunistic types *ex ante*.

Taken together, the dual assumptions of bounded rationality and opportunism describe an organizational man who is computationally less competent, but motivationally more complex, than his predecessor, the economic man. Absent either of these assumptions, interesting problems of economic organization vanish.

Matching Modes with Attributes

A preoccupation with production functions recedes into the background, and interest in alternative modes of contracting is enhanced, as attention is focused on human agents and their behavioral characteristics. There is, however, no single superior organizational form with respect to which alternatives can be ranked in a descending hierarchy. Rather, organizational form matters in a conditional way. Assessing this is largely a transaction-cost exercise and requires that transactions be dimensionalized. The analyst, however, must also allow for both economies of scale and economies of scope in reaching an optimizing match between transactional attributes and governance structures.

A sensitivity to scale economies is obvious: A firm is poorly advised to produce for itself items that can be produced more cheaply by suppliers that realize economies of scale by aggregating demands. Economies of scope are commonly given as reasons for firms to integrate; however, this construes the issue too narrowly. The fundamental point is this: Activities that experience economies of scope are advantageously located within *some* organization rather than split between several autonomous entities. This does not, however, imply that a firm that needs a good or service for which scope economies obtain should itself offer the full commodity mix to which these economies apply. On the contrary, economies of scope—especially at the distribution stage—often warrant that a firm produce rather than integrate into the activity in question. Thus, although the marketing of eggs arguably benefits from sale in conjunction with dairy products and other groceries, producers of eggs do not need to own and operate supermarkets for this reason. Efficiency is served by bringing the relevant set of activities together; forward integration in this instance would be an extreme response.

Whereas economies of scale and scope are familiar production-function relations, transaction-cost economies raise a broader set of contractual issues. The dimensions I have found useful for studying the governance of contractual relations are: (1) uncertainty, (2) the frequency with which transactions recur, and (3) the degree to which durable transaction-specific investments are required to realize least-cost supply (Williamson 1979b). A nontrivial degree of uncertainty must exist if an interesting economic problem is to be posed (Hayek 1945, pp. 523–524). It will facilitate the argument to assume that an intermediate degree of uncertainty exists (whence the organization needs to adapt transactions at the interface) but otherwise to hold uncertainty constant.

It is convenient, if somewhat arbitrary, to recognize two frequency classes: occasional transactions and recurrent transactions. As compared with recurrent transactions (where the immediate parties themselves can often fashion an effective governance structure), occasional transactions benefit from third-party assistance. Economies of pooling and the ease with which reputation effects are enforced are the main factors explaining these differences.

The most important, though hithertofore neglected, dimension for describing transactions, is transaction-specific investment.[6] The issue is less whether there are large fixed investments (though this is important) than whether these investments are specialized to a particular transaction. Items that are unspecialized among users pose few hazards, because buyers in these circumstances can easily turn to alternative sources and suppliers can sell output intended for one buyer to other buyers without difficulty. Non-marketability problems arise when the *specific identity* of the parties has important cost-bearing consequences. Transactions of this kind may be referred to as idiosyncratic.

Occasionally the identity of the parties is important from the outset, as when a buyer induces a supplier to invest in specialized physical capital of a transaction-specific kind. Inasmuch as the value of this capital in other uses is, by definition, much smaller than the specialized use for which it has been intended, the supplier is effectively locked into the transaction to a significant degree. This is symmetrical, moreover, in that the buyer cannot turn to alternative sources of supply and obtain the item on favorable terms, because the cost of supply from unspecialized capital is presumably great. The buyer is thus committed to the transaction also.

Ordinarily, however, there is more to idiosyncratic exchange than specialized physical capital. Transaction-specific investments in human capital commonly occur as well. Specialized training and learning-by-doing economies in production operations are illustrations. Except when these investments are transferable to alternative suppliers at low cost (which is rare), the benefits of the setup costs can be realized only so long as the relationship between the buyer and seller of the intermediate product is maintained.

Additional transaction-specific savings can accrue at the interface between supplier and buyer as contracts are successively adapted to unfolding events and as periodic contract-renewal agreements are reached. Familiarity here permits communication economies to be realized: specialized language develops as experience accumulates, and nuances are signaled and received in a sensitive way. Both institutional- and personal-trust relations evolve.

The transactions on which I principally focus are those for which recurrent exchange is contemplated. Three degrees of asset specifically are recognized: nonspecific assets, semispecific assets, and highly specific assets. Whether a firm chooses to internalize a recurrent transaction (that is, make a component itself rather than contract with a supplier) turns on four factors:[7]

1. The ease (cost) of adapting the interface to changing circumstances.
2. The degree to which economies of scale are exhausted by their own requirements;
3. The degree to which economies of scope are sacrificed by undertaking one's own production;
4. The incentive and other disabilities of internal organization.

Chandler's discussion of the transformation from unitary to multidivisional structures (1966) and subsequent commentary thereon (Williamson 1970, chs. 7–9) disclose that the incentive and bureaucratic limits of internal organization vary with the way in which the firm is organized. The incentive and bureaucratic disabilities of internal organization, as compared with markets, nevertheless favor market procurement (Williamson 1975, ch. 7). As discussed above, outside procurement is also favored if economies of scale or economies of scope can thereby be realized. The distinctive advantage of internal organization is that adaptations at the interface can be more easily effected.[8]

Progressively increasing asset specificity has two effects, both of which favor internal procurement. For one thing, as the assets in question become more fully dedicated to the specific needs of the firm, the importance of scale economies necessarily decreases: the firm can realize steady-state supply economies itself as fully as an outside supplier would. Second, the hazards of interfirm trading relation increase with increasing asset specificity. As lock-in effects become stronger, the parties will be confronted with greater bargaining opportunities as unforeseen contingencies, and the potential gains of adapting responsively to them, appear.

The efficient match of governance structures with recurrent transactions thus varies as follows:

1. Classical market exchange prevails for transactions supported by nonspecific assets. Bureaucratic considerations favor this; scale and scope economies do likewise; and neither the buyer nor the seller has a special interest in the identity of the other, since alternative purchase and supply arrangements are easy to work out.

2. Classical market trading gives way to a more nearly bilateral exchange relation as asset specificity moves into the intermediate range. Bureaucratic considerations and production economies continue to favor outside procurement, but the specific identity of the parties now matters, since to interrupt the relation would be to sacrifice values embodied in the specialized assets in question. To maintain continuity, a specialized governance structure of an "obligational market contracting" kind is evolved to effect harmonious (albeit delimited) adaptations.[9]

3. Economies of scope aside, a unified governance structure—the firm—appears for transactions of a highly specific kind. Market procurement is still favored by bureaucratic considerations, but scale economies are no longer realized by contracting out for the work. Internal organization permits greater adaptation to changing circumstances because the profit strains that occur when autonomous parties are asked to adapt coordinately are greatly attenuated when a single ownership entity spans both sides of the transaction.

Intermediate Product Markets

Using the manufacturer as the point of reference, intermediate product-market transactions of three types can be distinguished: forward integration out of manufacturing into distribution; backward integration into processed and raw materials; and lateral integration into component manufacture. Only the first of these has been studied extensively, and it is the main focus of attention here. Both backward and lateral integration pose interesting contractual issues, however, and some of these are briefly addressed.

Forward Integration into Distribution

Description: The principal development that induced forward vertical integration into distribution was the appearance of the railroads in the second half of the nineteenth century (Porter and Livesay 1971, p. 55). To be sure, there were other significant technological developments, including the telegraph (Chandler 1977, p. 189); the development of continuous-process machinery (Chandler 1977, pp. 249–253); the refinement of interchangeable-parts manufacture (Chandler 1977, pp. 75–77); and other technological developments that supported mass manufacture (Chandler 1977, ch. 8). However, without the low cost, reliable, all-weather transportation afforded by the railroad, the incentive to integrate forward would have been much less.[10]

The extensive forward integration that occurred during the last thirty years of the nineteenth century was, however, highly varied. These differences are the conditions to be explained. From least to most, integration into distribution varied as follows: (1) none, in which case the prevailing wholesale and retail structure continued; (2) integration into wholesale but not retail; and (3) integration into retail (which usually included wholesale). A temporal dimension is useful to bear in mind in all of this, since the factors that favor integration at one time may not continue indefinitely. Also, mistaken forward integration warrants attention. Presumably such integration errors are less likely to be imitated or renewed, and for this reason are less widely reported. A predictive theory of forward integration, however, should explain both failures and successes.

1. Unchanged Distribution: The sectors of the American economy in which independent wholesalers continued to distribute goods to independent retailers included "the complex of goods sold through retail outlets such as grocery, drug, hardware, jewelry, liquor, and dry goods stores" (Porter and Livesay 1971, p. 214). Whether independent wholesalers and retailers provided the full set of support services, or whether manufacturers performed some, depended on product differentiation. The role of the middleman was reduced for branded products.

2. Wholesaling: Manufacturers became involved in wholesaling functions in three ways: preselling, inventory management, and facility ownership. The cigarette was the orphan of the American tobacco industry until 1880.

The appearance of the Bonsack machine for the continuous processing of cigarettes in 1881, together with its adoption by James Duke, quickly changed that (Chandler 1977, pp. 249–250). Duke cut the prices of cigarettes drastically to reflect manufacturing economies and coupled this with massive advertising (Chandler 1977, pp. 290–292). Although Duke continued to sell through jobbers and retailers, he also organized a network of sales offices in the larger American cities in which salaried managers worked to coordinate marketing and distribution (Chandler 1977, p. 291). The appearance of continuous-processing machinery and attendant economies of scale also gave rise to branding and subsequent efforts to presell product and manage distribution in "matches, flour, breakfast cereals, soup and other canned products, and photographic film" (Chandler 1977, p. 289).

An example of differential inventory management is the decision by Whitman to use two different merchandising methods in marketing candy. Wholesalers were bypassed in the sale of high-grade, packaged candies. Small, inexpensive bar and packaged candies, by contrast, were sold through the usual jobber and wholesale grocer network. Control of the wholesaling function for the former was arguably more important for quality-control purposes. These high-grade items were "sold directly to retailers so that the company could regulate the flow of the perishable items and avoid alienating customers" (Porter and Livesay 1977, p. 220). The customers were presumably prepared to pay a premium to avoid stale candy.

Ownership of wholesaling was reserved for products that required special handling, mainly refrigeration. Meat packing and beer are examples (Chandler 1977, pp. 299–302). Gustavus Swift was the leading innovator in meat packing. He recognized that the practice of shipping live beef to the East coast involved considerable waste, and proposed to eliminate this by slaughtering and dressing cattle in the Midwest and shipping the beef East in refrigerated cars. Implementing this transformation, however, was not easy. It met with resistance both from Eastern butchers, packers, and jobbers (Porter and Livesay 1971, p. 169) and from the railroad interests (Chandler 1977, p. 300). To execute his strategy, Swift had to build his own refrigerator cars and ice houses and construct a network of branch houses that provided "refrigerated storage space, a sales office, and a sales staff to sell and deliver the meat to the retail butchers, grocers, and other food shops" (Chandler 1977, p. 300).

Retailing. Integration into final sales and service represented a more ambitious variety of forward integration. Three classes of products can be distinguished: (1) specialized consumer nondurables; (2) consumer durables requiring information aids, credit, and follow-on service; and (3) producer durables requiring the same.

Kodak photographic film is an example of the first kind. George East-man developed a paper-based film to replace the glass plates in use in the early 1880s. The film required a special camera, however, and developing the film was complex. Meeting little success among professional photographers, Eastman and his associates set themselves to developing the amateur market. "To sell and distribute his new camera and film and to service their purchasers, Eastman . . . created a worldwide marketing network" (Chandler 1977, p. 297). He explained his decision to eliminate independent wholesalers as follows:

"The wholesaler or jobber is a detriment to our business because a large proportion of it is in sensitized goods which are perishable. . . . We have organized our distribution facilities so as to get the goods into the hands of the consumer as quickly as possible. Our sensitized goods carry an expiration date. Our own retail houses . . . have been educated to control their stocks very accurately so that the goods are kept moving" (Porter and Livesay 1971, p. 178).

Consumer durables for which forward integration into retailing was attempted were sewing machines and, later, automobiles. After the legal contests over patents were resolved in 1854, sewing-machine patents were released to twenty-four manufacturers. Only three of these attempted to integrate forward, and only these remained major factors in the industry. Singer had opened fourteen branches by 1859. The pattern was to staff each branch with "a female demonstrator, a mechanic to repair and service, and a salesman or canvasser to sell the machine, as well as a manager who supervised the others and handled collections and credits" (Chandler 1977, p. 303).

Although automobiles were mainly sold through franchised dealers rather than company-owned outlets, the Ford Motor Company and others required their dealers to "supply full demonstrations and instructions for customers unschooled in the operation of the new vehicles. Furthermore, the dealers agreed to instruct consumers in the proper methods of caring for the cars and to keep on hand a supply of parts and a force of mechanics capable of repairing the autos" (Porter and Livesay 1971, p. 195). Of course, independent wholesalers were eliminated entirely from the distribution process.

Alfred P. Sloan (1964) gives an interesting explanation of why the automobile manufacturers decided to franchise rather than own their dealerships. He observes that

. . . automobile manufacturers could not without great difficulty have undertaken to merchandise their own product. When the used car came into the picture in a big way in the 1920s as a trade-in on a new car, the merchandising of automobiles became more a trading proposition than an ordinary selling proposition. Organizing and supervising the necessary thousands of complex trading institutions would have been difficult for the manufacturer; trading is a knack not easily fit into the conventional type of a managerially controlled scheme of organization. So the retail automobile business grew up with the franchised-dealer type of organization (p. 282).

Not only, therefore, did the retail sale and service of automobiles require that transaction-specific investments be incurred, it also required (especially as trade-ins became more common) that judgments based on idiosyncratic local information be made. Centralized ownership reduced the incentive to exercise this judgment in a discriminating way, and posed severe monitoring problems. Rather than integrate fully into the retail sale of automobiles, an intermediate form, the franchised dealership, was developed instead.

Producer durables were distributed through two networks. Small, standardized machinery was sold through commission merchants and jobbers. Expensive, specially designed products that were technologically complex and required special expertise for installation and repair were sold through integrated marketing systems (Porter and Livesay 1971, pp. 183–184). Examples include the system developed by Cyrus McCormick, who pioneered the integrated distribution of farm equipment and set the stage for others to imitate (Livesay 1979, ch. 3). Office machines were another case where demonstration, sales, and service required specialized expertise and for which franchised dealers were instrumental to success (Porter and Livesay 1971, pp. 193–194.

The manufacturers of textile machinery, sugar-mill machinery, industrial boilers, and large, stationary steam engines were also ones where direct contact between buyer and seller were favored (Porter and Livesay 1971, pp. 181–182). The sale of electrical machinery posed special problems for customers that had "special needs and requirements that made standardization extremely difficult in the industry's early years" (Porter and Livesay 1971, p. 187). The sale, installation, and service of electrical generators and related central-station equipment required even closer attention. Forward integration in all of these areas was correspondingly extensive (Porter and Livesay 1972, pp. 182–190).

Mistaken Integration. Forward integration mistakes are not widely reported and, if reported are not always recorded as mistakes. An exception is American Tobacco's effort to expand its position in the cigar market by attempting to integrate both the wholesaling and retailing of cigars. Porter and Livesay (1972) record this effort as follows:

[American Tobacco] had much success in the nineties in extending its dominance from the cigarette business into other lines in the tobacco industry, including smoking tobacco, plug tobacco, and snuff. The cigar trade, however, proved much more difficult to conquer, primarily because it . . . was not subject to economies of scale in production. American Tobacco [turned instead, therefore, to forward integration]. . . . These efforts to move into the wholesale and even the retail end of the [cigar] industry proved very expensive, and American Tobacco endured substantial losses in its war on the cigar trade (p. 210).

Porter and Livesay (1972) also report that the "American Sugar Refining Co. engaged in a similar effort to drive its competitor John Arbuckle out of business by buying into wholesale and retail houses to discourage the sale of Arbuckle's sugar. The attempt failed miserably and proved very costly" (p. 211, n. 52).

Pabst Brewing, Schlitz, and other large brewers purchased saloons in the late 1800s and rented these to operators as outlets for their brands of beer (Cochran 1948, pp. 143–146). Whatever the merits of this might have been at the time—which, except as a short-run expedient, appear doubtful (Cochran 1948, p. 199)—the shift from kegs to bottled beer rendered it nonviable.

Transaction-Cost Interpretation. Chandler (1977, pp. 287, 302) and Porter and Livesay (1971, pp. 166, 171, 179) refer repeatedly to the "inadequacies of existing marketers" in explaining forward integration by manufacturers into distribution in the late 1800s and early 1900s. Presumably the same would be said of marketers in the 1950s, when IBM integrated forward in the sale and service of computers. But to what do these inadequacies refer? Judging from the differential response, the nature or degree of severity evidently varied considerably.

The explanation advanced here is at best suggestive. It appears, however, that scale economy, scope economy, and transaction-cost factors are all operative. In addition, a hitherto unremarked factor also appears: externalities.[11]

Externality concerns arise in conjunction with a branded good or service that is subject to quality debasement. Whereas a manufacturer can inspect—and thereby control—the quality of components and materials that it purchases from earlier stage and lateral suppliers, it is less easy to exercise continuing quality control over items that it sells to distributors.[12] This is not a special problem if the demands of individual destributors are independent of one another. If, however, the quality enhancement (debasement) efforts of distributors give rise to positive (negative) interaction effects, the benefits (costs) of which can be incompletely appropriated by (assigned to) the originators, failure to extend quality controls over distribution will result in suboptimization.

Failure to exhaust economies of scale is an impediment to integration of any kind. I will, however, ignore economies of scale on the grounds that

Table 6–1
Forward Integration into Distribution

Degree of Forward Integration	Economies of Scope	Externalities	Asset Specificity
None	+ +	0	0
Wholesale			
1. Preselling	+	+	0
2. Inventory Management	+	+ +	0
3. Ownership	0	+	+ +
Retail			
1. Consumer Nondurables	~	+	+
2. Consumer Durables	0	+	+ +
3. Producer Durables	0	+	+ +
4. Mistaken	+	0	0

these become progressively less important as assets become more specific. Accordingly, attention is focused on economies of scope, externalities, and asset specificity in interpreting the differential degrees of forward integration reported above. Letting + + denote considerable, + some, ~ uncertain, and 0 negligible, the attributes of the various degrees of integration reported by Chandler take on the pattern shown in table 6–1.

Specialized governance is needed wherever externalities and asset specificity appear. The concern in the first instance is with reputation effects, while bilateral trading problems appear in the second. Firms will be deterred from integrating forward, however, if economies of scope are sacrificed in the process. The pattern of forward integration reported by Chandler and summarized in table 6–1 appears to reflect these considerations.

Thus, full forward integration was never undertaken (except mistakenly) when it involved substantial sacrifice of scope economies. Externalities arising from product deterioration were often the reason to take on a management function, but integration forward into ownership (or into a tight bilateral trading relation, such as franchising) was usually reserved for products with great asset-specificity requirements.

As indicated, this is a highly provisional assessment. The qualitative assignments (from + + through 0) are judgmental and based on description; other factors that have a bearing on forward integration have been ignored. Temporal elements, including customer learning (which may reduce the need for sales and service assistance) have been ignored. Often, however, refined assessments are not needed to evaluate discrete structural alternatives (Simon 1978, p. 6). If, therefore, organizational innovation in the form of forward integration is driven mainly by transaction-cost economizing considerations (as I believe it is), and if crude assignments are acceptable, secondary or occasional factors can be neglected for first-pass purposes.

Backward and Lateral Integration

The distinction between lateral and backward integration is somewhat arbitrary. I include in the former the supply of components, body panels, and the like, and reserve backward integration for more basic materials. Lateral integration poses the typical make-or-buy decision and has been extensively examined elsewhere (Williamson 1971, 1975, 1979a; Klein, Crawford, and Alchian 1978; Flaherty 1981). Suffice it to observe that asset specificity is a crucial factor in these decisions, whereas externalities are less so.

No one has yet provided an historical overview of backward integration from manufacturing into earlier stages (or, depending on where one starts, forward integration from raw materials into processing) in the way that Porter and Livesay (1971) and Chandler (1977) have provided for forward integration out of manufacturing and into distribution. Backward integration is nevertheless interesting from a transaction cost point of view, and a few observations can be offered.

Backward integration into raw materials can occur for three reasons: (1) to realize prospective transaction-cost economies; (2) for strategic purposes; or (3) for mistaken reasons. Transaction-cost economies will warrant integration when the parties are tightly joined in a bilateral-exchange relation (whence problems of harmonizing the interface are crucial) and when integration does not sacrifice economies of aggregation. The acquisition of the Mesabi iron-ore deposits by steel companies may qualify (Parsons and Ray 1975), though others favor a strategic explanation (Wall 1970). Acquisitions of coal and limestone deposits by steel companies lack either transaction-cost or strategic purpose and were probably mistaken.

An illustration of what was held to be strategic backward integration, undertaken to forestall rivalry, is Alcoa's acquisition of bauxite deposits and hydroelectric sites. Allegations to this effect were made in conjunction with the antitrust case.[13] A careful assessment is beyond the scope of this paper. Transaction-cost benefits as well as strategic purposes may have been served by backward integration into bauxite deposits. This is less clear for hydroelectric sites.

Backward integration into the buying and storage of agricultural products was undertaken by American Tobacco, Campbell soup, and Heinz
(Chandler 1977, pp. 291, 295). Assuring a steady supply of tobacco, vege-
tables, and other perishables is reported to be the reason; however, more
detail would be needed to assess the nature of the market breakdown (if
such there was).

Manufacturers sometimes operate on the mistaken premise that more
integration is always preferred to less. From a transaction-cost point of
view, the following examples of backward integration appear to be mistakes
(and, I conjecture, have mainly been abandoned as renewal decisions have
presented themselves): (1) backward integration by Pabst Brewing into
timberland and barrel-making plants (Chandler 1977, p. 301); (2) backward
integration by Singer Sewing into timber, and iron mill, and some transportation (Chandler 1977, p. 305); (3) backward integration by the McCormick
Company into timberlands, mines, twine factories, and hemp plantations
(Chandler 1977, p. 307); and (4) Ford Motor Company's "fully integrated
behemoth at River Rouge, supplied by an empire that included ore lands,
coal mines, 700,000 acres of timberland, sawmills, blast furnaces, a glass
works, ore and coal boats, and a railroad" (Livesay 1979, p. 175).

To be sure, managers, like others, are reluctant to concede mistakes;
accordingly, mistaken integration may not quickly be undone. Moreover
some, like "the River Rouge behemoth," involve the construction of facilities in cheek-by-jowl proximity to each other. Such site specificity forces
the parties into a bilateral-trading relation; for this reason, integration is apt
to be continued. Distant twine factories, by contrast, can be sold off or
closed down with ease.

Site preemption issues aside, backward integration that lacks a transaction-cost rationale or that serves no strategic purpose will presumably be
recognized and undone. The discontinuation or sale of mistaken integration activities will occur more rapidly if the firm is confronted with active
rivalry.

Internal Labor Markets

What has come to be known as the "internal labor market" literature
(Doeringer and Piore 1971) poses an interesting set of organizational issues.
As I have argued elsewhere, many labor-market phenomena have transaction-cost origins, and the parallels between labor-market and intermediate product–market organization are numerous and striking (Williamson 1975, 1979a). The evolution of work organization from the putting-out
system through inside contracting to the authority relation has also been
assessed from a transaction-cost viewpoint (Williamson 1980). The history

and structure of labor unions are also matters on which transaction-cost economics has a bearing.

A number of interesting issues arise in this connection. What are the governance needs of labor? Do these vary with the nature of the task? How does the history of the labor movement bear on this? Although such a large undertaking is beyond the scope of this paper, the general nature of the transaction-cost approach to the study of labor organization can nonetheless be sketched and contrasted with the implications of alternative theories of unions.

Overview

The transaction-cost approach to the study of labor organization has implications at three levels. One of these has to do with the character of labor movements. A second deals with the details of labor governance. The third concerns labor performance. Differential efficiency drives the argument in all three cases.[14]

1. Labor Movements.

1. The potential efficiency gains from organizing labor will be greater in those industries where firm- and industry-specific investments in labor are relatively large. *Ceteris paribus,* these are the industries where labor will be organized first. Note in this connection that the issue is posed in terms of the organization, rather than unionization, of labor. The latter is a specific form of organization. Since issues of efficient governance need to be addressed whether there are labor unions or not, and since resistance to unions may arise for a number of economic and noneconomic reasons, efforts to create a governance structure ought to predate the appearance of unions in industries where labor specificity is great.

2. Efforts to organize the labor class, as opposed to efforts to organize particular types of labor, will, of necessity, emphasize broad distributional aspects at the expense of detailed efficiency aspects. The success of such efforts is more problematical, and will turn more on the politics than the economics of the proposed relation.

2. Labor Governance.

1. *Shop Floor:* Collective governance structures will be designed for shop-floor labor. The degree to which such collective labor-market governance structures are elaborated will vary directly with the investment specificity of the labor force.

2. *Staff and Executive positions:* Individualized governance structures will be more feasible for specialized staff and executive positions for which

numbers are few. Whether, however, such positions will be surrounded with protective governance structure to discourage unwanted quits and arbitrary dismissals will depend on whether firm-specific capital is great.

3. Labor Productivity.

1. Unionization is least apt to promote productivity gains in industries where specific labor capital is slight.

2. Labor strife and recourse to the political process will be concentrated in areas where nonspecific skills predominate or where the governance structure is not developed enough to deal with the complaints of specific labor in a discriminating way.

Some Evidence

While scarcely dispositive, Porter's remarks on labor organization (1973) are congruent with the transaction cost approach to the labor movement. Thus he observes that:

> . . . railroad workers were the first to achieve genuine collective bargaining and grievance channels through their national unions, the railroad brotherhoods. Initially these unions, like many other early American labor organizations, were social and mutual benefit societies. By the 1870s, though, they were evolving into modern unions. Like many of the craft unions which formed the American Federation of Labor in the 1880s, the railway brotherhoods derived their economic strength from the fact that their members had scarce and hard to replace skills. A strike by such a union was a real threat to employers, because it was extremely difficult to break the strike by bringing in outside workers ("scabs" in union parlance). Furthermore, the railway workers were additionally vital because they controlled the use and maintenance of expensive equipment. The unhappy history of unions that tried to include all the nation's working people, such as the National Labor Union and the Knights of Labor, indicated that it was very difficult, if not impossible, to create and maintain unions unless the members had scarce economic skills like the railroad workers and the members of the craft unions that made up the American Federation of Labor in the 1880s. The all-inclusive unions faced other difficulties as well. Gerald Grob's *Workers and Utopia* (1961) convincingly argued that the members and the leaders of such non-craft unions shared an ideological reluctance to accept the wage system (pp. 34–35).

The corollary to the efficiency hypothesis referred to earlier can also be explored. Thomas Cochran's remarks on preunion organization (1972) are germane

> In order to check the threatened spread of trade unions, thoughtful employers . . . experimented with ways of attaching the worker more strongly

to the company. . . . Employee representation plans were started by three companies in 1904, but were not widely adopted until World War I. While the leaders of such 'company unions' were all on the payroll, meetings gave an opportunity for expression of grievances (p. 168).

Since unions service a variety of purposes (of which efficiency is only one) and since the appearance of a union is attended by considerable uncertainty, the apprehension with unions to which Cochran refers is understandable. But the questions remain as to which were the more thoughtful employers and what were their purposes. The transaction-cost approach permits these matters to be addressed in a more discriminative way.

Thus, whereas the objective of forestalling unions applies to all industries, only some stand to realize efficiency benefits from collective organization. Those that do, moreover, will not merely create cosmetic front organizations to forestall unions, but will develop a governance structure of an economically meaningful kind. There is some evidence[15] that the "more thoughtful" employers were not merely generous-spirited, but recognized efficiency benefits in creating employee representation plans. This is suggested by the following:

1. The steel industry is an industry where specific skills are relatively great.
2. Seven steel firms had introduced employee representation plans prior to 1932.
3. The grievance procedures of these mainly followed those of the 1919 Bethlehem Plan of Representation.
4. Similar grievance procedures[16] and the same preunion division of labor and job hierarchies were retained when the industry was unionized.

Internal labor-market governance depends not merely on the grievance machinery but also on ports of entry, job ladders, promotion criteria, and bumping (Wachter and Williamson 1978, p. 567). Promotion ladders in firms where a succession of interdependent jobs are highly specific should be long and thin, with access restricted mainly to the bottom; promotion ladders in nonspecific activities should be broad and diffuse. Also, to the degree in which screening for specific skills is more difficult than for general skills, promotion on merit ought to be favored over promotion strictly by seniority in firms where jobs are more highly specific. Likewise, bumping ought to operate within narrow job ladders where skills are more specific. The pattern of governance practices adopted by auto workers as compared with steel workers is consistent with the differences between them in job specificity.

Consider finally the matter of the impact of unions on productivity. Richard Freemen and James Medoff (1979) contend that there are two faces of unionism. The monopoly view is that unions restrict employment and reduce productivity by placing "limits on the loads that can be handled by workers, restrictions on tasks performed, featherbedding, and so forth" (Freeman and Medoff 1979, p. 76). The second, less widely recognized view of unionism is the "collective-voice/institutional-response model." According to this view, unions can raise productivity by reducing quits, emphasizing seniority, tightening job standards, and improving channels of communication (Freeman and Medoff 1979, pp. 76–78).

The transaction-cost approach to unionism offers a third approach. In this view, productivity can be increased by a union-assisted governance structure, depending on the nature of the work. Unions will have mixed productivity effects[17] under this third view—positive in industries where human-asset specificity is great (in which event, harmonizing the interface between management and labor is valued); but mainly negative where asset specificity is negligible. More generally, the transaction-cost approach generates a whole series of comparative propositions for assessing unionism. To illustrate, the unionization of migrant farm labor, compared, say, with steel, ought to (1) appear later, (2) require greater support from the political process, (3) rely on a more primitive governance structure, and (4) yield performance outcomes more nearly consonant with the monopoly face of unionism.

A systematic assessment of these and related arguments requires that labor-market data be worked up in a more microanalytic way than previously attempted. The characteristics of various tasks and of the associated governance structures both need to come under scrutiny. Applications should include failures (such as the National Labor Union) and transient forms (such as inside contracting). With respect to successes, the issue is less whether an activity is unionized than whether collective organization appeared early or late, and whether governance structures and task attributes are aligned.

To be sure, a transaction-cost theory of labor markets is seriously incomplete. A full theory of labor organization will also allow for appropriate political factors. An economic approach in which transaction costs are featured by itself, however, generates testable implications regarding differences among unions in timing, structural, and performance respects. A monolithic view of unionism thus gives way to a more discriminating assessment.

Alternative Theories of Organizational Innovation

Economizing on transaction costs is purportedly responsible for the organizational changes reported above. This is not to say that it is the only factor, but other influences are usually weaker and very partial—some apply here, others apply there, but none apply in general. The leading alternative theories that have been offered to explain organizational changes are: domination theory, market power, technology, life cycle, pecuniary economies, and strategic behavior. Consider these seriatim.

Domination Theory

Domination theory focuses on human actors. Some possess economic power, and some do not. The organization of economic activity is under the control of those who possess economic power. The reason why one mode is chosen over another is because this permits those in control to extend and perfect their power.

This theory of organizational innovation presumably applies both to the relationship between capitalists and workers and that among capitalists themselves. I have previously examined the thesis that work is hierarchically organized to prevent workers from gaining power, and have found it wanting (Williamson 1980). Consider, therefore, whether power theory explains confrontations among capitalists.

Two applications suggest themselves. The first is the transformation of the merchant capitalist described by Porter and Livesay. The second is the resistance to the conglomerate.

Porter and Livesay (1971) report that during the "first two centuries after the initial English settlement on the North American continent, urban merchants dominated" (p. 5). These "urban merchant capitalists . . . were the wealthiest, best informed, and most powerful segment of early American society" (p. 6.). This all-purpose merchant nevertheless gave way to the specialized merchant early in the nineteenth century, which merchants then became "the most important men in the economy" (p. 8). The specialized merchant, in turn, found his functions sharply cut back by the rise of the integrated manufacturer late in the 1800s: "the long reign of the merchant had finally come to a close. In many industries the manufacturer of goods had also become their distributor. A new economy dominated by the modern, integrated manufacturing enterprise had arisen" (p. 12).

Power theory must confront two troublesome facts in explaining these changes. First, why would general-purpose (and later, special-purpose) merchants ever permit economic activity to be organized in ways that would remove power from their control? Second, why did power leak out selectively—why was the merchant role appropriated extensively by some manufacturers, but not by others? As developed above, the transaction-cost approach explains both in terms of efficiency. Perhaps power theory can add detail, but as an overall approach to the study of organizational change, power theory is bankrupt. Efficiency is the main factor driving organizational change.[18]

Market Power

Market-power arguments can be brought to bear on organizational innovation in two ways. One is that the possessors of market power simply prefer certain organizational arrangements. The second is that organization is used strategically as an impediment to rivals.

Porter and Livesay (1971) appeal to the former in explaining why manufacturers integrated into distribution in some industries and not in others. Thus they observe that the "incidence of oligopoly and large size was much less frequent" among manufacturers that did not integrate forward than among those that did (p. 214). It is noteworthy, however, that a number of large firm/concentrated industry groups are included among the nonintegrators (breakfast cereals, hand soaps, soup, and razor blades, to name a few). These industries would presumably be prime candidates for forward integration if oligopolistic preferences rather than efficiency were driving organizational change.

Technology

The argument that technological imperatives explain organizational structures is an old one. Joe Bain contends that meritorious vertical integration can be distinguished from nonmeritorious integration on these grounds. Thus he observes (1968) that the integration of iron with steel making is explained by thermal economies, and that where "integration does not have this physical or technical aspect—as it does not, for example, in integrating the production of assorted components with the assembly of those components—the case for cost savings from integration is generally much less clear" (p. 381).

As explained earlier, however, the common ownership of two stages operating cheek-by-jowl is a solution to a troublesome bilateral bargaining relation. Thermal economies could be realized by placing autonomous blast furnaces and rolling mills alongside one another; how to mediate the interface is a transaction-cost issue.

Forward integration into distribution is an anomaly if addressed in physical or technical terms. Chandler, however, has come forward with an alternative technological explanation for this condition (1977). Although he acknowledges that successful organizational innovations serve (among other things) to economize on transaction costs, the main factor is what he refers to as "economies of speed" (Chandler 1977, pp. 256, 281, 286; Chandler and Daems 1979, pp. 30–31). According to Chandler and Daems (1979), such economies "could only be realized . . . if a managerial hierarchy carefully scheduled the flows. . . . Therefore, when and where a new technology permitted mass production and when and where new markets permitted mass distribution, such administrative coordination turned out to be more efficient than when the movement of goods *between* units was a result of a multitude of market transactions" (p. 31).

Although economies of speed remain unspecified, appeal to an intuitive notion of such economies leads to a number of anomalous results. Why didn't manufacturers comprehensively integrate into distribution for the sale of cigarettes, beer, and branded packaged goods? Why were small, standardized producer durables sold through independent distributors, while manufacturers sold and serviced large, unique producer durables themselves? I submit that the human assets needed for the retail sale and service of cigarettes, other packaged goods, and standardized producer durables were quite interchangeable, which they are not for large, unique producer durables. The pattern of integration and nonintegration is explained by interchangeable versus noninterchangeable human resources, economies of scope available for the former set of products and not for the latter, and the diseconomies of bureaucracy that attend forward integration, rather than by differential economies of speed.

Life Cycle

George Stigler (1951) has advanced a theory of vertical integration in which life-cycle features are prominent. Extensive integration is favored at both the early and late stages of an industry's development, and less integration occurs at the intermediate stages. Integration in the textile industry is held to be consistent with the hypothesis (Stigler 1951).[19]

Both Porter and Livesay (1971, p. 132) and Chandler (1977, p. 490) read the evidence differently. Specifically, Porter and Livesay (1977) contend that "while large firms may pass through the three stages described by Stigler, they frequently engage in reintegration or extended integration as a result of rising, not declining, demand" (p. 132).

I submit that life-cycle analysis needs to be joined with transaction costs in order to explain the observed pattern of vertical integration. More interesting, moreover, than the disputed demand features referred to above is the following life-cycle phenomenon: As customers and independent middlemen become more knowledgeable of the technology and as the reliability of an item increases (whence service requirements decrease), the transaction-cost incentive to maintain a forward market presence by a manufacturer decreases. Accordingly, items that were once marketed by an integrated sales and service organization can often be returned to the wholesale and retail market in the later stages of a product's life cycle.

This has numerous ramifications, among which is the viability of discount houses for selling mature products. Also, public policy toward forward integration ought to make allowance for life-cycle features. The likelihood that forward integration is justified by transaction-cost considerations is much greater for products that are sold in the growth phase. Such integration, however, might also be continued at mature stages because it impedes the entry of competitors.

These issues relate to the differential performance of firms that have technologically satisfactory products but follow different marketing strategies. The success of IBM relative to Sperry-Rand (and, later, RCA and GE) may well turn on the intensive sales and support that IBM offered for its relatively unfamiliar, but complex, product in the 1950s, which were critical formative years in the history of the computer industry.

Pecuniary Economies

Vertical integration is sometimes adopted to avoid excise taxes (Coase 1937; Stigler 1951). Whether this has been an important factor in explaining vertical integration in the United States has never been established. I conjecture that it is of minor significance relative to the real transaction-cost savings reported above.

Tax incentives purportedly explain some of the conglomerate mergers that have taken place in the United States, especially in the period after World War II. Again, however, this remains to be investigated. Plainly tax considerations played a major role in the early postwar acquisitions of Royal Little (Sobel 1974, p. 356). They continue to influence conglomerate acquisitions to this day (the attempted takeover of the Mead Corporation by Occidental Petroleum is a recent example[20]). Whether assets, once acquired, will be effectively managed is an issue of organizational form. Whatever the immediate incentives to integrate, therefore, transaction-cost issues still need to be addressed. Conglomerates that adopted a holding-company rather than M-form structure would presumably be less well-suited to deal with complexity and adversity. These would tend to shake out as events progressed.

Strategic Behavior

Strategic behavior refers to efforts by dominant firms to take up and maintain advance or preemptive positions or to respond punitively to rivals. The object in both instances is to deter rivalry. An example of the first kind would be forward integration into distribution where transaction-cost savings are negligible. Punitive strategic behavior is illustrated by predatory pricing.

Since few industries are characterized by dominant firms,[21] and as much of the organizational change reported above occurred in nondominant firm industries, strategic considerations obviously explains little of the reorganization of American industry over the past 150 years. Strategic factors may, however, operate in some industries—if not in the decision to integrate forward, then in the decision to maintain a forward presence[22] after the industry has matured and the original transaction-cost incentives to integrate have weakened or vanished. This is a matter for separate investigation.

None of the six alternative theories of organizational structure and innovation discussed above makes more than a piecemeal contribution to an understanding of the reshaping of the American economy. Indeed, some are plainly misconceived. Transaction-cost economizing, by contrast, not only applies broadly to the changing governance of intermediate-product markets, labor markets, and capital markets, but it explains details as well as general movements. This is not to say that alternative theories should be disregarded. Refining transaction-cost economics as it applies to organizational innovation, however, would appear to be the more promising research direction.

Concluding Remarks

Schumpeter, Porter and Livesay, Chandler, Cochran, Cole, and Davis and North have argued persuasively that the American economy has witnessed numerous and significant organizational innovations during the past 150 years. This paper affirms and extends that judgment, and takes the argument a step further. I argue that efficiency is the main and only systematic factor responsible for the organizational changes that have occurred. Specifically, transaction-cost economizing is the previously neglected—but key—concept for understanding organizational innovation.[23]

The study of transaction-cost economizing entails an examination of alternative ways of governing exchange interfaces. Firms, markets, and mixed modes are recognized as alternative instruments of governance. Which is best suited for mediating a transaction (or a related set of transactions) depends on the underlying characteristics of the transactions in question. Dimensionalizing transactions, with special attention to their asset specificity features, is crucial to the exercise. Although tradeoffs between economies of scale and scope on the one hand and transaction-cost economies on the other can be important, the view of the firm as a production function is mainly subordinated to the view that the firm is a governance instrument.

While many of the benefits of successful organizational innovations originally give advantage to the firms that originate them, the benefits accrue to society at large as the competitive process unwinds. That Andrew Carnegie profited greatly (and sometimes at the expense of others) from the reorganization of steel is undeniable. Of greater economic significance, however, is that the steel industry was rationalized to advantage, and that lasting benefits were realized by society in the long run. This process of "handing on" always works "through a fall in the price of the product to the new level of costs" (Schumpeter 1947, p. 155) whenever rivals are alert to new opportunities and are not prevented by strategic restrictions from adopting them.

Natural selection forces do not always operate quickly, however. Firms can postpone the reckoning if they are buffered against change. For instance, some firms are buffered against product-market rivalry, as were European firms prior to the 1968 tariff reductions within the European Economic Community (Franko 1972). Others are buffered against capital-market discipline, as was the Ford Motor Company with its concentrated ownership and $600 million Depression bank account (Livesay 1979, p. 179). These, however, are the exception rather than the rule. Where incumbent managements are not pressed to adopt new procedures by economic events, successor managements (often led by a new chief executive) commonly will (Chandler 1966, ch. 7).

William Baumol contends (1968) that formidable difficulties beset a theoretical approach to entrepreneurship. He nevertheless holds out the hope that entrepreneurship can be promoted not by considering "the means which the entrepreneur employs or the process whereby he arrives at his decisions but by examining instead the determinants of the payoff to his activity" (p. 70).

Payoff determinants can be influenced in two ways. One is to take specific action to increase or decrease payoffs—by taking tax and other measures to encourage research and development, for example. Considering the diverse origins of organizational innovations, however,[24] direct measures are likely to be more useful for promoting technological than organizational innovations.[25] The second way of influencing innovations is by altering the climate in which they are received. Public policy toward organizational innovations was permissive through most of the nineteenth century (legislation against the trust being an appropriate exception).

Whereas public attitudes and public policy toward technological innovations have been mixed in recent years, as concern for the environment has become more widespread, public policy toward organizational innovations in the period after World War II has been skeptical, even hostile. The inhospitality tradition that antitrust agencies and other observers have maintained toward internal organization is especially inimical to organizational innovation. A former head of the Antitrust Division expressed his attitude toward vertical-market restrictions as follows: "I approach territorial and customer restrictions not hospitably in the common-law tradition, but inhospitably in the tradition of antitrust law."[26] The Federal Trade Commission, likewise, was quick to venture hostile views toward conglomerates with no appreciation whatsoever for the consequences in terms of efficiency.[27]

Considering the importance of organizational innovation to the vitality of an enterprise economy, such misguided public policy needs to be reversed. Instead of viewing organizational innovations with hostility, public policymaking should maintain the rebuttable presumption that organizational innovations have the purpose and effect of enhancing efficiency. To be sure, such innovations might also be used for strategic purposes. The circumstances, however, that support strategic behavior are special and easily recognized (Williamson 1979a, pp. 990–993). These aside, public policy ought to adopt a more permissive posture.

This will be accomplished as a deeper appreciation for the firm-as-governance-structure approach to the study of economic organization takes hold. Not only does this require that economic activity be examined in greater microanalytic detail than economists are accustomed to, but it also requires respect for the proposition that the form of the organization matters. Knowledge of and interest in organization theory may be essential—among academics and enforcement agencies alike.

Notes

1. See Chandler (1977), Sobel (1974), and Livesay (1979).

2. See especially Porter and Livesay (1971) and Chandler (1977).

3. See Davis and North (1971) and, for a commentary and survey, North (1978).

4. Sidney Winter (1980) expresses the mainline position succinctly as follows: "It is still standard practice . . . to represent the business firm abstractly by the production transformations of which it is capable, and to characterize these transformations by a production function or production set regarded as a datum" (p. 5). Also see Richard Nelson (1972) and Harvey Leibenstein (1968, p. 73).

5. Although I emphasize the development of internal organization, the same transaction-cost approach can be applied to a more general study of changing institutional forms. This would include legal forms (for in-

stance, the development of arbitration) as well as market forms (the appearance of the commodity dealer). As these are interrelated, a comprehensive analysis would look at internal, legal, and market forms simultaneously.

6. Recent applications of transaction-cost reasoning that use asset specificity extensively to explain economic phenomena include the vertical integration of production (Williamson 1971, 1975; Klein, Crawford, and Alchian 1978), aspects of regulation (Williamson 1976; Goldberg 1977), labor-market organization (Williamson, Wachter, and Harris 1975), and franchising (Klein 1980). This paper affirms the importance of asset specificity and extends the applications. For an early (predimensionalizing) study of firm versus market organization that introduces transaction costs, see Coase (1937).

7. Actually, there is a further consideration within the firm's control: component design. Specialized components can offer performance advantages, but they can also be expensive to produce or otherwise pose trading hazards. The overall optimization will take these factors into account.

8. Note the implicit assumption that contracts are incomplete. If it were feasible to write comprehensive contracts in which adaptations to contingent events were exhaustively stipulated in advance, adaptations could be smoothly implemented as events unfolded—at least if states of the world could be accurately discerned. Bounded rationality precludes such contracting.

9. For a discussion of obligational market contracting, see Wachter and Williamson (1978) and Williamson (1979b). Although such trading relations facilitate adaptations, they are not indefinitely elastic. Out of recognition that some forms of adaptation pose fewer hazards than others, the parties will generally restrict their adaptations to those with the least incentive hazards. Incentive hazards are ordinarily much lower for quantity adjustments than for price adjustments.

10. Not only did the railroad have a significant impact on the distribution of manufactured goods, but the organization of the railroad posed distinctive problems of its own (Chandler 1977, ch. 3), and servicing the supply needs of the growing railway industry had a direct impact on the organization of the iron and steel industry (Porter and Livesay 1971, pp. 55–62). The story of the railroads and of the organizational genius required by J. Edgar Thomson to fashion the structure and controls of the Pennsylvania Railroad, however, divert attention from the matter of principal interest here—namely, the nature and extent of forward vertical integration into distribution.

11. Externalities also have transaction-cost origins (Arrow 1969; Williamson 1975, pp. 5–6). It seems useful to examine distribution externalities of the free-rider kind separately, however, as this is a common reason for exercising controls over the distribution process.

12. As discussed below, this can sometimes be overcome by incurring

additional packaging or other expense—for instance, placing the item in a hermetically sealed container with an inert atmosphere—rather than by extending control over distributors.

13. *United States* v. *Aluminum Company of America,* 148 F. 2d 416 (2d Cir. 1945)..

14. For an elaboration and some case studies bearing on this approach to labor organization, see Scott Williamson (1980). Also see Wachter and Williamson (1978) for a discussion of the issues.

15. See S.R. Williamson (1980, pp. 31–39).

16. The grievance procedure was, however, slightly changed to discourage abuse. Thus although an "individual could still bring particular complaints to his foreman for redress, . . . thereafter the grievance had to be taken up by the union's grievance committee before it could be carried through the remaining grievance channels—which now ended in compulsory arbitration" (S.R. Williamson 1980, p. 39). As Archibald Cox has argued (1958), the practice of giving the union control over grievances better assures that collective interests will not be sacrificed for individual complaints that lack merit (p. 24).

17. Mixed productivity effects are what the evidence shows (Freeman and Medoff 1979, pp. 79–81). Whether the effects are mixed in the systematic way predicted by the transaction-cost hypothesis, however, remains to be investigated.

18. Power theory does somewhat better in explaining the conglomerate. To be sure, established firms have not blocked the development of the conglomerate form, but they have slowed its spread. Much of the legislation passed by states to impede takeovers was done at the behest of the managements of established firms (Cary 1969; Winter 1978, p. 43). Unable to suppress conglomerates by exercising economic power in the market place, incumbent managements turned to the political process instead. Possibly it is in this forum that power theory has the most to offer.

19. Although the textile mills were the first to introduce large factories to the United States, the industry is not the bellwether that many have thought it to be (Chandler 1977, p. 72). Factory organization, with its emphasis on the technology of production, falls well short of business organization, which deals with the organization of the firm itself.

20. *Mead Corp.* v. *Occidental Petroleum Corp.,* No. C-3-78-241 (S.D. Ohio, filed Aug. 18, 1978) and *United States* v. *Occidental Petroleum Corp.,* No. C-3-78-288 (S.D. Ohio, complaint dismissed without prejudice April 4, 1979).

21. I would define a dominant firm as one that occupies a 60 percent or larger market share in an industry where entry is impeded.

22. For a discussion of how a forward presence can deter entry by rivals, see Williamson (1979a, pp. 962–965).

23. This is not to say that others have not identified transaction costs as

a contributing factor. Chandler includes transaction costs, but he regards these as less important than economies of speed. He develops no systematic account of transaction-cost economies. Davis and North (1971) also include transaction costs as one of four factors giving rise to changes in organization (p. 12), and venture the opinion that the "organization and improvement of the flow of relevant economic information (one of many types of transaction costs) has probably been the major area of arrangemental innovation" (p. 20). But they do not get into a microanalytic assessment of organizational change from a transaction-cost point of view. For example, the changing distributional practices described here for intermediate product markets are dealt with in two pages and are accounted for in economy of scale terms (Davis and North 1971, pp. 200–201). As Chandler (1977) observes, North and his colleagues "have not yet focused on a detailed analysis of the historical development of any specific economic institution" (p. 5).

24. Adversity frequently operates as a stimulus, as in the M-form innovation. Recognition that the current structure is patently inefficient appears to be responsible in other circumstances—reorganization of steel by Frick and Carnegie is an example. Deep insights into latent opportunities are displayed by some innovators—the changes in meatpacking wrought by Gustavus Swift are in this category. The conglomerate appears to be a mixture of experiment and foresight.

25. An exception is the influence of tax credits on mergers. Certain conglomerate mergers were induced by tax incentives; the elimination of such incentives would remove the pecuniary gains that attend such mergers.

26. The quotation is attributed to Donald Turner (at a time when he was assistant attorney general in charge of the antitrust division) by Stanley Robinson, New York State Bar Association, *Antitrust Law Symposium,* 1968, p. 29.

27. U.S. Federal Trade Commission, *Report of the Federal Trade Commision on the Merger Movement; a Summary Report* (Washington, D.C.: Government Printing Office 1948), p. 59, offers the following assessment of the conglomerate:

> With the economic power which it secures through its operations in many diverse fields, the giant conglomerate corporation may attain an almost impregnable economic position. Threatened with competition in any one of its various activities, it may sell below cost in that field, offsetting its losses through profits made in its other lines—a practice which is frequently explained as one of meeting competition. The conglomerate corporation is thus in a position to strike out with great force against smaller business in a variety of different industries.

The economic properties of the conglomerate were regarded by others as a puzzle as late as 1972 (Posner 1972, p. 204). That the Federal Trade Commission was prepared to condemn the conglomerate form in 1948 discloses an inhospitality proclivity that is alien to organizational innovation in an enterprise economy.

References

Arrow, K.J. "Control in Large Organizations." *Management Science* 10 (September 1963):397–408.

———. "The Organization of Economic Activity." *The Analysis and Evaluation of Public Expenditure.* Joint Economic Committee, 91st Congress, 1969, pp. 59–73.

Bain, J.S. *Industrial Organization.* 2d ed. New York: Wiley, 1968.

Baumol, W.J. "Entrepreneurship in Economic Theory." *American Economic Review* 58 (May 1968):64–71.

Berle, A.A., and Means, G.C. *The Modern Corporation and Private Property.* New York: Macmillan Co., 1932.

Brown, D. "Pricing Policy in Relation to Financial Control." *Management and Administration* 1 (February 1924):195–258.

Bruchey, S. *Robert Oliver, Merchant of Baltimore, 1788–1819.* Baltimore: Johns Hopkins University Press, 1956.

Burton, R.H., and Kuhn, A.J. *Strategy Follows Structure.* Unpublished manuscript , May 1979.

Cary, W. "Corporate Devices Used to Insulate Management from Attack." *Antitrust Law Journal* 39 (1969–1970):318–333.

Chandler, A.D. *Strategy and Structure.* Cambridge, Mass.: MIT Press, 1962.

———. *The Visible Hand: The Managerial Revolution in American Business.* Cambridge, Mass.: Belknap Press, 1977.

Chandler A.D., and H. Daems. "Administrative Coordination, Allocation and Monitoring: Concepts and Comparisons," in N. Horn and J. Kocka, eds., *Law and the Formation of the Big Enterprises in the 19th and Early 20th Centuries,* pp. 28–54. Gottingen, Vandenhoeck and Ruprecht 1979.

Coase, R.H. "The Nature of the Firm." *Economica N.S.* 4 (1937):386–405, repr. in G.J. Stigler and K.E. Boulding, eds., *Readings in Price Theory.* Homewood, Ill. R.D. Irwin, 1952.

———. "Adam Smith's View of Man." *Journal of Law and Economics* 19 (October 1976):529–546.

Cochran, T.C. *The Pabst Brewing Company.* New York: New York University Press, 1948.

———. *Business in American Life: A History.* New York: McGraw Hill, 1972.

Cole, A.H. "The Entrepreneur: Introductory Remarks." *American Economic Review* 63 (May 1968):60–63.

Copeland, M.T. "The Managerial Factor in Marketing," in *Facts and Factors in Economic History*. Cambridge, Mass.: Harvard University Press, 1932.

Cox, A. "The Legal Nature of Collective Bargaining Agreements." *Michigan Law Review* 57 (November 1958):1–36.

Davis, L.E., and North, D.C. *Institutional Change and American Economic Growth*. Cambridge: Cambridge University Press, 1971.

Flaherty, T. "Prices versus Quantities and Vertical Financial Integration," *Bell Journal of Economics* 12 (Autumn 1981):507–525.

Franko, L.G. "The Growth, Organizational Efficiency of European Multinational Firms: Some Emerging Hypotheses," *Colloques international aux C.N.R.S.,* (1972):335–366.

Hayek, F. "The Use of Knowledge in Society," *American Economic Review* 35 (September 1945):519–530.

Klein, B., Crawford, R.A. and Alchian, A.A. "Vertical Integration, Appropriable Rents and the Competitive Contracting Process," *J. Law Econ.* 21 (October 1978):297–326.

Larson, H.M. *Guide to Business History*. Cambridge, Mass.: Harvard University Press, 1948.

Leibenstein, H. "Entrepreneurship and Development." *American Economic Review* 58 (May 1968):72–83.

Livesay, H.C. *American Made: Men Who Shaped the American Economy*. Boston: Little, Brown, 1979.

Nader, R., Green, M., and Selijman, J. *Taming the Giant Corporation*. New York: Norton, 1976.

Nelson, R.R. "Issues and Suggestions for the Study of Industrial Organization in a Regime of Rapid Technical Change," in V.R. Fuchs ed., *Policy Issues and Research Opportunities in Industrial Organization*, pp. 34–58. New York: Columbia University Press, 1972.

North, D.C. "Structure and Performance: The Task of Economic History." *Journal of Economic Literature* 16 (September 1978):963–978.

Pashigian, B.P. *The Distribution of Automobiles: An Economic Analysis of the Franchise System*. Englewood Cliffs, N.J.: Prentice-Hall, 1961.

Porter, G., and Livesay, H.C. *Merchants and Manufacturers*. Baltimore: Johns Hopkins University Press, 1971.

Porter, G. *The Rise of Big Business, 1860–1910*. Arlington Heights, Ill.: AHM Publishing Corporation, 1973.

Posner, R.A. *Economic Analysis of Law*. Boston: Little, Brown, 1972.

Schumpeter, J.A. *Capitalism, Socialism, and Democracy*. New York: Harper & Row, 1942.

———. "The Creative Response in Economic History." *Journal of Economic History* 7 (November 1947):149–159.

Smith, A. *The Wealth of Nations*. London: J.M. Dent and Sons, 1922.

Simon, H.A. *Models of Man.* New York: Wiley, 1957.

———. "Rationality as Process and Product of Thought." *American Economic Review* 68 (May 1978):1–16.

Sloan, A.P. *My Years with General Motors.* New York: Doubleday, 1964.

Sobel, R. *The Entrepreneurs.* New York: Weybright and Talley, 1974.

Soltow, J.H. "The Entrepreneur in Economic History." *American Economic Review* 58 (May 1968):84–92.

Stigler, G.J. "The Division of Labor is Limited by the Extent of the Market." *Journal of Political Economy* 59 (June 1951):185–193.

Stone, K. "The Origins of Job Structures in the Steel Industry." *Review of Radical Political Economics* 6 (Summer 1974):61–97.

Teece, D.J. *Vertical Integration and Divestiture in the U.S. Oil Industry.* Stanford: The Stanford University Institute for Energy Studies, 1976.

Wachter, M. and Williamson, O.E. "Obligational Markets and the Mechanics of Inflation" *Bell Journal of Economics* 9 (Autumn 1978): 549–571.

Williamson, O.E. *Corporate Control and Business Behavior.* Englewood Cliffs, NJ: Prentice-Hall, 1970.

———. "The Vertical Integration of Production: Market Failure Considerations", *American Economic Review* 61 (May 1971):112–123.

———. *Markets and Hierarchies,* New York: Free Press, 1975.

———. "Franchise Bidding for Natural Monopolies—in General and With Respect to CATV." *Bell Journal of Economics* 7 (Spring 1976):73–104.

———. "Assessing Vertical Market Restrictions." *University of Pennsylvania Law Review* 127 (April 1979):953–993.

———. "Transaction Cost Economics: The Governance of Contractual Relations." *Journal of Law and Economics* 22 (October 1979b): 233–261.

———. "The Organization of Work: A Comparative Institutional Assessment." *Journal of Economic Behavior and Organization* 1 (March 1980):5–38.

Williamson, O.E., Wachter, M., and Harris, J. "Understanding the Employment Relation: The Analysis of Idiosyncratic Exchange," *Bell Journal of Economics* 6 (Spring 1975):250–278.

Williamson, S.R. *A Selective History of the U.S. Labor Movement: The Transaction Cost Approach.* Undergraduate thesis, Yale University, 1980.

Winter, R. *Government and the Corporation.* Washington, D.C.: American Enterprise Institute for Public Policy Research, 1978.

Winter, S.G. "An Essay on the Theory of Production." Working Paper Series A #39, Yale School of Organization and Management, June 1980.

Part II
An Empirically Based
Framework

Some Insights Into The Entrepreneurial Process

Joshua Ronen

Introduction

Interviews conducted with twenty-three representative entrepreneurs form the basis of this chapter. Proceeding with open-ended questions and in-depth (if loosely structured) probings, this cluster of interviews had for its primary purpose the gathering of some fresh insights into the entrepreneurial game.

Questioned were the chief executive officers of large and mid-size firms representing diverse fields, mainly: agriculture, apparel, automotive, banking and finance, construction, entertainment, food, furniture manufacturing, high technology, metal fabrication, plastic industrial products, real-estate development, securities, various consumer leisure goods, and venture capital. Annual sales of these firms ranged from a minimum of $10 million to a maximum of $5 billion. In each, compounded rate of growth of sales had exceeded 10 percent over the past five years. All but three of the twenty-three executives had been with their respective organizations for at least twenty years; the three, approximately five years.

Here, two major dimensions of the process addressed are: special traits of the entrepreneur (including his modes of interaction with the environment) and characteristic decision making[1] (including ways of organizing individual businesses). A third segment attempts a synthesis proposing an (admittedly tentative) identification of entrepreneurism—with the emphasis on a generality of features noted among those interviewed. Here and there responses indicated differences, but the common elements abounded; it is these that constitute the thrust of the observations reported. The attempt is not to construct a model of the entrepreneur, but rather to delineate, if possible, the nature of those activities emerging as most typically entrepre-

This research is supported by the Price Institute. I am extremely grateful to the Institute's founder, Harold Price, whose enthusiasm for the subject of entrepreneurship created the impetus for writing this chapter.

I am heavily indebted to Julius Cherny for useful insights that he offered. Extensive comments received from and helpful discussions held with Mordecai Kurz led to some significant modifications in the chapter, especially in the section addressing risk taking. The comments of R. Ashton, W.J. Baumol, A. Bergson, J.M. Dutton, A.L. Gitlow, I.M. Kirzner, B. Koch, B. Levine, K. McGahran, A. Ovadia, H. Shapiro, G.H. Sorter, and A.M. Tinker are also gratefully acknowledged.

neurial. Such activities can then become the subject of more systematic inquiry, perhaps culminating in an overall theory of entrepreneurship. In conclusion, a number of major issues are formulated as questions. One can hope that these questions will help define an agenda for the ongoing analysis of entrepreneurial action.

It is to be said that previous such studies have often engaged the entrepreneurial black box, with intent to focus into view the psychological, cognitive, and perceptual attributes that could yield an understanding of the way of the successful entrepreneur.

Also, of course, there has been reflection, speculation by many, on the entrepreneur's contribution to economic equilibrium (or disequilibrium). Obviously, any pertinent theory then emerging must be dependent to a marked degree on the cultivated vision of whoever is doing the speculating.

The procedure herein described has most importantly put emphasis on (1) the environment in which entrepreneurs choose to operate, and (2) the manner of their decision making. An objective has been to gather cumulative knowledge of just what factors in the environment directly affect and facilitate entrepreneurial decisions, as well as identify examples that can help us focus (empirically *and* theoretically) on the entreprenuerial function. We are speaking of a lengthy process: the initial set of interviews here reported counts for only a first step. The work must be considered as ongoing.

Just how a given entrepreneur initiates, carries on and deploys, and brings to triumphant conclusion some chosen activity might be regarded as something of a mystery. There are those who would contend that any aspects of the entrepreneurial process so clearly identified as to make possible systematic imitation and manipulation would surely no longer be defined as entrepreneurial. Our present objective, first and foremost, is not necessarily to learn how one becomes an entrepreneur, but rather how to create an environment that stimulates the full play of socially useful entrepreneurial actions. To this end, we must define (or at least describe) whatever features we select for encouragement in such terms as to enable the interested observer to recognize them as unmistakably entrepreneurial. Past theorizing was somewhat plagued by countless numbers of transactions that were considered entrepreneurial, yet had no agreed upon rule of definition and exclusion: that is, without consensus as to whether or not manifesting entrepreneurship.[2] With this chapter, it is hoped that a project will have been initiated toward a surer identification of behavioral patterns clearly deemed entrepreneurial.

An obvious problem was the selection for interview of a sampling of executives with precisely the purpose to develop portraits of entrepreneurial engagement. How was one to identify, at the outset, individuals who could be referred to as "entrepreneurs?" A conceptual difficulty, but selection had to be made. Thus, we chose mostly owner-managers closely associated with innovative and growing businesses—a reasonable starting point. In the attempt to synthesize the impressions gained from the interviews (the concluding segment), it is projected that emphasis on characterization of entrepreneurial "events" and "acts," in addition to and as distinct from the description of traits of entrepreneurs, would offer analytical enrichment.

There is also the limitation of the interviewing method—the bias of self-selection. Here were successful entrepreneurs who had made it to the top; those who failed, who never made it, perhaps went bankrupt, could not be identified and interviewed. Whatever the effect, it could carry weight in many of the impressions offered as defining the entrepreneurial process—particularly in the discussion of risk taking. Indeed, a conscious effort was made during the interviews to elicit from the entrepreneurs descriptions of their decision processes and attitudes toward risk at the time they were about to undertake their very first entrepreneurial venture. The attempt (how successful?) was to minimize the bias introduced by ex post facto accomplishment. As in all such cases, the entrepreneurs are not necessarily the most reliable judges of their own motives and actions. The effort was made to distil essential facts by continued probing, addressing the same questions in varying guises.

Perhaps the most intriguing aspect of the entrepreneurial game is the way in which those who engage in it identify opportunities, assess their uncertainty, decide which to pursue and how. Can one observe common elements that characterize this process? Case histories of entrepreneurial action, additional in-depth interviews, and more close observation may lead to some answers.

Traits of the Entrepreneur

The Decision to Become an Entrepreneur

With most of the individuals questioned, the decision to become an entrepreneur would seem to have been motivated by two factors: a relative unattractiveness of known alternative employment possibilities (appendix 7A, note 1); and the eager eye: spotting of opportunities in the environment around. The latter would seem to play a decisive role. In some cases, the prime push was a dark fear (experience of the depression!) of having to go on living without money (appendix 7A, note 2). Or else, the urgent need for financial independence, for the way to come out from under the control of others. In other instances, the high need for independence was reinforced by distaste for conforming to the conventional patterns of behavior[3] (appendix 7A, note 3), especially as related to occupation and life-style of parents.

(Among most of those interviewed, however, the father had his own business, and thus probably played a role model.) While some said that the original entrepreneurial decision was taken out of sheer brutal need in the midst of relative wealth, it was, more than anything else, an inner pressure to be noticed, to be different, to gain power, prestige, recognition, and all this by being creative, by implementing new ideas, concepts that would elicit respect and admiration from peers.

All these factors appear to have been responsible not only for the entrepreneurial decision, but for the "success" (including money) that followed. It would seem, in fact, that the majority of the successful entrepreneurs interviewed might have decided to strike out on their own even if their previous employment or occupation had been relatively appealing: for them, "happiness" meant an environment offering full independence, unencumbered by organizational structure, open to experiment with the new.

The occupations chosen were those in which boredom was least likely to set in—where, indeed continuing innovation was essential for survival. And if the entrepreneur did, after all, find himself bound to a business that demanded little innovation, he became restless and yearned to move on into a different venture (appendix 7A, note 4).

There are those entrepreneurs who keep going even after having accumulated the wealth they envisioned for themselves and their children[4] (appendix 7A, note 5). Others—those who have accomplished most of their initial objectives—end up as executives of larger organizations. As a result, they may drop entrepreneurial habit: a new venture holds no lure.[5]

Objectives of an Entrepreneur

Freedom from control by others, the sense of "doing one's own thing," emerges as a salient objective of the entrepreneur. Not so the accumulation of wealth, not primary, but most often perceived as the means to a greatly desired independence. Extraordinary wealth leads naturally to power and authority over others and in our society of today it is this alone that guarantees the desired freedom from control by others. Such would seem to be the thinking.

Also valued is that measure of success that implies doing things better than others and better than before. Certainly, an important measure of success is commensurate with efficiency, a high rate of growth. And a general perception among entrepreneurs sees the accumulation of wealth to be a byproduct of excellence in whatever the endeavor pursued. In the experience of "making things work" the entrepreneur seeks to satisfy two important ego needs: first, to demonstrate to himself his ability to perform well, to do better than someone else, and with that feel the special thrill of discovery of a talent, of strength and power heretofore unknown; and second, to demonstrate to others, win recognition among peers, gain respect among all (appendix 7A, note 6).

Interaction with the Environment: Nature of
Entrepreneurial Ventures

Entrepreneurs are attracted to ventures that involve new products or processes—that is, those with which there has been little, if any, previous experience. Ideas of the new stimulate them; repetition, even if profitable, can turn their zeal off. It follows therefore that they are attracted to the kinds of opportunities characterized by uncertainty, wherein the probabilities attached to differing consequences are not easy to gauge: previous or similar experiences are lacking; events pertinent to the consequences of the venture are too few, scattered over time. It follows that entrepreneurs typically move into innovative and high-growth industries subject to wide fluctuations and to events or factors difficult to predict.

The types of environments in which entrepreneurs function can perhaps be related to Perrow's (1970) typology of technologies employed by organizations.

	Task Variability	
	Low	High
Unanalyzable	Craft	Nonroutine
Analyzable	Routine	Engineering

(Search behavior)

Source: C. Perrow, *Organizational Analysis: A Sociological View.* Copyright © 1970 Wadsworth Publishing Company, Inc. Reprinted by permission of the publisher, Brooks/Cole Publishing Company, Monterey, California.

Search behavior characterizes the individual's response to received stimuli (orders, signals, and so on); even the decision to ignore the stimulus and not to "see it" is a response. Search behavior is analyzable, according to Perrow, when the response pattern is fairly established:

If the stimulus is familiar and the individual has learned in the past what to do in the face of it, little search behavior is required. He may respond automatically or after a moment's thought. The response may be to turn to a pile of instructions, manuals, a computer, or a clerk, but the problem with which the stimulus presents him is analyzable; there are known ways of solving it, and little reflection or judgment is required after one has some experience with it. (p. 76)

On the other hand, if the problem presented by the stimulus is not analyzable, Perrow suggests, "The individual must rely upon a residue of something we do not understand at all well—experience, judgment, knack, wisdom, intuition." (p. 76)

The "nonentrepreneurial" manager, typically, is found to be engaged in the analyzable routine decisions; whereas decisions of entrepreneurs are more properly characterized by nonroutine. Circumstances can "push" an individual from the nonentrepreneurial into the entrepreneurial: difficult times may force him to search the environment for new opportunities.

Adjustment to the Environment

Entrepreneurs view themselves as adjusting faster than others to changes in environmental conditions and as being especially alert to exploiting such changes[6]—including those caused by the regulatory condition of the environment. Some pointed out that they might never have ventured forth as entrepreneurs if governmental regulation had been excessive at the time (appendix 7A, note 7).

Typically, those who do take the entrepreneurial plunge reach out to the innovative—looking to what is already there makes no appeal. They are in a hurry to gain the edge on their possible imitators, launch new products, to carry out new factor combinations. Developing a new resource, they straightway look for possible added uses for it.

Availability of resources and financing is an important factor in any entrepreneurial decision. The entrepreneur seeks such opportunity as will create profits for him beyond those called for to attract prospective investors. He then deploys the capital in such a way as to create the above-normal profits. Thus, the entrepreneur has always in perspective to secure his means of production from capitalists who have already accumulated their wealth (Kirzner 1979). Relatively efficient capital markets must exist; indeed, the ability to get financial backing emerges as probably the most crucial factor in embarking on any entrepreneurial project. The requisite capital market need not be perfect in the sense that one price for capital must be available throughout: "there is no 'imperfection' in a market possessing incomplete knowledge if it would not be remunerative to acquire (produce) complete knowledge (Stigler 1967, p. 291). An important obstacle to the ambitious entrepreneur, however, is information asymmetry: confident in his own judgment, he yet finds it difficult—in the absence of proven past track record—to convince owners of capital that he is capable and trustworthy, both. An entrepreneur of wealth could, of course, launch his project himself, thus saving the costs of persuading others of the soundness of his undertaking, and his certain ability to make it a success.[7] There is the suggestion here that for the independent entrepreneur (or the small entrepreneurial business) access to a capital market may be more difficult than for the innovative entrepreneur working within a large organization. The latter reaches out nearby to persuade decision makers inside his organization (they know more about him than any external capital markets) to finance the development of his innovative project through the organization's own resources (internal capital market). On the other hand, large organizations with internal resources can be encumbered by a bureaucratic internal capital-allocation mechanism militating against the financing of innovative research.

The cost of information asymmetry must prevail as long as the entrepreneurs vying for capital include incompetents or cheats, and as long as capitalists vying for entrepreneurial business outlets recognize such hazard. This cost of adverse selection (Akerlof 1970) can be mitigated through the market mechanisms (Securities Exchange Commission, accounting standard boards, and so on). What is important for the encouragement of entrepreneurship is identifying the least socially costly arrangement for minimizing the expense of transporting a brilliant (but penniless) entrepreneur from a state of unknown ability into one of recognized talent.

State of Alertness

Entrepreneurs see themselves as being more alert to opportunities in the environment than professional managers (appendix 7A, note 8). Somehow they "see" the potential lying out there, along with its possibility of reward. Even if they start in a given well-defined line of business, they do not restrict themselves to it. Nor do they go searching out information on opportunities; rather, they are quick to detect the revealed opportunity—a talent not shared by the nonentrepreneur.[8]

There is restlessness, tension in the entrepreneur; by contrast, what he perceives in the usual professional manager is preference for financial security within a structured environment. The restlessness of the entrepreneur spells outright boredom with routine—the urge is to innovate and forge ahead in new endeavors. Some of those questioned indicated that four to five years was the longest they could conceivably stay put with a given product or in one line of business. They were irresistibly drawn to the un-tried, the unknown—a new venture, a new company.

This emphatic restlessness could point to the notion that the marginal product of entrepreneurship is high only in the initial phases of the product cycle. As the enterprise matures, that marginal product diminishes, giving way to the same restlessness, pushing toward the initiation of something new.

Decision Making

Organizational Structure

Entrepreneurs organize businesses in a centralized fashion; they make the important decisions themselves. Decision making is not democratic. It might have the appearance of being participative: a "consensus" has been reached between entrepreneur and subordinates, a "group" decision has emerged. Yet the entrepreneur remains the sole maker of it. He listens to contradictory advice, considers the information offered by subordinates, but in the end processes the information in ways he sees fit, and guards for himself the final decision-making power[9] (appendix 7A, note 9). Nor does he tolerate much opposition from subordinates, exhibiting little patience with such organizational concerns as structure, hierarchy, clarification of tasks of personnel. He has in fixed view his own ultimate success, and his main interest therefore lies in the operations and growth of the enterprise, in innovations, not in organizational issues as such.[10]

In fact, most entrepreneurs questioned perceived a growing bureau-cracy as stifling to entrepreneurial initiative—the larger the organization, the more stifling. Its hierarchical structure, its formalized decision-making procedure, the need to justify plans, the lesser freedom of the individual—regardless of the autonomy accorded him—of necessity constrain an entre-preneur operating within the organization.

Risk Taking and Information Gathering

Few of the already successful entrepreneurs indicated that they are willing to take any great risk.[11] On the whole, they pay primary attention to the downside risk. Certainly the business promising large rewards attracts, but only if any maximum conceivable loss cannot threaten the entrepreneur's survival, his ability to continue on his course. Thus, established entrepre-neurs seek ventures which, being associated with new products, promise to yield large profits if they succeed, but, failing, will not be disastrous to a continuing entrepreneurial career. Still, these same entrepreneurs emphasized that at the very start of their venturesome journeys they *had* to assume the risk of ruin,[12] spelled out as exile from the high entrepreneurial community. The fear of not "making it" appears to leave an indelible mark on the behavior of the entrepreneur after he has met with a few successes. The strong impression emerges that the willingness to undertake ventures where risk is specifically viewed as the possibility of ruin shrivels away with the accumulation of accomplishments (or wealth). Perhaps, then, success can bring about the demise of entrepreneurship at the level of the individual entrepreneur (though not necessarily for the economy as a whole).

As has been said, entrepreneurs rely basically on their own judgment and interpretation in arriving at a decision. They disdain elaborate, formal analyses of costs and benefits. Valued more is the informal search for information linked to a knowledge of the individuals involved in the transaction, the entrepreneur's own experience with similar other situations, his special inner feelings, his own positive vision of the future. These the entrepreneur ponders (appendix 7A, note 10).

And so he gathers as much information as he can find and deems necessary with regard to a particular opportunity. On the basis of that information, he might well revise strong prior convictions formed from his own experience and intuitions. This is an approach to decision making consistent with the entrepreneur's optimistic and venturesome nature. If finally events prove his special intuitions right, he is reinforced in his actions. If events diverge from expectation and things turn out not as they should, he opens the "back door"—the loss-cutting strategy generally included from the very start in the original design. Right here we see how superficial is the analogy of entrepreneurial action to that of the gambler's. The average gambler does not hedge his bets; if the potential loss seems large enough, the entrepreneur does (appendix 7A, note 11).

Yet it is not easy for the entrepreneur attracted to projects where little past experience exists to gauge the probabilities of success or failure. Finally, then, he must form a quite subjective assessment of potential loss and potential gain. Such an assessment will, in turn, depend greatly on the entrepreneur's perception as to how much his very own skill and ability can influence events. Characteristically, he believes in his ability to make things work—he holds luck to have but a small share in the end result. Thus, subjective probability of success is higher among entrepreneurs than among nonentrepreneurs; conversely, the entrepreneur's subjective probability of failure is lower than that of the nonentrepreneur. Naturally, an "established" entrepreneur's subjective probabilities might be colored—perhaps wrongly—by the successive wins he has experienced. The novice entrepreneur might hesitate to put so high a trust in his (as yet untested) ability and skills; certainly the "failing" entrepreneur can have detected nothing in his experience of past failures to justify great optimism (high subjective probability of success). In any case, no one knows whether the would be entrepreneur undertakes a novel (and, by definition, risky) venture because he is by disposition less risk-averse than his nonentrepreneurial counterpart, or whether because he strongly perceives the project as being less risky (or perhaps both at the same time).

Typically, the nonentrepreneurial manager seems to seek more "formal" information than the entrepreneur does. For one thing, information-flow requirements are set up in organizations within which the manager functions. Entrepreneurs exhibit distaste for such requirements. The nonentrepreneurial manager and the formality-stressing organization perhaps select each other; alternatively, the entrepreneur perhaps comes to be less entrepreneurial from necessity to adapt to the formal structures he encounters in the organization.

It cannot be overemphasized that the role of information seeking in the entrepreneurial process is crucial. The process through which the entrepreneur seeks and gathers the information is not one that can best be characterized as "rational" search based on an expected net benefit from the search. For the innovating entrepreneur, information about unknown opportunities cannot be associated with *ex ante* quantifiable benefits. The information gathering assumes the larger aspect of experimenting with the environment (Dutton and Freedman 1980). Once opportunities are identified, however, rational cost-benefit calculations become important for obtaining efficiency in the (ultimately routine) operation. The entrepreneurial process thus involves in part an opportune search for knowledge, and in part a serendipitous find (Kirzner 1973, 1979).

When the innovative phase is over, procedural rationality sets in (see Simon 1956). Calculating methods become subject to uncertainty, however, and the disadvantage felt from restricting decision making to "rational" calculations in a world of uncertainty leads the entrepreneur to experimenting with the environment (internal and external) to find new advantages (Dutton and Freedman 1980; Burns and Stalker 1961; Downs 1966; Emery and Trist 1973).

Thus, imperfect knowledge of the environment leads to experimentation as a method of discovering for the organization. Such experimentation is most apt to take place when events involve new experience. That is, calculating per se is observed typically where rules are known and stable and existing associations can be employed. When the rules are unclear, the domain unknown, where cause and effect relations are uncertain, experimentation takes place to discover possible eventualities (Dutton and Freedman 1980; Weick 1979).

When one compares the responses of those who followed innovative endeavors through most of their business careers to the responses of those whose activities were more routine, it appears that the former—once established—are no more risk seeking than the latter. All aim to minimize the risk of losing large sums of money (appendix 7A, note 11).

Those defined as more entrepreneurial (in the sense of repeatedly seeking out the new) seem to have stumbled into situations of prevailing uncertainties—the very consequence of the new endeavors, new products, new markets. In these domains, there was no body of general accumulated knowledge to help orient the entrepreneur, no past experience with the same or similar endeavors to help dispel uncertainty, in small measure even. It becomes apparent that the more entrepreneurial adventurers move into an environment of such higher uncertainty not out of any lesser risk aversion, but out of a passion for novelty. The quest for newness, not the lure of risk as such, is uppermost.

However, investing irreversibly in a novel, highly uncertain venture—thus exhibiting full willingness to assume large risks—implies that the entrepreneurial man of business was in fact less averse to risk than the nonentrepreneurial who chose not to invest. (Unless, by virtue of his self-perceived superior ability, he does not view the risk as high.) It may be said then, that strong entrepreneurial activity indicates (if subjective probabilities of entrepreneurs and nonentrepreneurs do not differ systematically) a relatively low degree of risk aversion. In sum, it is probably not a positive "taste" for risk itself that is operative, but a willingness to accept high risk as the inevitable price of satisfying the taste for newness.

Now, a more careful scrutiny shows that diverse motivation in the initial entrepreneurial action leads to dissimilar reaction. Individuals whose taste for risk had induced them to act entrepreneurially apparently would have been content to continue to operate within the environment of high uncertainty once having embarked on a new venture. On the other hand, entrepreneurs purposefully aim at reducing such uncertainty. To that end, they invest resources in market testing, establish links with distribution channels, engage in whatever other activities they can calculate on to reduce probability of large losses.

Resources expended by the novelty-seeking entrepreneur on pilot-market experimentations are akin to an insurance premium. The less entrepreneurial the individual, the more he can afford to save such insurance outlays—he sees himself as deriving no great utility from novelty. Such "insurance premium" is hardly necessary for the manager who operates within the routinized and relatively certain environment of existing product lines, existing manufacturing processes, existing and well-known markets.

If this validly characterizes the difference between entrepreneurial individuals and those less entrepreneurial, one would expect the former to exhibit a higher rate of adoption of new technologies, larger investments in research and development, and more extensive market experimentation and testing. If economies of scale exist in research and development, market testing, and internal communication networks that facilitate experimentation within the organization one might expect the more entrepreneurial organization to grow in size within an ongoing process of identifying new ventures.

The profile of the entrepreneur now seen emerging combines the Schumpeterian innovator (see Schumpeter's "Economic Theory and Entrepreneurial History," in Aitken 1965) with the Knight (1940) view as formalized for special cases by Kihlstrom and Laffont (1979) and Kanbur (1979) among others. It is somewhat closer to the Schumpeterian view. For Knight, the entrepreneur performs the ". . . twofold function of (a) exercising responsible control and (b) securing the owners of productive services against uncertainty and fluctuation in their income" (Knight 1921, p. 278). Even though Knight emphasizes ability as well as "willingness [and] power to give satisfactory guarantees" as a factor that determines the supply of entrepreneurs (p. 283), anyone who performs a "managerial" function of "responsible control," and who bears the uncertainty of residual income after payments to productive labor, is an entrepreneur.

On the other hand, what is suggested from all the preceding is the existence of a *continuum* of entrepreneurship. The managerial, least entrepreneurial, individuals operate within the well-defined and prescribed domain of business activity: existing products, existing markets, existing processes. At the other extreme lies the constant and dynamic innovator, who incessantly seeks new endeavors that involve research and development, market testing, and other uncertainty-reducing activities.

Common to the continuum of entrepreneurship is the Knightian "exercise of responsible control"—that is, the function of business decision making under uncertainty. The entrepreneurial function is not restricted to top management, because situations of decision making under uncertainty can occur anywhere in the continuum of ranks and positions within a business organization. In any business, most operations are characterized by a measure of uncertainty and thus involve some decision making under uncertainty. It follows that the degree of such uncertainty varies with position and rank within the total continuum of organization. At the extreme of the continuum is the simple laborer, placed by Knight in contrast to the entrepreneur.

As previously argued, risk bearing by itself is not a characteristic that distinguishes the greater entrepreneur from the lesser entrepreneur, or even the entrepreneur from the laborer.[13] Within a capital market that facilitates trading in risk, laborers as well as entrepreneurs can partake of risk. A laborer as such need not be more risk averse than his more entrepreneurial fellow on the continuum—the laborer could hold riskier portfolios, perhaps be more prone to visit a gambling casino. Of necessity, however, the entrepreneur—unlike the nonentrepreneur—exhibits the willingness to bear the special risk of failure and bankruptcy—even, ultimately, of losing the right to continue as entrepreneur. It is in this sense and with respect to this special kind of risk that the Schumpeterian and the Knightian views come into mutual play.

To summarize: there is a continuum of decision making under uncertainty. At its lowest extreme is the laborer, his routine tasks characterized by minimal uncertainty. At the other extreme stands the most innovative entrepreneur.[14] Along the continuum, the most discriminative characteristic is the quest for novelty.

A Tentative Synthesis

It would not be useful to blur the distinction between the manager and the entrepreneur. Keeping the distinction clear will help crystallize the characteristics, decision making modes, and other aspects of the entrepreneurial function.

It may be reemphasized that the entrepreneur—in contrast to the professional manager—tends to seek novel ventures in the context of an environment of uncertainty. Within such an environment, the entrepreneur (unlike the manager, who typically maximizes expected return) limits downside risk by seeking projects with a possible maximum of losses that will not threaten his ability to survive as entrepreneur, but, contrariwise, give promise of very large returns. Unlike managerial decision making, the entrepreneur's is not truly a consensus decision. The entrepreneur thus pursuing his novel venture is the one now likely to be observed engaging in market testing, in research and development, so as to reduce uncertainty.[15]

Because of his passion for novelty, the daring entrepreneur may be willing to give up a measure of the low-risk return he might possibly secure elsewhere. More importantly, he must bear the risk of bankruptcy, which tends to be high from the very novelty of his project. To minimize this major threat to his entrepreneurial survival, he proceeds innovatively and resourcefully to devise the kind of complex financing arrangements that will lure capital. Thus, the entrepreneur's "Knightian" risk bearing—observed to accompany (of necessity) his "Schumpeterian" zeal for the new—triggers with its urgent immediacy yet another outburst of innovativeness, now in the area of a financing arrangement that seeks creative ways to avoid bankruptcy.

The entrepreneur rarely resides in a large, bureaucratic organization. The innovative ideas the entrepreneur seeks to implement (characteristically with highly uncertain prospects) sometimes require long periods of incubation. They are thus difficult to defend to those internal-capital allocators who are not so bold, who are less entrepreneurially inclined. This kind of innovative idea can run into a grim fate in a large organization given to incentive schemes that emphasize the short-run, visible-performance measures of management, militating against investment in innovative research. The uncertain results can be visible only in the longer run.

So we see the novelty-seeking entrepreneur shy away from the large, little-changing organization; conversely, the less-entrepreneurial, the managerial-type individual seeks association with (and is sought by) the large organization and, when there, discourages entrepreneur adventurers from joining its work force or staying in it. This mutual self-selection can induce a notable incidence of innovative research in small, entrepreneurial firms, while erecting within the large firm an internal capital-allocation mechanism of a bureaucratic and relatively nonflexible nature. It is the nonentrepreneurial, managerial type of individual who seems inevitably destined to house the executive suite.

A Metaphysical Digression

At the risk of being shrugged off as exhibiting an unduly high dose of metaphysical proclivities, I would also assert my strong impression that the entrepreneurially oriented are driven to continue to accumulate wealth (even after securing the consumption needs of themselves and their offspring) so as to gain a measure of "immortality." The capability of continued wealth accumulation commands power and works toward the attainment of other attributes essential to the entrepreneur: independence, prestige, freedom from outside control, and more. Very importantly, the piling up of business triumphs (and thus wealth) demands an ongoing process of action and *change*—for the intellectual entrepreneur, perhaps unexpected creativity, new ideas, continued research. Such process of continued change is antithetical to death, indeed may suppress the very awareness of one's mortality and that of one's genes. Death can be perceived as the "ultimate change": but repeated and successive "changes" (rehearsals) preceding it could blunt death's implied total discontinuity. Thus is gained some reassurance of continuity. Oblivion, too, is perchance inhibited. Worldly accomplishment, repetitive and varied—would they not be remembered?

If this metaphysical speculation has any germ of truth in it, it implies that utility functions of entrepreneurs are better specified throughout the life cycle with wealth (surrogating for immortality) as an argument in addition to the consumption vector. Also, wealth accumulation becomes a more salient objective (that is, as an argument in the utility function, wealth accumulation carries a greater weight) for those who attach less importance to what might or might not come to pass in the hereafter than to feats in the world of the living. One would then expect those whose ethos is manifest in notions of reincarnation (therefore, in due time, infinitely wealthy) to exhibit, *ceteris paribus,* a much lesser passion for the entrepreneurial attainment of wealth. Consider that for such as the Hindus (as perhaps contrasted with the Jews) the future state of infinite bliss (self-believed) must render far less urgent any entrepreneurial accumulation of worldly wealth.

Additionally, the entrepreneur's appetite for wealth seems to grow with its accumulation, thus implying a positive second derivative of utility in wealth (in contrast with accepted conventional wisdom). How, then, can a marginal utility that increases with wealth be reconciled with the observation that the more entrepreneurially oriented (successful) are no greater risk takers than those less entrepreneurially oriented? One possible explanation—which seems consistent with the interviews here reported—is that in the game of making money, winning (money gain) and losing (money loss) enter separately into the utility function with positive and negative sign, respectively. If so, one would have to formulate measures of risk aversion for the typical entrepreneur that incorporate explicitly (and separately) the signs of wealth changes.

Indeed, in their recent review of decision making, Tversky and Kahneman (1981) cite findings that are consistent with their prospect theory (1979). This theory predicts, among other things, that the value (utility) function is S-shaped—concave about a reference point (assigned a value of zero) and convex below it. Moreover, the response to losses is more extreme than the response to gains. If the reference point is continually adjusted to reflect the status quo, so that the decision maker views each choice incrementally in terms of a "minimal account" (Tversky and Kahneman 1981), then the departure from the expected utility model embedded in this aspect of prospect theory could reconcile the entrepreneur's exhibited risk taking behavior (which is no more risk seeking than that of the nonentrepreneur)[16] with a marginal utility that increases with wealth.

The immortality hypothesis above is not devoid of significant policy implications: promise of increased transfer payments after retirement (such as social security) need not increase the propensity to consume, and vice versa. Policy deliberations on such issues might, therefore, have to consider explicitly the weights attached to wealth accumulation among different groups in society.[17]

Entrepreneurial Acts and Events

As the entrepreneur becomes more managerial because of the managing-coordinating function needed in an enterprise, the decision-making process loses its entrepreneurial property. Since, then, circumstances can affect the degree to which a given individual exhibits entrepreneurial character, it would seem the more illuminating approach to discard the notion of "entrepreneur" and to concentrate on "entrepreneurial events," "entrepreneurial processes," the "entrepreneurial act." For example, Schumpeter states that "we maintain that someone is only then by definition entrepreneur if he implements new combinations—after which he loses his characteristic, where he then continues to manage the founded enterprise systematically" (p. 116).[18]

From the standpoint of encouraging entrepreneurship, what must concern us is identifying what might trigger an entrepreneurial move, regardless of how, in the given circumstances, the person engaged is identified, whether as entrepreneur or manager. Emphasis on the character "an entrepreneur" would compel us either to identify the individuals who have remained entrepreneurial throughout their lives, or find explanation for the changeover to nonentrepreneurial. On the other hand, concentrating on the entrepreneurial course must lead to closer identification of factors that encourage sparks of entrepreneurship among individuals hitherto not identifiable as entrepreneurial in any way.

A tentative description of an entrepreneurial process follows that appears to be consistent with the insights summarized above.

The Entrepreneurial Process

The entrepreneurial process consists of a sequence of entrepreneurial events. These may, or may not, culminate in a definitive entrepreneurial act. The act implies the prior occurrence of the events, however it is *not* implied that an entrepreneurial act will inevitably follow a given sequence of entrepreneurial events.

The first entrepreneurial set of events can be characterized as initiation, or invention. The set includes the following:

1. A complex evolutionary process continuously generates changing realities. These could take on fundamental forms of natural evolution (in a very long perspective), or they might appear in the form of new technological and social configurations (including, for example, changes in tastes resulting from wars, migrations, and so on).

New realities—and even some among the long-standing ones—can elude awareness. They do not exist in the consciousness of any individual until another event intrudes: their discovery. And until such reality impinges on the consciousness of the given individual, nothing can happen—no potential entrepreneurial act follows. Also, whoever does become aware of the reality might still remain totally unaware of its potential usefulness to society. The individual perceives the reality, but remains unaware that it might be useful to anyone. Thus the discovery can be obliterated from his memory and lead to no entrepreneurial consequences.

2. Discovering of the reality can lead to entrepreneurial consequences in one of two situations: (1) The discoverer might become himself aware of its potential use. (2) One of the individuals to whom he has diffused this knowledge now becomes aware of the potential uses to which it can be put. In *both* cases, we witness a diffusion of the discovery and recognition of its likely usefulness to society. Clearly, the likelihood of recognition is greater after diffusion has occurred than if the knowledge were to remain solely within the province of the original discoverer.

3. The individual who has become aware of the discovery might at once recognize the opportunity it offers. Such an individual makes the connection between the discovery and its possible supply and demand implications. The discovered object or reality can be exploited to satisfy an existing (or created) consumer demand; used as a cheaper substitute for a resource already employed in producing commodities that directly enhance consumer's utilities. Such immediate recognition is indubitably entrepreneurial. It could be the result of a serendipitous inspiration, or of a deliberate thought process initiated by the individual for the very purpose of discovering or recognizing new opportunities. It would be almost impossible to point to which process ultimately led to the given individual's recognizing the opportunity. The important fact is recognition—elsewise, for society, the discovery is waste, yields no good.

4. Until this point of time, the entrepreneurial events described have not resulted in a new entry into the economic stream. Nothing has happened yet that could be characterized or observed as economic activity. The step following the recognition of an opportunity is the one that introduces the entrepreneurial idea (recognition of the opportunity) into the economic stream. This step can be characterized as "instigation," or "promotion." In this event, the recognizer of the opportunity—the promoter—attempts to exploit his insight. He might create windfall profits either by selling his idea (the opportunity) to an entrepreneur, or by playing the entrepreneur himself, thus implementing the idea (along with other factors) into a finished product directly usable by consumers to enhance their utilities. Thus the promoter becomes the entrepreneur. But the promoter could merely attempt to sell his idea to some other entrepreneur: he may not himself have the ready resources to put together his own production factors or access to these might be too costly to finance (his track record is not good enough). Also, he may not wish to engage in the production process; just simply, adhere to the business of promotion. It follows that promotion might first require developing the idea to a stage in which it becomes salable to an entrepreneur, or acting to alert the entrepreneur to the existence of this purchasable idea.

5. The entrepreneurial act itself follows. Here a promoter directs the attention of the entrepreneur to the existence of an opportunity. His interest won, the entrepreneur makes a decision as to whether to implement the opportunity, and it is this decision to implement (for instance, by investing in research and development to examine the idea's feasibility or to develop appropriate manufacturing processes) that constitutes the entrepreneurial act. The entrepreneurial act is the culmination of the entire sequence of preceding events—these events are necessary, but not sufficient, conditions for the final act.

In making the decision to implement the idea, the entrepreneur has in mind its novel prospects—of necessity characterized by relatively uncertain distribution, but promising very high returns. (In fact, he believes he will be able to control events so as to minimize the downside risk.) Once the opportunity is implemented and its finished product has been introduced into the market, cost reducing moves are undertaken to routinize production and marketing and thus achieve efficiency. At this point, the entrepreneurial process ceases, the managerial begins. It should be noted that the process could culminate in an act either constructive or destructive. Innovative change for private ends can be initiated into the economic system in a way that proves either consistent with the social good—or inconsistent.

The Quest for Novelty

The quest for novelty has been emphasized as a primary criterion for distinguishing among different degrees of entrepreneurship. What is important to keep in mind is that innovativeness must be characterized by purposefulness. It is *purposeful human action* that defines an entrepreneurial act. Accidentally stumbling on a new market while engaging in routine improvements in the manufacturing process would not be a self-aware entrepreneurial act. To reemphasize, it is purposefulness of innovation in the market place that constitutes the essential entrepreneurial element. However, the degree of innovativeness counts, and we note how it differs along a continuum of entrepreneurship. For example, an innovation altering the sequence on five sewing machines in some apparel firm could be viewed as an entrepreneurial change in a manufacturing process. Obviously, it does not exhibit the same degree of entrepreneurship as, for example, a new method of transport from railroad to airplane. Though both entrepreneurial, factory change and revolution in travel, clearly the latter is by far the more significant. We see then that one clue to calibrating the degree of entrepreneurship is the nature of the innovation. If the innovation addresses only routine improvement of the input-output relation, making production more efficient but calling for little scanning of the outside environment for new ideas in production, the degree for entrepreneurship must be marked low. Whereas the individual constantly searching the wider environment for process or product innovation, or for changes in taste, is apt to exhibit a high degree of entrepreneurship. Commercializing a new means of transportation requires much interaction with the environment, whether through discovering an already existing means that may be usable, or through stumbling on an idea that can be developed inside the organization into some practical mode of transport. Thus, the higher the degree of interaction with the environment (broadly understood to include ideas and scientific discoveries), the higher the degree of entrepreneurship exhibited. Mere improvement of an existing routine that demands minor variations, with minimal excursions into the outer environment, typically introduces minimal shock into the system already there.

The Displacement Motive

Another of the forces in the push toward entrepreneurship was that some individuals felt "displaced," or were in dire need, or had little other choice. Low perceived opportunity costs can act as powerful inducement for exploring entrepreneurial ventures, for becoming an entrepreneur; therefore: the higher incidence of entrepreneurs among immigrants and other "outsiders", whose relatively restricted economic opportunities spell lower cost of opportunity than for established "insiders." This, certainly, is only one determinant of the supply of entrepreneurship. Furthermore, restriction of economic opportunity for "outsiders" need not necessarily be the result of discriminatory impositions. More often than not, such restrictions come down to the costs of gaining knowledge about the new community, costs of learning how to communicate effectively with economic agents who are insiders, and the costs of inspiring trust and credibility among financiers within the community ready to absorb the outsiders. These costs arise naturally, because different aggregates of people differ culturally, linguistically, and in the types of communication networks they have erected over time to facilitate the transacting of business. In a similar vein, a sociological tradition endows the displaced outsider with the perspective of cultural deviance or social marginality. Note Simmel's[19] concept of the stranger and Park's (1928) notions of the marginal man; also Veblen's interpretation of the contribution of Jews to economic and intellectual progress and Weber's emphasis on the impact of Protestantism's "worldly asceticism" on the rise of capitalism. Collins, Moore, and Uinwalla (1974) state the notion forcibly: "Our study suggests that the carriers of the basic entrepreneurial values of our society tend, paradoxically enough, to be those who are marginal to the established social networks" (p. 145).

Potential policy implications are clearly not artificially to lower (as through subsidy) the opportunity costs of either insiders or outsiders migrating from one community to another: this would be akin to subsidizing the cost of transporting workers from low-wage to high-wage regions. Rather, it would be sufficient not artificially to restrict entry from one region to the other. Potential entrepreneurs in regions with low opportunity costs might not hesitate to migrate to regions where the insiders, because of their own relatively high opportunity costs, shy away from entrepreneurial ventures. The migrators, of course, must perceive net gains above their opportunity costs plus the cost of learning how to transact in the new community and the cost of persuading financiers that they can be capable and trustworthy entrepreneurs.

The cost of inspiring trust and overcoming adverse selection (Akerlof 1970) can also explain what seems to be the higher incidence of entrepreneurship among individuals in entrepreneurial families (the father-role syndrome). Such families typically have accumulated sufficient wealth to finance the emerging new entrepreneurs of the family; furthermore, there is "the extended family aspect . . ." which "can be explained by the fact that gap-filling capacities depend in part on kinship relations in which there is a much higher degree of trust and through which one can draw on more diverse capacities than exist on a universalistic basis" (Leibenstein 1968, p. 81).

Thus, the costs of gaining credibility and of adverse selection are minimized within the closely knit network of communications among family, tribe, or neighborhood. Adopting innovations can also be facilitated when information transmission between the creator of the innovative idea and the entrepreneur (potential implementer) can be carried out at minimal cost—such as, for instance, within an organization that has developed elaborate and sophisticated communication networks for such purposes. Certain departments of banks and other financial institutions also specialize in screening and evaluating entrepreneurial ideas, as well as potential entrepreneurs ready to carry them out with the help of the bank's financing. These departments or venture-capital units exploit economies of scale in the specialized field of evaluating the credibility and trustworthiness of entrepreneurs and assessing the soundness of entrepreneurial opportunities.

Concluding Remarks

The dimensions of entrepreneurship here offered, together with our tentative synthesis, are speculations drawn from commonalities we perceived in the responses of the entrepreneurs during their in-depth interviews. At best, such speculations can but outline the rough contours of entrepreneurship; they are not refined enough to form a unit of analysis. More important, the entrepreneurial function as such remains hidden in a black box. Although the outline perhaps helps identify the series of entrepreneurial acts after they have been carried out, their antecedents remain a mystery: how *does* the entrepreneur stumble upon an opportunity; evaluate its potential and attending uncertainties; assess his ability to implement; persuade capital owners to finance; procure the labor resources and necessary managerial skills, and allocate risk between them and himself—the list is a long one.

The impressions outlined in this paper can perhaps be pulled together into a compendium of questions that form an agenda for future work. A promising procedure would be to include historical and contemporary case studies and experimentation, including the analysis of entrepreneurs who failed and the reasons for their failure. The major questions to be addressed:

1. What are the most important observable characteristics of entrepreneurial activities;

2. How are the objectives of return, quest for novelty, quest for power, quest for independence, reduction of risk, balanced in making entrepreneurial decisions; for example, will the entrepreneur sacrifice some returns in exchange for novelty, and will such exchange carry implications for the mode of organization of the business, for the multi-period investment strategy, and so on;

3. What are the effects of the fear of bankruptcy and the attempt to allay it on (a) mode of organization (b) multi-period investment decisions;

4. How is knowledge gained about existing opportunities hitherto unknown; how are probabilities assessed by the entrepreneur—that is, how do changes of probability space occur; how are decisions made, and how is the discovery of new opportunity evaluated in light of utility trade-offs (novelty, reward, risk, power, and so on) to form entrepreneurial decisions;

5. Is entrepreneurial activity subject to decay with accumulation of accomplishments or wealth (possibly along with increasing fear of bankruptcy), thus causing a shift in the locus of entrepreneurship; on the other hand, does the ability to undertake novel entrepreneurial projects increase with greater wealth;

6. How is information about discoveries diffused, what are the incentives for such diffusion; how are rewards distributed among entrepreneurs and other agents throughout the entrepreneurial process;

7. How are entrepreneurial activities aggregated, and what are the determinants of the supply of entrepreneurship; what causes entrepreneurial decay, or accretion, in the aggregate;

8. What are, in general, the effects of regulation and fiscal policy on the supply of entrepreneurship; specifically, can regulation create novel opportunities and thus increase entrepreneurial activity, and how are

novelty and rewards evaluated in the context of regulatory constraints. If regulation suppresses some entrepreneurial innovation, how is such depletion of the supply of entrepreneurship to be evaluated against the enhancement of public good the regulation is intended to bring about;

9. What are the effects of different incentive structures, modes of communication, and information networks on entrepreneurial activities in large organizations.

What became evident from the interviews is that motivational circumstances—including, importantly, profit incentives applicable to workers in organizations as well—count for as much in the sum total of entrepreneurship as any impact, negative or positive, from institutional rigidities or restrictive regulations. Thus, even in an environment with no restrictions or barriers to entry, one can encounter stagnation and reduced supply of entrepreneurship.

Some of the corners of the black box we call the entrepreneur must, over time, be illuminated (or at least what goes in and out of the box should be identified) if the effort to increase the supply of constructive entrepreneurship is to be successful. One might hope for—but despair the prospects of—such an ambitious endeavor. Yet, the challenge is too important to be missed.

Notes

1. Appendix 7A provides pertinent quotations from the interviewees' statements that supported insights reported in these sections.

2. Definitions of an entrepreneur vary over a wide spectrum. Webster's *Third New International Dictionary* (1961) defines the entrepreneur as "the organizer of an economic venture, especially one who organizes, owns, manages and assumes the risk of the business." The Funk and Wagnalls *Standard Dictionary* (1958) similarly defines him as "one who undertakes to start and conduct an enterprise or business, assuming full control and risks." Mill (1909) emphasized as entrepreneurial functions direction, control superintendence, and risk bearing. To him, risk bearing most sharply distinguished an entrepreneur from a manager. For Schumpeter, the distinguishing factor was innovation; risk taking, he believed characterized both the entrepreneur and the manager. McClelland (1961) did not even require an entrepreneur to own the business; any innovative manager could assume decision-making responsibilities. Weber (1930) considered the entrepreneur the ultimate source of formal authority within the organization, in that character distinguished from the manager. Today, many writers regard any owner-manager of a business to be an entrepreneur.

3. Indeed, it is argued that possessing value systems different from those characterizing mainstream society will contribute to unconventional patterns of behavior that often lead to entrepreneurship. For example, for Hagen (1962), deterioration in the status of a group within a society characterized by traditional values could result in the emergence of creative entrepreneurial activity. Older patterns of behavior of social group and family are no longer acceptable, and innovative ways must be sought to integrate the individual with society. Members of minority groups, exposed as they are to discriminatory treatment and prevented from obtaining established, high-status goals, are left with no choice other than venturing into the unknown (examples include immigrants and political refugees). That the urge not to conform to existing patterns of behavior can trigger the decision to become an entrepreneur is consistent with the high incidence of entrepreneurs founded among ethnic or religious minority groups: the Santri Moslems of Java; the Jains, Parsees, and Sikhs in India; the Indians and Chinese in Southeast Asia; the Lebanese in North Africa; the Ibos in Nigeria; the Jews in various parts of the world; and other minorities. (Roberts and Wainer 1966; Hagen 1962; Kasdan 1965; and DeVries 1977).

4. Whether continued accumulation of wealth becomes at some stage a proxy for immortality is a question ultimately best left to the immortals to answer. However, a few speculations are ventured in a subsequent section.

5. Review of general management and behavioral literature reveals fragmentary (and at times contradictory) evidence on the decision to become an entrepreneur. McClelland depicted indivduals with high need for achievement (n Ach) as those who take personal responsibility for solving problems and setting goals to be reached by their own efforts, together with a desire to obtain feedback pertinent to their task accomplishment. McClelland hypothesized that entrepreneurs would have high n Ach because they seemed to possess these same characteristics. In tests of this hypothesis, however, the findings McClelland interpreted to confirm the relationship between n Ach and entrepreneurial tendencies were based on a rather broad definition of an entrepreneurial occupation. Included in one of the studies, for example, were salesmen, management consultants, fundraisers, and officers of large companies, as well as actual owners of businesses. His tests, therefore, could not be used directly to establish a relationship between n Ach and the decision to own and manage a business. (See McClelland 1961, 1965, and 1969.) Still a later study (Komives 1972) revealed that twenty successful high-technology entrepreneurs were high in the achievement and decisiveness categories.

Achievement-training courses were not successful when participants' opportunities to act were stifled by the general business environment (Neck 1970) and when training in business skills was lacking (Timmons 1971). Studies that linked training and achievement motivation with entrepreneurial success were criticized (Miron and McClelland 1979) in that the observed increase in entrepreneurial tendency and profits could also have resulted from business training. Wainer and Rubin (1969) found associations between high company performance and high need for achievement along with a moderate need for power. However, Schrage (1965) found that successful research and development entrepreneurs did not have a consistently high level of achievement motive, nor were they consistent on the power motive. In all these studies, the sample was biased in favor of successful business owners, and their success could contribute to their high need for achievement rather than the reverse. No known research has attempted to correlate the decision to start a business with a natural need for achievement.

Compared to men in general, entrepreneurs scored significantly higher on the EPPS (Edward's Personal Preference Scale) reflecting need for achievement, as well as on the SIV (Gordon's Survey of Interpersonal Values) for independence and effectiveness of leadership. They scored lower on the need for support scale from the SIV. The OIS (Kuder Occupational Interest Survey) scores were not significantly different (Hornaday and Aboud 1971). Female entrepreneurs had higher EPPS scores on achievement, autonomy, and aggression than the general female population. Likewise, the SIV scores of the female entrepreneur were higher than the norm for leadership and independence. SIV scores in support, conformity, and benevolence were lower for both groups than the norm (DeCarlo and Lyons 1979). A related finding by Komives (1972) revealed that twenty high-technology entrepreneurs scored significantly higher than the general population on the leadership scale of the SIV, but significantly lower on the support and conformity scales of the SIV. Studies distinguished between *successful* entrepreneurs and the general population; they gave no index to differentiate between the general population and the entrepreneur who made an attempt and failed. Gasse (1977) found that English Canadians were more open-minded than French Canadians, less authoritarian and more tolerant. He, therefore, suggested that variety of industry might be appropriate for variety of subculture.

Entrepreneurs are significantly more satisfied than the general population with their jobs. Most dissatisfying to entrepreneurs appeared to be actual conditions of work itself: they were more unhappy with coworkers and supervisors than the average members of the normative population. In fact, entrepreneurs expressed less dissatisfaction with promotional opportunities than with the categories of work, coworkers, and supervision (Brockhaus 1980a). The data indicated that dissatisfaction with the actual work is a major source of a push from one's job.

Some (Roberts and Wainer 1966; Shapero 1971; Susbauer 1969; Collins and Moore 1964) document that an unusually high percentage of entrepreneurs had fathers who were themselves entrepreneurs. No studies were found comparing the careers of the fathers of entrepreneurs with those of the fathers of nonentrepreneurs. Brockhaus and Nord (1979) asked both managers and entrepreneurs working in new businesses if any close relative or friend had owned a business. No significant difference between the two groups was found.

Shapero (1975) referred to people without a present job (such as recent school graduates, discharged servicemen, and immigrants) and those between jobs as displaced persons. He argues that in this period, the displaced person is forced to act and make a career decision; unlike the working person, he cannot afford the luxury of staying put. Thus, displaced persons have a greater tendency to become entrepreneurs: the cost is insignificant, the regular salary of a prestigious position is not being sacrificed. Collins and Moore (1964) found that among 150 entrepreneurs interviewed in depth, 20 percent were foreign-born (the United States white population in 1960 contained less than 6 percent foreign-born). They reasoned that the foreign-born with limited opportunities found the ownership of small businesses more attractive than the native-born, who could choose from a variety of occupations.

The decision to become an entrepreneur is most likely to be made between the ages of 25 and 40 (Shapero 1971; Mayer and Goldstein 1961; Cooper 1973; Howell 1972). Liles (1974) suggested that in this age interval, an individual has acquired sufficient experience, competence, and self-confidence, but does not yet have financial and family obligations or a position of prestige and responsibility in some large company. It is a period in which the entrepreneur is most likely to be able to make a decision.

6. This is consistent with evidence reviewed by Schultz (1975) on the equilibrating performance of housewives, laborers, students, and farmers. It is also consistent with his conjecture that the ability to deal with disequilibrium is important for businessmen. For Schultz, this ability is a major element of the entrepreneurial function, and commands a price: "The ability to be among the first to act appropriately and to proceed most promptly in completing the reallocations has an economic value" (p. 842).

7. Hardly a deplorable state of affairs. At any point of time, distribution of capital ownership is such that a given percentage of capital owners are entrepreneurs, and a given percentage of those without capital are potentially capable (if penniless) entrepreneurs. Replacement of one distribution of capital ownership by another need not decrease the potential social cost of diffusing knowledge about entrepreneurial capabilities. Thus, a priori, no one particular distribution of ownership capital is superior to another (Kirzner 1979).

8. Changes in the environment tend to be viewed as opportunities by the entrepreneur and as threats by the nonentrepreneurial manager. Miles (1967) distinguishes between the general and specific segments of the envi-

ronment. "General environmental conditions" can be thought of as those that are potentially relevant for the focal organization. Moreover, the organization is not typically in touch with these elements on a day-to-day basis; it must create special environmental scanning and monitoring activities to deal with them. In the category of general environmental conditions Miles includes technological, legal, political, economic, demographic, ecological, and cultural elements. In contrast, he characterizes "specific environmental conditions" as those that have immediate relevance for the focal organization. These conditions include organizations or individuals that a focal organization directly interacts with. Miles's general segment of the environment characterizes the opportunity set faced by the typical entrepreneur.

Another perspective of the environment that can perhaps be helpful in analyzing entrepreneurship is the linkage model proposed by Emery and Trist (1965). They classify organizational interdependencies into three categories—(1) internal (L 11), (2) transactional (L 21, input and L 12, output) and (3) environmental (L 22)—by the "causal texture," or degree of interconnectedness (the extent to which a change in one portion of the environment affects another portion), and by movement (the rate of change in environmental elements). The latter two dimensions (interconnectedness and movement) can perhaps be used to partition cell 2 of Perrow's matrix (the nonroutine tasks) to further refine the characterization of the entrepreneur's environment.

9. This may partially explain the difficulty many entrepreneurial organizations encounter when they attempt to identify a successor to the original entrepreneur. The entrepreneur's preference for personalized relationships might also illuminate the difficulty some organizations have in growing. Growth necessitates an increasingly sophisticated information network and greater decentralization. Efficient and effective large organizations require managerial attributes—they cannot solely rely on the entrepreneurial spark.

10. Burns and Stalker (1961) studied the effects of the rates of change of technological innovation and markets on the management systems of twenty British and Scottish firms. As a result of their observations, they classified their sample organizations into two groups: mechanistic and organic. In the mechanistic organizations, "each individual pursues his task as something distinct from the real tasks of the concern as a whole; as if it were the subject of a subcontract. Somebody at the top is responsible . . . , operations and workmen behavior are governed by instructions and decisions issued by superiors. This command hierarchy is maintained by the implicit assumption that all knowledge about the situation of the firm and its tasks is, or should be, available only to the head of the firm." By implication, a mechanistic system does not adapt well to rapid changes in the environment.

Burns and Stalker state that "organic systems are adapted to unstable conditions when problems and requirements for action arise which cannot be broken down and distributed among specialist roles within clearly defined hierarchy. Individuals have to perform their special tasks in the light of their knowledge or the tasks of the firms as a whole. Jobs lose much of their formal definition in terms of efforts, duties and powers, which have to be redefined continually by interaction with others participating in a task. Interaction runs laterally as much as vertically. Communication between people of different ranks tends to resemble lateral consultation rather than vertical command. Omniscience can no longer be imparted to the head of the concern" (p. 121).

It would appear that the type of management system employed by the entrepreneur is a hybrid. The hybrid system possesses such mechanistic elements as: there is somebody "at the top," interaction within the organization is vertical, and instructions and decisions are issued by the entrepreneur himself. It also includes organic elements: the organization is adaptable, it consists of flat structures, jobs are redefined by interaction, and interaction runs laterally as well as vertically.

11. Among these, very few are willing to take much *financial* risk. Most, however, were willing to expose themselves to considerable social and psychological risks (a decline in prestige and status in the initial phase of entrepreneurship). While Knight (1940) viewed the entrepreneur as the assumer of nonquantifiable uncertainties, many entrepreneurs seem to be able innovatively to share uncertainties with investors whom they resourcefully identify and persuade to bear some of the risk burden.

12. Put differently, a relatively low degree of risk aversion is a necessary, but not sufficient, condition for entrepreneurship. The probability of exhibiting entrepreneurial activity under this condition is greater than under a relatively high degree of risk aversion.

13. McClelland (1961) determined that a high n Ach is associated with moderate risk taking propensities. Two of the major considerations in the decision to become an entrepreneur seem to be the perceived degree of risk and the probable consequences of the financially unsuccessful venture. The risks involved include damage to financial well-being, career opportunities, family relations, and psychic well-being (Liles 1974). Atkinson (1957) hypothesized that performance level would be highest when there is greatest uncertainty about the outcome (subjective probability of .5) Persons with strong achievement motives would prefer intermediate risks, while those for whom the motive to avoid failure is stronger would avoid intermediate risk, preferring either very easy and safe undertakings or extremely difficult and speculative ones. Presumably the person with the stronger motivation to avoid failure will either succeed with the safe task or find the failure of the very speculative task easy to explain.

McClelland (1961) speculated that the individual's perception of his degree of control and skill is most important in moderately risky circumstances, rather than in either very risky or very certain circumstances. No more than average ability is needed to perform a safe function, whereas no amount of skill can help in a situation of pure chance.

In a study by Brockhaus (1980b), no significant differences were found between the responses of entrepreneurs and managers on the choice dilemmas questionnaire (CDQ) developed by Kogan and Wallach (1964). For the purpose of that study, risk-taking propensity was defined as the perceived probability of success required by an individual before he is willing to subject himself to the consequences of failure. Moreover, data in the study indicated that the level of risk-taking propensity does not distinguish new entrepreneurs from either managers or from the general population. Also, no significant differences were found between the CDQ scores of entrepreneurs whose businesses still existed three years after the scores were obtained and entrepreneurs whose businesses no longer existed (Brockhaus 1980a). Thus, it appears that risk-taking propensity is not related to either the entrepreneurial decision or to the success of the enterprise. However, as the CDQ measures only one component of risk, other components might successfully distinguish between entrepreneurs on the one hand and managers and the general population on the other. Some of the pertinent other components are the perceived consequences of failure for a specific venture. Also, the probability of failure for any given venture can change with the acquisition of information about the competition, the amount of capitalization required, the managerial and technical knowledge and skills required, and so on.

Liles (1974) noted that the decision to start a business depends on the entrepreneur's perception of the risk involved and the degree of control he believes he will have over the venture's outcome. Rotter (1966) defined a belief in external control as the perception that reinforcement is not entirely contingent upon the individual's action, but rather is a result of luck, chance, fate, or the control of others. Conversely, when the person perceives events to be contingent upon his own behavior or on his relatively permanent characteristics, he is considered to believe in internal control. Various studies show that the belief in an internal locus of control is associated with a more active role by individuals in manipulating events. (Atkinson (1957); McClelland 1961; McGhee and Crandall 1968; Gurin, Gurin, Las, and Beattie 1969; Lao 1970; Shapero 1975; Brockhaus 1975; Borland 1974; and Brockhaus and Nord 1979). This general belief and its associated effort hold true for both successful entrepreneurs and successful managers.

14. This is reminiscent of Sawyer's speculation (1958) that entrepreneurship comprises "a more or less continuous set of functions running from the purely innovative toward the purely routine," performed within

business firms or other agencies "at many levels of initiative and responsibility—wherever significant decisions involving change are made affecting the combination and commitment of resources under conditions of uncertainty" (p. 439).

15. The observable characteristics of the entrepreneur delineated in this synthesis are consistent with, but extend beyond, commonly stated definitions—especially with respect to the mode of decision making. As an example, consider Leibenstein's four major characteristics (1968): "He connects different markets, he is capable of making up for market deficiencies (gap-filling), he is an input-completer, and he creates or expands time-binding, input-transforming entities (for example, firms)" (p. 75).

16. An approach similar to that of Kahneman and Tversky suggests that risk can be measured as a probability weighted function of returns below a target (Fishburn 1977). This approach and that of Kahneman and Tversky (in particular, its emphasis on a reference point or target return) found empirical support in the experimental work of Payne, Laughhunn, and Crum (1980).

17. Reacting to speculation on the possible connections between entrepreneurial wealth accumulation and the quest for immortality (together with the attending policy implications) my colleague, Professor Mordecai Kurz, affirmed that data he gathered in his research project on social security suggest that there is a human tendency to accumulate wealth, even after retirement, beyond what could be normally explained by the life-cycle hypothesis. This is consistent with an immortality hypothesis.

18. See Schumpeter (1931) as translated by M. DeVries (1977).

19. See Wolff (1950) for Simmel's treatment of this topic.

References

Aitken, H.G.J., ed. *Explorations in Enterprise.* Cambridge, Ma.: Harvard University Press, 1965.

Akerlof, G.A. "The Market for 'Lemons': Qualitative Uncertainty in the Market Mechanism." *Quarterly Journal of Economics* (August 1970).

Atkinson, J.W. "Motivational Determinants of Risk Taking Behavior." *Psychological Review* (1957).

Borland, C. "Locus of Control, Need for Achievement and Entrepreneurship." Doctoral dissertation, The University of Texas at Austin, 1974.

Brockhaus, R.H. "I-E Locus of Control Sources as Predictors of Entrepreneurial Intentions. *"Proceedings,* Academy of Management, New Orleans, 1975.

————. "Psychological and Environmental Factors Which Distinguish the Successful from the Unsuccessful Entrepreneur: A Longitudinal Study." Paper submitted for the Academy of Management Meeting, 1980a.

———. "Risk Taking Propensity of Entrepreneurs." Academy of Management Journal (September 1980b).

Brockhaus, R.H., and Nord, W.R. "An Exploration of Factors Affecting the Entrepreneurial Decision: Personal Characteristics vs. Environmental Conditions." Proceedings, National Academy of Management, 1979.

Burns, T., and Stalker, G. The Management of Innovation. London: Tavistock, 1961.

Collins, D.F., and Moore, D.G. The Organizational Makers. New York: Meredith, 1970.

Collins, D.F., Moore, D.G., and Unwalla, D.B. The Enterprising Man. East Lansing: Michigan State University Bureau of Business and Economic Research, 1964.

Cooper, A.C. "Technical Entrepreneurship: What Do We Know?" Research and Development Management (February 1973).

DeCarlo, J.F., and Lyons, P.R. "A Comparison of Selected Personal Characteristics of Minority and Non-Minority Female Entrepreneurs." Journal of Small Business Management 17 (October 1979).

DeVries, M.F.R.K. "The Entrepreneurial Personality: A Person at the Crossroads." Journal of Management Studies (February 1977):34-57.

Downs, A. Inside Bureaucracy. Boston: Little, Brown, 1966.

Dutton, J.M., and Freedman, R.D. "Calculating and Experimenting in a Theory of the Firm." Unpublished manuscript, New York University, 1980.

Emery, F., and Trist, E. "The Causal Texture of Organizational Environments." Human Relations 18 (1965).

———. Towards a Social Ecology. Plenum, 1973.

Fishburn, P.C. "Mean-Risk Analysis with Risk Associated with Below-Target Returns." American Economic Review 67 (1977).

Gasse, Y. Entrepreneurial Characteristics and Practices. Sherbrooke, Quebec: Rene Prince Imprimeur, 1977.

Gurin, P., Gurin, G., Las, R., and Beattie, M.M. "Internal-External Control in the Motivational Dynamics of Negro Youth." Journal of Social Issues (1969).

Hagen, E.E. On the Theory of Social Change: How Economic Growth Begins. Homewood, Il.: Dorsey, 1962.

Hornaday, J.A., and Aboud, J. "Characteristics of Successful Entrepreneurs." Personnel Psychology (Summer 1971).

Howell, R.P. "Comparative Profiles-Entrepreneurs versus the Hired Executive: San Francisco Peninsula Semiconductor Industry." Technical Entrepreneurship: A Symposium, 1972.

Kahneman, D., and Tversky, A. "Prospect Theory: An Analysis of Decision Under Risk." *Econometrica* (March 1979).

Kanbur, S.M. "Of Risk Taking and the Personal Distribution of Income." *Journal of Political Economy* (1979).

Kasdan, L. "Family Structure, Migration and the Entrepreneur." *Comparative Studies in Society and History* 7 (1965).

Kihlstrom, R.E., and Laffont, J.J. "A General Equilibrium Entrepreneurial Theory: A Front Formulation Based on Risk Aversion." *Journal of Political Economy* 4 (1979).

Kirzner, I.M. *Competition and Entrepreneurship.* Chicago: University of Chicago Press, 1973.

———. *Perception, Opportunity, and Profit.* Chicago: University of Chicago Press, 1979.

Knight, F.H. *Risk, Uncertainty and Profit.* 5th ed. Boston: Houghton Mifflin, 1940.

Kogan, N., and Wallach, M.A. *Risk Taking,* New York: Holt, Rinehart and Winston, 1964.

Komives, J.L. "A Preliminary Study of the Personal Values of High Technology Entrepreneurs." In A. Cooper and J. Komives (eds.), *Technical Entrepreneurship: A Symposium,* 1972.

Lao, R.C. "Internal-External Control and Competent and Innovative Behavior Among Negro College Students." *Journal of Personality and Social Psychology* 14 (1970).

Laughhunn, D.J., Payne, J.W., and Crum, R. "Managerial Risk Preferences for Below-Target Returns." *Management Science* (December 1980).

Leibenstein, H. "Entrepreneurship and Development." *American Economic Review* (May 1968).

Liles, P.R. *New Business Ventures and the Entrepreneur.* Homewood, Il: Irwin, 1974.

Mayer, K.B., and Goldstein, S. *The First Two Years: Problems of Small Firm Growth and Survival.* Washington, D.C.: Small Business Administration, U.S. Government Printing Office, 1961.

McClelland, D.C. *The Achieving Society.* Princeton, N.J.: Van Nostrand, 1961.

———. "Achievement Motivation Can be Developed." *Harvard Business Review* (1965).

———, and Winter, D.G. *Motivating Economic Achievement.* New York: Free Press, 1969.

McGhee, P.E., and Crandall, V.D. "Beliefs in Internal-External Control of Reinforcement and Academic Performance." *Child Development* (1968).

Miles, R. *Macro-Organizational Behavior,* Santa Monica, Ca.: Goodyear, 1967.

Mill, J.S. *Principles of Political Economy.* Edited with an introduction by Siv W.J. Ashley; Toronto and New York: Longmans, Green, and Co. 1909, as reprinted 1926.

Miron, D., and McClelland, D. "The Impact of Achievement Motivation Training on Small Businesses." *California Managment Review* (Summer 1979).

Neck, P. "Report on Achievement Motivation Training Program Conducted in Uganda." June 1969 to December 1970.

Park, R.E. "Human Migration and Marginal Man." *The American Journal of Sociology* (May 1928).

Payne, J.W., Laughhunn, D.J., and Crum, R. "Translation of Gambles and Aspiration Level Effects in Risky Choice Behavior." Management Science (October 1980).

Perrow, C. *Organizational Analysis: A Sociological Review.* Belmont, Ca.: Wadsworth, 1970.

Roberts, E.B., and Wainer, H.A. "Some Characteristics of Technical Entrepreneurs." *Research Program on the Management of Science and Technology.* Massachusetts Institute of Technology, 1966, pp. 145–166.

Rotter, J.B. "Generalized Expectancies for Internal Versus External Control of Reinforcement." *Psychological Monographs* (1966).

Sawyer, J.E. "Entrepreneurial Studies: Perspectives and Directions, 1948–1958." *Business History Review* (Winter 1958):434–443.

Schrage, H. "The R&D Entrepreneur: Profile of Success." *Harvard Business Review* (November–December 1965).

Schultz, T.W. "The Value of the Ability to Deal with Disequilibria." *Journal of Economic Literature* (September 1975).

Schumpeter, J.A. "Theorie der Wirtschaftlichen Entwicklung, e Aufl.," Munchen und Leibzig; Duncker und Humdlat, 1931.

Shapero, A. "An Action Program of Entrepreneurship." Multi-Disciplinary Research Inc., Austin, Texas, 1971.

———. "The Displaced, Uncomfortable Entrepreneur." *Psychology Today* (November 1975).

Simon, H.A. "Rational Choice and the Structure of the Environment." *Psychological Review* (1956).

Stigler, G.J. "Imperfections in the Capital Market." *Journal of Political Economy* (June 1967).

Susbauer, J.C. "The Technical Company Formation Process: A Particular Aspect of Entrepreneurship." Ph.D. dissertation, University of Texas, Austin, Texas, 1969.

———. "The Technical Entrepreneurship Process in Austin, Texas," in A. Cooper and J. Komives (eds.), *Technical Entrepreneurship: A Symposium.* Milwaukee: The Center for Venture Management, 1972.

Timmons, J.A. "Black is Beautiful—Is it Bountiful?" *Harvard Business Review* (November–December 1971).
Tversky, A., and Kahneman, D. "The Framing of Decisions and the Psychology of Choice." *Science* (January 1981).
Wainer, H.A., and Rubin, I.M. "Motivation of R&D Entrepreneurs: Determinants of Company." *Journal of Applied Psychology* (1969).
Weber, Max. *The Protestant Ethic and the Spirit of Capitalism.* Translated by Talcott Parsons. New York: Scribner, 1930.
Weick, K.E. "Cognitive Processes in Organizations," in B.M. Staw, *Research in Organizational Behavior,* vol. 1. JAI Press, 1979.
Wolff, K.H., ed. *The Sociology of George Simmel.* Glencoe: Il.: Free Press, 1950.

Appendix 7A

This appendix supplies quotations culled from interviewees' comments that supported insights presented in the text. The pertinent passages are indicated in the text by numbered references.

1. "I think he (the entrepreneur) would tend to be more of a free individual who has certain values which if they weren't met, he'd seek other applications of his abilities in other climates."
2. "The money I think became more important than it should have been. It was very important. The fear of not having it was very threatening."
3. "Even in my career, I'm a displaced person. I went to the opposite end of the world to get away from my background and it's perfectly understandable and rational."
4. "I soon realized that when you join a large organization you have two choices: you can either get in the corporate cocoon and rock along and not have any problems, well that certainly wouldn't be for me. I would have been bored to death . . ."

   ". . . all of sudden I look back and I say hey, come on guy, you're doing the same damn thing thirty years later, you've got enough, why don't you do something worthwhile? . . ."
5. "I think that 'X' is an example of it. He certainly accumulated a lot of wealth and continued to want to invent. Other people I think in history have shown that it isn't necessarily wealth that they aspire to . . . it's the productive creative mind."
6. "Authority is a better word than power. A man stripped of authority couldn't carry out his program to promote what he thinks would be a successful enterprise—if he didn't have the authority which you convey as power."

   "Once you are wealthy, you are financially independent, that objective is accomplished. It must be something in addition to that."

   "Surprisingly, it is not wealth, it is not money. It is some recognition that whatever the project was that became successful, the innovator or the entrepreneur has a sense of satisfaction that his judgment was better, witness the fact the enterprise was successful, and I think that's number one. Money follows, money comes, recognition of others comes if the enterprise is successful, so I think the driving force is the desire to demonstrate to others judgmental ability of the entrepreneur that he was correct in taking measured risk."

   "I think the primary objective of an entrepreneur is to create, to develop something new, to push back frontiers and to see that creation resolved in some commercial or let's say practical application.''

"No, I don't think so. I think, oh, if you went back into the late 19th century the whole game was to accumulate wealth, power, but I think today there's a great deal of ego involved. I think business is a lot of ego.''

"Oh, I think there's prestige, wealth, ego, power. I don't think wealth can be a single motivating factor. A good example of that is . . . stepping down from a $600,000 a year position to $100,000 a year position. It is a personal satisfaction.''

"There are some men that are never satisfied until they carry the top burden as I like to look at it, you call it power and authority. They are restless until they arrive at that.''

"This is his ego. He's an entrepreneur and I think this is what most people are.''

"I don't think it's just that. One of my friends referred to it as the power and the glory.''

"Security, yes. Security and recognition. He wants to be recognized for his achievement, be it by bonus, increase in merit, increase in perks, or whatever, but he's not trying to reach for the big ring, he wants to make steady progress. He doesn't want to be charged with too many mistakes because he doesn't want to mar his record.''

7. "Today as you well know, I assume that there are so many rules, so many regulations that it could be frightening sometimes.''

"Then on the other hand another department will prolongate regulations or operational laws which make it difficult to finance or get reward for financing or difficult to put the concept into practice because of environmental concern or social concerns . . . Yes, they fight each other, no question about it.''

"I think entrepreneurial activities are being discouraged by the government with their tax program.''

"I think government policy regulations are getting terrible.''

"There is a need. I'm not saying that government does not belong in business. What I'm saying is that they have overdone it, we've got too much government in business and the unfortunate thing is that the only way through which this has ever been overcome in other countries, has been through revolution and they wind up with a dictatorship.''

8. "Yes, an entrepreneur shoots from the hip most of the time in recognizing an opportunity.''

"Of course, yes, he sees it when no one else sees it. He has the vision to envision the development that isn't visible to the plodder.''

"I do believe that the distinction between a manager and an entrepreneur is an extra insight and alertness.''

9. "Yes. I could never really give up the management, the really important management controls to others. I did develop a group of officers, the conventional personnel people, computer people. I had an executive vice president whom I finally put in charge of operations but I held a very tight rein."

   ". . . An entrepreneur is an independent individual who believes himself capable of making most of the decisions that have to be made."

10. ". . . therefore the able man will get all the information. He will consult his advisors, engineers, bankers, specialists in that field. One who is driven to doing things emotionally is destined to be a failure because he hasn't the facts."

11. ". . . You really weigh all these pros and cons and if it has a risk that's reasonable . . . That's how your arrive at a decision. You have options to look at."

    "Is it fatal? It's like being on the battlefront. You don't mind getting a few shrapnel wounds but you don't want to be fatally pushed out of the picture."

**Part III
Entrepreneurship in
Yugoslavia and
the Soviet Union**

8

Entrepreneurship under Labor Participation: The Yugoslav Case

Abram Bergson

Introduction

In world affairs, Yugoslavia is often a focus of attention because of its strategic location between East and West and the ruling Communist Party's policy of nonalignment with either side. From an academic standpoint, though, it is perhaps of more interest as a country where the social system is socialist in a rather novel sense. Although private ownership of the means of production has been largely excluded, it has been superseded not by public ownership as commonly understood, but by "social ownership." The precise nature of that category is disputed by Yugoslavs themselves, but the devolution to workers of substantial responsibilities and rights normally associated with ownership is clearly among legal first principles.

Practice in Yugoslavia often diverges notably from legal doctrine, but the resulting social system still represents the most far-reaching application so far of labor participation in industrial administration. As such, it has attracted much attention from Western scholars. Yugoslav scholars too have not neglected their novel scheme; rather, they themselves have long been producing an impressive volume of research on it.

The resultant inquiries have only rarely focused on the impact of the new system on entrepreneurship (clearly a cardinal issue under any form of labor participation). Even though emphases tend to be elsewhere, however, the studies still often bear on that matter. Among other things, administrative and financial working arrangements that have been elucidated from other standpoints can be read, if only provisionally, as indicating entrepreneurial motivation. Not infrequently, they relate to entrepreneurship more generally. A review by a nonspecialist will hopefully provide further insight, while serving to underline knowledge gaps relating to an important theme.[1]

In economics, entrepreneurship means various things, but risk taking by producers is almost always a cardinal feature. Discussion of entrepreneurship in this sense often focuses on innovation (for instance, the intro-

To my profit, Stephen R. Sacks and Oliver E. Williamson commented on an earlier version of this chapter. I alone, of course, am responsible for any errors.

duction of new technologies and products) where risk is apt to be especially important. Risk taking, however, is also of interest in other contexts. Here, I consider producer risk taking in general terms, though I refer to innovation as an outstanding case.

Producer risk taking occurs when new production units are established and when existing ones are operated. Of these two sorts of activities, the first is more often innovative than the second, but by inquiring into the operation of existing production units, we can draw on a relatively developed body of theoretical analysis. Here, I focus on risk taking by existing production units, although the founding of new ones cannot be entirely ignored.[2]

The Communist Party (since 1952, the League of Communists) came to power in Yugoslavia immediately after World War II. In economic affairs, the new government began as all other newly communist governments in Eastern Europe were doing: wherever feasible (and sometimes where not especially so), it simply replicated Soviet economic working arrangements. These included the characteristic Soviet hierarchical administrative system, with workers serving as hired employees more or less as in the West.

These arrangements were in effect in the summer of 1948, at the time of the famous break of Tito with Stalin. It was not until 1950–1952 that the government took steps to supplant them with a mechanism stressing labor participation. The system that now prevails, however, could hardly spring into existence full-grown. Rather, it evolved in the course of years, not always in a linear way, and through a bewildering number of reforms. Arrangements for labor participation nevertheless reached a relatively mature form by the mid-1960s. Measures introduced in 1964–1965 and referred to collectively as the "economic reform of 1965" are often cited specifically as initiating such an advanced phase. As it turns out, these measures were hardly definitive, but the experience after they were enacted is of particular interest here.

Our concern is especially with agencies administering production units. The chief of these is the enterprise (*preduzeće; poduzeće*). The enterprise, like a Western firm, is in charge of one or more production units. This has been the primary legal entity administering the Yugoslav economy. Or rather that has been so until the last years. In the ever-evolving Yugoslav system of labor participation, even the status of the enterprise has lately been in flux.

Theoretical Considerations

Labor participation is a theme that lends itself readily to theoretical analysis. At all events, it has often been so treated. Although often inspired by

the experience in Yugoslavia, the analysis is notably abstract and is sometimes rather remote from Yugoslav practice. It can still serve here, however,
as a point of departure.

Relevant aspects for the most part are by now fairly familiar and need
be set forth only briefly. In this type of economy, firms administering production units obtain their inputs (apart from labor) and dispose of their outputs in conventional markets. These are usually envisaged as of a competitive sort. Each firm determines for itself the volume of nonlabor inputs it
will purchase. With the labor at its disposal, the firm also determines the
volume of its output.

The firm determines labor inputs too, but rather than hire workers in a
market, it in effect coopts them as members of the enterprise collective. It is
the collective that ultimately controls the firm. For their part, workers are
free to seek employment in one firm or another in accord with their preferences and talents. It goes without saying that households are also free to
spend their earnings as they wish in the market for consumer goods.

A "labor-managed" firm (LMF)—to use the usual designation for such
an enterprise—might be motivated variously. In theoretical analyses, however, attention is most often focused on one particular hypothesis. Workers
in an LMF are supposedly claimants to residual income that remains after
expenses for nonlabor inputs are met. The individual worker, therefore,
receives as his remuneration a share of this residual income rather than a
conventional wage. According to the hypothesis referred to, the firm, in
conducting its affairs, seeks to maximize residual income per worker.

To be precise, if Y denotes the firm's residual income, then

$$Y = p_x X - \sum_i q_i R_i \qquad (8.1)$$

where X is the firm's output; p_x, its price; R_i, the ith nonlabor input employed; and q_i, the price of R_i. For simplicity, the formula is given for a
firm producing a single product. For a durable capital good, q_i must be
considered a rental charge, compounded of interest and depreciation. If for
the moment the labor force is taken to be homogeneous, the hypothesis is
that the firm pursues as a maximand,

$$y = \frac{p_x X - \sum_i q_i R_i}{L} \qquad (8.2)$$

where L is the number of workers employed and thus sharing in residual
income. Residual income is also designated as net income, although in that
case the earnings in question are understood to be net before any charge for
labor inputs.

The behavior produced by the pursuit of *y* as a maximand has been the subject of extensive analysis. Suffice it to say that for the LMF (as for its private-enterprise counterpart) there is generally a determinate equilibrium of inputs and outputs.[3] For nonlabor inputs, the specific conditions for such equilibrium are similar for the two sorts of firms. Thus, as the primers teach, the private-enterprise firm employs each nonlabor input up to the point where the value of its marginal product equals its price. That is so for nonlabor inputs generally, even though for durable capital goods (which tend to be fixed in the short run) the equality can be realized only in the long run. In equilibrium, the value of marginal product and price must also be equal for nonlabor inputs in an LMF.

For a private-enterprise firm, however, that equality also obtains for labor inputs. For the LMF, the corresponding equilibrium requirement has the novel form:

$$p_x \cdot \text{MPL} = y \qquad (8.3)$$

where MPL is the marginal productivity of labor. This one singular feature is rather consequential. Because of it, the response of the labor-managed firm to changes in the prices of nonlabor inputs and the prices of outputs is apt to be different from that of the private enterprise firm; indeed, often paradoxically so.[4]

The foregoing refers to the equilibrium of the firm. Imposition of the usual requirement that prices are at clearing levels leads at once to the concept of the equilibrium for a market. As was done for a private-enterprise system, conditions are also elaborated for equilibrium for the economy in general. In addition to the simultaneous clearing of all markets, there must be no opportunity for workers to gain by leaving one firm for another that is prepared to coopt them, nor any incentive for firms in one industry to shift to another or for workers to leave firms that employ them in order to create new ones. The opportunity to form new firms supposedly also precludes involuntary unemployment.

In the diverse sorts of equilibria that thus materialize, only one feature, already implied, merits note here: the marginal value product (and hence earnings) of labor may differ in different firms. That is almost inevitable in the short run, when enterprise capital stocks, the particular firms in any industry, and the technologies that they use are given. In time, workers whose earnings suffer because of limitations in the capital goods and technologies they employ have an opportunity to remedy such deficiencies, either within the firms where they are employed or by creating new ones. By shifting their firm's output mix or industry, they might also repair any shortfall caused by the adverse state of demand. Such adjustments, however, might take a very long time.

At this point, then, the labor-managed economy is in dramatic contrast to the private-enterprise economy, where the marginal-value product and earnings of labor tend towards parity in different firms even in the short run. There is also a corresponding contrast of the two systems from the standpoint of efficiency, which requires that marginal-value products of any factor should be the same in all uses. This fact has often been stressed (no doubt properly) in the normative appraisal of labor management, but the comparative efficiency of that system and the private-enterprise economy is a complex and manysided matter that need not be systematically pursued here.[5]

I have been considering an economy with a homogeneous labor force. Since the labor force is homogeneous, all of the workers in any firm share equally in net income. Should income shares vary because of differences in labor skills and tasks, the firm's maximand is usually understood to be net income per standard worker. A standard worker is labor of a particular kind. Other kinds of work are expressed in terms of it by reference to their relative shares in net income per unit of labor. The comparative shares accruing to labor of different kinds might be determined independently by each firm, but in maximizing earnings per standard worker, each firm seeks to employ different kinds of labor so that their marginal productivities are proportional to their relative earnings per unit of labor. Different firms should also be impelled by market forces to align their schedules of relative earnings for different kinds of labor.[6]

Attention has been focused on the competitive case—strictly speaking, the case of perfect competition, in which each firm is too small to have any control over input or output prices. In theoretical analyses, alternative sorts of markets where firms exercise monopoly power have also been analyzed. As might be expected, monopoly power is in itself a source of divergencies of labor marginal products in different firms, but that, of course, is also true in the private-enterprise system.[7]

Attention up to this point has been focused on an essentially static economy. As in the private enterprise firm, the LMF must often decide on matters involving a choice between income in different time periods. The question is thus posed as to whether, and to what extent, income should be retained to finance investment. This question is not central here, but a basic aspect is the nature of the firm's maximand when income accrues over time to a staff whose personal composition may shift. That is also a matter that might be (and in theoretical writings, has been) treated variously, but one hypothesis is especially plausible: the enterprise is administered in the interest of the current collective.

To the extent that different workers might anticipate different tenures and have different time preference rates, the implied maximand could still be complex, but a corollary is fairly evident: the current staff has only limited interest in building up their equity in the firm by plowing back current income. The resulting increase in the capital stock, it must be understood, must remain indefinitely with the firm. In other words, the capital is not vested with the workers who generate it, and so does not accrue to them on their departure from the firm. Hence, if the current staff is to retain and invest earnings, rather than distribute them among themselves, they must earn a rate of return that compensates not only for their time preference but for the nonrecovery of principal.

Formally, let the workers' desired savings S be represented by a function

$$S = F(r) \tag{8.4}$$

where r is the rate of earned interest. Assuming that the principal is recovered, r also corresponds to the workers' marginal rate of time preference. Then the desired saving can be expressed as a function

$$S = F^*(R) \tag{8.5}$$

where R is the rate needed to induce S when principal is not recoverable. It can be shown that

$$R = \frac{r(1 + r)^n}{(1 + r)^n - 1} \tag{8.6}$$

Here n is the expected tenure of the current staff. I refer to a simple case where $S(r)$ and r are constant from year to year. With r as the rate of discount, an income stream of r times a principal sum over any period has a present value equal to the principal—provided the principal is recoverable. Without recovery of principal, the same equality obtains for an income stream of R times a principal sum over the period n. Evidently R (let us call it the adjusted marginal rate of time preference) must exceed r. Depending on n, the margin between the two rates could be wide. The margin declines, however, as n increases.

Should staff members withdraw earnings, they might still have the option, say, of depositing funds in a savings bank at interest. Since the principal presumably would be recoverable in that case, formula (8.4) indicates the individual savings that would occur in that way for any r equal to savings deposit interest. From formula (8.6), we see that self-financing would supersede such individual savings only if the rate of return on enterprise investment equals or exceeds the corresponding R.

Even so, self-financing of investment could occur (depending on the actual rate of return, but from the standpoint of the current staff, such action might still be groundless if another option were open. If unrestricted credit were available, the current staff would prefer to borrow rather than to finance marginal investments internally whenever the market rate of interest is, for the volume of investment in question, less than R.[8]

I have been considering the labor-managed firm as it functions in a risk-less world. For our purposes, the alternative environment where there is uncertainty is of particular interest, but again, what is chiefly in question is the enterprise's maximand. In theoretical writings, attention has focused on a natural extension of the maximand considered in the nonstochastic case: the concern of the firm is to maximize the expected utility of its staff members. Suppose, for convenience, that reference is again to a single period, that members of the collective derive income only from work for the enterprise, and that all have the same von Neumann-Morgenstern utility function, $U(y)$. The maximand of the firm is then[9]

$$y^* = EU(y) \tag{8.7}$$

One implication is obvious but nevertheless important here. It merits more attention than it has received in theoretical writings to date: In order to choose risky over safe options, the LMF requires a higher risk premium than a comparable private-enterprise one. That is to say, the LMF is more prone to risk avoidance than a comparable private enterprise one. Such a pattern derives from the fact that workers are apt to be less affluent than owners of a private enterprise and should, therefore, be subject to a greater degree of risk aversion on that account. A marked tendency to risk avoidance on the part of the LMF is offset to an extent because losses and gains are distributed over many workers, but a corresponding distribution over many owners is also realized in the corporate form of private enterprise.

Given that kind of organization, owners of a private enterprise are less inclined to avoid risk if they can diversify their investments. To achieve a comparable diversification, workers in the LMF would have to be members of many firms at the same time. Such diversification is not very feasible.

Theory teaches that, other things being equal, the greater risk premium that obtains in choices among stochastic alternatives, the less efficient (in a stochastic sense) is the allocation of the community's resources. Among decision makers with the same utility functions, the higher the risk premium, the greater the degree to which opportunities for costless gains from insurance against risk remain unexploited. The difference between the two sorts of enterprises in posture toward risk, therefore, are in that sense a source of economic waste.[10]

This posture toward risk might be manifest in various forms, but it should be particularly prominent in decisions regarding innovation, for risk is especially important there. Losses due to excessive risk premiums, therefore, should take the form of foregone innovations.

To finance investment out of retained earnings, the enterprise must earn a differential return (possibly a sizeable one) over the rate available to individual workers if the income in question is distributed to them and they deposit it in a savings account. If workers are averse to risk, the premium must be larger, for savings invested in the firm are necessarily at risk.

Theoretical writings are not too explicit about the status of banks in the labor-managed economy, particularly whether they too are to be labor-managed. In whatever way they are organized, the government presumably must reserve for itself revenues generated by the expansion of the money supply. The government will also earn interest on any funds it contributes to capital markets. If, as is appropriate here, natural resources are assumed to be publicly owned, rentals for their use would accrue to the government as well. Should the government require still more revenue, there is, or course, no bar to its levying taxes. As in a private-enterprise economy, however, these ideally must be lump-sum taxes; otherwise inefficiency is unavoidable for well-known reasons. The incidental result is that the government must ideally refrain from varying its levies in such ways as the use of surtaxes on high incomes, which would limit variations in labor earnings and in effect the incidence of risk on workers.[11]

All this, however, presupposes that workers in the LMF are indeed residual claimants to income. As such, like owners of a private enterprise, they become in effect primary risk-bearers, and (at least within presumably wide limits) fully absorb losses and gains from the enterprise's activities. Worker earnings, however, could thus be subject to a correspondingly wide fluctuation. In a community committed to labor management, one inevitably wonders whether such fluctuations would be tolerated.

From the standpoint of realism, one may wonder too about the theoretical neglect of management. By implication, management is simply another kind of labor.[12] In private enterprise, management needless to say often has a critical role of its own, especially where entrepreneurial activity is involved.

I said at the outset, however, that the theoretical analysis of the labor-managed firm is notably abstract. The foregoing queries only underline that fact. At any rate, in inquiring here into risk taking by the Yugoslav enterprise, it seems inappropriate to proceed as tends to be done regarding almost any aspect of Western enterprise behavior, that is, to take a theoretical maximum as a datum and to try to explain or predict the firm's behavior in that light. Rather a principal concern must be to explore the nature of the novel working arrangements in question and to try to gauge on that basis how enterprise motivation might be expected to compare with that depicted in theory. So far as a divergence from theory is indicated, we must also consider what the consequences might be for risk taking.

But, for the Yugoslav no less than for the Western firm, expectations must ultimately be tested empirically. In a review such as this, we must consider not only working arrangements but conduct. That is in order even though research on the latter aspect seems still to be at an especially early stage.

I alluded earlier to very recent shifts in Yugoslav working arrangements. The latest, while partially legislated in 1971, were only implemented on any scale after they were embodied in the new constitution of 1974 (Yugoslavia's third under communist rule) and in further legislation of 1976. These 1974–1976 reforms have still not been fully applied, but even if (as now seems doubtful) they were fully applied, they would often leave previous working arrangements intact. I will refer, however, to those earlier arrangements as the pre-BOAL system (PBS). The Basic Organization of Associated Labor (BOAL) is a cardinal feature of the 1974–1976 reforms.

Recall, though, that among earlier arrangements, those that prevailed after the mid-1960s are of particular concern. Unless otherwise indicated, these will be the ones under discussion. I will first explore PBS in some depth, and then consider how matters of interest may be affected by the 1974–1976 reforms. Among working arrangements concerning the enterprise, of special interest here are those affecting internal authority, external constraints, and income disposition. I consider each aspect in turn, and then examine in the light of such arrangements what is to be concluded as to enterprise motivation and risk taking.

Authority within the Firm

In theoretical analysis, just what is meant by labor management is more often implied than explicit. The presupposition, however, is clearly that workers can impose their will on the firm where they are employed, and so assure that the decisions taken will serve their interests. According to Yugoslav legal doctrine under PBS, the question thus posed is readily settled: authority within the Yugoslav firm under PBS was vested in the workers employed there. The enterprise was supposed to conform to existing law, but within its confines the workers were ultimately in charge.

We must heed here that proverbial legalistic view. The siting of ultimate authority in workers employed in an enterprise is the legal hallmark of the form of industrial organization to which the Yugoslavs came to be committed early on: labor management or, in their parlance, self-management (*samoupravljanje*).[13] Our concern, however, is not so much with doctrine as with practice, particularly the practice under PBS. That practice is by now a familiar theme, but the facts on it are rather complex, perhaps more so than some Yugoslav, as well as Western observers, seem to urge. Even a summary account, therefore, must set forth the available evidence, if only in the briefest terms. When an elusive question such as labor management is at issue, it is not surprising that the evidence is ambiguous, or at least difficult to interpret.

If workers are in fact in control of the self-managed firm (SMF) clearly one requirement is that the political process within the firm must be of a democratic sort. Workers thus must be able to determine freely either the policies pursued or the authorities who act for them. This requirement supposedly was met under PBS by means of the principal instrumentality through which the collective of workers exercised authority, the famous workers' council. Legally established procedures for electing members to the council were, by the mid-1960s, democratic in any usual sense of that word. Thus, voting was by secret ballot on candidates nominated at a general meeting of workers. Four sponsors sufficed for any nomination.[14]

Impressive as these arrangements were, they did not always prevail. For many years the trade union had been authorized to determine nominees for the council. Although a competing slate could be presented on the petition of ten percent of the work force, that had been rare. After the mid-1960s, the union was no longer authorized to shape council elections in this way, but it would be surprising if it thereby lost all of its influence. If it did, it soon regained it in some degree. These developments, however, will be considered later as part of the 1974–1976 reforms. An obvious anomaly under self-management, Yugoslav trade unions were mainly a post–World War II creation. Like the Party, with which they are closely allied, they clearly have a quasi-official status.

While acting in behalf of the collective, the council under PBS, was served in turn by a board of management. Limited in size (a membership of five was legally minimal) and meeting more frequently than the council itself, the management board consisted of members of the council together with the enterprise director, who could not serve on the workers' council. The director apart, the members of the management board had been elected by the council from the earliest days.

As for the designation of the director, here again participation by the collective was initially minimal. However, by 1965 the council had a major part in the process. This included substantial representation on a nomination committee, and the right to determine finally the appointment actually made.[15] On the other hand, the government of the locality or commune where the enterprise was located also participated. Although, under PBS, the government no longer formally had the decisive voice it once had, its factual role (for reasons to be explained) must have been consequential. At least at this important point, then, democracy within the firm was somewhat flawed, though by no means fatally so.

How democratic a political process will be depends also on the information available to the electorate. From that standpoint, self-managment surely qualifies as democratic; in fact, the volume of information made available to workers is a subject of complaint in Yugoslavia. It is held, no doubt with some basis, that the worker can hardly digest the often complex and bulky materials supplied to him.[16] Reference is made particularly to workers on the council, but such materials must also have been available (and no more digestible) to workers generally. Granting that, however, the need to provide such information, and its actual dissemination, must have constituted a constraint on willful executives. It has been plausibly argued (Granick 1975, pp. 378 *ff*) that one of the principal gains of the worker under self-management is his enhanced access to information.

In describing the political process within the SMF, I have outlined the diverse entities (the collective, the workers' council, the management board, and the director) that together were legally responsible under PBS for the operation of the enterprise. In earlier years, the trade union also had an important part in the enterprise's affairs—particularly in the election of council members. Under PBS, the union played a more general role in the enterprise's affairs, though usually it did not have independent operational authority. That was also true of the Party, but representatives of the union and the Party in effect acted for quasi-official organizations of national scope. Further discussion of their role, therefore, is best deferred to the section where I refer to external controls over the enterprise.

What is chiefly in question here, then, is the comparative roles in the enterprise of the different entities legally responsible for its functioning. This has been a subject of inquiry by Yugoslav scholars themselves. Although the scholars deal with power within the firm in general, their studies bear at once on the roles of organizational entities referred to. The precise periods to which reference is made is not always indicated, but the bulk of the inquiries clearly refer, among other things, to circumstances under PBS.[17]

Of particular interest are findings such as those Gorupić (1978) has summarized in this way:

> Empirical investigations thus far conducted on the structure of influence in the enterprise have shown that the formal self-managing structure often conceals concrete relations that are inconsistent with the idea of self-management. The enterprise's professional management has excessive influence, while workers have too little. Research has also shown that workers are not satisfied with their role, and that they demand the realization of their self-management rights (p. 131).

In the studies in question, this gap between formal structure and concrete relations is usually, though not always, found.[18] Sometimes it is distinctly wider than that described by Gorupić. According to Županov (1975), the inquiries even show

no difference in the distribution of "executive power" in the surveyed
Yugoslav organizations as compared with the American organizations: an
oligarchic pattern was found in both of them. This finding in itself should
not be disturbing since "executive power in democratic organizations
usully is distributed in accord with the pyramid structure of authority."
However, basically the same pattern was found in the area of "legislative
power" where, according to Katz and Kahn a completely different distribution should be expected; even here the top executives as a group are more
powerful than the workers' council. True enough, the workers' council is
perceived to have a "medium" amount of power, but further analysis
revealed that the two most influential groups within the council itself are
top executives and staff experts, while blue-collar workers are the least
influential group (pp. 82–83).

Coming from scholars in a society like that studied, these are striking
assessments. However, in weighing their import we must consider that none
of the studies in question was of a comparative sort, rather, data were
assembled on circumstances in the Yugoslav firm alone. Županov's conclusion on the comparative distribution of power there and in the U.S. firm,
therefore, represents something of an extrapolation, though certainly an
illuminating one from a distinguished sociologist.

The inquiries, moreover, utilize diverse indicators of power distribution, of which the principal one is simply the manner in which that distribution is perceived by workers generally. However, an investigation of authority within the enterprise on that basis has its limitations. One suspects that
many workers might perceive executives as possessing cardinal authority
even if they performed only delegated functions. Reports to the effect that
the executives themselves saw their role as preeminent (Županov 1969, pp.
251–252; Županov 1973) are perhaps more illuminating. Also ambiguous
are the results of further Yugoslav inquiries focusing on such aspects as the
sponsorship of proposals considered and adopted by the workers' council
and the extent to which different groups participated in council discussions.[19] Probably one of the more telling indications, however, of restricted
worker influence is the reported wholesale abstention on the part of worker
members from voting in the workers' council; however, reference is made
only to the experience in a single enterprise.[20]

In Yugoslavia, unlike in much of the socialist world, labor strikes are
not illegal. In affirming this, Yugoslav officials also affirm that such strikes
are also not legal, but they do occur and not infrequently. Some 1526 were
reported as occurring during the years 1961–1969. In 37 strikes during
1967–1969 for which there are data on the number of participants, the number of workers involved totaled 57,597.[21]

Strikes are an obvious oddity where workers are supposedly bosses.
Those in Yugoslavia are doubtless properly construed (as they have been
even in Yugoslavia[22]) as still another evidence of the breach between prin-

ciple and practice regarding self-management. Paradoxically, however, they may also indicate that under that system, workers' residual authority is often greater than it might have been otherwise. Thus, though the strikes were typically unsponsored even by unions, they were usually of brief duration. Yet, they very often culminated in the workers' essential demands being met. The reason for such easy success, Županov (1978-A) conjectures, may be that:

> Yugoslav executives are insecure about their power, which is very great in actuality but modest in its institutional definition. Thus, much of their power is illegitimate and makes them extremely vulnerable in case of a strike. That is, a strike puts executives on the spot by exposing publicly and dramatically the illegitimacy of their power; this in turn generates an urgent need to bring the strike to an end quickly regardless of cost (pp. 395-396).

As in the West workers strike most often over money—the amount of their earnings and the manner of their determination. These are matters over which the authority of Yugoslav enterprise executives has been relatively constrained, so the strikes need not always signify the kind of usurpation of power by executives that Županov refers to. Also, even Yugoslav scholars might not take enough into account that Western business enterprises do not characteristically need to bring a "strike to an end quickly regardless of cost." Given such an imperative, however, managerial personnel must be concerned to avoid strikes to begin with. By the same token, workers' interests and attitudes might have to be heeded even when not effectively expressed through formal representational procedures.

Authority within the Yugoslav SMF is among the topics dealt with in several case studies completed by foreign scholars who have visited in that country. It has also sometimes been of concern to foreign journalists. The resulting accounts are at best only suggestive, but a rather intricate pattern seems to emerge. Executive domination is certainly among the situations reported, but a meaningful and effective involvement of workers is not rare.[23]

I have been considering authority within the firm under PBS in general terms. Though we seek only a summary view, we must bear in mind that Yugoslav workers, like workers elsewhere, are more interested in some matters than in others. Judging from Yugoslav inquiries into the subject, ordinary workers have probably been relatively influential in some spheres of particular concern. I reserve for later discussion working arrangements as to income disposition (*raspodela dohotka*), but note that these working arrangements, understandably, were one area where the collective had an enhanced role.[24] Among other such spheres were labor discipline, dismissals, and working conditions.[25]

Županov (1974) has characterized the varying meanings of labor participation in different contexts in a related but different way:

Recent investigations into the problem of participation in industry, though far from being systematic and comprehensive, seem to suggest the following tentative conclusions: (a) intensity of participation is normally higher in a "crisis" than in "normal" circumstances; (b) participation is more extensive when human and "internal politics," rather than functional problems, are under discussion; and (c) participation is more intensive when distribution of personal income, rather than production problems, are in debate (p. 186).

    I have referred so far to *the* workers' council. As self-management was organized initially, there usually was, in fact, only a single council in an enterprise. In the course of time, however, councils were set-up in enterprise subdivisions—in different plants, if there were more than one in the enterprise, in departments within plants, and possibly in even more limited sectors.[26] In promoting this development, the government clearly intended to enable the ordinary worker to participate more effectively in the firm's affairs. Evidence adduced here on the limitations of such participation bears, however, on circumstances where the proliferation of workers' councils was already relatively advanced. At any rate, the impact of that trend on the workers' role in decision making has probably been modest (Neuberger and James 1973, p. 275; Granick 1975, p. 378). That will be of interest when we turn to the 1974–1976 reforms.

    I have been outlining evidence as to authority within the firm under PBS. The conclusion must be, I think, that power gravitated to executive personnel to a distinctly greater degree than official doctrine allows, though perhaps not quite as much as often held, even by Yugoslav scholars. Ordinary workers were probably more influential in some matters than others. Circumstances also varied between enterprises.

    Under PBS, who was the entrepreneur? Such a question is rarely easy to answer in the Western business firm; it is no easier here. In the conduct of any enterprise, Yugoslav or Western, risk taking is likely to be especially characteristic of technological and product innovation. In the West, executives usually play a key role in such matters, and the level of authority engaged is often commensurate with the magnitude of the financial commitment entailed for the firm. In the SMF under PBS, executives could hardly do otherwise. This is inevitable, if only because of their hierarchical status and their resultant command over and ability to construe relevant technical information. Such capabilities are especially important when new technologies and products are in question. Yet innovations might easily impinge on labor staffing and earnings—matters of particular concern to workers generally. Where they did, the collective could become involved, one way or another, in the decision-making process. As illuminating case studies illustrate (Adizes 1971, ch. 4), the involvement might be more than perfunctory.

    Here as elsewhere, then, self-management hardly conformed to Yugoslav doctrine. However, granting the cardinal role of executives, workers were by no means impotent. These facts will have to be considered when we turn later to motivation and risk taking.

Enterprise Autonomy

In theory, labor management derives its significance for resource allocation from the fact that the firm itself is an essentially autonomous entity. That is so in stochastic circumstances, among other things. The enterprise must procure inputs and dispose of outputs in markets, but it determines for itself how to respond to whatever trading currents confront it. At this point, then, the labor-managed firm is simply a replica of the firm in a private-enterprise economy.

Turning to the question that this raises concerning Yugoslavia, the government in organizing the economy initially reproduced the economic working arrangements of the USSR. Among these—and basic to all else— was the famous Soviet system of coordinating and directing enterprises bureaucratically through the extensive use of obligatory physical targets. Under these circumstances, enterprise autonomy was limited indeed. However, in turning subsequently to labor participation, the Yugoslav government also dismantled the elaborate controls erected previously. Of concern here, therefore, is not the initial system of centralist planning, but the mechanism that supplanted it.

That, it is often assumed, is a form of market socialism, where coordination and direction are accomplished essentially through market processes. Although economic plans are still formulated, these supposedly are of the indicative sort that excludes obligatory targets for the enterprise. The corollary is that the Yugoslav SMF has in fact approached the LMF of theory with respect to autonomy. Although only rarely explored systematically, such suppositions are doubtless broadly valid with respect to PBS (on which I still focus). Under that scheme, however, the enterprise was still appreciably constrained, and sometimes in ways that could possibly affect risk taking. I again defer discussion of one sphere in which that was so, that of income disposition.

Under PBS, another such sphere was price determination. In theoretical analyses of labor management, prices are generally market determined, but it does not matter for the functioning of the firm if the government determines them instead. If market forces rule, prices are data for the enterprise in any event except where there is monopoly power. Should the government fix prices to clear markets, the enterprise might behave in the same way in one case as in the other.[27]

The stipulation is essential, however. If it is not met, the enterprise might behave rather differently from the way theory envisages. It should be observed, therefore, that although centralist planning had long since been abandoned, the government under PBS still regulated prices. The regulation was of varying, but usually fairly extensive scope. It took diverse forms, including determination of fixed prices and trade margins, ceiling prices, requirement of prior approval of price changes, episodic overall price freezes, establishment of maximum benchmark increases, price rollbacks, and so on.[28]

More concretely, what was involved can be judged from the fact that a principal element of the economic reform of 1965, which ushered in PBS, was a radical restructuring of prices carried out in July 1965. The restructuring followed a brief price freeze. Producers' prices of some 65 percent of industrial output were subject to controls of one sort or another by the end of 1966. Of the total increase in living costs in the first quarter of 1973 (5.5 percent), nearly one-fifth manifested initiatives or approvals of federal authorities, and about one-third, initiatives or approvals of republican or local governments (Organization for Economic Cooperation and Developments, OECD, 1969, pp. 19–21; 1974, p. 18).

Government regulation of prices is of interest here, to repeat, only to the extent that markets are not cleared in consequence. Given the scope and nature of the Yugoslav regulation, it would be surprising if this were not often the case. Observers rarely report the kinds of retail-shop sellouts and queues that are so characteristic elsewhere in the socialist East; however, shortages and informal rationing sometimes occurred even for intermediate products, at least in the early years (Montias 1967, p. 405).

The economic reform of 1965 embraced, along with a revision of the price structure, an extensive reorganization of the banking system. Enterprises, however, continued to obtain the bulk of their new capital (beyond what they generated for themselves) in the form of bank credits. Such credits were used to meet long-term as well as short-term needs. This mode of external financing is in contrast to the traditional Eastern one involving budgetary grants (at least for long-term needs). The Yugoslavs themselves employed the latter form of financing under centralist planning.

Under the circumstances, the government necessarily came to use the banking system, itself of shifting structure, as an instrument for assuring macroeconomic balance. The more or less persistent inflation and sharply fluctuating tempos of change in physical volume testify that the effort was not exactly successful (Horvat 1971; OECD 1974). Of more concern here, however, is another closely related, but still distinct, function that the banking system was called on to perform.

Under PBS, the economic plans of the government were essentially indicative—that is, they did not include obligatory physical targets for the enterprise.[29] In the still imperfect state of planning of the time, one wonders how much of a constraint the plans (especially the longer-range ones) could be even for government entities themselves. The plans nevertheless did embrace diverse sectoral as well as aggregative targets, and banks were expected to heed them in granting credits. Whatever the degree of implementation of plan targets per se, political entities at all levels had development policies that they called on the banks to help promote. Government agencies also called on the banks to administer so-called earmarked funds, whose use might be restricted to particular regions or branches, or possibly to an even more limited sphere. In this way, government agencies could buttress to a degree their plans and development policies.

As for banks, they charged interest on their credits, but the rates levied were subject during the period in question to a ceiling, initially 10.0 percent and, later, 8.0 percent. With industrial producers' prices rising annually an average of 7.3 percent during 1966–1973, the banks (not surprisingly) were often able to impose higher rates, one way or another. For practical purposes, credit rationing was also widespread.[30] Not surprisingly, too, banks came to occupy an important role in the enterprise's affairs. In one Yugoslav empirical inquiry into self-management, banks outrank all other entities as an external influence on the enterprise.[31]

Just what this meant is not entirely clear, but bank credit policy was obviously politicized. Enterprise autonomy must have suffered as a consequence, if only from an expedient concern for orienting investment projects to bank, and ultimately political, interests. That was made more likely by the fact that, whereas the enterprise itself might be among the founders of, and hence have a voice in, the affairs of the bank, that was also true of political entities.

Under PBS, then, bank and political influence on investments must have been a constraint on enterprise autonomy in addition to that represented by price regulation. One of the political entities that had a voice in bank affairs, furthermore, was the commune government. Enjoying, as explained, a special status as a participant in the recruitment of the enterprise director, that agency was also a frequent sponsor of the firm when it was established, and a source of aid when it experienced financial and other difficulties. It was thus in an especially favorable position to influence enterprise investment activity. It apparently had an even larger role than that—it was able, as Županov (1974) put it, "to widen its influence on the business and personnel policies of the enterprise through formal and, to a greater extent, through informal means" (p. 190).

Banks and the commune government were significant constraints on enterprise autonomy, but two other external entities were also influential. Under PBS, one of these (the trade union) no longer had the formal status that it once had. However, it probably still had some role in council elections. Like strikes, a transparent incongruity under self-management, the union also had an impact more generally, if only in informal ways (Wachtel 1973, pp. 77–79).

To the extent that it did, however, it usually acted as a surrogate for another quasi-official body, the Party. As for that organization, it too was generally without legal responsibilities. Indeed, as seen by Edward Kardelj, a principal architect of self-management (quoted in Rusinow 1978, p. 217), the Party was supposed to play only a severely restricted part in the enterprise's affairs:

> The internal decision making and acts . . . of the bodies of self-management in working organizations must not be interfered with by Party organizations and their bodies except by means of political action, i.e., by persuasion, help, by providing information to the public, education, and similar methods.

As rhetoric, Kardelj's 1966 statement on the Party's role under self-management was by no means novel, but reformist currents of the time embraced politics as well as economics. Although the Party was once relatively potent, it clearly experienced something of a decline as PBS was being put in place. That trend encountered resistence within the Party, and was in due course reversed. But while it prevailed, Kardelj's prescription for Party behavior within the self-managed firm was more important than might be supposed.[32] We must read in that light further results of Yugoslav inquiries into the perceptions of power within the enterprise under circumstances prevailing in 1968–1969. The Party was seen as outranked by higher executive personnel. That was the perception of executives themselves, as well as of workers generally.[33]

Such results must in a degree reflect enduring forces. Whatever the larger political currents of the moment, Party activists had to be concerned not only with Party directives in general, but with the material success of the firm. However that might be construed, the Party activists had to temper their strivings for influence. The results, predictably, was that the executive who could manage successfully acquired "great power over the organizational environment."[34]

The director of the enterprise, of course, was himself often a member of the Party (Wachtel 1973, p. 80; Dirlam and Plummer 1973, p. 52; Granick 1975, pp. 441–442; Sirc 1979, p. 186). What is in question, however, is the degree to which the director was subservient to the Party organization in the firm. Often he was not.

The commune government, as noted previously, was a source of outside influence on the self-managed firm under PBS, partly because the commune government often sponsored the fledgling enterprise. More generally, under PBS, a political body at any level might be the founder of a new enterprise—which is to say that, among other things, it either had to arrange for the firm's financing or supply the needed capital itself (Sacks 1973). Service in that capacity, therefore, could be a source of influence for other political agencies as well as the commune. Enterprises, however, were also often founded by other enterprises. In principle, a group of citizens could also found an enterprise, although that procedure was of relatively limited importance.[35]

This chapter is concerned with risk taking. Risk taking is especially important in decisions on investment projects such as those that apply novel technologies or introduce new products. The SMF under PBS, we may conclude, had substantial autonomy, but regarding such investment projects it probably had to defer to some degree to authorities outside the firm, particularly banks and the local government. Even so, enterprise autonomy was much greater than it generally is under Eastern socialism, even in Yugoslavia itself, when it was under centralist planning. That is one of the more important ways in which market socialism, as found in Yugoslavia under PBS, differed from centralist planning. In trying later to gauge how the self-managed firm might behave in the face of risk, we must keep in mind the foregoing facts.

Income Disposition

A basic feature of the LMF of theory is the manner in which labor earnings are determined. Rather than being paid conventional money wages, workers have at their disposal the balance of income after nonlabor charges are met. If they wish, they can save part of this for use by the firm; the rest is available for distribution among them, supposedly in accord with their productive contributions. With all workers acquiring in this way the status of residual claimants, they also become primary risk-bearers, absorbing both gains and losses from varying performance. The behavior of the firm under stochastic conditions is shaped decisively by these arrangements.

Even if the same procedures prevailed in Yugoslavia, a firm there might behave rather differently in the presence of risk. As we have seen, the Yugoslav SMF often differs from the theoretic LMF in two basic spheres: authority within the enterprise and enterprise autonomy. Nevertheless, how labor earnings are determined in the SMF might well affect risk taking there. If we are to gauge risk-taking behavior under PBS, therefore, we must know how the SMF compared with the theoretical LMF regarding income disposition.

Although practice regarding income accounting for the self-managed firm has varied over time, we can grasp the essentials by referring to Yugoslav serial data on revenues remaining after charges for nonlabor operating expenses and depreciation (table 8-1). The data relate to revenues "realized

Table 8-1

Disposition of Net Income of Enterprises in Socialized Sector, Yugoslavia 1966-1971

(percent)

Item	1966	1967	1968	1969	1970	1971
All	100.0	100.0	100.0	100.0	100.0	100.0
Allocated to political-social institutions	40.0	43.0	44.0	43.2	42.9	39.5
Interest on credits	4.1	5.0	5.3	5.7	5.6	5.5
Interest of capital assets	2.5	3.2	3.0	2.8	2.2	0.2
Turnover taxes[a]	10.9	12.7	13.7	12.1	13.0	12.7
Taxes on personal incomes	20.2	19.5	18.8	19.5	19.0	17.6
Other	2.3	2.6	3.2	3.1	3.1	3.5
Retained inome of enterprise[b]	21.6	17.0	15.9	15.5	16.3	19.6
Net personal incomes	38.5	40.2	41.2	41.2	40.7	40.9
Discrepancy	(−).1	(−).1	(−)1.1	—	—	—

Source: SZZS (1973), p. 155. On the scope of the data, see also pp. 20-21.

Note: Reference is to realized income (see text). On the discrepancy see *n.* 36. Other divergencies between sums of indicated items and 100.0 are due to rounding.

[a]In addition to the turnover tax (*porez na pomet*), this includes a special surcharge (*naknada*) on the retail price of gasoline.

[b]Allocations to capital account, reserve funds, and various other accounts.

through the market''—that is, revenues apart from changes in stocks—but for our present purposes, that is just as well. As so understood, net income was devoted in part to paying interest on bank credit.[36] Although made at rates below clearing levels, such payments were simply a further nonlabor factor charge. Hence, there is, in principle, no departure from theory at this point.

Under PBS the net income remaining after the charge for interest on bank credit was divided among three uses: (1) taxes and other obligatory payments to governmental and other public institutions; (2) earnings retained in the enterprise; and (3) incomes paid out to the working staff. Of these three claims, the first had a prior character, whereas under self-management, retained earnings as well as take-home pay are viewed as worker income. Apparently, then, the immediate corollary is that in the SMF under PBS, theory was generally replicated with respect to income distribution. Workers were, in effect, both residual claimants and primary risk-bearers.

Or so it is often reasoned. The conclusion is not very wide off the mark, but for a more accurate appraisal we must also consider that even though taxes and the like are prior charges against net income, they might conceivably vary in ways that might dampen the impact of shifting enterprise fortunes on residual earnings. To the extent they did so, the residual claimant fails to bear the risk experienced by the enterprise as a whole. In fact, among three main sorts of Yugoslav levies,[37] one (yielding the least revenue) was simply a charge on the enterprise's net worth paid in addition to the interest paid to banks. Although likewise referred to as interest (*kamata*), this levy extended to the enterprise's self-financed capital, and is more properly considered a tax. Under PBS, a very low flat rate—for some time, 4 percent—was standard. While there were reductions for some kinds of capital and some industries, no further adjustments were scheduled that depended on the profitability of the individual enterprise.[38]

The so-called turnover tax (*porez na promet*), like the Soviet tax of the same name, was originally levied on sales turnover at different stages. It was transformed in 1965 into little more than a retail sales tax—or rather, a complex of such taxes, with federal, republican, and communal governments each levying charges of its own. Within any locality, however, the total percentage charge was uniform for any commodity—and, to a considerable extent, even among commodities.

Taxes on personal incomes, as recorded in the table, are in Yugoslav parlance "contributions" (*doprinosi*). They include payments by the SMF, not only into governmental budgets as such, but into special funds such as that for social security. What is to be noted here, however, is that under PBS the bulk of such charges were essentially levied as a flat percentage of sums allocated to worker incomes. Taxes were also levied at progressive rates on incomes, reported on individual declaration, but such charges were apparently directed primarily at super incomes. Socialized sector earnings over a wide range extending well beyond the usual income of an SMF director were subject to either a nul, or a relatively low, marginal as well as average rate. In any case, the taxes on income indicated on individual declaration were reportedly evaded in a wholesale way.[39]

The foregoing levies on the enterprise and its workers all differ from lump-sum taxes. To the extent that they do, income disposition under self-management deviates from theory. The divergence, however, has little practical import for our purposes, for such levies can have only a limited effect on the stochastic dispersion of earnings. The latter is what counts for risk taking.[40]

So much for variations in taxes and similar levies as a factor affecting the workers' status as a residual claimant and risk bearer. From the same standpoint, a further question arises concerning the enterprise's retained earnings—particularly the degree to which such allocations are determined by worker time preference. That they are so determined is presupposed by LMF theory. It is only on that basis that retained earnings can be viewed as on a par with take-home pay as worker income. Discussion of this matter is postponed; however, any close correspondence to worker preferences appears unlikely. Departures from worker preferences, moreover, could have served to dampen fluctuations in take-home pay.

Under PBS, then, the worker under self-management diverged to some extent from his theoretical counterpart as a claimant to residual earnings and as a risk bearer. The divergence becomes more pronounced (though still only partial) when we consider that the worker actually received at regular intervals an advance payment (*akontacija*) determined from the estimated income of the enterprise for its accounting period (most often, a year). While frequently referred to as a wage (*plata*), the advance payment was only provisional, for the worker periodically received supplementary payments as well that represented his share of net income after retention of earnings.

Or rather, he received such supplements if the net income was high enough. If net income instead fell below the projected amount, no earnings might be retained, but there would be no supplements either. On the other hand, the enterprise might be able to maintain worker earnings at the advance payment level for a time, even though net income did not actually suffice for this purpose. To do so, it might draw on reserve funds held for such purposes. It could also possible draw on corresponding communal funds to which it contributed jointly with other enterprises in the same area. With the support of the communal government, it might be able to extend its bank loans, or even negotiate new ones. It might delay paying its suppliers (a not at all unusual circumstance, especially if the banks themselves became restrictive). For a firm experiencing financial difficulties, tax waivers too were a possibility.[41] In a word, the *akontacija,* rather than being purely residual earnings, might become something like a conventional contractual wage.

The enterprise was obligated in any case to pay workers a legal minimum wage. Should it be unable to do so, the commune government was obliged to make up the shortfall. The minimum at the time in question, however, was not very effective, for it was well below the earning levels in most industries.[42]

A further obligation of the enterprise—established by law—was to maintain its capital intact. If an enterprise failed to meet its obligations, its commune government could place it under receivership. In that case, self-management was suspended, and the enterprise was administered by authorities appointed by the commune government. Alternatively, the enterprise might be declared bankrupt, and liquidated.[43]

In fact, workers tended to receive a modest supplement to their advance payments. These averaged, if we can judge from pre-1965 experience, about 7-12 percent of their total earnings.[44] However, such earnings varied downward as well as upward, sometimes markedly so. Although the precise magnitude of such drops were rarely indicated, delays in wage payment and reductions in wages were reportedly among the more significant immediate causes of strikes (Jovanov 1978, pp. 366-367). On the other hand, payments at projected levels did often continue for some time in the face of losses, and receiverships and bankruptcies were relatively infrequent. In 1968, for example, bank credit was being relaxed after the severe restraint of 1966-1967, but 36 percent of Yugoslav firms were reportedly unable to meet their contractual obligations. Of the 13,840 enterprises in the socialized sector, however, only 74 were put into receivership and 124 were liquidated.[45] Bankruptcy was rather rare according to Horvat (1971), "because the commune is obliged to find new employment for workers and so prefers to help the enterprise as long as possible" (p. 105). The commune government might also be required to assume the financial obligations of a defunct enterprise (Tyson 1977a, p. 288).

Let me try to sum up the worker's status with respect to income disposition. In the SMF under PBS, workers generally had only a rather limited part to play in decision making in the presence of risk. Paradoxically, however, they were nevertheless residual claimants to income. While not to the degree envisaged in theory, they necessarily were also risk bearers. More precisely, their earnings might be depressed should the enterprise experience an adverse conjuncture, though in one way or another the impact of such a development was dampened. Worker gains from enterprise successes might also have been limited through involuntary or quasi-voluntary variation in the rates of income retention by the enterprise.

I have been discussing total labor earnings under self-management. On the related question concerning the shares of different workers in that total, only one aspect—executive pay—is of particular interest here. However, it should be observed first that under PBS it was left to the enterprise—particularly the workers' council—to decide at what specific rates different workers should share in the total income available.

As in the socialist world generally, though, an authoritative ideology required that rewards conform to "work done." In implementing that precept, the government formerly intervened in detail in the sphere of labor remuneration, and under PBS, it still prescribed general principles to be observed. It was partly on that account that there was considerable uniformity regarding the essentials of enterprise practice. Thus, the relative earnings rates for different kinds of work were determined in each enterprise in accord with a detailed scale established in advance. Each job was placed in the scale according to diverse criteria, all familiar to a Western observer: skill and educational requirements, effort needed, working conditions, and the like. In establishing a scale and classifying tasks in it, the workers' council necessarily had to consider how other similar enterprises were dealing with the same matters. The state of the labor "market" in general might also be weighed, though with what effect is not too clear.

When the rates for different kinds of work were determined, the relative pay of the individual worker performing one or another job was also fixed. The worker's pay in a particular job, however, might also vary depending on his seniority, special proficiency, and so on. In piece work, which was often employed, the worker's pay also depended on his output. His pay might also include a bonus for, say, product quality that was determined in accord with established principles.[46]

On the basis of the foregoing procedures, the enterprise determined the worker's rate of advance payment (*akontacija*). Supplementary distributions might then be made simply in proportion to advance payments, though not necessarily. Here, particularly, the workers' council might endeavor to allow for market conditions.[47]

So much for the distribution of earnings among workers generally. As for executive pay, the main fact of interest becomes evident when we observe that, for the purpose of determining relative earnings rates, administrative personnel were essentially treated like all other workers. Their jobs too were classified in the enterprise's earning scale, and with due regard for the criteria considered in classifying workers generally.

The workers' council might also pay executives bonuses for successful performance, but special rewards were rather exceptional and, where available, tended to be quite modest.[48] Not very surprisingly, that was also true of executive incomes overall. In 1969, socialized-sector enterprise directors earned, on the average, only 3.3 times as much as unskilled workers (*Savezni Zavod za Statistiku,* SZZS, 1971, p. 271). Executive personnel also benefited from inevitable fringes, such as the use of a company car (Bajt 1972; Bučar 1978, p. 431). However—at least in self-managed enterprises—Yugoslav incomes were probably more egalitarian than Yugoslavs themselves often assumed.[49]

The role and status of executive personnel are rarely considered in the theory of the LMF. The supposition is that such personnel are simply another type of labor and, if rewarded as such, can be counted on in general to pursue the interests of the workers as those interests are conceived in theory. In the Yugoslav SMF under PBS, as we have seen, executive personnel often were the repository of inordinate power. The manner in which they were rewarded is, therefore, of particular interest. This has yet to be fully elucidated, but earnings must have tended to vary, much as did those of the rest of the collective, with the income of the enterprise. When we come to the behavior of the SMF with respect to risk, that will be a cardinal datum to consider.

Although executive pay is of special concern, it should be observed that earnings differentials from firm to firm for workers generally were here too very broad as theory envisages. With differentials apparently of a constricted sort, though, the earnings from different kinds of work are unlikely to have approximated the marginal productivities to which theory equates them.[50]

I have been discussing income disposition, but the deeper concern has been risk bearing and hence risk exposure. From that standpoint, we must consider that in adverse circumstances in the West, not only income but employment (which is not the same thing) can be at hazard for workers and executives alike. That is also true of the staff of the LMF of theory, although that fact tends to be neglected in the analysis of risk taking. In gauging risk exposure in the SMF, therefore, we must be aware that under PBS, as before, staff curtailment was legally a matter for final determination by the workers' council rather than by the administration (International Labor Office, ILO, 1962, pp. 180–185; Blumberg 1969, p. 203). Council members, according to a survey, considered themselves relatively influential in that sphere (Arzenšek 1978, pp. 377–381). In view of likely limitations in council representativeness, that could obviously mean various things. However, under self-management, staff curtailment in the face of an adverse market conjuncture was, in fact, relatively infrequent and limited. That might perhaps be inferred from reports of chronic overstaffing, but avoidance of staff curtailment is also a recurring theme of writings on the SMF.[51] Under self-management, then, while workers experienced risk as residual claimants to income, the additional risk posed by the possibility of dismissal in adverse circumstances was relatively modest. A corollary, though, is that earnings fluctuations must often have been greater than they would have been otherwise.

The foregoing deals with the risk of dismissal for workers generally. For executives, it might suffice to refer to the enterprise director. Under PBS, the occupant of that post was normally appointed for a term of four years and could then be reappointed. He could also be dismissed before completing his term. Here, the workers' council—at least de facto—shared power with communal authorities (Blumberg 1969, pp. 204–205; Granick 1975, pp. 363–364). At all events, dismissal was a possibility as was failure to be reappointed (which comes to much the same thing). That, in fact, was the fate of 15–19 percent of the directors whose terms expired between 1966 and 1970. Some of the persons in question were probably superannuated; others must not have been candidates for reelection to begin with. Directorial turnover during the years considered must also have reflected a Party policy of the time to deprofessionalize cadres.[52] Even without dismissal or failure to be reappointed, of course, the director's career might be impaired should the enterprise experience vicissitudes. In appraising risky ventures, the director had to consider such facts, along with the modest material rewards for success. We must read in that light reports of difficulties in recruiting directors.[53]

Enterprise Motivation and Risk Taking

In preceding sections, I have outlined working arrangements under PBS relating to authority within the firm, enterprise autonomy, and enterprise income disposition. The working arrangements are sometimes similar to, and sometimes different from, those envisaged in the theory of the LMF. We must now consider how risk taking under those working arrangements might compare to that predicted theoretically. Research on the actual behavior of the Yugoslav firm under PBS is still not very advanced, but we must consider whether something can be inferred from such research as well as from the prevailing working arrangements.

Activities of interest turn decisively on the motivation of relevant decision makers. In theory, such motivation in stochastic circumstances is represented by a particular enterprise maximand. A cardinal issue here, therefore, concerns the degree to which that maximand applies to the Yugoslav SMF.

As given by formula (8.7), however, that criterion is but a variant of an alternative one given by formula (8.2), which supposedly obtains where risk is absent. Such an environment is an analytic construct rarely encountered in the real world, but for many sorts of decisions uncertainty is often negligible. Whatever can be ascertained as to the applicability of (8.2) in such circumstances should also bear on the applicability of (8.7) under uncertainty. Similarly, whereas both formulas (8.2) and (8.7) abstract from time, we may be able to judge their relevance better if we consider also how theoretical principles relating to choices over time can be applied to the SMF.

In trying to gauge motivation for risk taking in the Yugoslav SMF under PBS, therefore, it is well to begin with the related issues posed by formula (8.2), concerning motivation in the absence of risk, and the further theoretical principles, just referred to, for choices over time. Formula (8.2) simply represents net income per worker—that is, net income after nonlabor expenses are met. In relating such income to employment, due allowance is made for differences in labor quality and conditions. These differences are supposedly reflected in corresponding differentials in earnings. What is in question, then, is the degree to which (8.2), so understood, represents a maximand that is applicable to the SMF under PBS. Reference is to circumstances where the concern is essentially with nonstochastic alternatives relating to a single time period.

In trying to appraise that matter, we must consider these aspects:

1. Theoretical analyses are rarely explicit on authority within the LMF. The presupposition is that the collective is effectively in charge and is able to impose its will whenever it wishes to do so. As we saw, that was formally true in the SMF under PBS; however, in practice, much power was in the hands of executive personnel, particularly the director.

2. On the other hand, labor earnings were determined more or less as theory posits—that is, as a residual after nonlabor factor charges. Before incomes accrued to workers, deductions were also made for diverse taxes. Since these diverged from the lump-sum taxes of theory, they could have distorted enterprise behavior in familiar ways not central here,[54] but they would not at all bar pursuit of a maximand such as that assumed by theory. Also not envisaged in the theory are diverse Yugoslav arrangements tending to cushion the impact on labor earnings of unexpected declines in enterprise income. However, those arrangements are of only limited interest in the nonstochastic context of immediate concern.

3. I have been referring here to the total earnings bill. Between different kinds of labor, earnings varied broadly (as in theory) depending on labor quality and work conditions. This was true not only of ordinary workers but of executives. In seeking their own pecuniary gain, therefore, executives had reason to seek that of workers generally. It also follows that, despite the inordinate power of executives, enterprise motivation need not have diverged from that in theory.

4. A well-known, yet curious, feature of the theoretical LMF is that, depending on the initial level of operations, maximization of net income per worker might call for a curtailment of the work force. With that maximand, then, some members of the collective could be expected to seek their financial gain by dismissing some of their fellow workers. A virtual corollary is, however, that the realism of the theoretical maximand itself is in question at this point. That is so even if the collective is fully in control, for *a priori,* such staff curtailment is hardly likely in a community where labor management is the rule.

5. In any event, the SMF under PBS could not have been too prone to staff curtailment. As explained, dismissals were relatively infrequent, and overstaffing was reportedly widespread. Thus, the operation of the theoretical maximand applied to the SMF under PBS was subject to a constraint against staff curtailment.

6. A feature of the Yugoslav labor market is chronic unemployment. Under PBS, registered job seekers exceeded 7 percent of the social-sector labor force (Dubey 1975, p. 87). The unemployment doubtless had diverse causes, but it is consistent with a persistent gap between the marginal productivity of labor and its supply price that is understandable in terms of the theory of an LMF economy.

7. A further implication of labor-management, as seen in theory, is that in a short-run equilibrium, earnings of workers doing the same kind of

work in different enterprises can diverge even in the same locality. Because of differences in capital per worker, in technologies, and (in the case of firms in different industries) product demand, the divergence in earnings could be substantial.[55] Such a divergence—so much in contrast with the relatively short-run erosion of earnings disparities expected in a private enterprise economy—is considered a hallmark of an economy where labor-managed firms seek to maximize net income per worker.

In fact, notably large differentials have been reported in Yugoslavia. Horvat, for example, cites Yugoslav data showing that the earnings of workers performing the same kind of job in Belgrade in 1967 differ by as much as 3:1 or 4:1 (Horvat 1971, p. 117).[56] Yugoslav earnings differentials, as analyzed more generally by Estrin (1981), also suggest behavior such as that predicted by LMF theory.

As Jaroslav Vanek (1977) and Vanek and Jovicic (1975) have argued, some of the variation in earnings for similar work could represent rents on capital in excess of the capital tax and bank-loan interest. To that extent, the variation simply reflects the nature of Yugoslav income accounting and in no way confirms the LMF theory. Much of the variation, however, is apparently due to other causes. While the precise nature of those causes is still not clear, the variation is not inconsistent with theoretical expectations.[57]

8. I alluded earlier to other (sometimes paradoxical) implications of the theoretical maximand. One of these is that the firm could find it useful—at least in the short run—to reduce output in response to an increase in its price. Since the prediction is conditional, not much can be settled by referring to one or another instance of actual price-output variation. According to Horvat (1975), however, no pattern of price-quantity variations such as that in question

> . . . *has been observed in the Yugoslav economy.* Increases in prices, as *signals of unsatisfied demand,* have been followed rather quickly by efforts to increase supply (vol. 2, p. 235; his italics).

We may, perhaps, properly demur at Horvat's view that to be satisfied as to the validity of his contention, "it suffices to read newspapers." We should also note, however, that exclusion of short-run curtailment of output comes to much the same thing as the constraint on employment cuts referred to earlier.

I sum up the foregoing considerations in this way: If only provisionally, the theoretical maximand represented by formula (8.2) can be plausibly ascribed to the SMF under PBS. Such motivation on the part of the SMF was seemingly induced by working arrangements within the enterprise regarding the disposition of income. As a result, executives tended to see their interests as broadly in accord with those of the collective generally, and in that way, in effect, with the theoretical maximand. In the perspective of theory, executive authority in the SMF must be considered inordinate. Without executive incentives to conform to the theoretical maximand, the enterprise could easily be impelled to pursue a rather different end. There is also some indication of motivation like that represented by the theoretical maximand in observed enterprise behavior—particularly in the notably large divergencies in earnings for the same kind of labor in different firms.

Most likely, however, the theoretical maximand had only limited application to the SMF when it called for staff curtailment. The disinclination of the SMF to take such action, though, testifies not so much to a breach with the preferences of the collective as to the lack of realism of the theoretical maximand as an expression of those preferences when staff curtailment is in question.

The LMF of theory pursues its maximand in a market system that functions effectively—that is, prices tend to be at market clearing levels. As we saw, for the SMF under PBS that may not be the case. Government controlled prices can deviate from clearing levels even more than is usual in market systems. It also follows that without being motivated differently from the LMF the SMF might sometimes be led to behave differently from that entity. Such distortions, if they occur, are not observable from the limited information at hand. They will be consequential, however, in a later context.

Similarly, the SMF could diverge from theoretically predicted behavior because of external constraints on its response to market conditions. Here, too, available data are not illuminating. However, at least one source of external pressure on the firm, the commune government, has sought ends that were more harmonious with than in conflict with those we impute to the SMF. Thus, other things being equal, that agency had diverse specific concerns (Neuberger and James 1973, p. 270). One of these was to expand its tax revenue. With rates subject to substantial federal constraint, that objective should have been broadly consistent with increasing net income—though not necessarily net income per worker. The latter could dictate a reduction in employment and total income. The commune government could be expected to oppose such action, however, to the extent that a further concern of that agency was to expand employment within its locality. The enterprise, in any case, was probably not inclined to curtail staff.

Available evidence as to the motivation of the self-managed firm under PBS, however, is rather limited as yet. That also implies that we cannot really rule out some hypotheses, rather different from LMF theory, that have been advanced mainly by Yugoslav economists. Among these, the chief is that of Horvat: the enterprise seeks to maximize, not net income per worker as understood here, but net income after deduction of labor charges at some target pay rate. This explains at once the asserted absence of a backward-sloping short-run supply curve; on the other hand, that is equally excluded by a constraint on staff curtailment. Horvat apparently considers such a constraint as applying in any case. Also, the resulting analysis is incomplete in that no explanation is provided of the target pay rate, or, more basically, for the earnings differentials observed among workers doing similar work in different enterprises.[58]

Enterprise choices among time periods (to come to that aspect) are involved in a sense in every decision on investment, but central to all such decisions is that on enterprise savings. To the extent that savings are invested and investment in the real world inherently entails risk, in exploring enterprise savings we cannot continue to exclude risk as we have done so far. Systematic discussion of risk taking, however, is still deferred.

When savings are in question, as we saw, the maximand of the theoretic LMF can become rather complex. From the standpoint of the current collective, however, the case for retaining income within the LMF, rather than distributing it, could clearly be rather attentuated.

To recall analytic essentials: the current staff will engage in self-financing only so far as the rate of return matches or exceeds an adjusted marginal rate of time preference, R. The latter rate exceeds the marginal rate of time preference because the required return must also compensate for nonrecovery of principal by the current staff. The excess over the time-preference rate depends on the expected tenure of the current staff. If workers have the option of depositing in savings accounts at interest sums that they save individually, the rate of return must also match or exceed the R for which the marginal rate of time preference equals savings-deposit interest. Finally, even if the rate of return matches or exceeds R, the current staff should prefer to finance investment through credits, should the credits be available at a rate of interest less than R.

What all this meant for the SMF under PBS, we can discern when we consider that interest rates on savings deposits over the years in question ranged from 5.0 to 7.5 percent (Dubey 1975, p. 228). With a marginal rate of time preference equal to, say, 6.0 percent, the corresponding R would vary as follows depending on the expected worker tenure:

Expected tenure (years)	(percent)
1	106.0
5	23.8
8	16.1
10	13.6
20	8.7

Under PBS, interest on bank credit was subject to a ceiling of 8.0–10.0 percent. With industrial producers' prices rising at an average rate of 6.4 percent, however, banks could often impose above-ceiling rates, while credit rationing was widespread.

Nevertheless, unless workers looked forward to a relatively long tenure, they had little incentive to engage in self-financing. If bank credit were available, there was instead a case for recourse to such funds to finance investment. Savings deposits too must very often have been relatively attractive.

The incentive to invest would have been low even if investment in the enterprise posed no risk. To the degree that there was risk, the rate of return required to induce self-financing would have exceeded R by an appropriate risk premium. Recourse to bank credit would be more appealing on that account.

Under PBS, enterprises nevertheless retained 15.5–21.6 percent of their income (table 8–1), or 27.4–35.7 percent of their disposable income (that is, income after taxes and other payments to political-social institutions). These totals include allocations both to investment and to diverse other purposes. However, investment allocations alone came to about 17.2–24.5 percent of disposable income.[59] By Western standards, such shares represent a notably high propensity to save for a country at the Yugoslav level. That is so even though, in the West, principal is recoverable. Yugoslav enterprise savings, moreover, were superimposed upon appreciable private savings by households (Dubey 1975, pp. 220–221, 227–228; SZZS 1973, p. 176).

One wonders, therefore, whether enterprise motivation at this point is not different from that posited theoretically. For well-known reasons, enterprise executives in the West often find it to their interest to promote growth, and retain profits to that end. If Yugoslav executives were similarly motivated, they could have sought, by use of their authority, to influence the enterprise to act accordingly. Their immediate financial rewards for promoting growth would be modest, but the resulting gains in status and prestige (Jan Vanek 1972, p. 205) could have been appealing.

Still, granting the possibility of such countertheoretical motivation, there were causes enough to explain the inordinate savings. Here again, markets were not as envisaged in theory. At this point, the divergence must have been consequential. I refer particularly to the limited availability of credit, and to the fact that the banks usually financed fixed investments only if the enterprise supplied some of the required funds. At least, that was the practice in earlier years, and apparently it persisted under PBS to some degree (Furubotn and Pejovich 1971, pp. 72, 87; Jan Vanek, p. 264).

Then too, before the economic reform of 1965, the division of enterprise income between retained funds and worker take-home pay was the subject of rather specific government guidelines. Under the reform, such regulation was abandoned, but informal external control of one sort or another can hardly have been entirely lacking. At any rate, prereform patterns sometimes persisted. Reinstitution of quasi-official (if not official) controls over earnings retention and worker take-home pay has been a feature of the most recent reforms, and some steps in that direction were already being taken as PBS waned.[60]

In short, the capital market was flawed, and the enterprise was constrained in ways favorable to high rates of savings. However, the enterprise for its part could still have been motivated as theory posits.

Under PBS, the share of income that the self-managed firm saved was impressive throughout, but it tended to decline over the course of time (table 8-1). The reason must have been the indicated shift regarding external controls. While informal constraints probably persisted after 1965, the abandonment of governmental guidelines doubtless stimulated an increased payout. In the process, enterprise savings should have come to diverge less widely from theoretical expectations.

Although the savings share was generally large, among different firms it tended to be larger the higher the level of worker take-home pay—or so we infer from industry data on income-retention rates (Wachtel 1973, p. 114 ff). Such a relation between savings and income is familiar in the West, and in itself need not represent any departure from theoretical expectation. In the Yugoslav case, however, the differential savings rates might have reflected the need of less prosperous firms to compete for labor with more prosperous firms. If so, workers weighing employment in different firms must have discounted enterprise savings relative to take-home pay. Theoretically, that would be understandable only if savings exceeded those that conform to workers' preferences. We have found reasons enough for this to be the case. The same causes that gave rise to the excess, furthermore, probably had much to do with the differential savings rates between firms with different levels of worker take-home pay.

Thus, it is not surprising that the egalitarian tendencies in earnings differentials between workers in different occupations operated here as well to limit the payout of more prosperous firms (Comisso 1979, pp. 107–108). Another related doctrinal strand bore more expressly on earnings retention: the enterprise should exclude from workers payout unearned gains such as those derived from a price increase. A tendency for the individual firm to plough back a larger share of earnings when business is good (Jan Vanek 1972, p. 246) would also have contributed to the variation in enterprise savings ratios with the level of worker take-home pay. That, however, could easily have occurred without any external constraints.

Policies and practices such as the foregoing have an immediate corollary for the main theme of this chapter: Given the apparent constraints on enterprise saving, workers' gains from stochastic variations in enterprise income should have tended to be restricted. There probably was thus a kind of symmetry involved—a high level of worker earnings was trimmed back, just as sharp cuts in pay were avoided.[61]

This brings us finally to risk taking. In choosing among stochastic alternatives, the LMF of theory would be notably prone to risk avoidance because, with workers ultimately in charge and primary risk bearers, the concern would be to maximize the expected utilities of the collective in general. Members of the collective will ordinarily be at income levels that are characterized by marked risk aversion. Unlike stockholders in the usual Western corporate enterprise, workers in the LMF will also be unable to limit risk through diversification.

In gauging to what extent the SMF under PBS was similarly prone to risk avoidance, our point of departure must be the tentative view of its motivation to which we have arrived thus far. Although the SMF contrasted sharply with its theoretical counterpart with regard to executive authority, under the existing income-disposition arrangements, executives and workers had an incentive to pursue ends more or less as theory postulates. Viewed as a hypothesis, the prevalence of such motivation can sometimes be discerned in enterprise behavior with respect to nonstochastic alternatives relating to a single time period. The theoretical maximand tends to lose effect, however, where staff curtailment is in question. As for choices among time periods, as manifest in enterprise savings, the enterprise diverges from theoretical expectation at this point, but the causes could easily be other than the pursuit of the relevant theoretical maximand.

In short, to the extent the hypothesis is valid, enterprise motivation in the face of risk must turn on how workers and executives in the SMF under PBS compare with the collective as a whole in the theoretical LMF in their degree of aversion to and exposure to risk. Should all those groups experience the same degree of risk aversion and exposure, the SMF is no less and no more a risk avoider than its theoretical counterpart. Should workers and executives in the SMF be adverse and exposed to risk in different degrees, the extent to which the enterprise seeks to avoid risks would depend additionally on the comparative influence of the two groups when risk taking was in question.

Turning to those matters, the essentials are readily stated so far as they are known. Workers in general are presumably equally risk averse, whether employed in the SMF under PBS or the LMF of theory. On the other hand, the SMF differed markedly from its theoretical counterpart regarding the exposure of the collective to risk, especially with respect to enterprise adversity. Unfavorable consequences for worker take-home pay were cushioned in one way or another, particularly in the short run. Repercussions on employment were also limited to the extent that there was a constraint against staff curtailment, although earnings fluctuations were correspondingly magnified. The worker was by no means completely sheltered from downside risk, but overall, his exposure was distinctly mitigated. Through more or less imposed variations in the retention of enterprise earnings, the workers' participation in gains from enterprise success was also circumscribed, but overall, workers in the SMF had less reason to be risk avoiders than those in the theoretical LMF.

With higher incomes than those of workers in general, executive personnel should have experienced somewhat less risk aversion than the latter. Their exposure to enterprise risk should have been broadly similar to that of the collective as a whole. Should the enterprise come upon adversity, however, executives might be affected inordinately—whether through dismissal, failure to be reappointed, or some other form of career impairment.

What can be said about the comparative influence of the collective as whole and executives in particular on decisions on questions involving risk must already be evident. Such questions arise most often in the case of investment projects that entail the introduction of new technologies and products. Here, to a greater degree than elsewhere, executives, together with their technical aides, tended to be relatively influential in the SMF under PBS.

Just what the foregoing facts mean as to the tendency of the SMF under PBS to avoid risk must to some extent be conjectural. This tendency, however, should not have been nearly as great as could be expected to characterize the LMF of theory.

I have tacitly assumed that under PBS workers were not only exposed to risk, but were aware of that fact. Results of a survey of workers in ten enterprises reported on by Županov (1967; 1969, ch. 1) indicate otherwise. When asked about the impact on their own earnings of a decline in the income of their enterprise, a great many responded either that they did not expect their earnings to be affected, or that they did not know what the effect on their earnings would be. The survey was conducted, however, in June 1966. As Županov indicates, it might not fully reflect circumstances following the 1965 reform. The survey questionnaire apparently did not distinguish between a short-term and a long-term reduction in enterprise income. That could be an important aspect, particularly as the first effect of a reduction in enterprise income might be felt only on the supplementary income that the worker received at the end of, say, a year. To the extent that workers were not clear about the downside risk to which self-management subjected them, however, the tendency toward risk avoidance under that form of organization would be less.

I refer to Županov's findings for the collective generally. Županov regrettably does not present any numerical data on the perceptions of managerial personnel alone, but apparently the majority were aware of the downside risk to which not only they, but ordinary workers, were exposed. There is no basis here, therefore, for discounting the tendency to risk avoidance.[62]

However weak or strong that tendency may have been, our ultimate concern is with risk taking. We wish especially to grasp how self-management may have affected decision making regarding innovation, where risk is apt to be relatively important. From that standpoint, although self-management probably did not skew decision making against risk as much as it would in the theoretical LMF, it still entailed significant diffusion of authority within the enterprise. That was true regarding innovation. Here, as elsewhere, decision making was an internal political process as well as a bureaucratic one. Not too surprisingly, the process often turned out to be cumbersome and one whose consummation in any practical action was rather uncertain—in short, a process hardly favorable to innovation. Here again, Županov (1978b) is an eloquent witness:

> Since there are no systematic data on anti-entrepreneurship, one can only cite individual examples from the press. Such argumentation nevertheless rests upon shaky foundations, since one can always find contrary examples. A true picture could be provided only by systematic research that demonstrates how many managers have attempted to behave in an entrepreneurial manner and—encountering disapproval and misfortunes—have abandoned that behavior. The number of defeated and resigned is unlikely to be small. Approximately 73 percent of directors and 62 percent of other managers interviewed expressed the view that new ideas create resistance and conflicts in the organization, making it difficult to predict whether directors would be successful in implementing changes. In any case, the labeling of entrepreneurial behavior with the reprehensible term "managerialism" speaks for itself (p. 83).

Županov is citing here the results of a survey of some 245 executives who attended a 1968 symposium.[63]

The self-managed firm, under PBS, we must again consider, was not entirely autonomous. In the case of investment projects, outside agencies—chiefly the commune government and the banks—played a significant part. If the commune government was motivated as argued above, it would not have discouraged enterprise initiative regarding investment projects, but the additional clearance involved could not have been helpful. Banks were often under the influence of the commune government, but they doubtless tended otherwise—as banks do almost everywhere—to inhibit risk taking, if only through qualitative credit controls.

While limiting downside risk for workers, the prevailing constraint on staff curtailment must also have acted by itself to thwart innovations. Still again, activites entailing risk in a theoretical context must have been even more risky in an environment such as that in Yugoslavia under PBS: an environment, that is, where shifts in working arrangements were numerous and frequent; where the economy itself manifested marked instability (Horvat 1971, pp. 90 *ff*); and where, as indicated, prices must have diverged frequently from clearing levels. Because of the latter, availability of materials for new technologies and products must sometimes have been uncertain.

The net of all forces affecting enterprise risk taking under PBS, considered together, can only be determined by further empirical inquiry. It would be surprising, though, if the SMF were not more entrepreneurial than the LMF of theory could be expected to be. I have been comparing the SMF with its theoretical counterpart, but it would also be surprising, I think, if the SMF under PBS were as entrepreneurial as the typical Western private enterprise firm.

The 1974–1976 Reforms

What I have called the BOAL system of self-management dates essentially from the promulgation of the latest Yugoslav constitution (in 1974) and the subsequent codification and elaboration (principally in legislation enacted in 1976) of the novel arrangements for self-management outlined there. Many features of the new system had already been introduced in June 1971 as a series of amendments to the previous (1963) constitution, but prior to the adoption of the 1974 constitution, these amendments remained largely inoperative. Even after the new arrangements were dealt with in the new constitution and subsequent legislation—most importantly, in the Law on Associated Labor of November 25, 1976—they were by no means put immediately into effect. According to the latest accounts, some legalities have still to be fully implemented. That fact must be kept in mind as we consider the more important of the changes made in working arrangements.[64]

Of these, the chief relates to the internal organization of the enterprise. Organs of self-management began to proliferate within the firm at an early stage. Among other things, there could be further councils in individual works and departments in addition to the enterprise-wide workers' council. That arrangement had already become widespread by the late 1960s, but under the latest reforms, it is being extended further and transformed dramatically. The BOAL, or Basic Organization of Associated Labor, is an administrative entity that can be organized for an enterprise division. It has its own organs of self-management, has gained legal authority over enterprise assets required for the division's functioning, and has become a separate and distinct commercial entity. Its relations with the BOALs established in other divisions of the same firm are supposed to be conducted accordingly. The different BOALs can continue to coordinate their activities and arrange for services to be used in common, such as legal counseling, marketing, and the like. However, that is supposed to be by agreement, and transfers of goods and services between divisions are to take place at agreed-upon prices.[65] At the same time, a BOAL administering a division formerly subordinate to one enterprise can enter into contractual relations with a BOAL adminstering a division formerly subordinate to another enterprise.

The new arrangements are to be established more or less generally in industry. To organize themselves into a BOAL, workers in an enterprise division must be performing labor whose results are expressible "in terms of value within the work organization or on the market," but the stipulation evidently is not highly restrictive. Wherever it is met, workers have not only the right, but the duty, to establish a BOAL.[66]

The mandated restructuring of industrial self-management is dramatic indeed. In effect, the BOAL is to supersede the enterprise as the primary agency for industrial administration. The resulting atomization of multi-divisional enterprises might be the envy of any Western trust-buster. As a mechanism for industrial coordination, however, the new arrangements are obviously quite complex, and what could be achieved by introducing them must have seemed problematic to many concerned. Understandably, the restructuring has also turned out to be often *pro forma*. While instituting the new arrangements on paper, many enterprises have reportedly functioned much as they did before (Comisso 1980, pp. 193, 201–203).

The new scheme has doubtless been widely implemented in a more or less meaningful way (compare Sacks 1980). Even where it has, however, the break with the past has been mitigated by the inevitable feature already mentioned: after divisions of an enterprise are organized into BOALs, they must still coordinate their activities. That is legally obligatory—at least, a BOAL cannot withdraw from the larger "work organization" of which it was a part if that should "lead to a major hindrance or prevention of work" elsewhere in the work organization (Constitution of 1974, art. 37).

In coordinating their activities, the different BOALs can also assign responsibilities to central-enterprise executive authorities and self-managed organs, including the workers' council. The latter is composed of delegates from the different BOALs. Arrangements of this sort must be more or less widely operative, although as a result of the very restructuring that has been in progress relevant statistical data are difficult to construe (Sacks 1980, p. 223).

The government had diverse aims in restructuring self-management in the foregoing manner, but not least was the obvious one of making that system more effective in assuring workers' control. To the extent that the new arrangements have come to operate at all effectively, they must have tended to weaken the authority of central executives in the enterprise (Comisso 1980; Sacks 1980). To what extent, however, the worker has gained in influence is an interesting question. The trend towards divisional self-management that prevailed before the BOAL was instituted apparently yielded the worker at most only limited gains in influence. Although the enterprise is being atomized, the government has also taken steps to assure that the trade unions can participate legally in the process of staffing executive posts in the BOAL and in other affairs of the enterprise. Partly on that basis, the unions (and also the Party) have recovered influence within the enterprise that they lost previously.[67] Yugoslav complaints about the limitations of the workers' role under self-mangement continue; so, on some scale, do strikes.[68]

Under the latest reforms, the government has also initiated a number of shifts affecting the institutional environment within which the enterprise operates.[69] Most importantly, it has sought to reestablish control over income disposition through the system of so-called "social compacts" and "self-management arrangments," early antecedents of which date as far back as 1968. Social compacts have now been concluded countrywide among political, social, and economic agencies at different administrative levels ranging from the federal to the commune. The agencies for a particular region or industrial branch determine in this way the principles of income disposition that are supposed to be implemented by self-management agreements among corresponding BOALs and enterprises.

Although this process is rather different from pre-1965 regulatory procedures, the principles established in the social compacts are apparently obligatory for BOALs and enterprises and must be heeded in their own self-management agreements. The compacts and agreements concluded so far have yet to be studied in any systematic way; however, what they mean for income disposition can be inferred from the fact that the post-1965 decline in the share of disposable income retained by the enterprise has been arrested, if not reversed.[70]

Under the new arrangements, disproportionately high retention rates have been imposed on high-income BOALs and enterprises.[71] That, of course, was to be expected. As we saw, the same pattern probably prevailed already under the informal constraints of the late 1960s. If a 1972 self-management agreement for Belgrade trade workers is at all indicative, though, progressivity has perhaps become more marked: A firm with income per standard worker amounting to as little as 61 percent of the projected Belgrade average could devote as much as 95 percent of its income to take-home pay. Should income per standard worker be as high as 212 percent of the projected Belgrade average, however, the permissible payout fell to 55 percent of income (Furubotn and Pejovich 1973, p. 293 *ff*).

According to the Law on Associated Labor (arts. 115, 128) income disposition within the BOAL is to conform to "common bases and scales" (*osnovi i merila*) established by the self-management agreement among different BOALs in an enterprise. We presumably must read in that light instances reported where extreme variations in income per worker among different BOALs within a firm gave rise to hardly any variations in payout per worker. The differences in earnings, we must infer, go rather to generate widely different rates of earnings retention.[72] The net impact of the BOAL system on executive pay is not clear.[73]

Control over income disposition is the principal, but not the only, use to which the system of social compacts and self-management agreements has been devoted. The government has also been seeking in the last years to use the accords as an instrument of coordination more generally. It has been endeavoring to assure that the plans of political, social, and economic entities will be more fully integrated with each other than was the case previously. To that end, self-management agreements are supposed to cover not only income disposition but matters of mutual interest to the signatories—particularly prices, quantities of goods traded, and joint investment projects. BOALs and enterprises are supposed to reach agreements on these matters with due regard to annual and medium-term plans that they formulate. The plans, in turn, must take into account guidelines established in social compacts. Through an interactive process, the plans of different BOALs within an enterprise are to be brought in harmony with each other, with those of BOALs in other enterprises, and with those of political and social entities.

Shortly after this scheme was introduced in 1976, the mechanism by which it would be implemented was described as "agonizingly vague" (Milenkovich 1977, p. 58). Its workings are still not too clear. The government claims not to have revived centralist planning. This might be true, but planning was not entirely indicative previously, and divergencies from indicative planning have no doubt increased. How fully the plans of different entities are being integrated is another matter, but self-management agreements that fix prices, quantities of goods traded, and investment pooling arrangements are being widely concluded.[74]

To come again to risk taking and innovation, the particulars of the new reforms are often uncertain. In any event, the changes are still in the process of implementation. It is not too early, however, to discern significant tendencies. It is difficult to avoid the conclusion that, overall, risk taking and innovation are probably being adversely affected. This is so despite some aspects that favor such activities—for instance, the fact that the self-management agreements, in effect, establish forward markets. The environment within which the enterprise operates might, in this way, become less stochastic.

Another feature, not yet noted, should have a mixed impact on risk taking. I refer to the explicit prohibition in the Constitution of 1974 (art. 32) and Law on Associated Labor (arts. 177, 213) of staff curtailment to implement technological and other innovations without arranging appropriate alternative employment for the workers affected. Not really very novel, the prohibition would tend to limit downside risk for workers, but even so could sometimes make infeasible otherwise admissible innovations.

Even if the foregoing features together tend to favor risk taking and innovation, still others should more than offset them. For instance, under the new controls over income disposition, the gains from successful outcomes have probably been restricted. Also, the atomization of the enterprise will limit risk pooling, despite such arrangements as those for joint investments by different BOALs. Likewise, under the BOAL system, relatively independent authorities in charge of different divisions of the enterprise must reach agreement on common action. This must often make the process of innovation even more cumbersome than before.

However, such tendencies might or might not persist. The outlook is especially uncertain when one is referring to such extraordinarily complex and sweeping reforms. One wonders how completely the reforms will ever be implemented, and, if they are implemented, how long they will endure before they provoke still further sweeping changes.[75]

Conclusion

This has been a lengthy inquiry. In conclusion, it may be advisable to summarize the discussion. The concern throughout has been with entrepreneurship as manifest in risk taking under the so-called "self-management" form of industrial organization in Yugoslavia. Risk is apt to be relatively important in the case of innovation, and attention has been directed especially to that aspect.

As a form of labor participation, self-management has been subject to extensive theoretical analysis. Theoretical writings refer particularly to an economy in which enterprises are labor-managed in a rather ideal sense. The resulting analysis is highly abstract, but is still serves as a point of departure. Of particular interest is the implication that, with workers ultimately in control and residual claimants to income—and hence primary risk-bearers—the labor-mangaged firm (LMF) should be notably inclined to risk avoidance. Innovation might suffer as a result.

Appraisal of this matter under Yugoslav self-management must consider that the relevant economic working arrangements have been notably fluid. I have focused particularly on the relatively developed system that came to prevail after the multiple institutional shifts known collectively as the economic reform of 1965. Reference was made at first to the pre-BOALs system (PBS)—that is, the economic working arrangements that prevailed prior to further reforms implemented after 1974–1976, and hence prior to the large-scale introduction of the so-called Basic Organizaton of Associated Labor (BOAL).

With respect to PBS, an initial finding concerns the behavior of the self-managed firm (SMF) in circumstances where risk is not consequential and enterprise savings are not in question: The enterprise probably pursued, at least to a degree, the maximand postulated for the LMF of theory. That is, it sought to maximize net income per employed worker. To determine the maximand, employment must be understood as calculated with due regard to differences in labor quality.

Depending on the circumstances, pursuit of such a maximand might theoretically call for staff curtailment. Hardly plausible to begin with in a labor-managed economy, such action could be expected under PBS only rather rarely and in attenuated form. However, sizeable divergencies in earnings for similar labor in different enterprises give reason to think that the theoretical maximand was otherwise pursued. That such divergencies should prevail in at least a protracted short run is an important analytic corollary of maximization of net income per worker.

Working arrangements that might have affected the behavior of the self-managed enterprise under PBS were nevertheless rather different from those assumed in theory. Most importantly, authority within the firm gravitated to a notable degree to managerial personnel, though perhaps not to the extent sometimes assumed in Yugoslav, as well as Western, discussion. Workers, however, generally had more or less the status of residual claimants to income that theory envisages for them. Granting the analytically incongruous authority of executives, such persons still found it to their interest to pursue the theoretical maximand along with workers generally. Under PBS, their incomes were determined essentially like (and varied with) the earnings of other members of the collective.

Under PBS, however, enterprise savings probably exceeded what might have been expected theoretically. Perhaps enterprise motivation at this point was other than theory envisages, but the inordinate savings can be explained otherwise in terms of credit rationing, the requirement posed by banks that enterprises supply matching funds, and the likelihood of informal external constraints on the share of enterprise income paid out to workers.

Under PBS, even if enterprise motivation in nonstochastic single-period choices and in decisions on savings had been such as theory presupposes, the SMF could not be expected to be as prone to risk avoidance as the LMF of theory was. True, in the SMF (as in the theoretical LMF) the collective's status as a residual claimant to income meant that risk-averse workers were also primary risk-bearers. However, for Yugoslav workers, exposure to risk of income curtailment in adverse circumstances was markedly limited by diverse mitigating arrangements. The risk of the loss of employment was also comparatively modest. Informal constraints on income payout probably tended at the same time to limit gains from successful performance, but with due regard to losses as well as gains, the expected payoff from risk taking should have been more favorable to such action than theory might suggest.

I have been referring to the collective generally. Under PBS, the attitude of managerial personnel towards risk was necessarily particularly important to enterprise risk taking. With their higher incomes, however, such persons should have been less risk-averse than workers, while their exposure to risk was broadly similar to that of workers.

Although the SMF was probably not as prone to risk avoidance as its theoretical counterpart, the SMF still was so inclined, perhaps sometimes markedly so. Moreover, however self-government affected attitudes towards risk, it often tended to thwart risk taking in the cardinal sphere of innovation. Granting the often preponderant authority of executives, power was still diffuse, with the result that obtaining clearances for innovations was notably cumbersome and uncertain. Additional clearances that might be required from external authorities, including both banks and commune officials, were not helpful. The constraint against staff curtailment must also have been an impediment.

So much for PBS. The shifts in economic working arrangements referred to as the 1974–1976 reforms have often been implemented only *pro forma* or not at all. To the extent that they have been implemented effectively, they are strikingly complex, and their impact on risk taking and innovation must be uneven, but overall adverse. To refer only to the most outstanding aspect, it is difficult to see how risk taking and innovation could benefit from establishing relatively independent self-management organs, or BOALs, to administer different divisions of the enterprise. Such atomization must tend to limit risk pooling and make the innovation process itself even more cumbersome than before.

Entrepreneurship under Yugoslav self-management is a relatively novel theme. In exploring it here, I have nevertheless been able to draw on much related Western and Yugoslav literature. A principal conclusion, however, is that still more research is needed. That it too evident from the often tentative nature of my findings to need laboring.

Yugoslav self-management is of interest not only for its own sake, but as an outstanding example of labor participation in management. From that standpoint, an inevitable question arises: How relevant is the Yugoslav experience elsewhere? In pondering this complex issue, the reader should consider the special circumstances under which labor participation evolved in Yugoslavia, particularly the relatively early stage of economic development there, the recent peasant origin of much of the labor force, and the nature of the political system—which, if not as authoritarian as elsewhere under socialism, is still authoritarian. If labor participation in Yugoslavia has often turned out rather differently than many proponents hoped, such circumstances are not the least of the reasons.

That must be so, among other things, with respect to the relatively limited role of the ordinary worker in managerial affairs—a denouement so much at odds with both the theory of the LMF and Yugoslav legal doctrine. On the other hand, the additional departure from theory represented by the dampening of downside risk for the worker must be inevitable in any far-reaching scheme of labor participation. Failure to consider that can only signify a lack of realism in the analysis. However, these are properly matters for separate inquiry, and cannot really be pursued here.

Notes

1. Much to the benefit of one who is not far along in his efforts to acquire Serbo-Croatian, a good deal of relevant Yugoslav scholarly work was originally published in English or has been translated.

2. My inquiry, thus, is complementary to that of Sacks (1973), which focuses on the founding of new firms. The latter study is an outstanding exception to the general neglect of entrepreneurial behavior.

3. The proverbial caveat as to scale, which holds in the linear homogeneous case for the private-enterprise firm, applies here as well.

4. See Ward (1958); Domar (1966); Jaroslav Vanek (1970); and Meade (1972).

5. Jaroslav Vanek (1970) provides an extensive discussion, though one that seems incomplete in interesting ways. For an example, see note 6.

To return to the variation in the marginal product of labor in different firms, note that for firms in the same industry applying the same linear homogeneous production function, a difference in capital stock will not cause marginal products to differ even in the short run. (See Jaroslav Vanek 1970, pp. 31–33.)

6. So Jaroslav Vanek plausibly argues. However, a definitive formal demonstration that relative earnings will be the same in equilibrium has yet to be provided.

7. In response to monopoly power represented by a downward-sloping demand schedule, however, the LMF tends to be more restrictive than the corresponding private-enterprise firm (Meade 1972; 1974).

8. The maximand that I assume applies in decisions on self-financing is essentially the one stressed in theoretical writings. Vanek, however, apparently adopted that maximand after first focusing on one of a rather different sort. On this and the conditions determining the volume of enterprise self-financing, see Jaroslav Vanek (1970), pp. 168–171, 296–298; and Jaroslav Vanek (1977), chs. 8–9. See also Furubotn and Pejovich (1974), pp. 227 *ff;* Pejovich (1973); Stephen (1980); and Furubotn (1980).

As indicated above, the LMF, like the private enterprise firm, employs a durable nonlabor input up to the point where the value of marginal product equals the rental charge corresponding to the rate of interest and depreciation. The rate of interest is supposedly that prevailing in the market, but one further assumes that the enterprise does, in fact, borrow at that rate.

For any likely market rate, that will usually be true, but a labor-managed firm might conceivably wish to meet all of its investment requirements out of its own savings. In that case, the rental charge is determined not by the market rate of interest, but by the R corresponding to r for the volume of savings in question.

9. The labor force is again supposed to be homogeneous. On the maximand for the labor-managed firm under stochastic conditions, see Hey and Suckling (1979).

10. I have been referring to absolute, as distinct from relative, risk aversion, and to risk premium in the sense of the excess of expected income over its certainty equivalent in terms of risk-taker utility. Also, in comparing enterprises under different systems, reference is to the risk premium, and hence to the expected return that is required—other things being equal—to induce risk takers to commit themselves to a given marginal project. On the foregoing, I have benefited from discussions with Jerry Green. Compare Arrow (1971), pp. 277–278.

11. From the standpoint of efficiency, however, the lump-sum taxes could also be differentiated between social states. For instance, in agriculture, a higher tax might be levied when there is rain than when there is no rain. Theoretically—though hardly in practice—income variation might be dampened somewhat in that way.

12. A rare exception is Furubotn and Pejovich (1974), pp. 227 *ff,* although reference there is to a nonstochastic environment, rather than to the stochastic one of interest here.

13. See, for example, Horvat et al. (1979), vol. 1, p. 25, and the 1974 constitution.

14. On elections to the workers' council, see Ward (1957); International Labor Office, ILO (1962): pp. 78–81; Blumberg (1969), pp. 196 *ff;* and Wachtel (1973), pp. 64 *ff.*

15. Different sources sometimes differ on the precise nature of the council's authority in selecting the enterprise director. See ILO (1962), pp. 100–104; Horvat (1971), p. 100; Wachtel (1973), pp. 70–71; Sacks (1973), p. 10; Granick (1975), pp. 363–364; and Sirc (1979), pp. 39, 183–184.

16. See *Radio Free Europe Research* (February 20–26), 1980).

17. A principal source here on the studies in question is Obradović and Dunn (1978). Some of the relevant essays by Yugoslav scholars collected in this volume are apparently revisions of papers previously published or otherwise circulated, but the empirical data still generally relate to PBS. On the other hand, the fact that the authors, in republishing their earlier essays, saw no basis to qualify conclusions that clearly followed from such empirical data is a fact to keep in mind when we assess the 1974–1976 reforms.

On the Yugoslav work on power distribution within the firm, see also Wachtel (1973), pp. 86 *ff;* Neuberger and James (1973), p. 276; Županov (1969), ch. 10; and Županov (1973; 1974; 1975).

18. For some dissident and also some corroborative views, see Wachtel (1973): pp. 86 *ff.*

19. As in Obradović (1978) and Vejnović (1978).

20. In Vejnović (1978), pp. 272 *ff.*

21. See Jovanov (1978), the report cited above on a book of the same author in *Radio Free Europe Research* (February 20–26, 1980), and the same serial for June 8–14, 1978.

22. *Radio Free Europe Research* (February 20–26, 1980).

23. See Adizes (1971) and *The Economist* (July 16, 1966; September 16, 1967; August 2, 1969). Although referring to a later period, the following accounts have implications for the PBS arrangements now being discussed: Comisso (1979), chs. 7–9; and *Wall Street Journal* (October 8, 1975).

24. *Raspodela dohotka* has usually been translated as "income distribution." However, in the West, that term is often used to refer to the division of income among individuals or households. For reasons that will become evident, the more general "income disposition" seems more accurate.

25. See particularly Obradović (1978), and Arzenšek (1978) in Obradović and Dunn (1978); also Županov (1969), pp. 248 *ff;* Zupanov (1973); Neuberger and James (1973), p. 280; and Wachtel (1973), pp. 91 *ff.*

26. According to a long-standing practice, however, no workers' councils were organized in very small firms; instead, the entire collective served as its own council.

27. The fixing of market-clearing prices by a Central Planning Board is, of course, an outstanding feature of the market socialism of Oskar Lange.

28. Pejovich (1966), p. 23 *ff;* Horvat (1971), pp. 108 *ff;* Dirlam and Plummer (1973), pp. 90 *ff;* OECD (1966; 1967; 1969; 1974; 1979); and Schrenk et al. (1979), pp. 119–122.

29. In Yugoslav parlance, economic plans are called social plans. Beginning in 1966, the annual plan at the federal level was superseded by a policy statement issued as a parliamentary resolution. On the state of planning at the time in question, see Pejovich (1966), pp. 36 *ff;* Horvat (1971), pp. 87 *ff;* and Dirlam and Plummer (1973), ch. 7.

30. The oft-noted Yugoslav experiment with credit auctions turned out to be just that—an experiment. It was employed only for a limited period after 1954. For more on the investment auctions, the state of post-1965 credit markets, and banking more generally, see Neuberger (1959); Horvat (1971), pp. 130 *ff;* Furubotn and Pejovich (1971); Dirlam and Plummer (1973), pp. 177 *ff;* Dubey (1975), pp. 66, 210 *ff;* Granick (1975), pp. 396 *ff;* and Schrenk et al (1979), chs. 4, 7, 8.

Given the prevailing inflation, the ability of the banks to impose extra ceiling rates and the prevalence of credit rationing do not seem inconsistent with the 9 percent rate of return that Jaroslav Vanek estimates is realized on the depreciated capital of self-managed enterprises.

31. Rus (1978-B), pp. 404 *ff* is not explicit as to the date of the survey data on which he relies. Although an original version of his essay was prepared for presentation to a conference held in August 1974, his conclusion about the status of banks, I believe, could apply to earlier years now of interest.

32. On the Party and self-management, see Wachtel (1973), pp. 79–82; on the Party's role in Yugoslav life more generally, see Rusinow (1978).

33. Neuberger and James (1973), p. 226; and Rus (1978-A), pp. 199 *ff*.

34. Bučar (1978), p. 427. The ascendancy that the executive achieved in this way over Party activists is reminiscent of circumstances long prevailing in other Eastern countries, where the secretary of the enterprise Party cell may find it expedient to collaborate with management even in violation of official norms. Bučar is also highly illuminating on the relation of the Party and trade union of self-management organs, although one wonders whether their control over the latter is nearly as complete as he implies. At any rate, the Party and the union were again on the ascendant in enterprise affairs towards the close of the PBS period, when subsequent arrangements began to come into play. Bučar may be referring particularly to circumstances at that time.

35. Founders, whoever they might be, had the right to repayment of any capital that they supplied. At least for citizen founders, repayment was with interest (Sacks 1973, pp. 12–13).

36. In the source cited, reference is the "net product" (*neto produkt*). However, that category comes to essentially the same thing as "net income" (*neto dohodak*) as that was used in Yugoslav accounting practice by 1969, or rather it is the same except that turnover taxes (exclusive of special charges on retail gasoline sales) are treated as a deduction before deriving net income.

As represented in table 8–1, net product is apparently rather different from the category of that name in Yugoslav national income accounting. That is necessarily so, if only because changes in stocks are excluded from net product in the table, but reference there is to initial and terminal stocks at acquisition prices. For purposes of national income accounting, initial and terminal stocks are valued at the prices on the corresponding dates.

Possibly there are other divergencies between the two output categories. At any rate, even apart from the treatment of stocks, net product as given in the table should not be identified with the category of that name as used in Western national income accounting, though there is clearly a broad correspondence.

On Yugoslav SMF and national income accounting, see Gorupić and Paj (1970), pp. 152 *ff;* Furubotn and Pejovich (1972); and Dubey (1975), ch. 9, appendix A.

SZZS (1973) provides no explanation of the discrepancy (*razlika*). It appears only for the three years 1966–1968, and is probably related to the manner of accounting for sales, which was changed in 1969.

37. On enterprise payments to social-political institutions under PBS, see Gorupić and Paj (1970), pp. 139 *ff;* Horvat (1971), pp. 145 *ff;* Dirlam and Plummer (1973), pp. 186 *ff;* Wachtel (1973), pp. 111 *ff;* and Dubey (1975), ch. 9.

38. The 4-percent rate was established along with the 1965 economic reform in July 1965. The tax was levied on the *poslovni fond* (business fond), which essentially corresponded to the net worth of a Western firm even though some self-financed special claims against the enterprise's assets were excluded (for example, so-called "reserve funds" and funds for "communal consumption" and housing. The *kamata* ceased to be levied in 1971. See Lepotinec et al. (1967), pp. 183 *ff;* Furubotn and Pejovich (1972), pp. 276–277; Dirlam and Plummer (1973), pp. 41–45, 192–193.

39. Although the progressive taxes under PBS served as a source of local finance, they were intially levied in accord with the schedule promulgated by the federal government. Subsequently, schedules were promulgated by republican (or sometimes local) governments. A schedule in effect in Croatia circa 1969, however, was more or less typical: annual incomes of up to 20,000 dinars were fully exempt from the tax. Should the taxpayer have any dependents, the exemption rose by 3,000–5,000 dinars per dependent. For incomes exceeding exempt amounts, the marginal rate of tax varied from 3 percent to 80 percent, the latter rate being levied on the excess over 80,000 dinars. For someone earning 45,000 dinars with no dependents, the marginal rate on the last 5,000 dinars earned was 13 percent.

For comparison, the average worker in the socialized sector of the economy earned 11,520 dinars in 1969. The corresponding figure for the director of an SMF was 28,404 dinars. (These figures, of course, represent earnings from employment in the SMF.) Income from outside work were also subject to the tax, although no doubt the tax was frequently evaded. See Jurčec (1969), pp. 77 *ff,* 160; Bakračlić and Stojanovic (1970); SZZS (1971), pp. 268, 271; Dirlam and Plummer (1973), pp. 190–191, and Dubey (1975), p. 250.

40. As a benchmark, it may be useful to consider that for an individual with an income of $100, an even chance to win or lose $10 means that his choice is between the certain income of $100 and the stochastic option of ($90, $110). With a lump-sum tax of, say $10, the alternatives become $90 and ($80, $100); and with a 10-percent income tax $90 and ($81, $99). For a risk-averse person, the stochastic option is somewhat more attractive with the income tax than with the lump-sum tax.

41. On the financing of enterprise losses, see Dirlam and Plummer (1973), pp. 49–51; Sacks (1973), pp. 75–78; and Tyson (1977a).

42. That was clearly so for a minimum fixed by federal law. A com-

mune government could, if it wished, fix a higher minimum for workers within its purview, but the commune rates too were relatively low. See Gorupić and Paj (1970), p. 167; Wachtel (1973), pp. 101–102; and Dirlam and Plummer (1973), pp. 50, 65.

43. Gorupić and Paj (1970), pp. 180–183; Horvat (1971), pp. 104–105; and Dirlam and Plummer (1973), pp. 49–51.

44. In relation to total earnings, supplementary payments in manufacturing and mining averaged in 1956, 7.2 percent; in 1959, 12.2 percent, and in 1961, 9.0 percent [Wachtel (1973), p. 110.] Reason to think that the corresponding relation under PBS may have been similar is found in data available for the socialized sector in Slovenia: supplements there in 1971 constituted 10.4 percent of total earnings. See Miovic (1975), p. 108.

45. Furubotn and Pejovich (1972), p. 280; Dirlam and Plummer (1973), pp. 49–50; SZZS (1969), pp. 128–129.

46. See ILO (1962), pp. 126 *ff;* 218 *ff;* Bajt (1966); and Wachtel (1973).

47. While according to ILO (1962), p. 222, proportionality had been traditional regarding supplementary payments, Wachtel (1973), pp. 108–111, cites data on the relation of full to variable wages for different groups of industrial workers to show that that rule had ceased to apply by the late 1960s. As Wachtel is aware, the highly aggregative data he presents are open to more than one interpretation from that standpoint, but divergencies from proportionality doubtless occurred.

48. Executive incentive payments tend to be neglected in writings on Yugoslav self-management. However, in a textile enterprise that Adizes (1971) visited in 1967, some executives might earn as much as 32 percent over their basic pay if the enterprise's plan were completely fulfilled in specified particulars. There were even bonuses for limited degrees of underfulfillment, while overfulfillment brought still larger rewards. See Adizes (1971), pp. 51–52. This bonus scheme apparently was an exception to the rule enunciated in OECD (1965), p. 36: ". . . managerial categories receive management bonuses which can amount to 10 percent of their salaries."

A further question concerns the extent to which such special bonus arrangements prevailed under PBS. The textile firm referred to is one of two visited by Adizes. He does not indicate whether a corresponding scheme was used in the other. Granick (1975), found that special bonuses were being paid to executives in only one of the eight firms that he visited during 1970 (pp. 358, 365). Professor Alexander Bajt informs me (by letter of February 3, 1981) that bonus schemes such as those described by Adizes are, in fact, exceptional. According to both Slovenian Chamber of Commerce and trade union officials, no more then ten percent of enterprises have special incentive arrangements for executives. Such arrangements were more frequent prior to 1972, a "year of . . . severe political criticisms of managerialism, technicratism, and similar tendencies among managers."

49. Yugoslav income disparities appear to have been rather contracted by Western standards. Among countries at a comparable development stage, they were very much so. See Lydall (1968), pp. 215–219; Wachtel (1973), pp. 126 *ff;* Michal (1973); Granick (1975), pp. 459 *ff;* and Chapman (1977). Brown (1977) finds that Yugoslav labor differentials are somewhat wider than those in Great Britain, but his data do not seem to reach to the top among executives of British firms (pp. 56–58). Among Western countries, furthermore, Britain has for some time been both relatively advanced and relatively egalitarian.

50. A further implication is that any tendency towards the equality between firms and industries of relative marginal productivities of different kinds of labor should have been attenuated.

Such attenuation is inevitable wherever income disposition is shaped in an egalitarian manner. In effect, a firm with superior executive and other highly skilled labor is apt to employ too few unskilled workers relative to a firm less well-endowed with executive and other workers of superior quality.

51. Blum (1970), pp. 182–185; Horvat (1971), p. 105; Adizes (1971), pp. 128–129; Bajt (1972), p. 6; Jan Vanek (1972), p. 240; Neuberger and James (1973), pp. 267–268; Dirlam and Plummer (1973), pp. 49–50, 51–52; and Sirc (1979), pp. 131–137.

52. On the dismissal and non-reappointment of directors, see Brekić (1967), pp. 337–339; and Granick (1975), pp. 339, 352. Sletzinger (1976), cites somewhat different data on the number of directors who were not reelected, but his data relate to socio-political as well as economic organizations, and might be broader in scope than Granick's (pp. 58–59).

53. Granick (1975), p. 355; Sirc (1979), pp. 183–186. See also Županov (1969), ch. 10; and Županov (1973).

54. I refer, of course, to the impact of the taxes on labor effort and the like.

55. The tendency could only be compounded if income distribution were egalitarian, as in Yugoslavia. See above, n. 50.

56. See also Jan Vanek (1972), p. 284.

57. From industry data on net income and capital assets per worker, Vanek and Jovicic inpute a rate of return of 7 or 9 percent to capital (the precise figure depends on whether capital is gross or net of depreciation). Reference is to net income including the capital tax and bank loan interest, but as Vanek and Jovicic point out (though with data somewhat at variance with those underlying table 8–1), interest at the imputed rates would exceed such charges. According to their calculations, however, the coefficient of correlation between net income per worker and gross capital assets per worker is only .48. When reference is to net capital assets per worker, the coefficient is only .53.

In a similar analysis, but with interest deducted from net income, Marschak (1968) found hardly any correlation to speak of between net income per worker and capital assets per worker (pp. 581–582). In their calculations, however, Vanek and Jovicic adjust employment for differences in skill; Marschak apparently makes no such adjustment. That could have been a factor in Marschak's relatively low correlation coefficients. Perhaps relevant circumstances in 1969, the year on which Vanek and Jovicic focus, were also rather different from those in 1959 and 1960. Marschak refers to the latter years.

58. In advancing his theory initially, Horvat sometimes took the charge in terms of which labor costs are calculated as corresponding to the *akontacija*. However, elsewhere reference is made to a target that includes supplementary pay. See Horvat (1971), p. 105; Horvat et al. (1975), vol. 2, pp. 234 *ff*. On other Yugoslav theories of the self-managed firm, see Milenkovich (1971), ch. 8.

I referred earlier to special bonuses sometimes paid to executives under PBS. Such bonuses tended to be unusual and, where paid, were rather limited in magnitude. However, to the extent they were paid, they might have affected marginal choices. It is of interest to note, therefore, that in the case described by Adizes (1971), executives were paid bonuses depending on how close they came to fulfilling plan targets for "profit from production," "cost" reduction, and sales (pp. 51–52). Adizes does not give these categories explicitly, but he informed me (by letter of February 12, 1981) that wages were probably not treated as a cost and expense before profits from production. To the extent that wages were not so treated, the bonus scheme represents an argument against the Horvat view of enterprise motivation.

59. The cited figures represent the sum of allocations to the "business fund" and one-half of allocations to the "fund for communal consumption and funds for housing construction." See SZZS (1973), p. 155.

60. Pejovich (1966), p. 31–32, 74; Bajt (1966), pp. 256–258; Furubutn and Pejovich (1971); Jan Vanek (1972), pp. 119–120; Furubotn and Pejovich (1973); and Sirc (1979), p. 138.

61. In the foregoing, I argued that large shares of disposable income saved under PBS must be understood in terms not of a maximand diverging from that of theory, but of market imperfections and external constraints. The latter constraints, though, became weaker in the course of time. Tyson (1977b) has urged a rather different view of PBS enterprise-saving rates. The maximand is still as theory posits, but enterprise savings essentially express propensities of a permanent income sort. For this view, Tyson can cite statistically significant (and often plausible) lagged relations between worker earnings withdrawals and enterprise income for different industrial branches. I wonder, though, if the same lagged relations are not consistent with market imperfections and external constraints that are especially

potent in initial years. If so, Tyson's view is not so very different from mine. Given the legal imperative to keep capital intact, Tyson's inclusion of depreciation in the enterprise's discretionary income also seems questionable.

62. In view of Županov's findings, one might wonder whether workers were subject to any downside risk at all. The evidence that they are, however, rules out any serious doubts on that score. Županov's findings for managerial personnel alone point to the same conclusion.

63. Reference is particularly to findings given in Županov (1969), pp. 247–248, and Županov (1973), pp. 55–56. In the same survey, the executives were asked to indicate in which of a number of spheres their authority should be increased. While one of the spheres in question was "technological decisions" (*tehnološke odluke*), most of the executives did not cite this as meriting an increase in their authority [Županov (1969), p. 249; Županov (1973), pp. 57–58]. Very possibly, they did not construe the technical decisions in questions as embracing consequential innovations. Although they might have felt that they already had sufficient authority to introduce major innovations, that seems unlikely. Compare, for example, Županov (1978b), p. 83.

64. The Constitution of 1974 and Associated Labor Act are available in English translation. On the latter, see Flanz (1979). For surveys of major facets of the BOAL system, see also Milenkovich (1977); Schrenk et al. (1979); Comisso (1980); Sacks (1980); and Tyson (1980).

65. The use of internal transfer prices among subdivisions of the enterprise has rather early precedents. See, for example, ILO (1962), p. 228.

66. See the Constitution of 1974, art. 36; also Law on Associated Labor, art. 320. The division must also be such that workers can realize "their socio-economic and other self-management rights." This almost lacks content; however, reference is made elsewhere to certain entities, such as units servicing several BOALs, banks, and so on, that are to form "work communities"—agencies similar to, but not the same thing as, BOALs. Among economic agencies, the stipulation is presumably to take cognizance of such exceptional entities. More difficult to interpret, as it has turned out, is another provision that a BOAL should focus on only one sort of activity. See Sacks (1980), pp. 212–213.

67. In the process, both organizations have come to serve as major instruments for imposing more or less novel controls to which I refer below. On the role of the Party and the union in industrial administration under the BOAL system, see the Constitution of 1974, art. 104; the Law on Associated Labor, arts, 36, 504, 505, 509, 590; Milenkovitch (1971), p. 59; Rusinow (1978), ch. 8; Comisso (1979), ch. 6; Comisso (1980); and *Radio Free Europe Research* (September 26, 1980).

68. Jovanov (1978); *Radio Free Europe Research* (April 7, 1977;

March 8, 1978; June 12, 1978; June 14, 1978; December 8, 1978; September 20, 1978; September 26, 1980; November 29, 1978; February 12, 1979; July 11, 1979).

69. The question may be raised, is it meaningful any longer to refer to the enterprise under the BOAL system? The answer is that the enterprise no longer has the clear legal identity that it had previously, but it still exists as a form of relatively close collaboration of BOALs. As such, it still has a status in Yugoslav law, though it is now referred to as a "work organization" or an "organization of associated labor" [compare Sacks (1980), pp. 217 *ff.*]

70. See Schrenk et al. (1979), pp. 151, 329. The apparent reversal, though, seems largely to reflect increments in inventory values caused by price increases. There are limited discrepancies between Schrenk et al., and table 8-1 in the data for 1966-1971. The reasons for this are not clear.

71. On social compacts and self-management agreements, see Furubotn and Pejovich (1973); Dubey (1975), pp. 237-239; Comisso (1979), pp. 124 *ff;* Schrenk et al. (1979); pp. 49 *ff,* 147*ff;* Sirc (1979), pp. 137-140; Comisso (1980); Sacks (1980); and Kardelj (n.d.)

72. Comisso (1980), pp. 202-203. In Slovenia, payouts in excess of norms have been made subject to a progressive tax [Dubey (1975), p. 238]. On other recent developments regarding enterprise taxation, see Dirlam and Plummer (1973), p. 193, and Comisso (1979), p. 126.

73. In the 1972 self-management agreement for Belgrade trade workers, differentials generally varied with educational qualifications; however, executives were to be paid 40 percent more than their educational level would indicate [Furubotn and Pejovich (1973), p. 296]. In the machinery firm that Comisso (1979) visited in 1974, the base rate of the director was 3.8 times that of a cleaning woman (pp. 142 *ff*). That spread is little greater than the 3.4 reported by Jan Vanek (1972) for a large undertaking in 1959 (pp. 129-130).

74. In addition to Milenkovitch, see Schrank et al. (1979), ch. 4; Comisso (1980); and Sacks (1980).

75. I have suggested the 1974-1976 reforms might be considered a kind of trust-busting program. The introduction of the BOAL system has also been referred to as a form of divisionalization (Sacks 1980). That characterization doubtless has its merit, but, in commenting on a preliminary draft of this chapter, Oliver Williamson pointed out that the key to effective divisionalization is to recognize opportunities for decomposability. Where there are such opportunities, he argues, operating responsibilities should be assigned to the parts concerned, but a general office should still be maintained that evaluates the performance of the individual divisions and is responsible for strategic resource allocation.

Although Williamson's formulation applies primarily to divisionalization in a Western firm, Williamson is surely right in assuming that there is an economic case for heeding the foregoing principles in respect to the Yugoslav SMF. Have they, in fact, been heeded under the 1974–1976 reforms? I cannot really pursue that matter here, but as Williamson conjectures, his principles have doubtless been violated often under the BOAL system.

References

AER: *American Economic Review*

EJ: *Economic Journal*

OECD: Organization for Economic Cooperation and Development.

QJE: *Quarterly Journal of Economics*

SZZS: Savezni Zavod za Statistiku

JCE: *Journal of Comparative Economics*

SL: *Službeni List SFRJ*

SFRJ: *Socijalistika federativna republika Jugoslavija*

Adizes, Ichak. *Industrial Democracy: Yugoslav Style.* New York: Free Press, 1971.
Arrow, Kenneth J. *Theory of Risk Bearing.* Chicago, Ill.: Markham, 1971.
Arzenšek, Vladimir. "Managerial Legitimacy and Organizational Conflict." In Obradović and Dunn (1978).
Bajt, Aleksander. "Income Distribution under Workers' Self-Management." In Ross (1966).
———. "Managerial Incentives in Yugoslavia." Mimeograph. Milan: Centro Studi e Recerche su Problemi Economico Sociali, 1972.
Bakračlić, Miodraz and Stojanović, Teodosije. *Zbirka propisa o doprinosima i porezima gradana.* Belgrade, 1970.
Blum, Emerik. "The Director and Workers' Management." In Broekmeyer (1970).
Blumberg, Paul. *Industrial Democracy.* New York, Schocken Books, 1969.
Bornstein, Morris, ed. *Plan and Market.* New Haven, Conn.: Yale University Press, 1973.
———. *Comparative Economic Systems,* 3d ed. Homewood, Ill.: Irwin, 1974.
Brekić, Jovo. "Analiza reizbornosti direktora." In Gorupić and Brekić (1967).

Broekmeyer, M.J., ed. *Yugoslav Workers' Self-Management.* Dordrecht, Holland: Reidel, 1979.

Brown, Henry Phelps. *The Inequality of Pay.* Oxford: Oxford University Press, 1977.

Bučar, France. "Participation of State and Political Organizations in Enterprise Decisions." In Obradović and Dunn (1978).

Chapman, Janet. "The Distribution of Earnings in Selected Countries, East and West." Mimeograph. Pittsburgh, (1977).

Comisso, Ellen T. *Workers' Control under Plan and Market.* New Haven, Conn.: Yale University Press, 1979.

———. "Yugoslavia in the 1970's: Self-Management and Bargaining." *JCE,* June 1980.

The Constitution of the Socialist Federal Republic of Yugoslavia. New York: Merrick, 1976.

Dimitrijevic, Dimitrije, and Macesich, George. *Money and Finance in Contemporary Yugoslavia.* New York: Praeger, 1973.

Dirlam, Joel B., and Plummer, James L. *An Introduction to the Yugoslav Economy.* Columbus, Ohio: Charles E. Merrill, 1973.

Domar, Evsey. "The Soviet Collective Farm." *AER* 56, 4 (September 1966):734–757.

Dubey, Vinod. *Yugoslavia: Development with Decentralization.* Baltimore: Johns Hopkins University Press, 1975.

The Economist. Various dates.

Estrin, Saul. "Income Dispersion in a Self-Managed Economy." *Economica* 48, 190 (May 1981):181–194.

Flanz, Gisbert H. *Constitutions of the Countries of the World: Special Supplement: Yugoslavia.* Dobbs Ferry, N.Y.: Oceana Publications, 1979.

Furubotn, Erik G. "Bank Credit and the Labor-Managed Firm: Reply." *AER* 70, 4 (September 1980):800–804.

Furubotn, Erik, and Pejovich, Svetozar. "The Role of the Banking System in Yugoslav Economic Planning, 1946–1969." *Revue Internationale d'Histoire de la Banque.* Geneva: Librairie Droz, 1971.

———. "The Formation and Distribution of Net Product and the Behavior of the Yugoslav Firm." *Jahrbuch der Wirtschaft Osteuropas* vol. 3. Munich, 1972.

———. "Property Rights, Economic Decentralization and the Evolution of the Yugoslav Firm, 1965–1972." *The Journal of Law and Economics* 26, 2 (October 1973):275–302.

———. "Property Rights and the Behavior of the Firm in a Socialist State: The Example of Yugoslavia." In Furubotn and Pejovich (1974).

Furubotn, Eric G., and Pejovich, Svetozar, eds. *The Economics of Property Rights.* Cambridge, Mass.: Ballinger, 1974.

Gorupić, Drago. "The Worker-Managed Enterprise (I): Stages of Institutional Development." In Obradović and Dunn (1978).

Gorupić, Drago, and Brekic, Jovo, eds. *Direktor u samoupravnim odnosima.* Zagreb, 1970.

Gorupić, Drago, and Paj, Ivan. *Workers' Self-Management in Yugoslav Undertakings.* Zagreb 1970.

Granick, David. *Enterprise Guidance in Eastern Europe.* Princeton, N.J.: Princeton University Press, 1975.

Hey, John D., and Suckling, John. "The Labor-Managed Firm under Price Uncertainty." Discussion paper 38, University of York, November 1979.

Horvat, Branko. "Yugoslav Economic Policy in the Post-War Period." *AER* 61, 3, part 2 (June 1971):71–169.

Horvat, Branko; Markovic, Mihailo; and Supek, Rudi, eds. *Self-Governing Socialism: A Reader.* vols. 1 and 2. White Plains, N.Y.: International Arts and Sciences Press, 1975.

ILO. *Workers' Management in Yugoslavia.* Geneva: ILO, 1962.

Jovanov, Neca. "Strikes and Self-Management." in Obradović and Dunn (1978).

Jurčec, Mijo, ed. *Zbirka propisa o doprinosima in porezima gradjana.* Zagreb, 1969.

Kardelj, Edward. *The System of Planning in a Society of Self-Management: Brioni Discussions.* Belgrade, n.d.

Komentar zakona o udruženom radu. Belgrade, 1980.

Lepotinec, Slavko; Djačić, Milan; Plivelić, Marijan; Šunjić, Ivo; and Vrsalovic, Berislav. *Zbirka propisa o sredstvima i dohotku.* Zagreb, 1967.

Lydall, Harold. *The Structure of Earning.* Oxford: Oxford University Press, 1968.

Marschak, Thomas A. "Centralized versus Decentralized Resource Allocation: The Yugoslav 'Laboratory.'" *QJE* 82, 4 (November 1968):561–587.

Meade, James. "The Theory of the Labor-Managed Firm and of Profit Sharing." *EJ* 82, 325S (March 1972):402–428.

———. "Labor-Managed Firms in Conditions of Imperfect Competition". *EJ* 84, 336 (December 1974):817–824.

Michal, Jan W. "Size Distribution of Earnings and Household Incomes in Small Socialist Countries." *Review of Income and Wealth* 19, 4 (December 1973):407–428.

Milenkovitch, Deborah D. *Plan and Market in Yugoslav Economic Thought.* New Haven, Conn.: Yale University Press, 1971.

———. "The Case of Yugoslavia." *AER* 67, 1 (February 1977):55–60.

Millikan, Max F., ed. *National Economic Planning.* New York, N.Y.: Columbia University Press, 1967.

Miović, Peter. *Determinants of Income Differentials in Yugoslav Self-Managed Enterprise.* Ph.D. thesis, Cornell University, 1975.

Montias, John M. "Economic Planning in Yugoslavia: Comment." In Millikan (1967).

Neuberger, Egon. "The Yugoslav Investment Auctions." *QJE* 73, 1 (February 1959):88–115.

Neuberger, Egon, and James, Estelle. "The Yugoslav Self-Managed Enterprise: A Systemic Approach." In Bornstein (1973).

Obradović, Josip. "Participation in Enterprise Decision-Making." In Obradović and Dunn (1978).

Obradović, Josip, and Dunn, William N., eds. *Workers' Self-Management and Organizational Power in Yugoslavia.* Pittsburgh: University of Pittsburgh Press, 1978.

OECD. *Economic Surveys: Yugoslavia.* Paris: OECD, various dates.

Pejovich, Svetozar, *The Market-Planned Economy of Yugoslavia.* Minneapolis, Minn.: University of Minnesota Press, 1966.

———. "The Banking System and the Investment Behavior of the Yugoslav Firm." In Bornstein (1973).

Radio Free Europe Research.

Ross, Arthur M., ed. *Industrial Relations and Economic Development.* London: Macmillan, 1966.

Rus, Veljko. (A) "Enterprise Power Structure." In Obradović and Dunn (1978).

———. (B) "External and Internal Influences on Enterprises." In Obradović and Dunn (1978).

Rusinow, Dennison. *The Yugoslav Experiment 1948–1974.* Berkeley, University of California Press, 1978.

Sacks, Stephen R., *Entry of New Competitors in Yugoslav Market Socialism,* Berkeley: University of California Press, 1973.

———. "Divisionalization in Large Yugoslav Enterprises." *JCE* 4, 2 (June 1980):209–225.

Schrenk, Martin; Ardalan, Cyrus; and El Tatawy, Nowal A. *Yugoslavia: Self-Management Socialism and the Challenges of Development.* Baltimore: Johns Hopkins University Press, 1979.

Sirc, Ljubo. *The Yugoslav Economy under Self-Management.* New York: St. Martin's, 1979.

Sletzinger, Martin C. *The Reform and Reorganization of the League of Communists of Yugoslavia, 1966–1973.* Ph.D. thesis, Harvard University, 1976.

Stephen, F.H. "Bank Credit and the Labor-Managed Firm: Comment". *AER* 70, 4 (September 1980):796–799.

Službeni list SFRJ.

SZZS, SFRJ. *Statistički godišnjak Jugoslavije 1971,* Belgrade 1971.

SZZS, SFRJ. *Privredni bilansi Jugoslavije, 1966–1971.* Belgrade, 1973.

Tyson, Laura D. (A) "Liquidity Crises in the Yugoslav Economy: An Alternative to Bankruptcy?" *Soviet Studies* 29, 2 (April 1977):284–295.

———. (B) "A Permanent Income Hypothesis for the Yugoslav Firm." *Economica* 44-176 (November 1977):393–408.

———. *The Yugoslav Economic System and Its Performance in the 1970's.* Berkeley: University of California Press, 1980.

Vanek, Jan. *The Economics of Workers' Management: a Yugoslav Case Study.* London: George Allen & Unwin, 1972.

Vanek, Jaroslav. *The General Theory of Labor-Managed Economies.* Ithaca, N.Y.: Cornell University Press, 1970.

———. *The Labor-Managed Economy.* Ithaca, N.Y.: Cornell University Press, 1977.

Vanek, Jaroslav, and Jovicic, Milena. "Capital Market and Income Distribution in Yugoslavia." *QJE* 89, 3 (August 1975):432–443.

Vejonić, Milos. "Influence Structure in a Self-Managing Enterprise." In Obradović and Dunn (1978).

Wachtel, Howard M. *Workers' Management and Workers' Wages in Yugoslavia.* Ithaca, N.Y.: Cornell University Press, 1973.

The Wall Street Journal. Various dates.

Ward, Benjamin, "Workers Management in Yugoslavia." *Journal of Political Economy* 65, 5 (October 1957):373–386.

———. "The Firm in Illyria: Market Syndicalism." *AER* 58, 4 (September 1958):566–589.

Županov, Josip. "The Producer and Risk." *Eastern European Economics* 7,7 (Spring 1967).

———. *Samoupravljenje i društvena moć.* Zagreb, 1969.

———. "Is Enterprise Management Becoming Professionalized?" *International Studies of Management and Organization.* Fall, 1973.

———. "The Yugoslav Enterprise." In Bornstein (1974).

———. "Participation and Influence." In Horvat et al., vol. 2 (1975).

———. (A) "Two Patterns of Conflict Management in Industry." In Obradović and Dunn (1978).

———. "Egalitarianism and Industrialism." In Obradović and Dunn (1978).

9 On the Nature and Location of Entrepreneurial Activity in Centrally Planned Economies: the Soviet Case

Herbert S. Levine

Introduction

Entrepreneurial activity in a centrally planned economy? These are strange bedfellows. What need is there for spontaneous, uncontrolled entrepreneurial activity in the planned, controlled environment of a centrally planned economy? It is the argument of this chapter, however, that there is such a need, and that this need is demonstrated by the experience of the Soviet Union.

We will treat entrepreneurial activity in a narrow, Schumpeterian sense as the introduction of new technology, excluding such other meanings as the Marshallian equilibrating activity. Schumpeter defined the entrepreneurial function as activity devoted to the promotion of innovation—that is, the introduction of new products and processes into production:

> . . . the function of entrepreneurs is to reform or revolutionize the pattern of production by exploiting an invention or, more generally, an untried technological possibility for producing a new commodity or producing an old one in a new way, by opening up a new source of supply of materials or a new outlet for products, by reorganizing an industry and so on. . . . To undertake such new things is difficult and constitutes a distinct economic function, first, because they lie outside of the routine tasks which everybody understands and, secondly, because the environment resists in many ways that vary, according to social conditions, from simple refusal either to finance or to buy a new thing, to physical attack on the man who tries to produce it. . . . [To] overcome that resistance, [is] the entrepreneurial function. This function does not essentially consist in either inventing anything or otherwise creating the conditions which the enterprise exploits. It consists in getting things done.[1]

I would like to thank Joshua Ronen for his comments on this chapter, and Judith Seldin and Susan Ziobro for their research assistance.

It might be thought that central planning like that of the Soviet economy removes the need for an entrepreneur, that the plan and its implementation "gets things done," including the introduction of new technology. However, from all of the research on Soviet planning experience, it is abundantly clear that Soviet planning is not frictionless, that not all parts mesh smoothly. The primary focus of Soviet planning is on production, including the production of new techniques through research and development. However, the introduction of these new techniques into an ongoing production process is itself not a production activity; it is more in the nature of a transfer. This transfer is resisted because of a number of factors, including inertia and risk aversion. Entrepreneurial action is required to overcome this resistance. The nature and location of such entrepreneurial activity in the Soviet economy is the subject matter of this chapter.

Before proceeding, several caveats are in order. In this chapter, we adopt two major limitations of coverage. First, we wish to focus on the operation of a developed centrally planned economy. Thus, we will discuss the current Soviet economy or the Soviet economy in the postwar period, not the Soviet economy in the 1930s, in its period of rapid development and structural change. Second, we will not include illegal economic activity, the major part of which is referred to as the "second economy." While such activity does exist in varying degrees in all centrally planned economies, and certainly involves considerable entrepreneurial activity (though perhaps more of the equilibrating type than of the new-technology type), it is outside the body of *planned* economic activity. We, therefore, have omitted it from this paper.[2]

The use of Russia (or any individual country) as a case study brings with it the problem of separating the effects of the given economic system from those of the country's history, traditions, and culture. Several times, what is seen in Soviet Russia under centralized planning can be related to what went on in Russia under the tsars, before the Communist Revolution. The effects of bureaucracy in the Soviet planned economy are similar to the effects of bureaucracy in Russia under the tsars. Are these effects of bureaucracy, or effects of some elements of Russian culture? For the purposes of this paper, we will assume that they are effects of the institutions of bureaucracy.[3]

By now, there is a very substantial Western literature on the organization and operation of the Soviet economy. We will draw heavily on this literature, especially the part of it concerned with innovation, or the introduction of new technology into the Soviet economy. Our angle of approach, however, is somewhat different from that of the standard literature.[4] Our aim is not to assess the process of innovation in the Soviet economy, but to build on such an assessment to identify the need for, and possible location of, entrepreneurial activity. This chapter, however, is at best an introduction to the subject. It sketches out the terrain, introduces some key features, and points the way to future research.

The chapter will begin by outlining the system of Soviet economic administration, emphasizing its bureaucratic, hierarchial nature. This will be followed by a brief description of the planning system, including the planning of research, development, and innovation. Next, we will examine the barriers to innovation that exist under Soviet centralized planning, then the possible location of entrepreneurial activity in the Soviet economy. In the concluding section of the paper, we will make some remarks about future prospects.

Soviet Economic Organization and Planning

Organization

The Soviet centrally planned economy has been described as a "command economy."[5] It is a felicitous phrase, for although Soviet economic reality is as complex and varied as that of any real economic system, the underlying nature of the Soviet system is well described as a command system. Commands, in the form of obligatory plan targets, are issued by the central leadership and communicated down through an administrative hierarchy, organized primarily by branch of production, to the basic producing units responsible for their fulfillment. Lines of authority are strictly delineated. Orders are issued by superiors in the hierarchy to their subordinates; information about production possibilities flows up the hierarchy. The Soviet economy is thus administered by means of a massive, comprehensive bureaucracy.

The goals of the system are established by the central leaders. For most of the period under discussion, these goals have stressed rapid economic growth with a strong priority on industry. As a consequence, the Soviet economy has operated under the constant pressure of excess aggregate demand at the macro level and of taut planning and little slack (with regard to outputs, inputs, and inventories) at the micro level. Planning, furthermore, has been output oriented. Ever-increasing levels of output are achieved through substantial infusions of labor and capital, rather than higher productivity and quality.

The Soviet economy is governed by two parallel bureaucracies—the state apparatus and the Communist Party apparatus. The state apparatus performs the operational administration of the economy, and the party apparatus performs important monitoring and control functions. The party leadership possesses ultimate power. It is dominant in the economy with regard to setting economic goals and policies.

The highest organ of the formal state apparatus is the Soviet Parliament (the Supreme Soviet). It meets infrequently, but it does pass some economic legislation. For example, at its fall meeting (usually in November) it ratifies the annual economic plan. It also (along with the Communist Party leadership) appoints members of the Council of Ministers, which is the administrative body at the top level of the state apparatus.[6] The Council of Ministers is currently composed of over sixty ministers, about forty of whom head up economic ministries. Roughly speaking, all of the enterprises producing a certain type of product are subordinated to a single branch ministry (ferrous metals, petroleum, chemicals, machine tools, and so on).[7] Furthermore, the ministries have centralized research and development institutes that serve all of the firms within an individual ministry. The ministry is organized in hierarchical fashion. At the top are the minister and his staff. Farther down are a number of intermediary organizations, called main administrations, responsible for either subgroups of the ministry's products or for a geographic subgroup of the ministry's firms. (There are also main administrations for functional activities—finance, investment, labor, supplies, and so on.) From there, the line of subordination runs to the basic producing enterprise. Thus, the ministries possess significant power. They control substantial sets of production enterprises, and in addition, have often developed their own supply agencies, sales agencies, and production facilities for material inputs required by their firms. Ministers and their deputies are essentially senior business executives or civil servants, not politicians in the Western sense. They are often former managers with engineering or technical backgrounds, and should be viewed more as technical executives than as policymakers. Policymaking in the Soviet economy is the domain primarily of the top Communist Party leadership and, to some extent, the 12–15-man executive council (Presidium) of the Council of Ministers, headed by its chairman, the Prime Minister.

At the base of the ministerial hierarchy is the Soviet firm ("enterprise," in Soviet terminology).[8] It is the organizational unit responsible for producing goods and services. Currently, there are over 40,000 enterprises. The Soviet firm does not differ much physically from its Western counterpart. In the manufacturing sector, for example, it consists of one or several plants containing the equipment and inventories necessary for production. The Soviet enterprise, however, is quite large when compared to firms in the West. According to data for the 1960s, 24 percent of Soviet enterprises employed more than 500 workers. In the United States, this figure was 1.4 percent and in Japan, 0.3 percent. Only 15 percent of Soviet enterprises employed fewer than 50 workers, compared to 85 percent in the United States and 95 percent in Japan.[9]

The managerial structure of the Soviet firm resembles that in the West. The chief executive officer is the director. He bears full responsibility for fulfilling all of the plan directives set for his enterprise. He is appointed to his position by his minister and high Communist Party officials, and he retains his position as long as his performance is considered satisfactory or until he is moved upward in the bureaucracy. The director is assisted by a chief engineer (who serves as a deputy director) and by a managerial staff of functional and line officers. The functional officers head departments responsible for such matters as planning, accounting, finance, supply, sales, labor, design, and so on. The line officers, or shop chiefs, are in charge of such production departments as foundries, machine shops, and assembly shops. The shop chiefs are responsible for the general production operations of the enterprises.

The table of organization of the Soviet firm, together with the obligations and rights of its managerial personnel, have been standardized and strictly fixed by Soviet laws and regulations. The powers of each official are established under what is referred to as the principle of "one-man responsibility." Under this principle, the line official at each level assumes full responsibility for the operation of his unit, and only he is empowered to give orders to the people under his jurisdiction. Thus, if the director, deputy director, or the head of the planning department wants something done in a particular shop, he may not, under this strict hierarchical system, issue an order directly to workers or to a foreman. He may issue orders only to the shop chief. In similar manner, the shop chief may not issue orders directly to workers, but only to his foreman.

Technically speaking, the Soviet firm does not own its assets; all means of production are owned by the state. As the agent of the state, however, it has the right and obligation of employing the means of production in pursuit of objectives laid out in the plans issued by the state.

Soviet economic plans are not the product of one planning organ, but of a hierarchy of planning organs. These extend from Gosplan, the State Planning Committee attached to the Council of Ministers (at the top) to the planning department of the enterprise (at the bottom). This hierarchy is the organizational structure through which instructions from the top are combined with specific knowledge from below. There is actually more than one planning hierarchy; there is a geographical hierarchy and an industrial-branch hierarchy. They both start from Gosplan at the top, but the geographical hierarchy runs from there to the planning committees of the republics, provinces, and localities, whereas the branch hierarchy runs to the planning departments of the ministries, main administrations, and enterprises. Gosplan is a functional organ, not a line organ. It has no direct administrative authority over any ministry or enterprise—that is, it is not authorized to issue direct orders to them. It does, however, possess significant administrative power through its role as advisor to the Council of Ministers and that body's authority to issue direct orders. Furthermore, neither the geographic nor the branch-planning hierarchy contains organs that are administratively subordinate to one another. That means that the planning department of a ministry (or of a republic council of ministers) is subordinate to the ministry (or to the republic council of ministers), not to Gosplan. Nor does the planning organ of a ministry have any administrative authority over any main administration or enterprise within the ministry. The geographic planning hierarchy is concerned primarily with economic activity of a local nature. The planning of economic activity of national significance is the responsibility of the branch-planning hierarchy.

The functions performed by Gosplan, at the top of the planning hierarchy, include working out the five-year and annual plans, coordinating the draft plans of the ministries, checking the fulfillment of the plans, and sponsoring scientific research on economic problems. The primary mission of Gosplan is not initiating and formulating major objectives, but achieving a feasible, consistent plan while preventing and eradicating disproportions within the economy. This was its primary task from its inception in 1921, but Gosplan's role as a coordinating body acquired increasing importance in the late thirties and after World War II as more and more specialized industrial ministries were formed, creating and intensifying the need for a body to coordinate their individual plans and activities.

At the head of Gosplan is a chairman, who is a member of the Council of Ministers, and a governing board (collegium) that contains (in addition to the chairman) the deputy chairman, the chairmen of the planning committees of the union-republics, and a number of important heads of Gosplan departments, all of whom are appointed by the Council of Ministers and the Communist Party.[10] The governing board directs the work performed by Gosplan's numerous departments. One rung below the governing board is a general department that deals with the national economic plan. This department reviews the final draft of the annual economic plan and tries to settle the differences that arise between the ministries and the departments of Gosplan. The basic work done at Gosplan in constructing the economic plan is done in branch-production departments and in branch-coordinating departments. The branch-production departments are, as a rule, organized in parallel to the existing industrial ministries. They deal with the output side of their respective industries, with the adequacy of the drafts of output plans submitted by the ministries, and with their correspondence to the tasks set by the government. The branch-coordinating departments, together with a general department of balances and distribution plans, check and coordinate the plans developed by the individual departments.

Although the coordination and elaboration of consistent, feasible plans are the main tasks of Gosplan, it is also involved in planning technical progress—research, development, and innovation. To this end, it has a department for the Introduction of the Achievements of Science and Technology into the National Economy. This consults with several outside organizations, primarily the State Committee on Science and Technology and the Academy of Sciences; however, the responsibility for constructing plans for technical progress rests with Gosplan.

The State Committee on Science and Technology is the chief advisor to the state and party leaders on national technological policy. This involves allocating research funds to competing projects and lines of development. The USSR Academy of Sciences supervises the bulk of scientific research work in the country. Its attention is concentrated in the natural and social sciences, and primarily on basic (rather than applied) research.

In addition to the state organizations already discussed, there are several others that play an important role in the administration of the economy and in the process of innovation. These include the Ministry of Finance, the State Bank, and the Bank for Construction (which are involved in financing economic projects and invesment); the State Committee on Construction (which supervises large construction projects); and the State Committee on Supply (which administers a substantial part of the interfirm flows of intermediary materials and equipment). Furthermore, if an economic activity entails imports or exports, the Ministry of Foreign Trade will be involved.

Parallel to the state apparatus is the apparatus of the Communist Party of the Soviet Union. The preeminent body in the party is the Politburo, usually composed of 10–15 senior party officials. The Politburo is the highest policymaking body in the country. Nominally, the Party Congress, composed of over 5,000 delegates from all levels of the Party hierarchy holds supreme power in the Party. The Party Congress normally meets once every five years to discuss (among other matters) the draft five-year plan. It elects the Central Committee of the Communist Party to administer the Party between congresses. The Central Committee, a rather cumbersome body of approximately 400 full and alternate members, is not constituted to wield power directly. However, it does play a significant role in party administration. It elects (albeit formally) the members of the Politburo and the Party Secretariat (an administrative presidium of the Party), and on a few occasions, it has been used to resolve conflicts among members of the Politburo.[11] It normally meets in plenary session twice a year (prior to November 7th and May 1st), at which time it considers matters of economic policy brought to it by the party. Finally—but perhaps most important for our purposes here—the Central Committee apparatus has a number of departments that monitor and supervise various sectors of the economy, thus duplicating to some extent the work of Gosplan and of the ministries. These sectors include heavy industry, machine building, defense industries, the chemical industry, light industry, the food industry, agriculture, construction, transport and communications, trade and services, planning, and financial organs.

At the republican, provincial, and local levels, branches of the Communist Party duplicate the various state agencies; thus for each state agency, there is a parallel party branch. This applies even to the lowest administrative echelons. At the enterprise level, a party branch monitors enterprise activity.

Planning

Our aim in this chapter is to examine the extent to which central planning can bring about a desirable level of innovation. To this end, we now turn to briefly discuss Soviet economic plans and their construction.

The Soviets construct a number of types of plans that differ as to the time period and part of the economy covered. Among the economywide plans, the five-year plans are perhaps the best known, if not the best understood. The five-year plan, referred to as a "perspective plan," provides a broad-stroke view of the terrain to be traversed. However, the relatively limited, highly aggregated data in it do not form the basis of commands to ministries and enterprises. At best, five-year plans have served as orientation for the construction of annual plans. There is now, however, some movement toward making the five-year plan more operational so as to lengthen the time horizon of Soviet managers.

The method of constructing five-year plans has never been well described. It can be surmised, however, that key roles are played by the growth and structure goals of the regime, technical information and studies, the Soviet "method of balances," and the calculation capacity of the planners at Gosplan (that is, desk calculators, adding machines, and—only very recently—computers). Presumably the planners collect estimates of initial production capacities, confer with political leaders' policy decisions as to desired rates of investment, and delineate their views on the desired structure of the economy. On the basis of these and other inputs, they then construct output targets for major economic sectors. In doing this, they use much technical information concerning present and planned levels of technologies in the different sectors, and try to take into account the effects of the projected levels of certain sectors on other sectors. The plan is supposed to be constructed with the participation of lower levels of the planning hierarchy; however, for several (if not most) of the plans, the work was actually done primarily at the center. The process seems to be one of separate sectoral planning, the results of which are tied together while roughly checking such overall balances as the planned uses and sources of materials and primary factors, national income, money flows, and others.

The primary objective is the construction of a realizable plan in general conformity with the desires of the political leaders. There is, however, little emphasis on scanning alternative production processes in search of an optimal plan. The aim is more to assure that a satisfactory plan is feasible. Soviet planners, however, do not have the knowledge, techniques, or time to construct even such feasible long-term plans. It is still frequently charged that many planning decisions are not based on sound economic calculations, but are arbitrary, willful decisions that lead to unbalanced, unrealistic plans.

The operational plan in Soviet planning practice is the annual plan, with its quarterly and monthly subdivisions. It is operational in the sense that the numerous and less highly aggregated data in it do form the basis for direct commands to producing units in the economy. The construction of the annual plan is not complicated by the uncertainties involved in long time periods or the complexities of capital planning. Furthermore, because it is the basis for commands to the economy, it requires a much higher degree of precision than the long-term plan.

Again, the emphasis is on consistency, not optimality. The plan is constructed in cooperation with ministries and enterprises in a flow-counterflow system. Instructions about output levels and input use flow down the planning hierarchy from Gosplan to the enterprises; information about production technologies and resource availabilities, together with counterproposals about output levels and input needs, flow back up the planning hierarchy.

The process of annual-plan construction begins with an intensive study of the statistical picture of the economy. With the aid of this information—and in relation to their long-term and short-term policies—the political leaders formulate and communicate their priorities for the forthcoming year to the central planners. Subsequently Gosplan constructs a preliminary, consistent set of highly aggregated output targets and input limits (using 200–300 product designations) and transmits these control figures to the ministries, which in turn subdivide them among their subordinate producing enterprises. The enterprises estimate their output possibilities in terms of somewhat more detailed designations and, using input coefficients (norms) established for them at different levels of the hierarchy, calculate their input needs. The plan proceeds back up the hierarchy, being debated, altered, and consolidated at different levels, until it returns finally to Gosplan at the top. At this stage, it is Gosplan's job to work out the internal balance of the plan. For this purpose, it records on simple T-accounts (called material balances) the quantities of planned demands for, and sources of supply of each of the centrally allocated materials and equipment (750–2,000 product designations have been used at various times). Through methods to be discussed in a moment, it then tries to balance the two sides of each material balance. The draft of the plan prepared by Gosplan is sent to the Council of Ministers, where it is frequently hotly debated (the careers of economic ministers are affected by the plans they get). And after some changes, it is confirmed as a law binding on all economic units.

The process of plan construction, however, does not end here. The output targets from the confirmed plan (addressed to ministries) are subdivided and passed down to the enterprises, which now calculate their input needs at a very detailed level. The detailed input requirements come up the ministerial hierarchies and are sent to central agencies, where again material balances are drawn up. (This is done currently for 18,000–20,000 product designations. Their quantitative dimensions, however, are supposed to be just disaggregations of the data in the state plan.) Ties between producing enterprises and consuming enterprises are established, and formal contracts between them are signed, ending the process of plan construction.

Two elements in this process—the input norms and the method of material balances—warrant further comment. The input norms, which establish the production processes to be employed and thus play a key role in formulating the plan, are constructed primarily on the basis of an engineering approach. There is no systematic calculation of the relative scarcities of inputs; therefore, the plan is far from optimal (in the sense that it is on a static production possibility frontier).

Furthermore, it is doubtful whether the plan is ever consistent. Many of the most important norms are constructed at the top, far from the producing enterprises. The difficulties involved in such an endeavor are so extensive, and the Soviet information collection and handling system is so hopelessly inadequate, that the norms tend to be remote from reality. Second, the material balances method is too primitive to cope with the task assigned it. To balance a material balance in which initially planned demands exceed planned supplies (the usual case), either the production of the deficit commodity must be increased, or the use of it must be decreased. If the input norms are held fixed, this requires changes in the output levels of all inputs into this commodity or of all products into which it is an input. This, of course, is merely the beginning of a long stream of such indirect effects. It is clear from the literature that the Soviets have not been able to handle these indirect effects. Consequently, significant (though not exclusive) reliance is placed on avoiding indirect effects by tightening or forcing the input norms—that is, by calling for more output without an increase in inputs, or decreasing inputs without decreasing outputs. This tightening of norms sometimes just reduces the safety margin producers built into their plans, but it sometimes also reduces norms excessively and leads to the construction of unrealistic, overly taut plans.

Thus the annual plan is deficient on a number of counts: it is decidedly short of optimal, it is frequently not even internally consistent, and furthermore, it requires a long time to construct (it is rarely complete by the beginning of the plan year). On the other hand, it does respond to the dominant priorities of the political leaders by concentrating output and resources in the growth-producing sectors.

With specific regard to the planning of new technology and innovation, the system is as follows.[12] The annual plan contains a section entitled, "State Plan of Scientific Research Work and the Introduction of the Achievements of Science and Technology into the National Economy of the USSR." This part of the plan is constructed according to roughly the same chronology as that of general planning. The control figures issued by Gosplan to the ministries contain certain innovation assignments. These are generally innovations of major importance and size that reflect high-level decisions on technological policy adopted by Gosplan and the State Committee on Science and Technology. The ministries, in turn, distribute these assignments to specific enterprises, along with certain innovation tasks that are not specified by Gosplan but that are part of the planned technological development of the ministries.

When an enterprise receives its innovation assignments, they are turned over to the appropriate enterprise departments for elaboration. In many cases, an ad hoc Enterprise Innovation Commission is established. This is chaired by the director or the chief engineer, and includes the heads of the major administrative departments, representatives of the trade union and party, and prominent workers and technical personnel. The commission studies the innovation assignments and determines (a) whether they can be carried out, and (b) which officials and production shops should be given the tasks. The commission also receives proposals from enterprise departments and decides which should be undertaken. When the list of planned innovations is established, it is submitted to the various functional departments for integration into the overall enterprise plan. The functional departments might decide, after analysis, that the preliminary list of projects is not feasible. If so, the commission will revise it, if necessary. In principle, when the work is done, the innovation section of the enterprise draft plan is fully articulated with the other sections and meets all of the innovation assignments specified in the control figures. If it proves impossible to meet all of the innovation assignments, the director must be prepared to battle with the ministry, armed with the documentation provided by this committee.

In addition to the enterprise draft plans pouring into the ministry, there are the draft plans submitted by all the research-and-development (R&D) and engineering-design organizations of the ministry. Their draft plans— also based on control figures previously issued to them—consist of lists of the projects on which they propose to work, with estimated completion dates, materials and equipment requirements, cost and productivity estimates, and financial requirements. Among the planning tasks of the ministry is the coordination of the R&D organizations. If a production enterprise has accepted an assignment to commence work on a new product model at a certain time in November, the ministry must assure that the R&D organization's plan provides for the completion of development work on that model sufficiently ahead of that time, and that the engineering-design organization's plan provides sufficient resources to have the blueprints ready on time.

The consolidated draft plan of the ministry identifies separately each of the projects specified in its control figures—that is, the projects of national importance that will later appear in the annual plan. All other innovations of ministrywide or enterprise-level importance are included only in summary form. The ministry draft plan is submitted to Gosplan, and a copy of the section that deals with R&D and innovation is submitted to the State Committee on Science and Technology.

A parallel stream of draft plans flows upward through the Academy of Sciences network of research institutes. The tasks of adjusting and coordinating these draft plans takes place at the highest level of government. In general, the vast set of draft plans requires extensive adjustment. They might (as a group) require a greater volume of resources than have been allocated for science and R&D, and some proposed projects might have to be dropped or reduced in scope. Likewise, some high-priority project might not have been given sufficient attention, and some ministry might have to take on an additional task it had not anticipated in its draft. Other adjustments must be made for purposes of coordination, particularly across ministry lines. The Ministry of the Chemical Industry might insist that it cannot develop a major new process until the research people in the Ministry of the Ferrous Metals Industry come up with a new alloy that can withstand the temperatures. The draft plans of the latter would then have to be changed. For these reasons, the ministries sometimes end up with a final set of planned innovation tasks very different from those provided for in their draft plans.

While general Soviet economic planning has a long history going back to the 1920s, the planning of new technology and innovation is of postwar origin. Not until 1949 did Soviet economic plans contain a section on introducing new technology. In precision and coordination, technological planning still lags far behind general planning. The reasons are found in the inherently greater difficulty of constructing technological plans. Because of the greater degree of uncertainty, it is much more difficult to construct time schedules for R&D work, to foresee the materials and equipment needs far in advance, to anticipate the date on which an innovation can be expected to commence production, and to estimate the future productivity of the innovation. Hence, although formal technological planning is an ongoing and extensive activity, it is not yet closely integrated with the other portions of the general plan.

Barriers to Innovation

We have described the bureaucratic organization of Soviet economic administration and the system by which its economic plans are constructed. We can now turn to examine the effectiveness of Soviet centralized planning in fostering the introduction of new technology. If one approached the issue through a reading of Western theory and research on the relationship, in market economies, between bureaucratic organization and innovation,[13] one would expect to find substantial resistance to innovation in the Soviet centrally planned economy. Indeed, one does. Analysts of the Soviet economy, both in the Soviet Union and in the West, generally agree that with regard to research, development, and innovation, the Soviets do fairly well with research (especially basic research), less well with development, and poorly with innovation.

We will organize our discussion of resistance to innovation in the Soviet economy in terms of seven characteristics of bureaucratic organization and innovation that play a prominent role in Western literature on this issue:

Strict hierarchy of authority

Narrowly specialized units

Striving for stability

Risk aversion

Measurability of performance and reward structure

Role of slack

Competition and bankruptcy

While the order in which we have listed these characteristics is not random, it is neither in perfect analytical sequence nor in order of importance. Furthermore, it is not complete. We do not, for example, discuss such important matters as prices, costs, information, and returns to investment.[14] Finally, although we will analyze these characteristics individually, they frequently interact—sometimes strengthening the individual tendency, but under some conditions possibly working in the opposite direction.

Strict Hierarchy of Authority

One Western analyst has labeled an organization with a strict hierarchy of authority a "monocratic" organization, and has described it in the following terms:

According to this stereotype, the organization is a great hierarchy of supe-rior-subordinate relations in which the person at the top, assumed to be omniscient, issues the general order that initiates all activity. His immediate subordinates make the order more specific for their subordinates, the latter do the same for theirs, etc., until specific individuals are carrying out specific instructions. All authority and initiation are cascaded down in this way by successive delegations. There is complete discipline, enforced from the top down to make certain that their commands are faithfully obeyed. Responsibility is owed from the bottom up. Reports on the carrying out of orders and the results obtained flow upwards to the top where they are compared with top management's intentions. As a result of this com-parison, orders are modified and again flow down the line, and the cycle is repeated. The organization is perceived to be a feedback loop.[15]

This hierarchy leads to a number of consequences that inhibit innova-tion. First, in such a hierarchy, proposals for changes in products or methods of production that come from below face an approval-veto pro-cedure that favors the veto. As the proposal moves up the authority hier-archy, a veto will kill the proposal (normally, a subordinate cannot appeal a decision of a superior). An approval, however, merely moves the proposal to the next level of the hierarchy, where again a veto will kill it, and an approval will move it up. Thus, it takes a number of approvals to adopt an innovation in such an organization, but only one veto to kill it. Second, this process involves what has been termed "bureaupathic behavior."[16] As the proposal moves up the hierarchy, the conflict increases between an admin-istrator's competence to make a decision and his authority to make a deci-sion. That is, those toward the top of the hierarchy are increasingly re-moved from the technology concerned and, thus are less capable of making a good decision on the proposal. This lowers the quality of decision making. In time, because of bad past decisions, it leads as well to a decreased willing-ness to take chances on such proposals. Finally, the strict hierarchy of authority, with its great number of gatekeepers, aggravates problems of red tape and produces long lead-times between the original submission and final acceptance of a proposal.

All of these comsequences are evident in Soviet experience. Soviet bureaucratic organization is well described by the stereotype of the strict authority hierarchy. There are concerns about the discrepancy between competence and authority in innovation decisions, and great concern about the virulence of bureaucratic red tape and the delays caused by the vast number of gatekeepers involved in approving such proposals. It normally requires about 25 separate approvals at different bureaucratic levels to introduce a new machine. One Soviet economist indicated that to build a new system of 10 to 15 machines, 400 to 500 approvals (mostly sequential) can be required.[17] According to studies conducted by the State Committee on Science and Technology, it often takes as long to get all of the required approvals and to move documents from one organization to another as it does to do all of the R&D work involved in the new technology. In other words, the bureaucratic process of moving research results consumes as much time as the R&D itself. Many promising proposals languish on the shelf. Nearly 700 completed R&D projects were proposed by the Siberian Division of the Academy of Sciences for introduction into production in the 1960s, but were not actually introduced for various reasons. Almost 300 of them became obsolete while waiting for approval.[18]

Narrowly Specified Units

A second characteristic of a monocratic (or "mechanistic"[19]) organization is its subdivision into narrowly specialized, compartmentalized units:

> Although tight, narrow, exclusive mission assignments are justified as needed "to pinpoint responsibility," they actually encourage irresponsibility in regard to new problems and ideas. They facilitate "buck-passing." It is always possible for any individual (or unit) to say: "This is not my problem; it does not fall within my jurisdiction; let somebody else take care of it." It is becoming increasingly evident that a somewhat more untidy structure, one with overlapping and duplicating efforts to solve the same problem, achieves more outstanding and novel solutions, in less time and with less expense, than does the tidy monocratic structure with "responsibility pinned down" in exclusive jurisdictions.[20]

The problems created by the barriers between narrowly specialized units—"departmentalism," in Soviet terminology—are endemic to the Soviet Union. For the Soviet economy, they manifest themselves most critically in the departmental barriers between the individual branch ministries. In general, the interest of the ministry is in meeting its own targets and obligations, not in meeting the overall goals of the economy.

Departmentalism also has specific effects on the innovation process. With exclusive bureaucratic lines of authority established over each branch of production, the development of new technology in one branch ministry (which often requires new or higher-quality inputs from other branch ministries) is impeded because of the cross-ministerial negotiations needed and the focus of each ministry on its own interests and requirements. A second consequence of departmental barriers is that dynamic, creative groups from other branches are prevented from invading a stagnant branch. Such "innovation by invasion" has caused significant introduction of new technology in market economies.

A third effect has to do with the separation between R&D and production within each ministry. The decision was taken early in the development of Soviet economic institutions to pursue the presumed advantages of scale and specialization, and to concentrate R&D within branch institutions rather than to have individual R&D departments at each enterprise. This separation of R&D units from production units extends to the separate subordination of each to different channels of planning, finance, and supply. This has proved a considerable barrier to the transfer of new technology from the laboratory to production. Similar Western experience clearly demontrates how important it is to maintain a close linkage between the management of production and that of R&D, to coordinate the two activities, and to ensure that the new technology is compatible with the technical production procedures and organizational characteristics and needs of the adopting enterprise. The separation of R&D and production thus inhibits innovation in the Soviet economy.

Striving for Stability

Bureaucracies tend to operate on the basis of standardized, repetitive, routine methods and procedures.[21] They resist new approaches that threaten to upset the established routine, and thus threaten to upset the bureaucracy's stability.

In the Soviet Union, bureaucratic stability involves the routine fulfillment of Soviet growth plans. Although innovation, if successful, would improve the growth performance of the economy, at the same time it threatens the stability of routine growth. It can be argued that (in the past at least) not only subordinates, but the Soviet leaders themselves were often willing to trade off the instability of innovation for stable growth through routinized plan fulfillment.[22]

Risk Aversion

Bureaucracies exhibit a high degree of risk aversion. This is partly because they value stability, and thus tend to penalize failure more than they reward innovational success. Another factor, however, is the critical importance to a bureaucrat of his "file":

> Whereas failure of yesterday's entrepreneur simply meant the loss of money (someone else's), failure for the modern bureaucrat means the loss of part of his identity. A report of his failure goes into his file—his paper identity, a paper alter ego that follows him inescapably through life and alters his identity unfavorably. Innovation is more risky for the bureaucrat than for yesterday's entrepreneur. Loss of identity is far more serious than loss of money, even one's own.[23]

The "file" factor is of great importance in the Soviet economy. Failure, negative entries in a file, might mean the loss of opportunities for promotion, or even the loss of managerial or administrative status. The loss of such status is very serious. In the Soviet Union, many aspects of material well-being are derived primarily from managerial or administrative status, rather than from high income and wealth: a good, well-situated apartment, access to special stores (where goods in short supply are available, usually at lower than official prices), a country house, vacation and travel facilities, and educational and career opportunities for one's children. These "perks" come with the position. Soviet bureaucrats are, therefore, very averse to taking risks that will endanger their positions. Because of the risks involved in introducing significant new technology, this feature of Soviet bureaucratic organization produces substantial negative effects on innovation.

Other aspects of this characteristic affect its significance in the Soviet environment. There are, in general, three types of uncertainty associated with a new technology. One is its technical feasibility: will it work? A second is its novelty: are competitors developing something similar? The third is its marketability: if it is a new product or service, can it be marketed? Only the first is really relevant in the Soviet case. This contributes to a lower problem of innovation risk in the Soviet economy as compared to a market economy. On the other hand, the scale of production and the size of firms is larger in the Soviet Union than in the West. This tends to increase the cost—and thus risk—of change.

Measurability of Performance and Reward Structure

In a bureaucracy, clear, quantifiable measures of performance are characteristically developed and used to evaluate the performance of subordinates. When a subordinate is confronted with such measures and when his rewards and penalties are functions of them, he responds by performing within the narrow confines of those measures, avoiding risky, innovative activity. Two American management specialists blame a good part of the recent decrease in U.S. productivity growth on the use of simple, quantifiable performance criteria by large U.S. corporations employing profit centers as the primary unit of managerial responsibility:

> Use of profit centers necessitates, in turn, greater dependence on short-term financial measurements like return on investment (ROI) for evaluating the performance of individual managers and management groups. Increasing the structural distance between those entrusted with exploiting actual competitive opportunities and those who must judge the quality of their work virtually guarantees reliance on objectively quantifiable short-term criteria.

Although innovation, the lifeblood of any vital enterprise, is best encouraged by an environment that does not unduly penalize failure, the predictable result of relying too heavily on short-term financial measures—
a sort of managerial remote control—is an environment in which no one
feels he or she can afford a failure or even a momentary dip in the bottom
line . . .

"Especially in large organizations," reports one manager, "we are observing an increase in management behavior which I would regard as excessively cautious, even passive; certainly overanalytical, and, in general,
characterized by a studied unwillingness to assume responsibility and even
reasonable risk."[24]

Among the Soviet economic institutions that affect the ability of the
economy to introduce new technology, the one that receives primary
emphasis in both Western and Russian literature on the Soviet economy is
the managerial reward mechanism, which has more or less dominated the
Soviet scene since the 1930s. In the past decade and a half, the Soviet Union
has been undergoing certain administrative changes. Although the current
picture is not totally clear, the incentive mechanism is still basically related
to the fulfillment of performance targets. In any situation such as this, there
are two ways of assuring success or increasing the possibility of success: (1)
performance and (2) keeping the target within reasonable distance. The
second aspect of target-type rewarding is particularly detrimental to innovation. Innovation always involves risk. The compensation for risk contained
in the reward for plan overfulfillment is reduced by the Soviet policy of
planning from the achieved level. Success today means a higher target
tomorrow, and managerial success in the system and the maintenance of
managerial status require the rather regular meeting of targets. Thus, managers resist innovation and try to keep targets low. There is much discussion
in the Soviet Union about how to get around this problem, but nothing very
effective has been introduced so far. Indeed, no significant results should
perhaps be expected from such attempts as modifying specific forms of success indicators, introducing cost sharing and pricing devices, and changing
the length of the plan time-period against which enterprise results are
evaluated. What is perhaps necessary is a change in the basic evaluation and
control philosophy itself: instead of making managerial income and promotion rewards direct and immediate functions of measurable objective performance indicators, perhaps these rewards should be decided upon by
superiors using less precise subjective criteria.[25]

A related issue is the fact that the short-run effects of innovation on
production-target fulfillment are almost always bad. Innovation interrupts
the rhythm of production work. Even if the introduction of the new
technology is going tolerably well, it usually takes more time than planned
to reach rated capacity; thus output, sales, and profit levels in monthly and

quarterly plan-fulfillment figures go down, and the manager is in trouble. The same applies to the use of enterprise labor, materials, and equipment for experiments with new technology.

Role of Slack

Slack plays a crucial role in the innovation process. On the supply side, it takes the form of surplus funds or resources that facilitate the provision of funds for innovation:

> One of the main consequences of slack is a muting of problems of scarcity . . . distributed slack is available for projects that would not necessarily be approved in a tight budget. . . . the tighter the budget, the more expenditures will be controlled by essentially conservative rules. Slack provides a source of funds for innovations that would not be approved in the face of scarcity . . .[26]

On the demand side, slack takes the form of inadequate demand for goods and services in the economy, this also plays a role in stimulating innovation. Its absence, however, inhibits innovation more than its presence stimulates it. That is, under conditions of a "sellers' market" the stimulation to innovate is missing:

> The problem is the lack of institutions and organizations which despite all obstacles can effect the introduction of revolutionary new technical innovations, accepting all the risk concomitant with this work, including that of failure, the struggle against conservatism and deep-rooted habit.
>
> Why should an enterprise director accept this risk and take up a struggle when . . . he is able without such effort to sell the products of his firm easily? With the buyers lining up for the firm's old product, why take upon oneself all the trouble involved in the introduction of a new product?
>
> Certainly, we do not rely on one factor to explain the lack of the introduction of revolutionary new products. A number of problems also may play a role. However, it is our conviction that all other factors are of secondary importance as compared to the cause discussed above; in the "sellers' market," there is no real incentive to introduce new products.[27]

Under Soviet centralized planning, both types of slack are usually absent. Until the most recent period, the dominant economic objective of Soviet leaders has always been rapid growth. In pursuit of this objective, they have exerted continuous, intensive pressure on producing units to increase output, to get more output from given inputs, and to uncover hidden reserves of productivity. Soviet plans were not intended as tools to achieve harmonious operation of the economy, but as tools to mobilize resources for rapid growth. It was a conscious policy, that plans were taut, exerted pressure on producing units. This presence is intensified, consciously and unconsciously, by the process of plan construction and implementation.[28] Consequently, there is little slack between the full productive capacity of the enterprise and the output demanded of it by plan targets. Coupled with a controlled supply of consumer goods below the level of consumer demand, this leads to a situation where a manager of a firm never has to worry about selling his output. His problem is acquiring the inputs needed to meet his output targets, not marketing the output.

Thus, from both the supply side and the demand side, the absence of slack in the Soviet economy inhibits the introduction of new technology.

Competition and Bankruptcy

In competitive market economies, the innovational process responds in a positive way to both high rewards for successful innovation and the firm's fear of being driven out of business by dynamic competitors. Indeed, the drive for survival is perhaps more important to innovation in the economy than the drive for high rewards. It is this defensive innovation that is the major factor in diffusing a successful innovation throughout the economy, and it is the diffusion of new technology that raises the general technological level of the economy.

Soviet firms do operate under a formal budget constraint—that is, they have to cover their costs from their revenues. However, the lower costs of an innovating firm do not lead to lower industry prices putting pressure on the revenues and profits of noninnovating firms and pushing them toward possible bankruptcy. In the Soviet Union, prices are set centrally for the industry, normally on the basis of average industry cost. The prevalence of sellers' markets means firms have no problems selling old products. However, even if the revenues of a firm fall below its costs, it does not go bankrupt. The budget constraint, as one analyst puts it, is a "soft" budget constraint.[29] The state will bail out a firm that is losing money through grants, subsidies, emergency credits, and allowed higher prices, and the firm will continue to operate. With the extension of public ownership and control over the economy, the creative-destruction aspect of innovation (the new drives out the old) is thus severely weakened in the Soviet Union. In a bureaucratized economy, those who operate the existing types of activities can protect themselves very well against the threat of new activities and new technologies. In this respect, one of the advantages of a private-enterprise system is that is does not internalize within the state decision-sector the destruction of the old technology. The price paid for new technology is absorbed privately by individual elements in the society, rather than publicly by the society as a whole.

The absence of competition, bankruptcy, and creative destruction in the Soviet economy removes the most potent force behind the diffusion of new technology—the fear of death and the drive to survive.

A final aspect of competition is the foreign sector. The Soviets have focused their efforts to develop new technology, both domestically and through imported foreign technology, primarily for domestic growth rather than international competitiveness. Once the new technology is in place, there is no pressure on those using it to keep up to changing foreign levels, and the technology languishes. This argument in part explains why the Soviets are much better in military technology than in civilian technology. Military equipment is by nature competitive; its performance and utility can be judged only relative to the equipment possessed by the (potential) enemy. This is not true of nonmilitary equipment.

The Possible Location of Entrepreneurial Activity

In view of these systemic barriers to innovation in the Soviet centrally planned economy, one would anticipate a very low rate of introduction and diffusion of new technology in the Soviet Union, compared with the advanced market economies of the West. While measurement problems make comparisons difficult, recent research shows that the Soviets are clearly behind the West in this respect. However, the relative position of the Soviet Union is perhaps not as bad as one might expect.

The compendium on Soviet technology produced by the Birmingham Centre depicts much of what is expected.[30] The Soviets pursue, in general, a traditional pattern of industrial production. They continue to emphasize such products as steel and cotton, while in the West, plastics and synthetic fibers are replacing these materials. Within each industry, concentration is on traditional products and processes. In the Soviet steel industry, for example, the use of traditional production techniques continues to increase even after the introduction of oxygen smelting and continuous casting. In the Western market economies, the new processes tend to drive out traditional techniques. It took the Soviet Union 16 years from their first industrial installation of the oxygen steelmaking process until it accounted for 20 percent of all steel produced. This compares with 5–12 years for the major industrial nations of the West.[31] However, the 12 years is for the United States. It took West Germany 11 years, and Japan and the U.K. both 5 years. Other similar data presented in the volume give the same impression.

Martens and Young calculated the time between the registration of inventions and their introduction into production in different countries. Whereas the United States and West Germany introduced about 65 percent of their inventions within two years, it took the Soviet Union 4 years to implement 65 percent of their inventions.[32]

Both of these measures have to be treated carefully, and further research might modify the picture. But as it stands, although there is clearly a gap between Soviet and Western performance, the gap is somewhat smaller than expected. To the extent that this is true, it might indicate (1) that the factors inhibiting Soviet innovation and diffusion are not as powerful as thought, or (2) that there are forces at work that modify the systemic resistance to innovation and diffusion.

The second point is the one we wish to pursue. Among the forces that counteract the resistance to new technology is entrepreneurial activity outside the firm. To be more precise, what we have in mind is what Ronen, in his chapter, calls "instigation." That is, there are forces or groups outside the firm that instigate innovation, energize the introduction of new goods and processes into production. They apply pressure on the firm to innovate; they push the manager to engage in entrepreneurial activity.

At the present stage of our research, all we can do is indicate where this activity might be located. We will start with a brief review of entrepreneurial activity at the level of the enterprise.

Enterprises

In most definitions, the entrepreneurial act is defined as the actual introduction of a new product or process into production. Thus, the focus of attention is on the firm, and normally the head of the firm (in the Soviet case, the director of the enterprise). We have argued that entrepreneurial activity at the Soviet enterprise is greatly inhibited by the Soviet bureaucratic structure and by the planning and control methods employed in the Soviet economy. The enterprise director is reluctant to generate new technology and is resistant to innovation-plan assignments. The enterprise director has considerable ability to resist plan assignments. "There are ways known to master bureaucrats all over the world of avoiding, delaying, altering, reconsidering, and generally frustrating the intentions of higher agencies; and always supported by incontestable good explanations of why something cannot be done."[33]

It is interesting, however, that according to some data for the 1960s, only 20–30 percent of all work on new technology was included in national economic plans.[34] Some of the remainder came perhaps from the ministries outside of annual national-plan channels. The data indicate, however, that more than half of all work on new technology (measured by cost) is generated at the enterprise itself, based on proposals from the enterprise's small research departments, as well as from workers. Undoubtedly, the new technology generated at the level of the enterprise embodies only minor changes from existing technology. The experience of other countries indicates, however, that small changes from the workplace can have a significant cumulative effect.

To counteract what is regarded by Soviet authorities as an insufficient level of entrepreneurial energy, special monetary bonuses have been instituted for the introduction of new technology. On balance, however, these appear to have been too low to have much effect.[35] Indeed, at least one Soviet economist argues that no monetary bonus, no matter how high, will induce Soviet managers to take on the risks associated with entrepreneurial activity.[36]

Ministries

The ministries possess significant power to influence and control their subordinate enterprises. They, along with the Communist Party, can hire and fire managers, set and change the levels of a manager's bonuses, and exert considerable influence on the path of a manager's career.

The ministries are pressured by higher party and government bodies to improve the introduction of new technology in their branches of the economy. The ministries, in turn, pass on this pressure to their subordinate enterprises. It is hard to say how intensive this pressure turns out to be. Although the ministries are held responsible by Gosplan and top party and government officials for the successful implementation of innovation plans, they are also held responsible for fulfilling production plans. Each ministry is very much in the same family with all its enterprises, and is therefore subject to the same systemic inhibitions on innovation.

It is probably safe to say that entrepreneurial-instigation activity at the ministerial level is muted. It is most likely limited to the most important, most publicized projects (especially those identified with individual political leaders) and at the other end of the spectrum, to the least radical, most evolutionary changes.

*Gosplan and the State Committee on
Science and Technology*

With regard to the introduction of new technology, these two state committees are primarily involved in constructing innovation plans, coordinating the activities of different ministries, and planning the supply of the required material and equipment. In the process, they have the important function of developing and transmitting information on the basis of which innovation decisions are made. However, they also exert pressure to bring about the implementation of innovation plans.[37]

The State Committee on Science and Technology focuses mainly on R&D activities. It maintains close contacts with ministries in regard to R&D matters, and encourages and pushes them toward implementing new technology. It has a rather sizeable science budget at its disposal, and it can extend funds to ministries for experimenting with particular types of new technology. It can also sign contracts for importing foreign know-how (importing equipment is in the domain of the Ministry of Foreign Trade) and can encourage ministries to have their enterprises try it out.

Gosplan is probably more engaged than the ministries in entrepreneurial-instigation activity. It is responsible for monitoring the implementation of the annual and five-year plans. If it observes noncompliance with an innovation plan, it can call in the offending ministry and try to pressure it to comply. It cannot, however, issue direct orders to a ministry or to any enterprise to comply. It can, though, get the Council of Ministries to issue such an order if the matter is important enough. In any case, Gosplan, wields power at the top of the economic hierarchy, and ministries prefer to stay on its good side.

R&D Institutes

There is a wide array of R&D institutes in the Soviet Union covering the entire gamut from basic research through applied research and development to engineering design and construction, including the building of prototypes.[38] Those concerned with basic research are attached primarily to the Academy of Sciences; those concerned with applied R&D (the bulk of the institutes) are attached to the branch ministries. In addition, there are R&D institutes attached to the universities that do primarily applied work under contract with industrial enterprises.

The R&D institutes—those attached to branch ministries and universities—maintain close contact with enterprises, and have staff who work with the enterprises to help introduce the new technology they have developed. These institutes are very interesting candidates for the location of entrepreneurial-instigation activity—they have a direct interest in seeing their products implemented. While it is true that the plan targets for R&D institutes are in terms of research products, in the longer run the prosperity and survival of the institute is affected by the actual use of its products in the economy. Thus, although some R&D institutes feel that their work ends with the development of a new product or process, there are others who actively promote the use of the new technology they have developed.

The Foreign Sector

The Soviet Economy, which operates in an environment of more advanced industrial nations, has been able to reap the benefits of backwardness by importing advanced, tested technology from other nations. One great advantage of this process is the reduction (though not elimination) of risk. The major entrepreneurs and promoters in this area—beside the foreign (capitalist) firm out to sell its technology—appear to be the State Committee on Science and Technology and the Soviet enterprise or ministry that has not been able to acquire the benefits of the new technology domestically.

The Communist Party

The Communist Party is the dominant entity in the Soviet Union. Its "power and authority extend into every fold and seam of the social fabric.[39] The leaders of the Party set policy for the economy, and the Party apparatus plays an important role in implementing economic plans.[40]

Much of the power that the Party apparatus exercises over the enterprises derives from what is called the *Nomenklatura* system. This system involves a list of all administrative positions (including enterprise director and chief engineer) for appointment to which the consent of some level of the Party apparatus is necessary. Furthermore, all enterprise directors of any importance are members of the Party. Therefore, the director's Party file is of crucial importance. The more criticisms and reprimands it contains, the more difficult it will be for that director to advance up the ladder or even remain as director.

Thus, the Party apparatus possesses significant power to influence the actions of enterprise directors. The question is, how does it use this power? It is clear that one of the ways it exercises influence over the economy is by helping correct the deficiencies of an erratic industrial supply system. If a Party official in one region has a firm that needs certain input materials to keep operating, he will call a Party official in a region where that material is produced and arrange to have some of the output of that material diverted to his needy firm.[41] The Party apparatus also puts pressure on enterprises to meet production targets. Does it, in addition, instigate the introduction of new technology?

The answer to this question is not clear, and Western specialists on the Soviet Communist Party disagrees on the issue. Berliner, a leading specialist on Soviet innovation, stated the following:

> One of the major responsibilities of the Party organizations is to maintain the pressure on enterprises to innovate. No action earns a Party organ such praise in the press as its intervention to force a cautious innovator to introduce an invention or new work technique. It is no accident that the conflict between an energetic Party secretary and a conservative manager over the question of technical innovation is one of the most recurrent themes in the Soviet novel on contemporary industry. One of the developers of a major Soviet innovation, the turbodrill, reports that after a series of failures and reverses, the project encountered great hostility and skepticism on the part

of the oil industry officials. It was only the strong Party support they received that enabled them to proceed.

As one might guess, Party officials do not always act as they are supposed to in theory. There are certain pressures upon them to "look the other way" at enterprises that may not be performing very well, and there are contrary pressures that push the Party from time to time into such close supervision of the enterprise as to constitute interference with the proper responsibility of management. But overall the Party does constitute a source of general pressure upon the economic units, among them enterprises, to innovate. The enterprise that fails to do so may expect, among the many unpleasant consequences, to be called before the Party and made to explain and to promise to do better next time.[42]

It may well be, however, that the Party is more active in promoting equilibrating entrepreneurial activity than innovational entrepreneurship.

The Top Political Leaders

A brief word is appropriate about the role of the top leaders as entrepreneurs-instigators. With regard to key projects like the Togliatti auto factory, the Kama River truck plant, and the Urals gas pipeline, the top leaders take a direct interest and thereby stimulate the entrepreneurial activity of the heads of these projects. Another, more pervasive role is conditioning the environment for innovation by inaugurating campaigns for introducing new technology into specific industries or into the economy in general. These command the attention of the bureaucracy, and usually get results. However, compliance with such campaigns often produces merely artificial, simulated new technology.

Finally, long-term, broad programs such as the program for the Scientific-Technical Revolution, or Detente with the West, condition the environment, make new approaches and new technology more socially desirable, and thus, in a sense, reduce the risk involved in innovative activity.

Summary and Conclusions

In this chapter, we have drawn on extensive Western literature on the Soviet innovation process to argue that innovation is not effectively handled by central planning—that at best the routinization of technical change leads to small changes and slow technological growth. Thus, even in a centrally planned economy, the energizing, instigating of entrepreneurial activity is needed, and takes place. We identified a number of places where this entrepreneurial-instigation activity most likely is located and explored in a preliminary way what the activity might be like at each location. If this subject is to be pursued, further in-depth research is needed, including actual case studies of successful and unsuccessful innovations in the Soviet Union.

What now can we say about future prospects with regard to new technology in the Soviet Union? It is clear that Soviet leaders are quite dissatisfied with the level of technological innovation in the Soviet economy. This dissatisfaction grew more acute in the 1970s as the pace of Soviet productivity growth diminished (in recent years, productivity growth has actually been negative). The prospects for future Soviet economic growth depend crucially on increases in productivity, which, in turn, require significant improvement in the Soviet innovation process. One of the most quoted statements is that of Brezhnev: "We must create conditions that will compel enterprises to produce the latest types of output, literally to chase after scientific and technical novelties, and not to shy away from them as the devil shies away from holy water."[43]

To this end, the Soviets have undertaken a number of experiments since the end of the 1960s, and have introduced several reforms. We will very briefly discuss two of these: the scientific-production association, and the innovation firm.[44]

The scientific-production association was introduced in 1968 to improve and speed up the introduction of new technology. It is an organization that combines an R&D institute, a design bureau, experimental production facilities, and one or more production enterprises. The R&D institute is normally the lead organization, with the head of the institute the director of the association. The hope is that this would raise the attention given to innovation. Their numbers have grown slowly; there were only about 150 of them by the end of the 1970s.

The scientific-production association is not primarily a production organization. Its main purpose is to develop a new technology and then transfer it out to the regular producing enterprises (or to the new production associations, which are combinations of enterprises). To facilitate this transfer, some scientific-production associations have special startup plants and installation groups that assist other production facilities in introducing and debugging new technology. One such association has a department that sets up and installs computer systems in other organizations.[45]

The scientific-production associations have been somewhat successful. They have produced greater opportunities for the practical implementation of new technology than have the R&D organizations that are not associated with production enterprises. However, they have their own problems that cover many organizational aspects of the forcible unification of diverse units. One major problem is the identification and measurement of their output. Their ministries sometimes treat them as production units and establish targets for them in terms of output rather than in terms of the development and introduction of new technology. At the present time, the debate about their usefulness continues; the original enthusiasm that supporters had for them, however, has severely diminished.

While some scientific-production associations have developed groups and departments for the active transfer of new technology to other organizations, such groups are the exception, not the rule. But in the 1960s, encouraged by the original decentralizing spirit of the 1965 economic reforms, there was a mushrooming of informal innovation firms (really, consulting firms) whose sole purpose was aiding innovation in client enterprises. These were groups of scientists and engineers who, working on their own, offered their services to industrial enterprises in all ministries for the testing and introduction of new technology. They operated on a profit and loss basis, and for a time they flourished. But opposition to them grew—primarily on the grounds that they did not fit into the planning system. Financial agencies, in particular, were opposed to them because they upset financial planning and control. In the 1970s, there were only two of them left. Many supporters are now calling for their reintroduction or for organizational forms similar to them.[46]

This is not the place to develop at length a set of proposals for improving innovation and entrepreneurial activity in the Soviet economy. Let us just conclude by saying that to achieve such improvement, Soviet political leaders will have to make decisions with regard to two major policies that they have consistently maintained over the years. One is the application of extreme pressure on the economy. This has resulted in a constant state of excess aggregate demand—absence of slack—which has deleterious effects on entrepreneurial activity. This pressure from the top will have to be reduced if the level of entrepreneurship is to improve in any substantial way.[47]

Second, successful entrepreneurial activity requires a significant increase in the entrepreneur's decision-making autonomy. The entrepreneur needs more autonomy in negotiating for R&D services, finding financial backing, negotiating with suppliers in different branches of the economy, locating customers, and setting prices.

It can be argued that decisions in these directions can be made without destroying the essential benefits that Soviet political leaders believe they derive from their centrally planned system. It will take a new generation of Soviet leaders, however, to make such decisions.

Notes

1. Schumpeter (1947), p. 132.
2. For a fascinating account of entrepreneurs in the Soviet second economy, see Simis (1981).

3. This basic methodological problem of separating system from culture is reflected in a popular Soviet anecdote. Question: "Why is it that East Germany, operating with socialist economic institutions similar to ours, is efficient, and we are so inefficient?" Answer: "Nobody has yet devised an economic system that can prevent Germans from working hard."

4. Among others, see Amann et al. (1977), Bergson (1964), Berliner (1976), Bornstein (1981), Granick (1975), Gregory and Stuart (1981), Levine (1981), Neuberger and Duffy (1976), and Nove (1977).

5. See Grossman (1963).

6. The Soviet Union is composed of fifteen union republics. Each union republic has a state apparatus that parallels the national apparatus. Beneath the republic governments are the provincial and local governments.

7. There are actually three types of ministries: The all-union ministry runs the enterprise under its control directly from Moscow, and its enterprises are not answerable to regional authorities. The union-republic ministry has offices both in Moscow and in the various republics, and the enterprises under its control are subject to the dual authority of Moscow and the republic council of ministers. The republic ministry directs enterprises within the republic and has no direct superior in Moscow. The heads of the first two ministries are members of the USSR council of ministers; those of the third are members of the republic council of ministers.

8. See, in particular, Berliner (1957), pp. 12–17, and Berliner (1976), pp. 32–34.

9. Kvasha (1967), p. 27, cited in Berliner (1976), pp. 33–34.

10. For an organization chart of Gosplan, see Dadaian (1974), p. 84.

11. In 1957, when Khrushchev was outvoted in the Politburo in connection with a massive reorganization of economic administration, he was able to bring the dispute to the Central Committee. There, he was supported.

12. This section is taken from Berliner (1976), pp. 43–47, with only slight revisions. For a detailed account of this process, see Nolting (1978).

13. See, for instance, Burns and Stalker (1961), Cyert and March (1963), Hayes and Abernathy (1980), Sayles (1974), Thompson (1961), Thompson (1969), and Zaltman et al. (1973).

14. See Berliner (1976) for a discussion of these matters.

15. Victor Thompson, *Bureaucracy and Innovation* (University, Ala.: University of Alabama Press, 1969), pp. 15–16. Reprinted with permission.

16. Thompson (1961), pp. 152–177; Zaltman et al. (1973), p. 124.

17. Kanygin (1974), p. 225, cited in Cocks (1978).

18. Cocks (1978), pp. 8–9.

19. See Burns and Stalker (1961), especially pp. 119–122.

20. Thompson (1969), pp. 24–25. Reprinted with permission.

21. See Grossman (1966), p. 118.

22. See Bergson (1978a), pp. 43–44.

23. Thompson (1969), pp. 4–5. Reprinted with permission.

24. Robert H. Hayes and William J. Abernathy, "Managing Our Way to Economic Decline," *Harvard Business Review* (1980):70–71. Copyright © 1980 by the President and Fellows of Harvard College; all rights reserved. Reprinted by permission of the *Harvard Business Review.*

25. See Granick (1975). He argues that the Soviet managerial system is essentially Taylorism, which was originally designed to increase the direct productivity of semiskilled workers, not the administrative and innovative activity of managers.

26. Cyert and March (1963), pp. 278–279.

27. Kornai (1971), pp. 288–289.

28. See the earlier section on planning, and Levine (1966).

29. See Kornai (1980).

30. Amann et al. (1977). See especially chapter 2.

31. Amann et al (1977), p. 55.

32. Martens and Young (1979), pp. 502–507.

33. Berliner (1976), p. 56.

34. Berliner (1976), p. 55. The data are from *Ekonomicheskaia gazeta* 2 (1966):30.

35. Berliner (1976), pp. 449–461.

36. Dudkin (1980), p. 401: "Measures commonly proposed for increasing management's interest in taking effective decisions cannot induce executives to take serious risks of any sort since no possible material or other incentives in the case of a success could compensate for the possible losses (particularly loss of job) that the executive might incur in case of failure." [Lev. M. Dudkin, "A System of Personalized Funds: A Proposal for a Centrally Planned Economy," *Journal of Comparative Economics* 4, no. 4 (1980):401. Reprinted with permission.] For a view that argues there is a level of monetary reward that can induce Soviet managers to assume entrepreneurial risks, see Bergson (1978a) and (1978b).

37. See Cocks (1978) and (1980), and Nolting (1978) and (1979).

38. See in particular, Cocks (1980), Nolting (1976), and Berliner (1976).

39. Grossman (1978), p. 5.

40. See Hough (1969).

41. See Hough (1969), especially pp. 214–234.

42. Joseph Berliner, *The Innovative Decision in Soviet Industry* (Cambridge, Mass.: MIT Press, 1976), p. 41. Reprinted with permission.

43. Brezhnev (1971), p. 81.

44. See Cocks (1978) and Cooper (1979).

45. Dzhavadov (1978), p. 195.

46. See, for instance, Dudkin (1974) and (1980),

47. In an important recent book, Janos Kornai argues that the absence

of slack is a systemic part of a socialist economy. It results, he says, from a lack of financial restraint ("soft budget constraint") and a paternalistic relationship between state and firm. He argues that slack would not increase even if the state removed its pressure on the economy. See Kornai (1980).

References

Amann, R., Cooper, J.M., and Davies, R.W. *The Technological Level of Soviet Industry.* New Haven, Conn.: Yale University Press, 1977.

Artemev, E.I., and Kravets, L.G., *Izobreteniia-uroven' tekhniki-upravlenie* (Inventions—the Level of Technology—Management). Moscow: Ekonomika, 1977.

Bergson, A. *The Economics of Soviet Planning.* New Haven, Conn.: Yale University Press, 1964.

———. "Entrepreneurship and Profits in the USSR," in Bergson, A. *Productivity and the Social System—the USSR and the West,* pp. 38–44. Cambridge, Mass.: Harvard University Press, 1978a.

———. "Managerial Risks and Rewards in Public Enterprises." *Journal of Comparative Economics* 2, 3 (September 1978b):211–225.

Berliner, J. *Factory and Manager in the USSR.* Cambridge, Mass.: Harvard University Press, 1957.

———. *The Innovative Decision in Soviet Industry.* Cambridge, Mass.: MIT Press, 1976.

Bornstein, M. *The Soviet Economy: Continuity and Change.* Boulder, Colo.: Westview Press, 1981.

Brezhnev, L.I. "Report to the 24th Party Congress," in *XXIV s'ed KPSS: Stenograficheskii otchet* (24th Congress of the Communist Party of the Soviet Union: Stenographic Report), vol. 1. Moscow: Politizdat, 1971.

Burns, T., and Stalker, G.M. *The Management of Innovations.* London: Tavistock, 1961.

Cocks, P. "Organizing for Technological Innovation in the 1970's." Conference on "Entrepreneurial Response and Economic Innovation in Russia and the Soviet Union." Kennan Institute, Washington, D.C., November 1978.

———. *Science Policy: USA/USSR* (Volume 2: Science Policy in the Soviet Union). Washington, D.C.: National Science Foundation, 1980.

Cooper, J. "Innovation for Innovation in Soviet Industry." Mimeo, CREES Discussion Papers, University of Birmingham, Birmingham, England, June 1979.

Cyert, R.M., and March, J.G. *A Behavioral Theory of the Firm.* Englewood Cliffs, N.J.: Prentice Hall, 1963.

Dadaian, V.S. *Ocherki o nashei ekonomike* (Essays on Our Economic System). Moscow: Znanie, 1974.

Dudkin, L.M. "Ekonomika riska. Kak uskorit vnedrenie izobretenii?" (The Economics of Risk. How to Speed Up the Introduction of Inventions?) *Ekonomika i organizatsiia promyshlennogo proizvodstva* 5 (1974):69–84.

———. "A System of Personlized Funds: A Proposal for a Centrally Planned Economy." *Journal of Comparative Economics* 4, 4 (December 1980):399–414.

Dzhavadov, G.A. *Upravlenie nauchno-tekhnicheskim progressom* (The Management of Scientific-Technical Progress), Moscow: Znanie, 1978.

Granick, D. *Soviet Introduction of New Technology: A Depiction of the Process.* Mimeo, SSC-TN-2625-7, SRI International, Washington, D.C., 1975.

Gregory, P.R., and Stuart, R.C. *Soviet Economic Structure and Performance,* 2nd ed. New York: Harper and Row, 1981.

Grossman, G. "Notes for a Theory of the Command Economy." *Soviet Studies* 15, 2 (October 1963):101–123.

———. "Innovation and Information in the Soviet Economy." *American Economic Review* (May 1966):118–130.

———. "The Party as Manager and Entrepreneur." Conference on "Entrepreneurial Response and Economic Innovation in Russia and the Soviet Union." Kennan Institute, Washington, D.C., November 1978.

Hayes, R.H., and Abernathy, W.J. "Managing our Way to Economic Decline." *Harvard Business Review* 58, 4 (July–August 1980):67–77.

Hough, J.F. *The Soviet Prefects: The Local Party Organs in Industrial Decision-Making.* Cambridge, Mass.: Harvard University Press, 1969.

Kanygin, Iu. M. *Nauchno-tekhnicheskii potentsial* (The Scientific-Technical Potential). Novosibursk: Nauka 1974.

Kornai, J. *Anti-Equilibrium.* Amsterdam: North Holland, 1980.

———. *Economics of Shortage,* vols. A & B. Amsterdam: North Holland, 1980.

Kushlin, V.I. *Uskorenie vnedreniia nauchnykh dostizhenii v proizvodstvo* (Speed Up the Introduction of Scientific Achievements into Production). Moscow: Ekonomika, 1976.

Kvasha, I. "Kontsentratsiia proizvodstva i melkaia promyshlennost." (Concentration of Production and Small-Scale Industry) *Voprosy ekonomiki* 5 (1967):26–31.

Levine, H.S. "Pressure and Planning in the Soviet Economy," in H. Rosovsky (ed.), *Industrialization in Two Systems: Essays in Honor of Alexander Gerschenkron.* New York: John Wiley, 1966.

———. "Soviet Economic Development, Technological Transfer, and

Foreign Policy," in S. Bialer (ed.), *The Domestic Context of Soviet Foreign Policy.* Boulder, Colo.: Westview Press, 1981.

Martens, J.A., and Young, J.P. "Soviet Implementation of Domestic Inventions: First Results," in U.S. Congress, Joint Economic Committee, *Soviet Economy in a Time of Change,* vol. 1, Washington, D.C.: U.S. Government Printing Office, 1979, pp. 472–509.

Neuberger, E., and Duffy, W. *Comparative Economic Systems: A Decision-Making Approach.* Boston: Allyn and Bacon, 1976.

Nolting, L.E. *The Financing of Research, Development and Innovation in the USSR, by Type of Performer.* U.S. Department of Commerce, Foreign Economic Report No. 9, Washington, D.C., 1976.

———. *The Planning of Research, Development and Innovation in the USSR,* U.S. Department of Commerce, Foreign Economic Report No. 14, Washington, D.C., 1978.

———. *The Structure and Functions of the USSR State Committee for Science and Technology.* U.S. Department of Commerce, Foreign Economic Report No. 16, Washington, D.C., 1979.

Nove, A. *The Soviet Economic System.* London: Allen and Unwin, 1977.

Sayles, L. "The Innovation Process: An Organization Analysis." *Journal of Management Studies* 13, 3 (October 1974):190–204.

Schumpeter, J.A. *Capitalism, Socialism, and Democracy,* 2nd ed. New York: Harper and Brothers, 1947.

Simis, K. "Russia's Underground Millionaires." *Fortune* (June 29, 1981): 36–50.

Thompson, V. *Modern Organization.* New York: Alfred A. Knopf, 1961.

Thompson, V. *Bureaucracy and Innovation.* University, Ala.: University of Alabama Press, 1969.

Zaltman, G., Duncan, R., and Holbek, S. *Innovations and Organizations.* New York: John Wiley, 1973.

**Part IV
Commentaries**

10 The Neglect of the Entrepreneur

Harold Demsetz

The entrepreneur is important enough to disrupt—and then restore—equilibria, to fuel economic development, and to bring a nation out of the depths of a recession. He perceives and acts upon opportunities that escape mere maximizers, yet he himself is only dimly perceived in the studies that attribute these roles to him. Does he sport a bright coat of arms, purchased at depression prices with the aid of a loan from some capitalist, or does he wear the gossamer cloth of economic mythology? Why do we not know more about this notorious personage?

The chapters in this book testify to our difficulty in dealing directly and analytically with the entrepreneur and his activities. Ronen's paper is the only one of the present collection that addresses the entrepreneur directly, but (as Ronen clearly states) it does so in a nonanalytical manner—it is a report of interviews, spiced with some speculative observations. The remaining chapters treat subjects at best only tangentially related to entrepreneurship. Arrow argues that small and large firms are likely to house different types of research activity. Such research, however, is not usually germane to entrepreneurial action. Green and Shoven give examples of how risk and bankruptcy can cause outside financing of research to be nonoptimal. This is more a study of the cost of information and of risk-averse behavior than it is of entrepreneurship, and its conclusions are applicable to any risky investment. A convincing case is made by Williamson for viewing the managerial revolution as a major innovative contribution to productivity. However, this is not itself a study of entrepreneurship. Bergson's discussion of the labor-managed firm in Yugoslavia presents the puzzle of the reinvestment of a large fraction of the revenue of these firms in capital renewal. Why worker-managers, who have no clear title to such firm-specific assets, should reinvest on a large scale is an interesting problem in property rights, but one that is quite distant from entrepreneurship. Baumol explicitly denies that he is analyzing the entrepreneur per se, setting for himself instead the task of modeling the interaction among regulation, an entirely abstract notion of the quantity of entrepreneurial activity, and economic growth. With the exception of Ronen's paper (and perhaps Baumol's), these papers could have been written without any reference to the entrepreneur and his social role. He is not the inventor, nor is he the funder of either inventions or capital assets. The organizations of large firms might, indeed, be a result of innovative activity, but they are themselves neither the entrepreneur nor his activities.

I note this neglect of the entrepreneur, not critically, but to underscore the intellectual puzzle of his resistance to analysis. Indeed, Baumol's observation that "the entrepreneur is universally acknowledged to play a leading role, and yet seems always to remain invisible in the models used to analyze [the firm and economic development]" suggests the theme of the present paper—why is our understanding of the entrepreneur so meager?

The neglect of the entrepreneur has not gone unnoticed by students of the history of economic thought, although it has hardly been their central interest. Professor Kirzner notes several explanations for this neglect in classical writings.[1] Some explanations are based on the nature of the real economy of the nineteenth century, particularly the submersion of the entrepreneurial function into that of the capitalist owner. Allegedly, the nonspecialized nature of businessmen during that century kept entrepreneurship hidden from view. Other explanations are based on a preoccupation by classical economists with the labor-capital input dichotomy. But, because entrepreneurship can be viewed as a form of labor services, this preoccupation does not imply neglect of the entrepreneur. In this vein, Kirzner notes the belief of Cannon that early classical writers were trapped by their belief in the wage-fund theory, a theory that asserted that wages are paid from the capital of employers, not from the output of the firms. Since the entrepreneur's return is received on the basis of the success of his ventures, not on some contracted wage agreement, the classicalists assertedly had no framework for treating the entrepreneur. Then there is the Schumpeterian opinion that classical economists viewed production as an automatic process not calling for active decision making.

It is improbable that these are correct explanations (although Schumpeter's explanation bears a superficial relationship to one I will propose later). The emerging industrial economies of the nineteenth century were noteworthy and well noted for innovation and private risk-taking. Classical writers, astute in such matters, could hardly have failed to perceive the entrepreneurial function. They were not blinded by the fact that the entrepreneur and the capitalist were frequently the same person. After all, they quite clearly separated conceptually the wages of management from the profit of owner-managers, and also the rent of land ownership from the income of farmers. No great intellectual leap was needed to disentangle the return to entrepreneurship from other factor payments. By the same token, the classical economists surely could have added entrepreneurship to the classical triad of land, labor, and capital if it had suited their purpose. Furthermore, they understood that production requires decisions. Smith clearly viewed the equalization of profit rates as the product of conscious decisions to seek a greater profit. Such nonautomatic decisions played no large role in theory—not because classicalists thought the economy ran automatically, but because such decisions were not very germane to the problem with which they wrestled. If discussing the entrepreneurial function would have furthered their theoretical objective, entrepreneurship would have received a prominent and insightful treatment in their writings.

The problem central to classical and neoclassical interests certainly was not the trade cycle, which, in Schumpeter's hands, is closely associated with entrepreneurial activity. Except for Smith's emphasis on the beneficent impact of specialization and free trade on a nation's wealth, and Malthus's discussion of population growth, these economists were not concerned with economic development. Even the dynamics of the movement from one equilibrium to another was tangential to the basic problem attacked by eighteenth and nineteenth century mainline economists. They surely recognized these problems and, in a general way, the role of the entrepreneur—or, as he was called in some of the writings, the undertaker of economic ventures—but their primary problem required no careful discussion of any of this. So, for 150 years, the main tradition in economics called for the neglect of entrepreneurship.

The problem they focused on instead was that of understanding how a *decentralized* economic system allocated resources. This demanded fundamentally an equilibrium analysis that would allow them to analyze the coordinating role of prices. They were quite willing to presume that prices and outputs would change in response to some alteration in an exogenous variable, such as a change in taste or in technology—changes that might in many cases be attributed to entrepreneurs—but they were not particularly interested in the change itself, or even in the path of adjustment. They sought an understanding of equilibrium prices and allocations. Wants and technology were taken to be exogenous to the coordination problem, and self-interest was assumed to respond effectively to profit opportunities. These assumptions were appropriate and advantageous for developing such an analysis. An appreciation of how the coordination problem of a decentralized economy is resolved would have been delayed if attention had been diverted to problems of economic change.

To understand the role of the price system, neoclassical economists gradually developed a limiting case of the problem posed by decentralization—the perfect competition model. This model is unfortunately named, for it has little to say about competition and much to say about decentralization. No wonder those who seek to incorporate the entrepreneur into economic analysis are so dissatisfied with it. Viewed from the proper perspective—as a model of *perfect decentralization*[2]—it is a remarkable intellectual achievement. The achievement, never fully appreciated even by those most responsible for its development, is in its abstraction from authority.

Perfect competition conceptualizes the protection of all decision makers from any element of authority. That is the substantive content of competition as it is used in the perfect competition model. (Entrepreneurship requires a different notion of competition.) All decision makers are price takers in this perfect decentralization model; so, no one exercises authority (that is, centralized control) over anyone else. Since prices are determined by the aggregate of individual decisions, there is a complete absence of authority or centralization in the model. The coordinating role of the price system, and the resource allocation that the price system tends to bring about, are clearly visualized with the aid of this limiting case of decentralization. Entrepreneurship was neglected because the problems of economic change would simply have made it more difficult to focus on the coordination problem. There are other reasons for this neglect, but for the period of classical and neoclassical economics, I believe that this was an important reason.

Coordination problems of a somewhat different type occupied economists after the great recession of the 1930s. Aggregative problems of unemployment and inflation did not go unnoticed prior to this, but there was a premise (based on monetary theory and Say's law) that coordination at this level would clear markets if various sorts of price rigidities could be purged from the decentralized economic system. While this premise became suspect after 1930, the approach to these problems remained essentially an equilibrium analysis of coordination through prices. There was, for example, the important question of whether interest rates could clear the capital markets at full employment. Moreover, the compartmentalization of economic actors into households and business firms continued as it had before, except that there was greater emphasis on the behavior of aggregates of individuals. Tools such as the marginal propensities to consume and to invest, along with the entire mode of analysis that culminated in the IS-LM framework, clearly reflected this compartmentalization. The new entity was a sham government sector, conveniently assumed to be motivated primarily to maintain full employment. Even the rational-expectations analysis of more recent vintage, though less naive about the functioning of government and the decisions of consumers and businessmen, follows quite consistently in the tradition of basing economic analysis on the standard economic actors of traditional economics.

These theoretical predispositions might correctly address the problems toward which they were directed, but they were hardly congenial to the recognition and analysis of entrepreneurship. Entrepreneurial actions do not fit neatly into an equilibrium analysis of households, firms, and a beneficent government.

Schumpeter and his followers took another approach, deemphasizing the importance of equilibrium and explicitly considering changes in wants and production functions. They noted, for instance, that change did not proceed in a balanced manner. Instead, a few lines of economic activity surged ahead of and strongly influenced other lines of activity, and prices during these periods of "creative destruction" went into a state of flux. Such occurrences could not be explained easily with traditional households and firms, and especially not with a passive money supply and a beneficent government. A new economic agent was needed, one that would not be constrained by given technology and given wants.

The chosen instrument was the entrepreneur, and the source of his earnings was the successful new combination of resources—the new product or new economic organization. The importance of the entrepreneur in this approach cannot be overstated easily, but his analytical substance can hardly be understated. This new economic agent was—and remains—as substantively pale as the government is in post-Keynesian analysis. In the Schumpeterian models of business fluctuations and economic development, the entrepreneur is neither an object of analysis nor of research, but is rather a deus ex machina of economic change.

To this charge there is an exception. The Schumpeterian entrepreneur does not cope well with fluctuating, disequilibrium prices. This single item of substantive behavior is sufficient for him to move great economies through chaotic fluctuations and uneven progress. When prices have settled into a recession equilibrium, when input prices are low and stable, he can visualize new techniques of production and new products that on average, will yield to him a handsome profit. So, when the economy has settled into an equilibrium, at less than full-employment, he begins to disrupt old ways. As entrepreneurial breakthroughs take place, the economy is driven upward from its recession lows. The creatively destructive impact of innovation spreads through the economic system, and imitators rush to take advantage of the opportunities revealed to them by entrepreneurial success. Things grow chaotic as full employment is reached. Input prices are forced upward into a state of disarray as inflationary pressures mount. Entrepreneurs, unable to make their economic calculations with any certainty—and by now reaping the rewards of their success—cash in and retire to the sidelines. Their absence not only removes an important real stimulus from economic activity, but their cashing in leads to a contraction of the money supply, starting the economy downward toward a new (but nonetheless wealthier) recession low.

The entrepreneur's contribution to business fluctuations is tied to his greater ease of calculation when prices are stable, and to his optimism that inputs are a good buy at the bottom of a recession. It is difficult to find much more of substance in the Schumpeterian entrepreneur. Nonetheless, Schumpeter's entrepreneur fired the imagination of many economists, and still seems to be the key element in the economics of change. Surely this is a tribute to Schumpeter's promotional skills.

Schumpeter, of course, is not the sole source of enthusiasm for the entrepreneur. Entrepreneurship had been an important topic in recent Austrian economics, where there has been a continuing effort to contrast market process with neoclassical equilibrium statics. I will not comment at length on this comparison here, but it would be unfair to my topic not to note that the entrepreneur in this literature contains little new substantive content. Indeed, one of the points emphasized in the Austrian writings undercuts the single substantive element in Schumpeter's entrepreneur—his inability to make the necessary economic calculations when prices are in flux during disequilibrium. Professer Kirzner writes:

> By contrast (to Schumpeter's) my own treatment of the entrepreneur emphasizes the equilibrating aspects of his role. I see the situation upon which the entrepreneur impinges as one of inherent disequilibrium rather than of equilibrium—as one churning with opportunities for desirable changes rather than one of placid evenness. . . . For me the changes the entrepreneur initiates are always toward the hypothetical state of equilibrium. . . .
>
> My emphasis on this difference . . . underscores the crucial importance of entrepreneurship for the *market process*. A treatment such as Schumpeter's . . . is likely to convey the impression that for the *attainment* of equilibrium no entrepreneurial role is, in principle, required at all.[3]

The Schumpeterian view is that the entrepreneur acts decisively to innovate when prices have settled into a recession stability, and decisively to abandon innovation when disequilibrium price fluctuations dominate the scene. The Kirzner view is that the entrepreneur—although he is a promoter of change—fundamentally acts when prices are in flux, and finds little opportunity for action when prices are in stable equilibrium.

The combination of these two views can be interpreted as saying that the entrepreneur attempts to profit by buying cheap and selling dear whenever he sees an opportunity for doing so, and that these opportunities include modifying tastes and technology. The problem in analyzing entrepreneurial behavior is not so much that the behavior defies standardization—as Baumol claims—but that it is not easily distinguished from the economic behavior of all economic actors. A positive response to perceived profit opportunities excludes very few maximizers from the entrepreneurial club. Furthermore, neither Schumpeter nor Kirzner requires exclusivity. Neither views entrepreneurship as an activity carried on only by a few specialized individuals. Rather, most players of the economic game behave entrepreneurially to varying degrees. Some of these players rely to a greater degree than others on entrepreneurship as a source of income, but no special species of entrepreneurs is claimed. The new element is really not the entrepreneur—it is the expanded opportunity set for maximizers, one that includes changing the parameters that the older economics found useful to take as given. Entrepreneurship is little more than profit maximization in a context in which knowledge is costly and imitation is not instantaneous.[4]

This expansion in the opportunity set theoretically facing maximizers permits them to profit by (and lose from) activities of the type associated with entrepreneurship. It also gives rise to tactical and strategic problems and to problems of authority and control, all of which are difficult to fit into a framework designed to explore the limiting case of perfect decentralization. Time and timing are important in this new opportunity set, as are risk and uncertainly. Not only is it possible and desirable to study these aspects of economic action, but there already exists a large literature on technological change, information, risk, and tactical and strategic behavior. The study of changing wants is still sparse in economics, but it is likely to become increasingly important. An understanding of economic action in these dimensions is entirely feasible without considering the entrepreneur explicitly.

The literature on entrepreneurship offers only one truly distinguishing characteristic that separates entrepreneurship from maximizing behavior: "alertness." On this, I turn again to Professor Kirzner:

> When we extend economic analysis to a world of imperfect knowledge it becomes possible to find place for an entirely new economic role . . . a decision-maker whose *entire* role arises out of his alertness to hitherto unnoticed opportunities.[5]

> All [the entrepreneur] needs is to discover where buyers have been paying too much and where sellers have been receiving too little . . . To discover these . . . opportunities requires alertness. Calculation will not help, and economizing and optimizing will not of themselves yield this knowledge.[6]

> The discovery of a profit opportunity *means* the discovery of something obtainable for nothing at all. No investment at all is required.[7]

> The difficulty with conceiving of entrepreneurship in terms of superior knowledge arises from the need to distinguish sharply between entrepreneurship and factors of production. . . . [P]ure profits implies a role in the market which cannot be reduced to just a special kind of productive factor . . . the services of men who possess knowledge, can, after all, be hired in the factor market.[8]

> The aspect of knowledge which is crucially relevant to entrepreneurship is not so much the substantive knowledge of market data as *alertness*. . . .[9]

If this is the essence of entrepreneurship, there is a more familiar name for it—luck. What is being described is the stumbling onto a profit possibility without any intent (that is, without any deliberate, focused investment of time, energy, or other resources). It is Pierre and Marie Curie noting the unexpected exposure of a photographic plate that had been placed without foresight next to ore containing uranium. It is striking crude oil and recognizing its value while drilling for water. Such discoveries do happen while persons are busy doing other things, so they are free opportunities to profit. All that is required is to note them when they occur. Alertness is the only requirement, and although I do not really believe that alertness is achieved without any cost, I am willing to accept the notion that this cost would trivially differ from zero in many instances.

Entrepreneurship can thus be factored into two parts. One is an impure component deriving from the fact that the economy works under conditions of imperfect knowledge. Thus, the discoverer of petroleum can invest in bringing his product to market before imitators reduce its price. The study of this component is the study of investment and risk taking of a planned, conscious sort. While the term entrepreneur is useful grammar for discussing such ventures, it adds no new economic agent or variable to the study of competition under conditions of imperfect knowledge. This is true even though such risk-bearing planned ventures may be the most important source of economic progress.

The second part is the pure component discussed by Kirzner. This component might or might not loom important in economic progress. Just how much of our wealth can be attributed to the pure mix of luck and alertness, and how much to risk-bearing investment in innovative enterprise, is difficult to say. But even if this pure component is the more important source of economic progress, it is, in a sense, beyond the scope of scientific analysis. For luck by any name is the unexplainable occurrence.

There are thus three reasons for our neglect of entrepreneurship.

1. The problem of understanding perfect decentralization that occupied neoclassical economists did not require that economic change be given much attention.
2. Problems of change that become important in a context of imperfect decentralization, such as those caused by imperfect information, are addressable without analytical appeal to entrepreneurship.
3. Problems of change associated with unforeseen and unforeseeable events are beyond the scope of analysis.

This leaves little room for the analytical treatment of pure entrepreneurship. Once an important unforeseeable event has occurred, we can analyze how people react and adjust to the event. These accommodations to an unforeseen event require the planned diversion of resources from other uses, so that costs are incurred. The problem becomes one of investment under uncertain conditions. Strictly speaking, this is also true of alertness. It is not enough to recognize that oil, not water, is coming from the ground—although even this involves the prior acquisition of the knowledge needed to distinguish the two. A mind must devote itself to considering the prospect and judging its potential. That is a mind diverted from other tasks; therefore, there is a cost to maintaining alertness. Alertness itself is a form of investment under conditions of uncertainty. The case of pure entrepreneurship, then, is in principle indistinguishable from the analysis of such investment problems. If the political system allows persons to retain a larger fraction of the profit created by being alert to lucky events there will be more alertness—a response difficult to reconcile with a belief that alertness requires no resources.

The only distinguishing component of pure entrepreneurship that remains is luck. I do not mean to say that luck is unimportant or uninteresting, or that investments in reacting to luck cannot be analyzed. I claim only that *pure* entrepreneurship—as a distinct analytical tool, or as an object of scientific study—has been neglected because it has not yet been linked to a systematic behavioral response to uncertainty.

Notes

1. Kirzner, I.M., *Perception, Opportunity, and Profit* (Chicago: University of Chicago Press, 1979), pp. 37–90.

2. A fuller discussion of the perfect competition model as one largely devoid of competitive activity can be found in my DeVries lectures, *Economic, Legal and Political Dimensions of Competition* (North Holland Press, 1982.)

3. Kirzner, I.M., *Competition and Entrepreneurship* (Chicago: University of Chicago Press, 1973), p. 73. Reprinted by permission of The University of Chicago Press.

4. This causes some difficulty for Schumpeter's theory of business fluctuations, based as it is on the special timing of entrepreneurial activity. Since we are all maximizers, there is no clear reason why the entrepreneurial function must exhibit the timing attributed to it by Schumpeter; or, at least, there is no reason for such timing to be identified exclusively with entrepreneurial behavior. Maximizing consumers are not prevented by clearly stated constraints from deciding that the depth of the recession offers especially good opportunities for consuming cheaply. Stable prices facilitate consumer calculations also, and if prices are lower than they should be, well, why not increase consumption? The same could be said for investment.

5. Kirzner, *Competition and Entrepreneurship,* p. 39. Reprinted by permission of The University of Chicago Press.

6. Kirzner, *Competition and Entrepreneurship,* p. 41. Reprinted by permission of The University of Chicago Press.

7. Kirzner, *Competition and Entrepreneurship,* p. 48. Reprinted by permission of The University of Chicago Press.

8. Kirzner, *Competition and Entrepreneurship,* p. 66. Reprinted by permission of The University of Chicago Press.

9. Kirzner, *Competition and Entrepreneurship,* p. 67. Reprinted by permission of The University of Chicago Press.

11

Entrepreneurs and the Entrepreneurial Function: A Commentary

Israel M. Kirzner

It is by now notorious that for many decades economic theorists virtually ignored the entrepreneurial role. Their models were peopled by agents who displayed few of the characteristics of—and encountered few of the problems faced by—the flesh-and-blood entrepreneurs whom we know both from business and economic history and from everyday casual observation. It has been gratifying during the past few years to witness the reawakening of interest in entrepreneurship among scholars working in several disciplines.[1] The chapters in this book offer us the opportunity to assess the progress made among scholars in economic theory. These chapters were written by outstanding economists; each aims to advance understanding on some aspects of entrepreneurial activity in a variety of institutional contexts. It is with much interest, therefore, that we examine these chapters to discover the extent to which entrepreneurship has become a vital area of study, and to savor the fresh insights into the entrepreneurial role that this new work has perhaps inspired. This chapter consists of the reflections precipitated by one such examination.

This writer would be less than candid if he did not express—along with his admiration for these contributions—a certain sense of disappointment. Each chapter is a conscientious and competent—even brilliant—exploration of its chosen topic within the overall theme of entrepreneurial behavior. Yet, for all their virtues, it appears that these chapters have pushed out the frontiers of the economics of entrepreneurship only slightly. It is apparent that we still have far to go before any recognized and useful economics of entrepreneurship will be part of the settled body of modern economic thought. The road to be traveled before we can hope to reach such a stage, moreover, promises to be rocky and treacherous. What is a matter for concern is not so much that the distinguished contributors to this book lack any commonly shared understanding of what the essence of entrepreneurship *is*, as that they hardly recognize the importance of a clear and satisfactory analytical idenfication of pure entrepreneurial activity. In the light of this observation, it comes as no surprise to note that these chapters lack a unifying theme. They all relate, of course, to some aspect of entrepreneurship.

But because the term "entrepreneurship" does not necessarily mean to one writer what it means to another, and because little attention is paid here to the definition of entrepreneurship as such, the sense of a lack of theme remains. It may be helpful, before discussing the elusive essence of entrepreneurship, to consider why modern economics has, until now, avoided paying the entrepreneur any attention at all.

The Entrepreneur and Economic Analysis

One would think that the figure of the entrepreneur, the active businessman, would be one of the last features of capitalist society to escape notice. The active businessman may be more or less innovative, more or less daring, more or less energetic—but he is still the figure in the market to whom one looks for energy, daring, and innovation. The seething activity in the market that we associate with energetic, bold, and innovative decisions is an item in the capitalist scene that is both striking and characteristic. How, then, have these seemingly essential features of the market society succeeded in effacing themselves for so long from the analytic picture constructed by economic theorists?

A plausible explanation for this puzzle might run as follows: The seething market activity that we associate with energetic, bold, and innovative decisions has been, in an important sense, precisely the element in the market from which it is necessary for economic analysis to abstract. After all, it is this activity that appears to defy all efforts at imposing an orderly, systematic analytical framework upon market phenomena. The vision that economic theorists brought to their work was that, *in spite of* the seemingly rudderless course of entrepreneurial events, market phenomena were nonetheless ultimately constrained and guided by systematic market forces. Beneath the facade of apparently unpredictable, energetic, bold, and innovative business activity, there resides a system of powerful coordinating forces to which, sooner or later, the seemingly free decisions of market participants must, willy-nilly, conform. It is the given underlying conditions of production and the given patterns of consumer preferences that, in the last analysis, govern market phenomena. To understand how such governance is exercised, it was *necessary* for theorists to ignore the superficial agitation of market phenomena, and to search for the underlying powerful realities that truly dominate the course of market events.

From this perspective, equilibrium analysis in economics constitutes a special kind of analytical feat—the discernment and explication of regularities that are masked from the eyes of the superficial observer by the apparently unsystematic gyrations of prices and of the quantities of resources and output. From this perspective, attention to the activities of the entrepreneur not only is unnecessary to the economic analysis, but in fact is a hindrance. It is reasonable, therefore, to assess Schumpeter's pioneering work on the entrepreneur in terms of this explanation for the neglect of the entrepreneur.

For Schumpeter, casual observation revealed that the capitalist process over the years was a series of spasmodic, discontinuous changes. The discontinuity of the changes that make up this process contrasts sharply with the theoretical picture of the "circular flow"—a picture that Schumpeter himself spelled out in detail[2] as the foundation upon which to construct his theory of (discontinuous) development. Schumpeter's appreciation, on the one hand, of the Walrasian theory of general equilibrium (the theoretical model of the circular flow) and on the other hand, his awareness of the need for a theory of dynamic, discontinuous development, together guided his own prolific contributions from his *Theory of Economic Development* (1911) and *Business Cycles* (1938) to his *Capitalism, Socialism, and Democracy* (1942). For Schumpeter, the Walrasian theory was the highest theoretical achievement in economics;[3] yet throughout his career, he was impatient with his colleagues for failing to see how limited equilibrium theory is, and how inadequate it is for understanding the *process* of capitalist development. For Schumpeter, a full understanding of capitalism thus required an appreciation of the way the Schumpeterian-entrepreneurial theory of development is superimposed upon the Walrasian theory of the circular flow.

From the perspective outlined above, it can be seen that Schumpeter fully accepted the need to pierce the agitated surface of capitalist reality to perceive the powerful forces beneath that bring about the circular flow. What impelled Schumpeter to focus analytical attention on the entrepreneur—and what sets him apart from all of his contemporaries who failed to understand the entrepreneurial role—was his perception that this agitation on the surface of capitalist reality is *more* that just fuzzy noise. What appears as functionless agitation from the perspective of equilibrium theory emerges, in the Schumpeterian vision, as necessary steps in the process of creative destruction that constitutes capitalist development. Thus, Schumpeter's vision permitted him to have, so to speak, the best of both worlds. On the one hand, he could endorse Walrasian general equilibrium theory by abstracting from entrepreneur-driven market agitation; on the other, he was able to perceive in that agitation an important—indeed essential—feature of the capitalist process.

However, the developments in twentieth century general-equilibrium and growth theories have perhaps made it *less* easy for economic theorists to focus attention on the entrepreneur than it was for Schumpeter. After all, modern extensions of equilibrium theory to include interaction between intertemporal, multiperiod decisions offer a vision of intertemporal growth equilibrium with respect to which Schumpeter's process of discontinuous development, too, must appear as fuzzy noise. The modern effort to discern the true underlying forces governing the course of economic activity through time thus calls for a resolute disregard of the surface discontinuities occasioned by precisely the entrepreneurial innovations that were, for Schumpeter, the essence of capitalism.

The current resurgence of interest in the theory of entrepreneurship recognizes, we hope, that such resolute disregard—whatever its merits might be for limited purposes—should not be maintained so consistently that it prevents us from seeing important systematic market forces arising out of entrepreneurship. Our discussion of these matters suggests a classificatory framework for possible theories of entrepreneurship. It will be useful to set forth this framework as a background for appraising the various approaches represented in this book.

Theories of Entrepreneurship: Four Levels

The discussion in the preceding section suggests that we can identify four levels at which one might, in principle, develop theories of entrepreneurial activity. Moreover, the essence of entrepreneurship at one level of theory might not be very useful at one of the other levels. Let us return to the flesh-and-blood entrepreneur—one of those, perhaps, interviewed by Joshua Ronen.

A flesh-and-blood entrepreneur takes decisive action along a variety of dimensions. He forms companies, he introduces new product lines, he initiates new techniques of production, he cuts prices, he strikes out for new markets, he seeks sources of finance, he innovates new forms of internal organization, he brings in new personnel, he reassigns existing personnel. It is not difficult to imagine the degree of agitation injected into the market by these kinds of activities. The economic theorist might grapple with these activities, or with their market consequences, at one or more of four levels:

1. The economic theorist might try to fit the decisions of this entrepreneur-businessman into the standard theory of the profit-maximizing firm with full relevant information. Each innovation, each pricing change, would then be viewed as a simple profit-maximizing reaction to some apparent shift in the arrays of revenue and production possibilities that confront the firm. Such a theoretical perspective rules out error (or the spontaneous discovery of earlier error), and also surprise. It can, with more or less difficulty, be stretched to include the decisions made by the firm to acquire additional information. However, the degree of information sought and possessed—and thus the degree of ignorance accepted—is at all times viewed as optimal. At this level, the theorist seeks to explain the firm's decisions within the theory of the profit-maximizing firm. For this level of entrepre-

neurial theory, the term "entrepreneur" simply connotes the imagined center of profit-maximizing decision making. This decision maker is assumed to possess, at all times, full relevant information, including full information concerning the worthwhileness of seeking additional information and full information concerning the sources of such information.

2. The economic theorist might recognize that, at a second level, the decisions of our entrepreneur-businessman cannot be fitted into the standard theory of the firm without unacceptable artificiality. At this level, the theorist recognizes that such human qualities as leadership, boldness, energy, persistence, resourcefulness, creativity, and judgment can crucially affect the decisions taken. There are, obviously, great variations between different would-be entrepreneurs with respect to these human qualities. This makes it highly implausible to view decisions as simply the calculated solutions to maximization problems presented by objective sets of data equally and fully perceived by all entrepreneurs. Instead of seeking to understand the decisions of our entrepreneur-businessman in terms of profit maximization, this second level of theory will seek a framework that transcends maximization. At this level, the theorist would seek theories that explain where their springs of creativity comes from, and under what circumstances they will assume Knightian uncertainty, or what makes them notice opportunities overlooked by others, and so on. For this level of entrepreneurial theory, the essence of entrepreneurship might be seen in any one (or in a combination) of many characteristics generally present in entrepreneurial activity. One theory might see the essence of such activity, for example, in its innovativeness, and might then construct a framework to account for different degrees of innovativeness. (Such a theory, of course, might be a psychological theory rather than a purely economic theory.) Such a theory might show how the degree of innovativeness is affected by economic constraints, regulatory climate, and the like. Another theory might see the essence of entrepreneurial activity in its speculative aspect, and might then trace the psychological or other lines of causation that govern the businessman's willingness to venture into the unknown.

3. A third level for the theoretical explication of entrepreneurial activity might address, not the determinants of the decisions of entrepreneurial individuals, but rather the *market consequences* of such decisions. Schumpeter's was a theory at this level of analysis. Such a theory views entrepreneurial activity as superimposed upon an equilibrium pattern of nonentrepreneurial interacting decisions. Without seeking to account for the particular creative, innovative, or speculative decisions of individual businessmen, a theory at this third level might, for example, illuminate the extent to which market phenomena, in fact, fail to correspond precisely to the conditions consistent with equilibrium. Thus, for Schumpeter, the activity of entrepreneurs is seen as disrupting the circular flow of equilibrium.

For this level of theory, the essence of entrepreneurship will probably be identified by a particular market phenomenon thought to be specifically generated by entrepreneurial activity. For instance, Schumpeter, who links his entrepreneur with dynamic, discontinuous market innovations, sees "creative destruction" as the essence of entrepreneurship: the entrepreneur can break away from the standard mold, initiate change and innovation. The point is that at this level, one's view of the entrepreneur is likely to be related to the ultimate market-theoretical purposes for which he is to be analytically deployed.

4. The fourth level at which a theory of entrepreneurship might be attempted is, like the third, not primarily concerned with the decisions of entrepreneurial individuals. It, too, is concerned rather with the market consequences of these entrepreneurial decisions. However, at this fourth level, such market consequences are not seen as superimposed upon an otherwise equilibrium world. Indeed, one does not take at all for granted that the market would at all times be in equilibrium in the absence of entrepreneurially driven agitation. At this level, the theorist considers the possibility that entrepreneurial activity is not merely a disturbing fuzzy noise masking the true, dominating forces of market equilibrium, but that such agitative activity might, in fact, be the only element on which we can rely to steer market decisions toward an equilibrium pattern. For a theory successfully sustaining this latter possibility, entrepreneurially driven market agitation is not a ruffled surface beneath which can be discerned the true balance of forces in equilibrium. Rather, the economists' vision of the market in equilibrium is relevant only to the extent that agitation leads eventually toward it.

At this fourth level (as at the third level), one's perception of the essence of the entrepreneur will depend a great deal upon the particular theory of market process for which the entrepreneur is being deployed. In work directed to this level of theory, the writer has identified pure entrepreneurship as consisting of pure alertness to as yet unexploited—because unnoticed—opportunities.[4] The purely formal sense in which the notion of alertness is used is closely linked with the fact that alertness, in that work, accounts for the equilibrative character of the market process.

Entrepreneurs and Entrepreneurs

Our classificatory schema has not only suggested a variety of different levels at which the economic theory of entrepreneurship can be pursued; it has suggested further that the theorist's analytical conception of entrepreneurship can depend on the level at which the theorist is pursuing his investigation. The flesh-and-blood entrepreneur of everyday encounter is a bundle of complex motivations, potentials, and perceptions. The ways in which his decisions can be tackled by the theorist are correspondingly multiple. Over the centuries, indeed, economists have identified the entrepreneur in a wide variety of different ways:

1. Many economists referred to entrepreneurial activity—at least part of the time—as merely a specific kind of labor service. Thus, some writers (including Say, Mill, and Roscher) see pure entrepreneurial profit as no more than a kind of wage.

2. For many other economists, the essential feature of the entrepreneur is his assuming the risk (or of the Knightian uncertainty) involved in business ventures. These economists include Cantillon, a pioneer entrepreneurial theorist, as well as Mangoldt, the major nineteenth-century profit theorist, and the prominent U.S. profit theorists F.B. Hawley and Frank Knight.

3. For yet another group of writers, including Say and, of course, Schumpeter, the essence of entrepreneurship is its innovativeness. The Schumpeterian entrepreneur, as we have seen, is an innovator, the initiator of discontinuous change.

4. For some economists, again, the core of the entrepreneur is his location between different markets. The entrepreneur thus serves as a middleman or arbitrageur, buying resources cheaply and selling output more expensively.

5. An important additional view of the entrepreneur is that he is essentially a coordinator, organizer, or gap-filler. An early statement from J.B. Clark along these lines was echoed independently in recent years by T.W. Schultz.

Besides these five quite distinct, major alternative definitions of pure entrepreneurship, a number of other attempts can be found in the literature. Here, the entrepreneur has been seen (among other things) as

6. providing leadership;

7. exercising genuine will;

8. acting as a pure speculator;

9. acting as an employer;

10. acting as a superintendent or manager;

11. acting as a source of information;

12. being especially alert to opportunities as yet overlooked in the market.

A particular writer sometimes appears to endorse more than one definition of the term at the same time. Sometimes the writer wishes to stress that it is this conjunction of several disparate functions that is essential to the entrepreneurial role. In other cases, the writer holds that one attribute of the entrepreneur is implied by a second attribute, and that only the latter attribute is in fact the essential defining characteristic.

Let us turn now to the chapters in this book. From the perspective of the classificatory schema outlined earlier, these chapters have rather different degrees of relevance to entrepreneurial theorizing. We shall take them up, very briefly, in rough order of *increasing* relevance.

On the Question of the Relevance, or Blackness, of Boxes

Oliver Williamson's exhaustive and fascinating account of organizational innovation provides us with an excitingly plausible transaction-cost framework for understanding the history of organizational change. Unfortunately, it throws little light on the nature or consequences of entrepreneurial endeavor as such. The entrepreneur is not merely an elusive figure in Williamson's paper; he is absent entirely. Instead, there is an impersonal process of organizational change that tends to somehow conform to requirements dictated by transaction-cost efficiencies.

The impressive chapters by Kenneth Arrow and by Jerry Green and John Shoven add valuably to our understanding of the constraints governing the innovative process. They suggest interesting implications for the ways in which the market determines the size of the firms in which innovations are developed and introduced, and how the market selects ideas to be financed. The focus, however, is not on the activity of entrepreneurs, but on the innovative process. The innovative process is, of course, important, and we expect it to offer scope for entrepreneurial activity. However, an understanding of entrepreneurial activity or its implications is not necessarily advanced by analyses of innovative processes from which consideration of entrepreneurial behavior—except perhaps in its most limited sense of maximizing behavior—is virtually excluded from the outset.

Abram Bergson's encyclopedic study of decision making under labor participation presents us with the challenge of considering what the entrepreneurial possibilities are when the enterprise is "labor-managed." Professor Bergson identifies entrepreneurial behavior with risk taking (with some supporting role for innovation). He offers us a thorough account of the Yugoslav institutional environment, together with an imaginative exploration of the way in which the goals of the labor force are likely to be translated into the decisions of the enterprise they manage. However, it is doubtful that this study can help significantly in understanding the springs of entrepreneurial behavior in *any* institutional setting, or the implications of such behavior upon market processes.

William Baumol has given us an elegant and resourceful method of attacking the problem of how to arrive at systematic conclusions about so elusive an entity as entrepreneurship. In so doing, Professor Baumol has put his finger on the "analytic intractability" of entrepreneurship with brilliant precision. No matter what the specific definition one adopts for entrepreneurship, it is inherently not routine—it defies analysis because of its very nature. Baumol, therefore, avoids a futile frontal assault on the problem. Instead, he turns pragmatically to suggest that one might obtain interesting results by considering that the very success of entrepreneurship might create opposition to it, leading to governmental restrictions on the exercise of entrepreneurship. Professor Baumol can certainly extract interesting implications from this ingenious idea. Yet one is left somehow feeling that this model of the entrepreneurial process was made possible only, as it were, by accident (an idea of which Professor Baumol's alertness has enabled him to take full—and altogether legitimate—advantage). The essential features of the entrepreneurial process have not been captured by this model. The blackness of the box labeled "entrepreneurial activity" is so utterly impenetrable that the very label calls forth challenge. How would Professor Baumol's model change, one wonders, if one replaced that label by another reading simply "business"?

Professor Ronen's paper is an enormously ambitious attempt to distil every ounce of information from his in-depth interviews with real, honest-to-goodness, successful entrepreneurs. Ronen has skillfully organized that information so as to focus on just about every possible angle of interest to potential entrepreneurial theorists. Moreover, his notes and references provide a highly useful guide and key to a rapidly expanding literature in economics as well as other disciplines. Yet Ronen's contribution runs into a fundamental conceptual problem. His interviews are with flesh-and-blood entrepreneurs, not with analytical abstractions. Still, one must subject the resulting raw information to some analytical sifting process if we are to focus on the entrepreneurial elements in this information without being distracted by nonessential, nonentrepreneurial trivia and irrelevancies. Therefore, we must begin our absorption of the interview material with some prior theoretical preconceptions. Ronen senses this at a number of points in his paper, but does not appear to be prepared to face up to the problem directly. After all, the definition one wishes to employ for the essence of entrepreneurship must grow out of the level at which one's theory is being pursued and out of the purposes for which one's theory is being envisaged.

The Economic Theory of Entrepreneurship

That the concept of entrepreneurship remains elusive is, after reading these chapters, more apparent than ever, The writer is emboldened, therefore, to offer a suggestion. As was explicitly acknowledged by Professor Baumol (and was implied, at least, in virtually all the chapters in this book), a frontal theoretical attack on entrepreneurial decision making is doomed unless one artificially and unhelpfully straps it to the Procrustean bed of maximization theory. In other words, referring to the four-fold framework developed earlier (and dismissing the first "maximizing" level, for obvious reasons), one is led to abandon all but the third and fourth levels as avenues for theoretical exploration in economics. Perhaps the practitioners of other disciplines can, in their continued work, offer more and more insights into the roots of successful entrepreneurial decision making. But for economists, the most fruitful task is that of pursuing the implications, *within market processes,* of entrepreneurial activity—that is, economists should work at developing theory at the third and fourth levels. The writer believes that consistent work at these levels will continue to prove its value. Despite our reservations concerning the chapters in this book, they, too, contain much of significant help in this regard. We have much reason to be grateful to Professor Ronen and his distinguished collaborators for their courage in pioneering in so difficult an area.

Notes

1. For a recent collection of papers on entrepreneurship and entrepreneurial research contributed mainly by noneconomists, see Kent, C.A., Sexton, D.L., and Vesper, K.H., *Encyclopedia of Entrepreneurship* (Englewood Cliffs, N.J.: Prentice Hall, 1982).

2. Schumpeter, J.A. *The Theory of Economic Development* (trans. R. Opie), (Cambridge, Mass.: Harvard University Press, 1934), p. 64 note. The first German edition was published in 1911.

3. Schumpeter, J.A. *History of Economic Analysis* (New York: Oxford University Press, 1954), p. 827. See also O'Donnell, L.A., "Rationalism, Capitalism, and the Entrepreneur: The Views of Veblen and Schumpeter." *History of Political Economy* 5 (Spring 1973):199–214.

4. See Kirzner, I.M. *Competition and Entrepreneurship* (Chicago: University of Chicago Press, 1973); and Kirzner, I.M., *Perception, Opportunity, and Profit; Studies in the Theory of Entrepreneurship* (Chicago: University of Chicago Press, 1979).

12 Entrepreneurial Activity in a Complex Economy

Mordecai Kurz

Introduction

History textbooks present a romantic view of the nineteenth-century entrepreneur as an English landlord who decides, during the Industrial Revolution, to take great risks by breaking new ground, starting new industrial ventures, and leading the parade of social change. Although this imaginary and simplistic economic actor is a gross historical approximation, it is probably true that the twentieth century has presented the entrepreneur with such a complex arena that just the identification and definition of the entrepreneurial function is subject to debate. Is the function organizational in nature, or does its essence lie in risk taking? Does it necessarily entail innovations and technical improvements, or does it include the acts of profiting from existing and known techniques that may have been ignored by others?

Equally perplexing is the question of whether entrepreneurial activity, by nature, is the domain of the individual, or whether it can be undertaken by collective bodies such as families, corporations, investment committees, or other industrial groupings.

Finally, how does public policy affect entrepreneurial activity, and to what extent do high taxes and public regulations curtail the activities of entrepreneurs in our society? This question is particularly crucial today, because one of the pillars of supply-side economics is the idea that a vast entrepreneurial potential associated with additional work and additional investments will be unleashed in the U.S. economy if the volume of regulations is reduced, taxes are cut, and the size of government is curtailed.

The diversity of views expressed in this book is a clear testimony to the complexity of the issues. In this note, I will attempt to highlight the main ideas developed in four of these papers (Arrow, Baumol, Green-Shoven, and Ronen), but at the same time integrate the discussion of the relevant issues.

The Entrepreneur and his Motives

The chapter by Professor Ronen provides us with a remarkable array of facts about the entrepreneurial process and entrepreneurial motives. To gather this information, Ronen carried out in-depth interviews with twenty-

The author thanks J. Ronen and E. Sheshinski for valuable comments on an early draft of this chapter.

three established entrepreneurs. The information presented is rich in potential implications. I note here only one of Ronen's most crucial characterizations of the entrepreneurial motives—namely, the passion for novelty. Ronen does not reject the traditional economic motive of profit maximization, but supplements it by an even stronger urge to make profits by introducing *something new*. Would an entrepreneur accept any substitution between profitability and novelty? From Ronen's material, I deduce that such substitution exists, but he does not directly discuss the issue.

An important problem arises with respect to the interview technique as a method of identifying the characteristics of entrepreneurs. Ronen recognizes that his sample is not representative. More specifically, one notes that his sampling technique induces a very drastic selection: the entrepreneurs interviewed represent a sample of the successful ones—those who made it to the top—while the technique of interviewing identifiable entrepreneurs could not include those who failed (and perhaps went bankrupt). Therefore, one cannot deduce with any degree of certainty from the interviews with the successful entrepreneurs which entrepreneurial properties are likely to lead to success.

An important effect of this bias is reflected in the discussion of risk taking by the entrepreneur. Ronen is caught between the Schumpeterian view, according to which the entrepreneur is an innovator who is not a risk taker, and Knight's view, according to which the entrepreneur is inherently a risk taker (although, according to Knight, this function entails the dual function of responsible control and securing the owners of productive services against uncertainty and fluctuations in their income). Ronen resolves this dilemma by defining a continuum of entrepreneurial activities. On one extreme, the entrepreneur is nearly a manager operating within a well-defined and prescribed domain of business activity, on the other, he is the dynamic innovator who seeks novelty. However, Ronen also suggests that he "leans toward the Schumpeterian view," because most of the entrepreneurs in his sample expressed a clear distaste for risk taking and a consistent desire to engage in activities that would *reduce* the uncertainty. This is hardly surprising. A successful entrepreneur will, in fact, be much closer to the Schumpeterian managerial type—he has to manage his business affairs, and given his success, he has far more to lose than a starting entrepreneur. Moreover, a successful entrepreneur is not likely to want to risk bankruptcy again.

If Ronen had been able to interview a random sample of *starting* entrepreneurs, his main impressions would have been very different. I conjecture that the members of his sample would have appeared as dynamic, innovative, and creative as he visualizes them. However, I think that a good portion of the interview would have dealt with the fear of bankruptcy and its effect on—and meaning to—the entrepreneur. The investors who provide venture capital take the risk of losing a fraction of their capital, but prudent owners of capital can always diversify among many good projects to reduce the risk to a level commensurate with the expected return. It is only the entrepreneur who must risk bankruptcy: if the enterprise fails, the entrepreneur often cannot continue as an entrepreneur because bankruptcy makes it so much harder for him to start all over again. One must then conclude that the burden the entrepreneur fears most is the burden he must bear most. It is this tragic reality that is at the bottom of his economic function as a leader and innovator. Clearly, like any rational economic agent, the entrepreneur will take all possible precautions to reduce the risk of bankruptcy; however, it is his ability to accept this risk, in conjunction with all the benefits of the venture, that enables him to function as an entrepreneur.

I conclude that the search for novelty is a crucial characteristic of the entrepreneurial activity. However, the view obtained from interviews with successful entrepreneurs tends to obscure the essential prerequisite for being an entrepreneur, which is the ability to sustain the economic war of survival in which the greatest risk is bankruptcy.

This discussion is intimately related to the very imaginative chapter by Professors Green and Shoven, who deal explicitly with the problem of bankruptcy in the context of developing leveraged enterprises. Green and Shoven attempt to model the enterprise as a joint venture of the owners of capital and the entrepreneur. They present six examples to demonstrate the complexity of the financing arrangements, their effect on the incentives of the participants, and the way bankruptcy can occur. The analysis is based, however, on a very limited set of possible financing arrangements, and the introduction of more complex financial instruments would modify their results. It appears to me that the critical step which Green and Shoven take is to model the relationship between the entrepreneur and his financial supporters as a *noncooperative* game. They can then show that an equilibrium may be socially inefficient. I suspect that a more complex view of this matter will regard the participants in the venture as playing a *cooperative* game in which the financial arrangements aim only to establish rules for the division of the cost and the benefits.

The difference between these two views is critical. In the noncooperative situation, each side adopts a strategy to maximize its own return. This narrow view can lead to the destruction of a sound enterprise if, somewhere along the way, it has cash flow problems, is temporarily unable to pay its obligations, and is thus pushed into bankruptcy. In addition, the outcome in their examples does not include any special penalty to the entrepreneur that results from the bankruptcy; thus, the entrepreneur has no special motivation to prevent the bankruptcy. One hopes that even in the noncooperative context, the future work of the authors will take into account this essential cost to the entrepreneur.

A cooperative view of a venture assumes that the parties will act as a unit and that as long as the enterprise as a whole is sound, it will not go bankrupt. The relative shares and division rules within the venture will be altered if conditions change, but the financing rules become only flexible tools of division. Here the entrepreneur clearly performs the Schumpeterian organizational function by adopting a flexible strategy that accommodates all of the conflicting needs within the venture. However, equally critical is the Knightian function of being the main bearer of bankruptcy risk.

Entrepreneurial Activity and the Optimal Size of Firms

It is a long standing view of microeconomic theory that the factor of entrepreneurship and managment is a fixed factor of production. Therefore, as the size of the firm rises, the marginal productivities of all other factors decline and the optimal size of the firm is determined by their prices. Yet we have witnessed in modern times the growth of giant-size enterprises, which suggests that the limitations of entrepreneurial or managerial abilities are not necessarily important limiting factors on the size of firms. Moreover, in contemporary economies, large and small firms compete and coexist side by side, implying that the textbook view of the fixed factors determining industrial organization must be replaced. An alternative theory would stress that different sizes of firm have different relative advantages and disadvantages, implying that, under certain conditions, each size of firm might serve specific functions. Given the technological and demand conditions of an industry, an equilibrium size distribution would then emerge endogenously.

The individual entrepreneurial function is usually associated with the small, newly established firm, whereas the managerial function is more critical to the large enterprise. This suggests that the entrepreneur and the industrial manager perform distinct economic functions that find their place in an industrial equilibrium structure.

The paper by Professor Arrow is developed along the above lines. It presents an exciting hypothesis that should receive both attention and additional research efforts. Arrow's view is that in evaluating the informational efficiency of any organization, there are two basic factors that must be taken into account:

1. The information channels of the organization are of limited capacity.
2. There are strong incentive effects that reduce the reliability of the information transmitted.

These factors operate within each firm, but they become critically important when information needs to cross the boundaries of the firm. In the process of innovating or developing an innovation, information flows are relatively inexpensive and efficient among the people who are intimately related to the innovation. They all understand the nature of the innovation and have reasonably clear communication on its economic value. However, the further the group needs to go to communicate its activities, receive approval, and obtain the capital for further development, the more sharply the cost of information rises and the reliability of the communication channel falls. With these the quality of the evaluation of the innovation deteriorates.

With the above model in mind, one sees that small firms can provide an open and intimate environment for developing innovation, but the information flows across the boundary of the firm in search for additional capital are very expensive. This deterioration in the quality and reliability of information translates itself into an increased cost of outside capital. Large firms have the advantage of a more secure capital base, but a more bureaucratic internal capital-allocation mechanism. As a result, information transmission within the firm is more distorted, and the mechanism for identifying desirable innovations is less efficient.

An important conclusion is that small firms are more likely than large firms to engage in ventures based on novel research concepts, whereas large firms will fund such projects at a less than optimal level. This analysis is confirmed by the casual observation that a novel industrial idea is often transformed into economic reality by a small firm created to develop it. Such firms sometimes merge into larger firms after the initial development is successfully completed.

The conclusions drawn by Arrow and Ronen are quite complementary. Ronen identifies the entrepreneur by his quest for novelty, whereas Arrow identifies the small firm as the organization with a relative advantage in carrying out novel projects. Together, these two writers imply that small firms will be led by entrepreneurs, whereas large firms will be led by industrial managers. Moreover, given their respective advantages, entrepreneurs in small firms will carry out and develop innovations, whereas giant firms, which are essentially financial empires, can undertake and manage large-scale projects and still diversify their portfolios to keep the total return on their activities reasonably safe. It seems that these ideas regarding the characteristics of the entrepreneur lead to very important testable hypotheses.

Arrow's idea that small firms have a relative advantage in information processing brings to the surface an important first point. Additional research will concentrate on other characteristics of the entrepreneur that associate him with the small firm. One possibility is the search for independence—a trait emphasized in Ronen's paper. An alternative direction of research might concentrate on the possibility that *larger* size might also provide a natural environment for the entrepreneur. The natural example that comes to mind is the recent wave of innovative activities in the banking and financial service industries. The outcome of this innovative entrepreneurial activity has been an improvement in the quality and diversity of financial services offered to the public. The entrepreneurial work, however, is associated with large financial firms that have been able to bring these improved services to market through combinations and the introduction of computerized technology. In these cases, it appears that a larger, rather than smaller, firm is the natural place for entrepreneurial activity.

Supply-Side Economics and the Effect of Public Policy on Entrepreneurial Incentives

Perhaps the most important issue in the current debate on economic policy is the extent to which public policy can influence the degree of entrepreneurial activity. Recent writings under the heading of supply-side economics suggest that government taxes and regulations have had a decisive negative effect on the desire of entrepreneurs to work, invest, or innovate in the United States. The proponents of this view suggest that removing regulations, abolishing taxes, and drastically reducing the size of the public sector would unleash a tidal wave of individual incentives to work, innovate, invest, and create new enterprises. Such a policy, it is argued, will restore productivity growth to the United States.

In this brief note, we will divide the discussion into two parts. First we will concentrate on the effect of public regulations on entrepreneurial activity. The analysis of this issue is important for the theme of this book, even apart from its implications for public policy. Second, we want to comment on the likelihood that the current economic policy will have the hoped-for effect on entrepreneurial activity.

Entrepreneurial Activity and Public Regulations

The paper by Professor Baumol deals directly with this issue. Our review of this paper will provide the basis for our later discussion.

Without stating it in such terms, Baumol's paper represents an attempt to model the dynamics of supply-side economics as it applies to the aggregate level of entrepreneurial activity. Baumol's construction consists of two critical ingredients on the supply side: taxation and regulations. As he formulates it, taxation directly reduces the compensation for entrepreneurship, while regulations directly restrict the amount of possible entrepreneurial activity. Thus, Baumol assumes that taxation curtails the supply of entrepreneurship, while regulations restrict the equilibrium level of entrepreneurial activity.

Next, Baumol constructs a dynamic model in which the rate of growth of output is determined by the level of entrepreneurial activity. Because this activity is restricted to specified boundaries, the model predicts a cyclical pattern of economic activity. Economic growth accelerates on the way toward the entrepreneurial ceiling; then, after bumping into the constraints imposed by regulations, the economy turns down to initiate the next cycle. Thus the formal models delineate a theory of a cyclical supply of entrepreneurial activities limited by an absolute regulatory constraint.

In assessing the effectiveness of public policy, Baumol concludes that high taxation changes only the qualitative pattern of the equilibrium level of entrepreneurial activity—that is, it slows down the growth rate of entrepreneurial activity. It does not, however, alter the ultimate level of output and entrepreneurial activity that the economy achieves—these depend more critically on the existing set of regulations. According to Baumol, high taxation just slows down the pace of reaching the peak, thus increasing the time it takes the economy to reach it. Baumol seems to believe that regulations are more decisive and critical in curtailing economic growth and thus are the real villains in limiting the availability of entrepreneurial talent. Yet, upon examining the kind of regulations Baumol has in mind, I find that he concentrates mainly on regulations desired by business firms that wish to limit and curtail competition or free entry. He specifically mentions the runner-up business firm that utilizes the regulatory power of the public sector to oppose the introduction of innovations by a competing and innovative firm. Baumol proposes the very reasonable view that the opposition of unions to labor-saving innovations is often short-sighted, and that perhaps our society should emulate Japan or the Israeli kibbutz and grant job security to the unions in exchange for full cooperation in the introduction of innovations. The resulting acceleration in the growth rate would more than cover cost of job security.

The aggregative nature of Baumol's model suggests that the most important next step in this analysis is to develop the micro foundations of a model from which the postulated macro relationships can be derived. Since this is a basis on which one can criticize almost any macro model, let me turn to some very specific issues that I believe should be addressed.

The most important fact to notice is that many—if not most—public regulations are intended to protect the public interest, and thus induce the production of public goods. Public health, air quality and safety regulations are such examples. Other regulations attempt to correct informational defects, such as the regulations regarding the conduct of financial markets, truth in lending, and disclosure of the composition of products offered for sale. All these regulations aim to provide the public with some welfare, though perhaps at the expense of the industry that produced the commodity up to that time without such a regulation. Clearly, such regulations restrict the profits of firms in the industry, but do they necessarily curtail entrepreneurial activities? Moreover, consider any regulation, prohibition, or limitation that aims to reduce the level of an undesirable activity. Does such regulatory action necessarily put a limit on incentives for entrepreneurial activity?

One can hold the view that public limitations or regulations do not necessarily restrict incentives or curtail entrepreneurial activities; indeed in some cases they can *increase* entrepreneurial effort. Moreover, most regulations that aim to provide some public good can induce both an increase in entrepreneurial activity as well as an expansion of social welfare. The case of regulations that cause a decrease in both entrepreneurial activity and social welfare is perhaps a rather special one.

The above follows from the observation that imposing a regulation immediately creates a new area of activities in which an innovation that satisfies the regulation might become very profitable. Japanese firms, for example, innovated important changes in their engine design to meet U.S. clean-air regulations. By satisfying air-quality standards at a lower cost than other firms, they were able to maintain, or even increase, their profit margins. Similarly, a drug manufacturer that discovers a new drug satisfying the safety conditions imposed by law attains a highly profitable position relative to the runners-up that have not. These two examples certainly show how regulations can encourage entrepreneurial activity. Also, despite the current antiregulation mood, most observers regard the clean air in U.S. cities and the high quality and safety of the U.S. drug industry as important contributors to social welfare. If the social benefits of clean air or drug safety exceed the social costs, we have examples of regulations that induce both increased entrepreneurial activity and increased social welfare. The "public goods" nature of air quality implies that no firm has the incentive to offer, and no consumer has the incentive to purchase, a car with a more expensive, pollution-free engine. Thus, setting air-quality standards is *one* way to create this desired public good.

To put the above examples in a broader context, I suggest that promulgating a regulation that aims to serve a social need is equivalent to creating a new, profitable market for providing that public good. In this market, entrepreneurs compete for innovations that will satisfy these needs while conforming to the regulation. Such new regulation might indeed depress the profit margins of existing unregulated industry, but the reduction of its output might be regarded as desirable. In addition, the entrance of new innovators into the field might well give rise to a wave of investments and entrepreneurial activities.

Going one step further, we note that regulations and legal limitations on free business activities may also induce a very active entrepreneurial activity in the black, or illegal, markets. For example, if the U.S. legalized the production and distribution of marijuana, this commodity would be produced and distributed in as routine a manner as tobacco is provided today, and no more than regular managerial input would be used in that activity. By declaring these activities illegal, society provides the motivation for very ingenious entrepreneurial activities in both the production and distribution of such commodities. I do not doubt that the attempt to regulate such industries as transportation and public utilities resulted in too many cases in which the regulating agency actually protected inefficient firms from innovations and competition. However, this was not the public purpose of such regulations. Furthermore, practically any regulation can be abused in some way to favor one economic agent over another. However, all this is far from equivalent to the simplistic view proposed by some supply-side supporters that all regulations serve no public need and that they only restrict incentives and entrepreneurial activity.

Is Entrepreneurial Activity Sensitive to Public Policy?

One would expect entrepreneurial activity to be somewhat sensitive to tax rates and other parameters of public policy. However, I seriously doubt that reducing tax rates, simplifying government processes, and removing counterproductive regulations as proposed by supply-side public policy will result in a tidal wave of entrepreneurial activity in the United States.

Some of the most perplexing facts of economic analysis come from comparisons between economic activities in different societies. Modern attempts to study different economic systems have revealed only that there are crucial differences in consumption, savings, investments, innovations, and general entrepreneurial activities that we cannot explain with the tools at our disposal.

Any attempt to explain a low level of entrepreneurial activity by high tax rates must also explain why high tax rates did not prevent Scandinavia from attaining some of the highest standards of living in the world, and why Britain has not been able to reverse its long-term trend toward stagnation, in spite of drastically lowered taxes and significant tax concessions for investing industries.

Similarly, any attempt to insist that the completely free individual entrepreneur is the most efficient vehicle for economic growth must find the Japanese experience perplexing. History provides numerous examples of social institutions that attained dramatic entrepreneurial achievements with drastically varying degrees of individualistic characters. In some societies, the tribe provides the basic unit from which incentives spring, in others, the family does. The Japanese corporation and the Israeli kibbutz provide modern examples of highly efficient entrepreneurial institutions in which the organization of incentives seems to function very well.

Even within Soviet society there are dramatic differences in the ability to innovate and carry out collective entrepreneurial activity. Soviet agriculture is well known for the complete failure of its collective entrepreneurial work, yet Soviet innovation and entrepreneurial work have been impressive in such fields as hydroelectric power, aircraft production, and space exploration.

Across the world we see creative and innovative entrepreneurial activities taking place within a variety of institutions that differ in their degrees of collective responsibility and in their compensation structures. The assumption that the only form of effective entrepreneurship is the individually operating captain of industry is nothing but "Ayn Rand" economics. The practice of such economics would only retard our understanding of the crucial role played by entrepreneurial activity in economic development.

One must conclude that social institutions and cultural frameworks have something fundamental to do with the entrepreneurial motive. Religious beliefs and ethical precepts might, indeed, be as important to entrepreneurial activity as science and technology. We have not yet developed the tools to study these interrelationships. No doubt, such studies would entail an important interdisciplinary view of the entrepreneurial role in society. From this, however, one must conclude that it is far from clear how entrepreneurial activity will respond to changes in taxation and other parameters of public policy. In some cultural frameworks, the response may be drastic; in others, it may be negligible, depending upon the circumstances.

The decrease in productivity growth and level of investments in the United States during the past decade is a perplexing phenomena for which clear and decisive explanations are still unavailable. In their stead we have the simplistic notions of supply-side public policy, which promises that reducing taxes and cutting down the public sector will reindustrialize the U.S. economy by creating a tidal wave of entrepreneurial incentives. Although I think that there are many desirable features of the supply-side policy proposals, my analysis here suggests that the expected wave of productivity increases will not materialize as fast as it is proposed. The social framework of economic activity in the United States—and in the world as a whole—is not the same in the 1980s as it was in the 1950s or 1960s. Given these changes, and without a better understanding of the sources of entrepreneurial activity, any quantitative prediction of the effect of public policy should be considered subject to a large prediction error.

13

Economics and Entrepreneurs

Sherwin Rosen

The connections between economic growth and entrepreneurial activity are intimate and well charted in economic history. The facts of economic progress throughout the world are replete with myriad examples of magnificent entrepreneurs and feats of entrepreneurship. The exploits of Law, Ford, Rockefeller, Whitney, Watt, Singer, Mellon, Barnum, Vanderbilt, Swift, Pullman, Eastman and countless others, both large and small, have been carefully documented as significantly altering the course of economic progress, sometimes for the worse, but most often for the better. Reviewing these episodes reveals that we lack a satisfactory definition of what entrepreneurs do and what social function they perform. Evidently we can recognize an entrepreneur when we see one (a successful one, at any rate). Yet it is difficult to know where to look and what abstract criteria to apply when predicting where entrepreneurial activities will or will not occur. Thus, the study of these activities is and has been essentially backward looking. Once an entrepreneurial act occurs and is identified as successful, imitators join the rush who no longer deserve such labels. Furthermore, the nature of new entrepreneurial acts is unpredictable and highly uncertain to the outside observer.

The problem of definition occurs because the entrepreneur has virtually no status in contemporary economic theory. It is precisely this lack of a theory, in conjunction with the many empirical observations about the entrepreneur's obvious importance, that makes the subject such a fascinating one to ponder and to study.

The problem is plainly one of theory, not of fact. Yet to interpret the facts requires the organizing device of a theory to help identify the common elements of all these episodes, to separate out what is crucial about them, and to bring them more clearly into focus. Otherwise the subject will be merely a string of distantly connected and dimly related case studies, not without interest, to be sure, but nevertheless on the periphery of mainstream economics.

Another aspect of the difficulty is that economists have so far failed to arrive at a satisfactory theory of the firm. As Oliver Williamson argues, the firm in economics is completely described by a production function—and that is all. The concept of fixed, indivisible, and nontradable "entrepreneurial capacity'' is invoked merely to place restrictions on the feasible size and scope of the firm. Otherwise, it plays no active role. Where does this production function come from? How is it arrived at, and how does the entrepreneur establish property rights to it? In fact, a case can be made that pure economic theory can make do with technologies, that is, production sets, and no firms at all. It is supply conditions in the market as a whole that are central to the major positive and normative propositions of the theory, and these are determined by technology and factor supplies. The technology is given from outside the system, and so is the available menu of goods and services over which choices can be made. Under these conditions, we might as well call each individual productive agent a ''firm'' and be done with it. Firms, after all, are nothing more than complex sets of contractual commitments that bind agents together. But all economic activities can be described by contractual commitments, so why should one subset have greater claims than any other?

Pursuing this line of reasoning does not take us very far. If every agent is his own firm (and, in an important sense, this is a truism), then practically every economic decision is an entrepreneurial one. By extending the scope of the definition so broadly, we explain either everything or we explain nothing; most likely the latter, for the bulk of these decisions are readily analyzed within the confines of the existing analytical apparatus. A more narrow definition is required.

It is a remarkable comment on the power of economic theory that so much can be obtained from so little. The main economic problem—allocating resources among competing objectives—is solved by confronting consumers' tastes with known production technology and resource constraints through the intermediaries of product and factor markets. In this scenario, competitive market organization is an exceedingly benign social institution that imposes great constraints on individual behavior and strongly limits the scope of individual actions. Each consumer merely chooses the quantities of consumption items conditional upon market prices and his income, and also decides which of his resources to offer to the factor market at given factor prices. Similarly, firms decide which goods to supply, how to produce them, and in what volume to produce them on the basis of these same product and factor prices. The prices themselves are determined in such a way as to satisfy everyone's choices and exhaust all gains from trade.

Thus, no individual possesses market power, and all rest content with making quantity decisions only—how much of each good to buy or sell at market prices. The decisions themselves are readily characterized by relatively simple rules: equate price to marginal cost, equalize marginal utility per dollar spent on all goods consumed, and so on. However, these decisions are better described as ''managerial'' than as ''entrepreneurial.''

Even the monopolist hardly does more than go through the additional computation of ascertaining marginal revenue. Furthermore, these markets and the transactions they effect are highly impersonal: the personal identities of transactors are of no consequence. Consequently, there is no room for the activities of a Ford or a Mellon beyond the ordinary industrial organization theories of imperfect competition.

I therefore conclude that in the presence of complete markets in all transactions (which itself implies a kind of complete information), there is no role for the entrepreneur to play, no scope for the entrepreneur at all. Since a good part of the work of economists over the years has been to set forth the details and implications of this particular model, it is no puzzle that the entrepreneur and his activities do not loom large there.

But markets in all kinds of economic exchanges are incomplete. Of course, some markets that could exist are not active because demand is small relative to supply, that is, only a subset of the goods and services that could be traded at any given time actually are traded. More importantly, the list of available or potential goods and transactions changes from time to time as circumstances change. Two types of change must be distinguished. The first are normal changes in income, factor supplies, and the like that call forth reallocations through the existing market structure and that are readily handled by it. At the individual level, they involve changes in the parameters relevant to those managerial decisions that support the market; the actual decisions change, and market allocations and prices change too. There is nothing entrepreneurial in this kind of dynamics, which is best described as a kind of moving equilibrium. The second type of changes are less routine. These call forth the creation of new markets, new goods, new services, and new ways of doing things. It is these kinds of events that give rise to entrepreneurial activities.

We are arriving at a definition of the entrepreneurial function by the back door, so to speak. If a complete market system eliminates the need for these activities, they must occur only when markets are incomplete. Markets are the central organizing institutions in an economy with known resources, preferences, and technologies, and as we have seen, all economic agents play extremely passive roles in that situation. Therefore, entrepreneurial activities must involve the organization of resources that are initially outside the existing market system. That is, they are activities that, in effect, create new markets, new forms of organization that didn't exist before. Economic organization through the market mechanism is a substitute for economic organization through entrepreneurial ventures, and vice versa. Whereas market activities are passive and closely constrained by prices and the activities of others, entrepreneurial activities are not so constrained because the entrepreneur *is* the market (or the market maker) and must play a very active role. A number of implications follow from this.

1. We see immediately why entrepreneurial activities are so ephemeral. Once the entrepreneur creates a new market (I use the term "market" in its broadest sense), then imitators subsequently enter. A formal market structure becomes established in which managerial decisions perform well. A successful creative entrepreneurial act ultimately gets used up and cannot be repeated in the same field (although it may breed a subsequent string of related organizational innovations opening as it does a new territory). The gains are exhausted when the more organized market takes over.

Entrepreneurial activities must therefore be described as a kind of stochastic process. Opportunities appear or are recognized at random, are exploited, and then become part of the established market economy. In this sense, entrepreneurial ventures are a generalized type of arbitrage activity, and serve the same economic function of allocating resources more efficiently. (Readers familiar with the efficient-market theory of finance will recognize certain parallels here.) This feature also explains why entrepreneurship is much easier to study from the backward perspective of hindsight and history than from the forward and predictive point of view. If one could easily predict where new markets would appear, discerning entrepreneurs would have already exploited those opportunities, and further entrepreneurial activity would not be observed.

2. A substantial volume of entrepreneurial activity should take place in the organization of new firms or in the reorganization of old firms. Following Coase, the rationale for the firm is to remove transactions from the market place and substitute a command system of organization instead. More generally, market systems do not function well where there are significant transaction costs. Hence we expect that entrepreneurship should be very active when transaction costs are important, especially when innovations in transaction-cost technology and mechanisms of control, together with growth in potential market size, allow further innovations in the organizational structure. Williamson's discussion of organizational innovations within firms is an important application of this general point.

Still, entrepreneurship is not exclusively confined to new methods of control of firms, for incomplete markets occur throughout the economy. Several examples present themselves as important vehicles for these activities.

a. Financial markets are incomplete because it is too costly to identify and verify all potential states of nature (the probability space) in advance. This presents fertile grounds for innovation in new financial instruments or operations, such as straddles, puts, options, and new futures contracts that offer new and attractive risk-spreading opportunities and make the market for risk bearing more complete and more efficient.

b. Organized forward and futures markets occur in very few commodities, yet the efficient intertemporal allocation of resources requires that agents take account of the future in making their current decisions. This is the basis for rational-expectations theories of economic dynamics and also why those theories are so compelling. Implicit expectational markets are substitutes for explicit futures markets in resolving intertemporal allocations, and often take the form of asset speculations (for instance, purchasing real estate now in anticipation of increased future demand) that have effects similar to a true forward market and promote efficiency.

c. A somewhat different class of ventures improves efficiency via previously unrecognized opportunities for internalizing externalities. Assembling land and redeveloping a new complex over previously separately owned parcels is the prototype example of this sort. The tender offer and the takeover are others. All are related to reorganizing several firms into a new and more efficient one, as mentioned previously.

3. Markets are indivisible objects. They either exist or they don't. In making new markets or completing existing one, entrepreneurs make quantum jumps. Perhaps their activities occur in fits and starts. This is in marked contrast to ordinary exchange, which evolves more continuously and in marginal increments. The minimum scale created by these indivisibilities is tantamount to a scale economy, and explains why the monetary gain from a successful operation can be enormous, many orders of magnitude greater than that obtained from the more usual market activities. That is why successful entrepreneurs are often so wealthy. Another implication of the indivisibility is that successful entrepreneurship often carries with it some degree of market power because of the implied barriers to further entry. The resulting monopolistic advantage is another element of the private return that induces people to undertake these activities.

4. Entrepreneurial projects are risky precisely because thay take place outside the established market mechanism and, therefore, always involve unknown—and perhaps unknowable—elements. Thus uncertainty is an inherent aspect of all entrepreneurial ventures. But it is not risk per se that is crucial for entrepreneurship; rather, risk is an inalienable byproduct of entrepreneurial activities arising from the incompleteness of markets. Failure to recognize this distinction often leads analysts to mistake risk taking and gambling with the entrepreneurial act itself, which involves the creative extension of the market mechanism. It is the creative idea that is the crux of the matter, not the risk. However, if risk is a byproduct of the idea, there is again a potential for financial barriers because of the substantial uncertainty and because of the asymmentry of information on probable outcomes. Green and Shoven's paper illustrates by example how these elements can interact with the actual outcomes of such ventures when debt instru-

ments are used. Equity financing circumvents many of these problems, as long as the venture is not too large. This explains why entrepreneurs are often associated with many ventures successively, and why they do not necessarily stop after an initial success. Previous successes allow them to finance subsequent ventures more easily. Personal wealth is therefore an important element in their undertaking—another reason why entrepreneurs tend to be wealthy.

This view of the entrepreneurial process is squarely in line with the ideas of both Schumpeter and Knight. It touches bases with Schumpeter in stressing the creative and innovational elements of entrepreneurial ventures. However, the aspect of creative destruction that Schumpeter emphasized is not necessarily crucial to the introduction of a new market, although of course monetary losses might be imposed on agents who were previously engaged in activities for which new organizations are substitutes and that are not sustainable in the new market structure. It is related to Knight's theory in both the stochastic nature of the process and in the elements of uncertainty to which they give rise. It perhaps departs from his vision of the entrepreneur as the residual-income recipient and ultimate risk-bearer, because the bearing of risk can be accomplished in the market, at least to the extent that the financial barriers mentioned above are not binding. To this extent, it is closer to Knight's views on uncertainty as distinguished from risk, and it is commensurate with his views of the entrepreneur as organizer. Indeed, the organizational role of the entrepreneur outside the formal market setting is the key feature, in this view, of the entrepreneurial process.

This view is also quite consistent with Ronen's empirical investigation of what sets entrepreneurs apart from other agents in the economy. His stress on innovation and on boredom with projects after they become established indicates the takeover of the formal market and managerial decision making after the new market has been created. The lack of interest his interviewees showed in formal organization and in the subordination of decision making is another manifestation of innovative market-making behavior. So is the use of intuition and the lack of stress on organized information, for organized information has unreliable virtues in the uncertain environment where these activities take place. The finding that entrepreneurs are rather risk averse is consistent with the idea that it is the creation of new markets that is the key feature of their ventures, not risk bearing in and of itself. In short, virtually all of Ronen's findings suggest that the entrepreneur is an organizer and promoter of new goods or new ways of doing things that substitute for the organizational attributes of formal market structures. The market mechanism does not contain within it any means of extending itself and creating new markets; there are no "markets" for new markets, as it were. The entrepreneur is the economic agent responsible for this important task in society.

My definition is also closely related to the Austrian view, best represented in modern literature by the work of Kirzner, that entrepreneurial activities are associated with disequilibrium phenomena. (The stress on disequilibrium and recognizing heretofore unseen opportunities is also emphasized in the recent writings of T.W. Schultz, though not from the Austrian perspective.) The whole concept of equilibrium in economics rests on the competitive-market mechanism of balancing demand and supply. The creation of new demands and supplies does not play a part in it; to that extent, entrepreneurship involves the closing of gaps that one associates with disequilibrium. However, in another sense—the sense of random stochastic process—entrepreneurship might be described as an organic equilibrium process with random elements in which available opportunities are being continually exploited commensurate with costs and perspective benefits.

Now that we have identified what entrepreneurship is, there remains the much more difficult task of ascertaining its determinants and, from the normative point of view, making welfare statements about how much is desirable. In a steady state with unchanging conditions, the amount of entrepreneurship would tend to a limit of zero. If we could imagine an economy beginning *de novo,* the creative process described above would be exhausted when all relevant transactions were carried on through the market place, and when markets were complete up to allowable transaction costs. There is nothing bad or good about this. It just follows from the fact that no social function would be served, in the limit, by entrepreneurial activities under such conditions.

Hence, a sustained rate of entrepreneurial activity occurs in a society that is constantly in a state of flux, forever changing. This is what makes it possible for new markets to appear. To that extent, one might say that invention is the mother of entrepreneurship. However, entrepreneurial activity is not invention. Rather, it is exploiting the new opportunities that inventions provide, more in the form of marketing and developing them for widespread use in the economy than developing the knowledge itself. This leads to an organic view of economic development in which the process of invention is in part determined by what is happening in the rest of the economy, and subsequently affects its future course of development through entrepreneurship.

Invention and innovation do not lend themselves to adequate economic modeling, and I can hardly improve on that situation. Nonetheless, it seems fair to say that the forces determining the pace of inventive activity are not immune from economic forces. Scientific knowledge about the way the world works is perhaps the basis of new technological advances, but even new advances in science depend on the social uses to which the knowledge are put: there is a tendency for society to invest greater resources in inventive activities that will yield greater social returns. Hence the search for labor-saving devices when wages are high, or the search for fuel-efficient capital stock under current market conditions. Some analysts have gone so far as to say that virtually all inventions are by demand; for example, the airplane was not invented in the eighteenth century because the value of time was not sufficiently high to warrant it. We do not have to carry things to that extreme to recognize the element of truth in that proposition. Invention alone, however, is insufficient, for it needs to be organized and put to good use by the entrepreneur.

William Baumol's interesting contribution is, by and large, consistent with the ideas put forth here, even though he does not clearly state why entrepreneurial activity, or the lack thereof, is something that should be promoted. He envisions an economy in a constant state of flux that would sustain a continual flow of new entreprenerial activity if unconstrained. On the other hand, if entrepreneurial activity is constrained, it tends to decay because existing entrepreneurs do not find it attractive to undertake ventures that would have been profitable previously, and because the available pool of entrepreneurial talent becomes depleted as new generations do not replace those who are dying off. To this general picture, he adds a constraint on entrepreneurship arising through the legal and governmental system that is itself endogenous. It is practically inevitable that new entrepreneurial activity creates losses for those entrenched in the existing market system, because such innovations invariably substitute for existing market arrangements. In Baumol's model, when these entrenched interests get powerful enough to garner the resources of the legal system, they are able to effectively constrain subsequent innovations. Hence the model gives rise to cycles: entrepreneurial activities initially go forth unconstrained, but ultimately bump up against constraints that are themselves reactions to prior innovations. At that point, the pace of activity falls off and decays until some new shock to the system starts it up all over again. These swings are accompanied by corresponding swings in the rate of growth of output. Baumol's model certainly has a thoroughly Schumpeterian flavor.

Two points of difficulty arise in this model. One is that entrenched interests fight to maintain existing wealth positions, whether the threat arises from acts of entrepreneurship or not. Thus all price changes in the economy impose losses on producers who could previously sell at high prices and who now cannot. The political-economic constraints in the model are in no sense specific to entrepreneurial activities. To the extent that is true, the model is a much more general one of the interaction between economic growth and constraints on growth applied via the political process. What determines political power? When can entrenched interests impose constraints on innovators, and why do these constraints apparently differ at different points in history? Completing the model requires a much more detailed structure on the determinants of the role of the State in economic affairs, including its role in encouraging entrepreneurs as well as discouraging them.

Second, the model downplays the importance of natural constraints on the pace of entrepreneurial activities, namely the tendency toward making markets complete. This force suggests a kind of diminishing returns to entrepreneurship in a given environment as the gains are exhausted (that is, the UU curve in Baumol's figures might cross the forty-five degree line, which is a potential rest point in the model). At a given point in time, there are potential gains from market creation not yet realized. An analogy with fishing is appropriate. Entrepreneurs seek out these opportunities by investing in information on what the profitable ventures might be. Sometimes they strike one, and sometimes they don't. As more and more strikes are made, the fishing grounds can become exhausted. Counterbalanced against this is the aforementioned possibility that new strikes might open entirely new fishing grounds. Thus, it is an open question whether there are diminishing or constant returns. If they are diminishing, the pace of entrepreneurial activity will eventually fall off. It may get started again if important inventions or unforeseen resource scarcities make new prospecting worthwhile again. Then we get a dynamic process, including waves of innovation and entrepreneurship, that does not depend at all on a theory of political economy to motivate cycles. This alternative model is consistent with Baumol's general framework, but I conjecture that it would be very difficult to distinguish the alternative from the version with the political constraint motivation of cycles.

The analogy with fishing and prospecting has another interesting implication related to some of the problems associated with common property resources. In a sense, the potential for market creation is common property, and the resulting indivisibility creates enormous gains to those who develop the idea first because of barriers to entry by latecomers (at least for a time). Our legal system does not generally assign property rights to organizational ideas. Hence without indivisibility, imitators could easily share the fruits of innovation and too little entrepreneurial activity would take place. If indivisibility creates barriers to subsequent entry and some degree of monopoly profits, then there is a great incentive for being first and some overinvestment (over fishing) is to be expected. This aspect of competition is more in line with the conventional layman's definition of the term, like horse racing. Again, benign competitive-market organization does not provide any scope for this kind of behavior.

Another source of innovation and creation of new markets lies in overcoming transaction costs. This is intimately related to economies of scale. As I mentioned earlier, organized markets do not function well when transaction costs are significant, because the return from engaging in market (as opposed to nonmarket) exchange is not worth its cost. For example, we do not expect market behavior to be important when the market is thinly traded, because the costs of operating it are too large. Hence the use of markets becomes increasingly important, that is, new markets are opened, as the volume of economic activity increases. This is nothing more than Smith's point that the division of labor is limited by the extent of the market.

Williamson's paper gives substantive content to this idea by giving examples of internal organizational innovations within firms used to overcome transaction costs. I think it would be useful to read it with Smith's theorem in one's mind. The innovations that he discusses are often only feasible when the volume of transactions is large enough to sustain a high rate of production, that is, when the economy has reached a sufficiently high rate of development and interaction. His work also suggests that this source of innovation depends on inventions that improve the technology of the control of large-scale enterprises. Information processing is an interesting area in which there has been great recent development. Yet I believe Williamson goes a little too far in casting aspersions on the received notion of the firm as a production function, and I prefer to read his work as one in which the internal organization of the firm itself defines the production function. The production function is not just some engineering relationship that occurs outside the economic system. It is an economic construct itself. It combines the engineering technology and the control technology into a final outcome that represents an efficient method of production at the given scale of transactions, transaction costs, labor and management skills, and available knowledge about the structure of capital equipment and interpersonal control. In that sense, the derived production function is a *result* of the internal organization, the end product of the entrepreneurial process, and not an exogenous constraint on the definition of the firm. Perhaps thinking of the firm in this way, as an explicit engine of both production and control whose elements combine into a production function, will ultimately provide an analytical basis for a more thoroughgoing theory of the firm than we have at present. The goal should be to explain the productive organization of the firm, not take it as a datum.

In conclusion, I believe that my central theme of treating entrepreneurship as essentially dynamic market-creating activity can provide an organizing focus for the bulk of activities that have been previously identified as entrepreneurial. The scientific and operational content of this idea will remain unclear until we are able to define abstract and measurable criteria on what markets actually are and how they can be identified empirically.

Index

Academy of Sciences (Soviet Union),
241, 258
Accounting procedures, 102
Achievement, need for, 140–141,
163–164, 171–172
Adizes, Ichak, 224, 226
Age of entrepreneurs, 161
Alcoa, 115
Alertness of entrepreneur, 139,
143–144, 278
American Federation of Labor, 118
American Sugar Refining Co., 113
American Tobacco, 112–113, 116
Antitrust program, 35, 127
Arbitrage, 287, 304
Arbuckle, John, 113
Arrow, Kenneth, 4, 6, 10, 11, 15–27,
102, 271, 288, 294, 295
Asset idiosyncracy, 12
Asset specificity, 3, 104, 125, 128; and
backward integration, 115; and
forward integration, 107, 108, 114
Austrian economic school, 15, 276, 307
Automobile industry, 111
Autonomy, 9–10

Backward integration, 109, 115–116
Bain, J.S., 122
Bajt, Alexander, 224
Bankruptcy, risk of, 1–2, 3, 49–74,
149, 157, 292–293; and Soviet
Union, 9, 11, 254–255; and
Yugoslavia, 199
Banks, 19, 156; and innovation, 296;
and Soviet Union, 241; and
Yugoslavia 192–193, 206–207, 211,
217, 221–222
Basic Organization of Associated
Labor (BOAL), 185, 212–216
Baumol, William, 9–10, 11, 29–47,
88, 89–94, 97, 127, 271, 272, 276,
288–290, 296–297, 308
Bearse, Peter, 47

Beer industry, 110, 113
Bergson, Abram, 6–7, 11, 177–229,
271, 288
Berle, A.A., Jr., 15
Berliner, J., 259–260
Bethlehem Plan of Representation,
119
Birmingham Centre, 255
Black markets, 298–299
Bonsack machine, 110
Boredom, fear of, 140, 306
Borel-Cantelli Lemma, 94
Bounded rationality, 105, 128
Brezhnev, Leonid, 261
Brockhaus, R.H., 161, 164
Brown, Henry Phelps, 255
Bruchey, Stuart, 101–102
Bučar, France, 222
Bulow, J., 59
Bureaucracies, 107–108, 149; and
Soviet Union, 7–9, 236–249,
250–253
Bureaupathic behavior, 248
Burns, T., 162–163
Business Cycles (Schumpeter), 283

Campbell Soups, 116
Canadians, 160
Cantillon, Richard, 287
Capital supply, 51–52; and
entrepreneurs, 142–143, 149–150,
156; graphics, 80; and
labor-managed firm, 181–184,
192–193, 198, 226–227; and large
firms, 4, 5, 19–20, 24, 143; model,
52–74; and profits, 49–50; and
research and development, 22–23
Capitalism, Socialism, and Democracy
(Schumpeter), 283
Carnegie, Andrew, 3, 102, 126, 130
Causality and models, 79
Central Committee of Communist
Party, 241, 263

Central planning, 191–193, 195, 221, 235–265; and technology, 256
Chamberlin, E.H., 17
Chandler, Alfred, 101, 103, 107–108, 113, 122–123, 125, 130
Change, 10, 83, 303
Cherney, J., 98–99
Chinese, 159
Choice dilemmas questionnaire (CDQ), 164
Cigarette manufacturers, 109–110
Cigar industry, 112–113
Clark, J.B., 287
Clean air regulation, 10, 298
Coase, R.H., 19, 304
Cochran, Thomas, 118–119, 125
Cole, Arthur, 102–103, 125
Collins, D.F., 155
Comisso, Ellen T., 228
Command economies, 237
Commodity graphs, 80–81
Commune governments, 193, 194–195, 198, 205, 223–224
Communist Party: in Soviet Union, 237–242, 259–260; in Yugoslavia, 178, 186, 187, 194, 213–214
Competitive entrepreneurs, 33
Complexification of models, 88
Component design, 128
Computer industry, 124
Concepts, 20–21
Conglomerates, 124, 129, 130–131
Constitution of 1974 (Yugoslavia), 215
Consumer durables, 110, 111–112
Consumer nondurables, 110–111
Continuous-processing machinery, 109, 110
Contraction of models, 88
Copeland, Melvin, 105
Costs: bankruptcy, 50, 51, 55–56, 62; coordination, 19; and entrepreneur's effect, 85; and innovation, 18; organizational, 3
Council of Ministers (Soviet Union), 238, 239–240, 243–244, 258
Cox, Archibald, 129
Credit auctions, 221–222

Croatia, 223
Crum, R., 165
Cultural influences, 29, 31, 37
Curie, Marie and Pierre, 277–278

Daems, H., 123
Davis, Lance E., 47, 125, 130
Debt, 2, 50–52; and labor-managed firm, 196; modeling, 52–74
Decentralized economic system, 273–274, 278
Decision making, 6–7, 8; and entrepreneurs, 138, 144–149, 151–152; models of, 83–84; and size of firm, 15–17, 19–20
Definition of entrepreneur, 85, 158, 286–288, 301
Demsetz, Harold, 5, 271–279
Deterministic laws, 77
Direct problems, 77
Displacement motive, 155–156
Disposable income and entrepreneurs, 37, 44
Domination organizational theory, 121–122
Drug industry, 298
Dudkin, L.M., 265
Duke, James, 102, 110
Dunn, William N., 220
Du Pont, Pierre, 102
Dynamics of systems and modeling, 83, 88

Eastman, George, 102, 111, 301
Economic conditions and entrepreneur, 89–90, 94
Edison, Thomas, 103
Edward's Personal Preference Scale, 160
Efficiency, 305; and organizations, 3, 101, 121–122
Electrical machinery manufacture, 112
Emery, F., 162
Enterprise, 178, 238, 256–257. See also Labor-managed firms
Entrepreneurial flow system model, 79–87

Entry barriers, 305, 307
Environment and entrepreneurs, 10,
    138, 140, 141–143, 161–162
Equilibrium, 17, 54, 294; and
    entrepreneur, 276, 282–284,
    285–286, 307; and modeling, 89,
    95–96
Equity financing, 2, 23, 50–52, 56,
    306
Estrin, Saul, 204
European Economic Community, 126
Externalities, 113, 114, 115, 128, 305
External state variables, 81, 87–88, 89

Factory organization, 102
Federal Trade Commission, 127
Female entrepreneurs, 160
Financial industry, 296, 304. *See also*
    Banks
Five-year plan, 242
Focus and modeling, 86–87
Ford, Henry, 3, 102, 301
Ford Motor Co., 111, 116, 126
Forward integration, 109–115,
    122–124, 125
Freemen, Richard, 119–120
Frequency of transaction, 106
Frick, Henry, 130
Furoboth, Erik, 220
Futures market, 304–305

Game theory, 17, 54, 95–96, 293
Gasse, Y., 160
GE, 124
Gosplan, 239–241, 242–244, 245, 246,
    257–258
Goupic, Drago, 187
Granick, David, 224, 264
Green, Jerry, 1–3, 49–74, 88–89, 93,
    220, 271, 288, 305–306
Grob, Gerald, 118
Growth and entrepreneurship, 33–34,
    36–38, 42, 140, 297

Hahn, F.H., 17
Hawley, F.B., 287

Heinz Soup, 116
Hierarchies, 7–8, 247–248. *See also*
    Bureaucracies
Horvat, Branko, 199, 204, 205–206,
    226

IBM, 124
Ibos, 159
Idealization of models, 76
Immigrants as entrepreneurs, 159, 161
Immortality, search for, 150–151,
    159
Incentives, 4; and Soviet Union, 8,
    251–253
Income, 179–180, 195–204, 207–208,
    214–215, 223, 225
Independence, need for, 139–140, 157,
    173, 295
Individual innovation, 15–16
Information, 144–149, 157, 173, 285;
    asymmetry, 143; degradation, 5, 22,
    23, 26; and large organizations,
    3–4, 12, 20, 21, 241, 294–295
Innovation: and labor-mangaged firm,
    177–178, 183, 235–236; and
    organization, 101–131, 294–295;
    and size of firm, 295; and slack,
    253–254; in Soviet Union, 245–260,
    300
Insurance principle, 20, 24
Interchangeable parts, development of,
    109
Interest rates, 32, 206, 219–220, 225,
    274
Intermediate product markets,
    108–116
Internal labor markets, 116–120
Internal state parameters, 81–82,
    87–88, 89
Inventions, introduction time of, 255,
    307–308
Inventory management, 110
Inverse problems, 77
Investment diversification, 74
IS-LM framework, 274
Israel, 11, 12, 46–47, 297, 299

Jains, 159
Japan, 10, 11, 12, 46–47, 238, 297,
    298, 299
Jews, 155, 159
Job satisfaction, 160
Jovicic, Milena, 204, 225–226

Kahneman, D., 151, 165
Kama River truck plant, 260
Kanbur, S.M., 148
Kardelj, Edward, 194
Keynes, J.M., 31–32
Khruschev, Nikita, 263
Kibbutzim, 11, 12, 46–47, 297, 299)
Kihlstrom, R.E., 148
Kirzner, Israel, 5, 30, 33, 272, 276,
    277, 278, 281–290, 307
Knight, F.H., 2, 148–149, 163, 285,
    287, 292, 294, 306
Knights of Labor, 118
Kodak film, 111
Kogan, N., 164
Komives, J.L., 160
Kornai, Janos, 264–265
Kuder Occupational Interest Survey,
    160
Kurz, Mordecai, 5, 10–11, 165,
    291–300

Labor-managed firms, 179–229; and
    authority, 185–191; and autonomy,
    191–195; and economic theory,
    178–185; and income disposition,
    195–202; reforms, 212–216
Labor-saving innovations, 11, 46, 297,
    307–308
Labor unions, 46, 297; and transaction
    costs, 117–120; and Yugoslavia,
    187, 188–189, 193–194, 213–214
Laffont, J.J., 148
Large firms: and capital allocation,
    4, 5, 19–20, 24, 143; and
    information, 3–4, 12, 20, 21, 24,
    294–295; and innovation, 23–26;
    and research and development,
    4–6, 20–21, 23–26
Larson, Henrietta, 103

Lateral integration, 109, 115–116
Laughhunn, D.J., 165
Law on Associated Labor, 212,
    214–215, 227
League of Communists, 178
Lebanese, 159
Leibenstein, H., 165
Levine, Herbert, 7–8, 235–265
Life cycle and organization
    structure, 123–124
Liles, P.R., 164
Little, Royal, 102
Livesay, H.C., 112–113, 121, 122, 123,
    125
Lorenz curve, 18
Luck, 277–278, 279

McClelland, D.C., 37, 158, 159,
    163–164
McCormick, Cyrus, 3, 102, 112
Malthus, Thomas, 273
Marginal value product, 180–182
Marijuana, 298–299
Market power, 302–306, 309–310; and
    organizational innovation, 16, 122
Marschak, Thomas A., 226
Martens, J.A., 255
Mathematical analysis and modeling,
    78
Mead Corporation, 124
Means, G.C., 15
Meat packing industry, 110, 130
Medoff, James, 119–120
Mergers, 4, 17, 124, 130
Mesabi iron-ore deposits, 115
Meta-models, 95–97
M-form innovations, 124, 130
Miles, R., 161–162
Mill, J.S., 158, 287
Minority groups, 159
Monocratic organizations, 247–248,
    249–250
Monopoly, 17, 303, 305; and
    labor-management firms, 181, 219;
    and unions, 119–120
Moore, D.G., 155
Motives of entrepreneurs, 2–3, 85,

139-141, 147, 149, 154-156, 163-164, 291-294
Multidivisional firms, 19, 102

National Labor Union, 118, 120
Net product, 222
Nord, W.R., 161
North, D.C., 125, 130
Novelty, quest for, 2, 147, 149, 154-155, 157, 293, 295

Objective function and model, 77, 78, 84
Obradovic, Josip, 220
Occidental Petroleum, 124
Optimality, principle of, 95-96
Optimizing behavior, 17, 105
Organizational entrepreneurs, 2-4, 101-131, 144

Pabst Brewing, 113, 116
Parents of entrepreneurs, 139-140, 160-161
Parsees, 159
Payne, J.W., 165
Peer approval, 32
Pejovich, Svetozar, 220
Pennsylvania Railroad, 128
Perfect decentralization model, 273-274
Perrow, C., 141-142
Politburo, 241, 263
Pooling, economies of, 106
Porter, G., 112-113, 118, 121, 122, 123, 125
Power theory, 121-122, 129
Price: and decentralized economic system, 273; and labor-managed firm, 191-192, 211, 215, 221; and regulation, 17, 35; in Soviet Union, 254
Process of entrepreneurship, 152-154
Producer durables, 110, 112, 123
Production function, 302, 310
Productive entrepreneurship, 9, 33
Productivity, 18, 85, 251-252, 300; and

labor-managed firm, 180; and unionization, 118-120
Profitability, 284-285, 287; and capital supply, 49-50; function, 24-25, 28; as reward, 32
Promotion, 119
Prospect theory, 151
Protestantism, 155
Public-policy issues, 10-11, 291, 296-300

Quality control, 113
Quotas, 34

Railroads, 109, 118, 128
Rational-expectation theory, 305
Raw materials, backward integration and, 115-116
RCA, 124
Regulation: effect on entrepreneurs, 3, 34-35, 36, 142, 157-158, 172, 291, 296-299; and efficiency, 3, 46; and innovation, 9-10; and public interest, 10-11, 291, 296-300
Religious beliefs, 29, 31, 32, 155, 300
Reputation effects, 106, 114
Research Center in Entrepreneurial History, 103
Research and development, 4-6, 126; and entrepreneur, 147, 154; and innovation, 21-23; and large firms, 4-6, 20-21, 23-26; sale of, 26-27; in Soviet Union, 245-246, 248-249, 257-258, 261-262
Retailing, 110-112
Rewards to entrepreneur, 32-34
Ricardo, David, 46
Risk, 1, 2, 145-149, 163-164, 292, 305-306; and bureaucracies, 250-251; and central planning, 236, 250-251; in Communist countries, 6-8, 195, 208-212, 215-216, 217-218, 236, 250-251; and financing, 59-66, 74; and labor-managed firm, 183
River Rouge complex, 116

Ronen, Joshua, 1–12, 98–99, 137–165, 256, 271, 284, 289, 291–292, 295, 306
Roscher, Wilhelm, 287
Rosen, Sherwin, 5
Rotter, J.B., 164
Rubin, I.M., 160
Runner-up business, 9–10, 30, 35–36, 46, 297
Rus, Veljko, 222

Sacks, Stephen R., 219
Santri Moslems, 159
Sawyer, J.E., 164–165
Say, Jean, 274, 287
Scale, economies of, 3, 18, 148, 156; and large firms, 20, 24; and transaction costs, 106, 107, 108, 113–114, 125–126, 309
Scandinavia, 299
Schlitz Brewing, 113
Schrage, H., 160
Schultz, T.W., 161, 287, 307
Schumpeter, Joseph, 2, 15, 16, 33, 38, 102, 125, 148–149, 152, 158, 235–236, 272, 273, 274–276, 283–284, 285–286, 287, 292, 294, 306
Scientific-production association, 261–262
Scope, economies of, 3; and transaction costs, 106, 107, 108, 114, 125–126
Search behavior, 141–142
Sequential-probability-ratio test, 96
Sewing machine industry, 111
Shapero, A., 161
Shapiro, Harold, 10, 75–99
Shoven, John, 1–3, 49–74, 88–89, 93, 271, 305–306
Sikhs, 159
Simmel, George, 155
Simulation models, 77–78
Singer Sewing Machine, 111, 116
Size of firms, 294–296. See also Large firms; Small firms

Slack and innovation, 253–254, 262, 265
Sletzinger, Martin C., 225
Sloan, Alfred P., 102, 111–112
Slovenia, 224, 228
Small firms: decisionmaking, 6; and information, 5, 294–295; and innovation, 4, 23–26, 294–295; and research, sale of, 26–27
Smith, Adam, 104–105, 232–233, 310
Social rewards, 85
Social welfare, 10–11, 291, 296–299
Soltow, James, 103
Soviet Union, 235–263, 300; and Yugoslavia, 178, 191
Specialization of innovation, 4–5, 11, 16–17
Speed, economies of, 123, 130
Sperry-Rand, 124
Springfield Armory, 102
Stability, striving for, 250
Stalin, Joseph, 178
Stalker, G., 162–163
State Committee on Construction, 241
State Committee on Science and Technology, 241, 245, 246, 248–249, 257–258, 259
State Committee on Supply, 241
Steel industry, 115, 119, 122, 126, 128; in Soviet Union, 255
Stigler, George, 123
Stochastic laws, 77, 78, 306, 307
Strategic behavior, 124–125, 127
Strikes, 188–189, 193, 199, 214
Supply of entrepreneurs, 37–38; time path, 38–44
Supply-side economics, 296–300
Supreme Soviet, 238
Survey of Interpersonal Values (SIV), 160
Swift, Gustavus, 102, 110, 130, 301

Takeovers, 4, 17, 68–73, 129, 305
Tariffs, 34, 126
Taxes, 9, 126; effect on entrepreneurs, 31, 33, 34, 36, 44–45, 49, 74, 89,

291, 296–297, 299; and
labor-managed firms, 184, 196, 197,
203, 205, 220, 223, 225; and
runners-up, 30
Taylorism, 264
Team entrepreneurship, 11–12
Technology: and central planning,
235–236, 248–249, 254–255, 261;
and organizational structure, 109,
122–123
Telegraph, 109
Textile industry, 102, 112, 129
Theory of Economic Development
(Schumpeter), 283
Thompson, J. Edgar, 102, 128
Time and models, 76–77
Tito, 178
Tobacco industry, 109–110,
112–113
Togliatti auto factory, 260
Transaction costs, 3, 101–131, 288,
304, 309–310
Transaction-specific investment,
106–107
Transfer pricing, 19
Transition operator, 83–84
Trist, E., 162
Trust, 4, 12, 156
Turner, Donald, 130
Turnover tax, 197
Tversky, A., 151, 165
Tyson, Laura D., 226–227

Uinwalla, D.B., 155
Uncertainty, 3, 12, 16, 285, 306; and
debt repayment, 10; and
transaction-cost economics, 106
United Kingdom, 225, 299
United States: employment, 238;

invention, 255; productivity,
251–252, 300
Urals gas pipeline, 260

Vail, Theodore, 102
Value system of entrepreneurs, 159
Vanek, Jaroslav, 204, 219, 222,
225–226
Veblen, Thorstein, 155
Vertical integration, 122, 123–124
Von Neumann, John, 96, 183

Wachtel, Howard M., 224
Wage-fund theory, 272
Wainer, H.A., 160
Wallach, M.A., 164
Walrasian theory of general
equilibrium, 283
Wanamaker, John, 102
Wealth and entrepreneurs, 85, 140,
150–151, 171–172, 306
Weber, Max, 155, 158
West Germany, 255
White, M.J., 74
Whitman, Candies, 110
Whitney, Eli, 3, 102
Wholesaling, 109–110, 111
Williamson, Oliver, 3, 12, 101–131,
228–229, 288, 301–302, 304
Winter, Sidney, 127
Workers' council, 186–188, 190,
200, 221; and BOALs, 213; and
risk, 201

Young, J.P., 255
Yugoslavia, 6–7, 8, 177–229

Zupanov, Josip, 187–188, 189–190,
211, 227

About the Contributors

Kenneth J. Arrow received the Ph.D. from Columbia University in 1951 and is presently the Joan Kenney Professor of Economics and professor of operations research at Stanford University. He is a member of the National Academy of Sciences and is the recipient of the Nobel Memorial Prize in economic science, the John Bates Clark Medal of the American Economics Association, and numerous honorary degrees. Professor Arrow served as president of the American Economic Association in 1973 and is a Distinguished Fellow of that association. He has also served as president of the Econometric Society. His fields of interest are rational behavior of organiations, collective decision making, resource allocation especially under uncertainty, and energy economics.

William J. Baumol received the Ph.D. from the University of London in 1949 and is currently professor of economics at Princeton and New York Universities. He is president of the American Economic Association, past president of the Association of Environmental and Research Economists and of the Eastern Economic Association and is a member of the American Philosophical Society. He holds a BSS degree from CCNY. He is author and coauthor of 12 books, most recently, *Economics, Environmental Policy, and the Quality of Life* (1979).

Abram Bergson received the Ph.D. from Harvard University in 1940 where he is presently George F. Baker Professor of Economics. A former director of the Russian Research Center there, he was a member of the U.S. delegation to the Moscow Reparations Conference in 1945. He has also served as chairman of the Social Science Advisory Board, U.S. Arms Control and Disarmament Agency, and has been a consultant at various federal government agencies and at the RAND Corporation. He is a Fellow of the Econometric Society and American Academy of Arts and Sciences, and a member of the American Philosophical Society and the National Academy of Sciences. He is the author of numerous books and articles in economic theory and socialist economics; his most recent book is *Productivity and the Social System: The USSR and the West* (1978).

Harold Demsetz received the M.A., M.B.A., and the Ph.D. in 1959 from Northwestern University. He is presently professor at the University of California at Los Angeles, where he served until 1980 as chairman of the economics department. Dr. Demsetz has been a consultant to the RAND Corporation and to General Motors, and is presently consultant to ARCO.

Jerry R. Green received the Ph.D. from the University of Rochester in 1970 and is now professor of economics at Harvard University. He is the editor of *Economics Letters* and has served on the editorial boards of the *Quarterly Journal of Economics* and *Econometrica*. His research encompasses topics in the economics of information and uncertainty, the economics of incentives, and taxation and corporate finance.

Israel M. Kirzner received the Ph.D. from New York University in 1957. He has extensively analyzed alternative conceptions of economics during the history of the science. He is a professor of economics at New York University.

Mordecai Kurz received the Ph.D. from Yale University in 1961. He is currently professor of economics at Stanford University and the director of the Economics Section of the Institute for Mathematical Studies in the Social Sciences, Stanford University. Professor Kurz has written in the areas of capital theory, general equilibrium theory, public policy and welfare. He has been a consultant for S.R.I. International and the World Bank, a special economic advisor to the government of Canada, and an economic consultant to the President's Commission on Pension Policy. Professor Kurz is a member of the Econometric Society and the American Economic Association and is a research associate of the National Bureau of Economic Research.

Herbert S. Levine received the Ph.D. from Harvard University in 1961. He is an internationally known expert in Russian economics and planning and is professor of economics at the University of Pennsylvania. Dr. Levine is consultant to the United States government on the Soviet economy and east/west trade. He is currently chairman of the Board of Trustees of the National Council for Soviet and East European Research. Dr. Levine has made major contributions to the analysis of Soviet economic growth and planning, and the effect of political pressure on planning.

Sherwin Rosen is professor of economics at the University of Chicago and research associate at the National Opinion Research Center and the National Bureau of Economic Research. He has written widely in the fields of labor economics and industrial organization. His current research interests include the organization of hierarchical firms, optimal-assignment problems and principal-agency problems. He received the Ph.D. from the University of Chicago in 1966.

Harold N. Shapiro received the Ph.D. from Princeton University in 1947 and is currently professor at the Courant Institute of Mathematical Sciences, New York University. His focus of study and research is the pursuit of mathematics and its application.

John B. Shoven received the Ph.D. from Yale University in 1973 and is presently professor at Stanford University and vice chairman of the department of economics. He specializes in public and corporate finance and in the development of general equilibrium computer models of the U.S. economy. He currently is director of the National Bureau of Economic Research's program to study private and public pensions, is a senior adviser to the Brookings Institution, and is the principal investigator on research programs sponsored by the U.S. Treasury, the National Science Foundation, the Sloan Foundation and the Electric Power Research Institute.

Oliver E. Williamson received the Ph.D. from Carnegie-Mellon University in 1963 and is now Charles and William L. Day Professor of Economics and Social Sciences at the University of Pennsylvania. He is a member of the American Economic Association and a Fellow of the Econometric Society. He has consulted for the National Science Foundation and the Federal Trade Commission and is editor of the *Bell Journal of Economics.*

About the Editor

Joshua Ronen received the Ph.D. from Stanford University in 1969. He taught at the University of Chicago and is now a professor at New York University Schools of Business, where he is director of the Doctoral Program in Accounting. He has been a Senior Research Scholar of the Vincent C. Ross Institute of Accounting Research, and president of the Price Institute for Entrepreneurial Studies. His many professional memberships include the American Accounting Association, the American Economic Association, and the Management Science Institute. He is the author of four books and a large number of articles in accounting, economics, finance, and behavioral science academic journals and publications. He is also a contributor to the *Encyclopedia of Economics*. Dr. Ronen has served as special editor of, or on the editorial boards of, several journals in accounting, economics, finance, and management science. Dr. Ronen also has extensive experience as consultant to business and government organizations, in giving expert opinion in litigation cases, and in serving in professional committees and on company boards.